Exploring Western Civilization

To 1648

A WORKTEXT FOR THE ACTIVE STUDENT

THOMAS J. KEHOE

HAROLD E. DAMEROW

JOSE M. DUVALL

KENDALL/HUNT PUBLISHING COMPANY
4050 Westmark Drive   Dubuque, Iowa 52002

Cover photos
Left: Courtesy of The Metropolitan Museum of Art, Rogers Fund, 1931.
Right: Courtesy of The Metropolitan Museum of Art, Gift of the Edith and Herbert Lehman Foundation, 1969.

Maps on pages 17, 20, 47, 57, 58, 76, 140, 168, 216, 258, 261, 268, 278, 288, 318, 343, 356, 357, 362, 371, 438, 439, 462, 476 from King, C. Harold. _A History of Civilization: Earliest Times to the Mid-seventeenth Century_. Second Edition. © 1964 by Charles Scribner's Sons.

CONTENTS

EXPANDED CONTENTS

FOR EACH SUBCHAPTER*

---

   * Each subchapter (numbers 1 through 15) corresponds to approximately one week of subject matter in a one semester course lasting fifteen weeks.

PREFACE

The present is part of a chain of events that links the past and the future. Since we can not explore the future, it is only by studying the past that we can try to understand the present and, maybe, discern a glimmer of what is to come. Many of the readers of this book will live in the United States. At the end of the twentieth century, the American past is shaped by several traditions. One of the most important is its continuing relationship and historic roots in Western Civilization.

America is an offshoot of European civilization; and while other, non-European, cultures are increasingly contributing to the unfolding of the New World, the European element is still the main stream of the American heritage. Thus for all residents of the United States, whatever their origins, knowledge of Western Civilization remains an important key to understanding the society in which they live.

As we look into the European past, we discover that Columbus was the product of 1000 years of what is commonly called the Middle Ages. These Middle Ages began when illiterate Germanic tribal peoples brought down a decaying Roman Empire. This Roman Empire had conquered and ruled all the peoples surrounding the Mediterranean Sea. The origins of this Roman state bring us back another 1000 years. When the Roman Republic began as a single city-state, in 509 B.C., Carthaginians, Etruscans, Greeks, Persians, Babylonians, Israelites, Egyptians, and many other peoples already had proud histories. The earliest civilizations were those of the Sumerians and the Egyptians, beginning about 3500 B.C.

Looking further into the past, we learn to appreciate the beginnings of the agricultural revolution only some 10,000 years ago. Beyond that lie the millions of years of the Paleolithic when mankind evolved as a forager, scavenger, and hunter. Also acknowledged are the beginning of life on Earth—some 3 billion years ago, the formation of our Solar System—some 4.6 billion years ago, and even the Big Bang origins of the Universe—some 15 billion years ago.

Western Civilization did not develop in isolation. Its roots reach back into the common heritage of mankind. It is not even a culture produced exclusively by Europeans. Neither the Minoans nor the Hebrews were European; yet their cultures form part of what is quintessential to the Western tradition. But the West is individualistic, rationalistic, and more egalitarian than the other cultures mentioned. This makes it different from other civilizations and worth studying for its own sake.

This worktext explores the evolution of Western Civilization from its origins to 1648, the end of the Wars of Religion engendered by the Reformation. A companion text,[*] published earlier, examines the modern period of Western Civilization from 1600 to the present. Each book has five chapters with three sections in each chapter—a total of 15 sections per volume. These sections correspond to approximately one week of subject matter in a one semester, fifteen-week course. Together, these two volumes can serve as the textbooks for the traditional, introductory Western Civilization courses given in the freshman year of college.

The authors designed this book as a worktext. It combines the features of a text, book of readings, and study guide. We want you to use this book as a study guide. We want you, the student, to write in the margins, answering the sidebar questions about the subject matter. If you read, and write immediately about what you have read, you will learn and retain much more than if you only read about some area of history. We want you to answer the multiple choice questions printed at the end of each chapter. We want you to identify the terms presented and give responses to the essay questions. The pages of this book can be torn out.

---

[*]Thomas J. Kehoe, Jose M. Duvall, and Lawrence J. Hogan, <u>Exploring Western Civilization: 1600 to the Present</u> (Dubuque, Iowa: Kendall/Hunt Publishing, 1994).

This is deliberate. We want you to use this book. It is a worktext. We do not want you to save this book, display it in your bookcase, or leave it as a bequest for your children. The messier and more used this paperback becomes, the more you learn and the happier will be the authors.

Acknowledgments

The authors would like to thank the following persons for their careful reading and valuable suggestions for this manuscript:

Hermann J. Bielefeld
John D. Madden

We are especially thankful for the support and patience of our spouses:

Toni Damerow
George B. Duvall
Jane C. Kehoe

Without their considerable understanding, the completion of this work would have been impossible.

Chapter I

FROM THE FIRST HUMANS TO THE GREEK CITY-STATES

1

Human Beginnings and the Mesopotamians

From the Beginning to the Mesopotamians

The Universe

The universe began from a single point in a giant explosion some twelve to fifteen billion years ago, according to the dominant scientific theory called the **BIG BANG THEORY**. All matter and energy now existing in the universe was concentrated in that single, almost incomprehensibly small location. The background noise or radiation from that explosion can still be heard today; indeed, it is the scientific measurement of this background radiation which provided the main scientific evidence for the Big Bang Theory.

Since the Big Bang, the universe has evolved to its present shape and is still evolving. There is a life cycle of stars and galaxies. If you are interested in this subject then you might want to study astronomy, physics, astrophysics, or cosmology.

The Solar System

Our own sun is a second or third-generation star system. We were formed out of stellar dust, that is out of the remains of

Explain the Big Bang Theory.

Figure 1.1 (opposite page). *Sphinx of Hatshepsut.* Thebes. Egyptian. XVIII Dynasty, c. 1503-1482 B.C. This red granite sphinx with the body of a lion and the face of a pharoah shows the only woman ever to govern the New Kingdom in her own right. Hatshepsut made Egypt into a splendid country by encouraging trade and foreign commerce. *Courtesy of The Metropolitan Museum of Art, Rogers Fund, 1931.*

Distinguish between the universe and our solar system.

previous generations of stars. This parent cloud of dense, mainly hydrogen, gas gave rise to the sun, nine planets with their moons, several thousands of minor planets called asteroids, and who knows how many comets.

Our solar system is located at the edge of the Milky Way Galaxy, which is only one of thousands of galaxies. We are not at the center of the universe, as mankind for many thousands of years had believed.

The Earth

The Earth and its Moon formed about 4.49 billion years ago. The science of geology explores the history of the earth. The earth is made up mainly of iron and silicates. For the first 500 million years of our history, the earth had a solid core. Radioactive decay heated up the core, melted the iron, which settled at the center of our planet. Surrounding the molten core, a semi-solid and still radioactive mantle, made up mainly of silicates, developed. Above the mantle is the Earth's crust, five to twenty-five miles thick. The earth's continental plates float on that mantle.

Discuss the formation and composition of the earth.

Life

Life on Earth is carbon-based, cellular, and, in all but its most primitive forms, dependent on the sexual exchange of DNA or deoxyribonucleic acid. Such cells have been in existence on Earth for more than one billion years. There are more primitive single-celled life forms which depend on fission: the simple division of a cell into two identical new cells. Blue-green algae divide in this manner and have been around for more than three billion years. Even such simple forms of life are miracles of chemistry. Scientists have demonstrated that inorganic chemicals, in existence during the formative period of Earth, through the influence of lightning and sunlight, can form organic compounds that are essential for life.

Single-celled life forms slowly evolved into multicellular fungi, plants, and animals. Multicellular green algae first established themselves on land about 1.2 billion years ago and biologists believe that modern plants evolved from them. By the Cambrian Period on the Geologic Time Scale, about 600 million years ago, invertebrate animals, like sponges, jellyfish, worms, shellfish, starfish, and crustaceans, abound in the fossil record.

During the Mesozoic Era, which lasted from 225 to 65 million years ago, insects and reptiles were the predominant land animals. The Mesozoic is the era of the dinosaurs. Their abrupt extinction is still unexplained, but was perhaps caused by a meteorite. Its impact threw so much dust into the atmosphere that sunlight could not get through. The cooling of the Earth for several years until the dust settled may have triggered the extinctions. The dinosaurs' extinction opened the door for the rapid evolution of birds and mammals. The age of the mammals is part of the Cenozoic Era (65 million years ago to the present) and our own human evolution.

The Evolution of Man

Mankind evolved over millions of years. The earliest primate fossils date back 70 million years. About 45 million years ago, more advanced primates had developed which were quite similar to modern lemurs. Primitive monkey-like primates appeared about 35 million years ago. True monkeys and apes first appeared about 22 million years ago, at

What are the origins of life?

What forms of life distinguish the Mesozoic from the Cenozoic Era?

What do humans share with African apes and chimpanzees?

the beginning of the long geological epoch known as the Miocene.

Modern geneticists have demonstrated that the DNA in modern humans and chimpanzees is very closely related, differing by about 2 percent. This has led to the view that our human ancestors split from the common stock which we share with the Great African Apes no more than eight million years ago. Many physical anthropologists hold that the genus of *Australopithecus* may have been part of the ancestral line from which the genus *Homo* emerged.

What were the distinguishing characteristics of *Australopithecus?*

Australopithecus existed from 5.5 to 1 million years ago, solely in Africa. Apparently walking upright and lacking the fangs (projecting canine teeth) characteristic of the apes, *Australopithecus* lived in the open woodland and grasslands of Africa, rather than in the forests like the apes. For these reasons it has been classified as a member of the HOMINID primate family. The brain of *Australopithecus* was small, similar to the apes rather than humans. Whether *Australopithecus* used tools, while probable, is still being debated. At least three distinct species of Australopithecines have been identified.

One of these, *Australopithecus afarensis*, was discovered in East Africa. In 1973 a young paleoanthropologist, Dr. Donald C. Johanson, found female fossil bones and a partial skull on a dig in Ethiopia. Because of the supreme ecstasy and jubilation at Johanson's camp, a Beatles song, "Lucy in the Sky with Diamonds," played all night long. Since that night, the female was dubbed "Lucy."[1] Lucy's bones showed her to have been an erect-walking hominid with a brain as large as a softball—a very early human-like ancestor, almost 3.5 million years old. Lucy is one of the most complete skeletons of an adult female australopithecine ever found.

Homo Habilis is the name given to the earliest human species. While like the australopithecines in many ways, it had a larger brain and clearly used tools. *Homo habilis* also had a much more complex social organization with a division of labor. It engaged in food gathering and hunting. The tools associated with these people belong to the OLDOWAN culture. Some of the earliest fossils date from 2 million years ago.

Homo Erectus By about 1.6 million years ago, physical and cultural changes of a sufficient magnitude occurred which have led anthropologists to classify the available fossil skulls, bones, and stone tools as belonging to a different type of human called *Homo erectus*. The brain is larger than that of *Homo habilis*, the teeth are smaller, and the jaws are less massive. Hand axes, belonging to what is called the ACHEULEAN culture, are found alongside the fossils. *Homo erectus* probably originated in Africa, but spread throughout the habitable world. By 500,000 years ago, he had learned how to utilize fire. He became extinct about 250,000 years ago.

Homo Sapiens Also, by about 250,000 years ago, humans which have been classified as *Homo sapiens* had evolved. These ARCHAIC HUMANS included what is popularly called NEANDERTHAL MAN or, more scientifically, *Homo sapiens neanderthalensis*. These archaic humans had large brains, similar in size to our own, but physically were still quite different with a large face, big teeth (compared to ours), a low skull with heavy brow ridges, and little or

What was the earliest human species?

Describe the distinguishing characteristics of Homo habilis, Homo erectus, and Homo sapiens.

**What do we know about Nean-
derthal man?**

**How closely interrelated are the
different groups of humans who
populate the earth today?**

no forehead. The LEVALLOIS culture of chipping flint tools is associated with these archaic humans.

NEANDERTHAL MAN, who flourished between 100,000 to 40,000 years ago, produced the MOUSTERIAN culture. This culture included the practice of burying the dead, leading to the assumption that some kind of religious belief was involved. Whether Neanderthal Man had a developed spoken language is unclear because some anthropologists believe that he had poorly developed vocal chords. Recently, paleoanthropologists have unearthed caves in Croatia and Spain where marks on the skulls and bones of Neanderthals show an excising of the flesh similar to the way animals are butchered.[2] Were these early hominids cannibals? Did Neanderthals disappear because of famine and an Ice Age or did they intermix with modern Cro-Magnon man? Because these heavy-browed, stocky hominids left no written records, much of their intriguing story is yet to be discovered.

Homo sapiens may have developed first in Africa, reached the Middle East about 100,000 years ago, where he may have lived side by side with Neanderthal Man, and gradually spread to Europe 40,000 years ago, to Asia at about the same time, and to the Americas through a land bridge that connected Siberia with Alaska about 20,000 years ago. All human beings on Earth today belong to this species. By 40,000 years ago, these modern humans replaced Neanderthal Man and all other species of *Homo sapiens*.

CRO-MAGNON MEN were modern humans although on average somewhat more muscular than we. They were extremely skilled big game hunters who lived during the last Ice Age. Several cultural stages have been identified for these people as follows: The AURIGNACIAN, PERIGORDIAN, and MAGDALENIAN cultures. During the latter period, their famous cave art was produced. Their cultures became extinct when warmer weather brought an end to the big herds of animals on whom these people depended.

Cro-Magnon Men were the first humans to develop art. Their cave paintings at ALTAMIRA in Spain and LASCAUX in southern France were done more than 15,000 years ago. They depict various animals like mammoths, bison, horses, deer, wild cattle, goats, and boars. The woolly rhinoceros, antelope, cave lion, wolf, cave bear, birds, and fish are more rarely painted. Even more rarely are human beings shown. The purpose of this art is still unknown, though it may have had a religious or magic significance.

Cultural Evolution

The evolution of human beings is closely related to changes in the natural environment. The latest geological epoch of the Earth's history which is called the PLEISTOCENE EPOCH. It began about 1.7 million years ago. The Pleistocene was a time of the Ice Ages. Thick sheets of ice covered much of Europe and North America. Africa had a much milder climate than it does today. These sheets of ice expanded and receded at least four times during this 1.7 million year period. All life had to adjust to these fluctuations in climate. Perhaps the australopithecines and *Homo habilis* died out at the beginning of these Ice Ages because they could not adjust to the harsher climate facing them.

For at least the last 40,000 years, *Homo sapiens sapiens*, our species, has had the world for themselves. Biological evolution is slow and it takes thousands of generations to produce noticeable changes.

For the past 100,000 years the biological evolution of *Homo sapiens sapiens*, our

What do we know about the culture of Cro-Magnon humans?

Distinguish between biological evolution and cultural evolution. Which form of evolution has had the greatest impact in the last 40,000 years?

When did the last Ice Age end?

species, has been supplemented by cultural evolution as the dominant factor in shaping our evolution. Tools are evidence of that cultural change. But cultural evolution requires a system of classification similar to that used for cataloguing biological changes.

We are living in the FOURTH IN-TERGLACIAL PERIOD which began about 15,000 to 10,000 years ago, after the latest Ice Age, the WUERM glaciation, ended. It is this warmer climate which helped to produce the age of agriculture which continues to shape our lives.

The Quest to Understand the Past

Is history dependent on written records only? Explain.

It should be noted that two hundred years ago, in George Washington's time, none of this knowledge about the evolution of the universe, the earth, life, and mankind existed. And it is only within the last fifty years that science has begun to fill in the details of the history outlined above. Radioactive Carbon-14 dating methods and new fossil finds in Africa at Lake Rudolf (Kenya) and Olduvai Gorge (Tanzania) have helped to confirm crucial pieces of these scientific theories.

History, as should be obvious by now, is an exploration of the past. Geologists and paleontologists are historians of a sort because they explore the geological layers of the earth for the information that may be found. Digging into the earth or gazing into the stars is a look into the past. What is closer to the surface or nearer to our planet is more recent in time than what is further or deeper down.

Classifying the Archeological Record

The first step in creating a scientific theory is often to catalog and then to classify the empirical data. When human-like skulls and bones were found, in various rock formations, together with stones, which had obviously been shaped deliberately into tools, then strong evidence existed that these fossilized creatures were, indeed, more than animals. It also became obvious that mankind and the Earth were much older than had been believed before modern times. A literal reading of the Bible had suggested that the Earth was only about 6,000 years old.

Christian Thomsen, a Danish museum curator and antiquarian, in 1836 proposed a three-fold classification system in order to catalog various artifacts. He proposed that iron tools were of more recent origin than bronze, and bronze more recent than stone tools. The English antiquarian, Sir John Lubbock in 1865 proposed that the Stone Age be divided into an old and a new one, Paleolithic and Neolithic. These classification systems have been kept; but as our knowledge has increased, these divisions have become increasingly problematic. Tools are important indicators of human cultures, but they are not its sole defining characteristic. Moreover, the Neolithic has been linked increasingly to the agricultural revolution, rather than particular kinds of stone tools. Since the agricultural revolution did not take place simultaneously throughout the world, we have become more interested in how agriculture spread and how farming cultures lived side by side with hunting societies and with civilizations, once those developed.

The study of the past always begins from a given moment in the present. When scientists in the nineteenth century began their research into the unknown past, their starting point was what they did know. They knew the history of Europe, Rome, and Greece. They knew a little about Egypt and less about Mesopotamia. What they knew was derived from books. History had to do with

How old is the earth according to the Bible? Do you think this is correct?

Mention a Dane and an Englishman who helped to develop ways of classifying the archeological record. Explain their contributions.

How has our understanding of "prehistoric" societies changed?

writing. Only people who left written records which could be read had a history. People who could write were civilized; those who could not were classified as either barbarians or savages. But as our knowledge of preliterate societies grew, it became obvious that such people did have histories.

Prehistory | The term prehistory was coined to distinguish research into preliterate societies from studies concerning societies with written records. Preliterate societies have continued into the twentieth century. Cultural anthropologists have done extensive field work studying primitive societies. They have discovered that hunter-gatherer societies and preliterate agricultural societies are quite complex and developed. The insights of cultural anthropologists studying contemporaneous preliterate societies are assumed to have relevance to preliterate societies of the Neolithic and Paleolithic eras.

Why do the authors argue that a new archeological classification system is needed?

The techniques developed by prehistorians have become very sophisticated. It is amazing how much can be learned from a 20,000-year old refuse heap using modern scientific methods. Those same techniques are increasingly used by all archeologists. Digging out the remains of a lost city and finding written records in a script which cannot be deciphered is no different from digging at preliterate Jericho. Even at archeological sites in Greece, Egypt, and Mesopotamia, whose ancient writings can be read, new research techniques are giving us new and deeper insights into those civilizations.

Terminologies which once helped us to understand the past are becoming more and more confusing as they overlap with each other. An entirely new classification system may be required and maybe one of you will create it. Until then, it is hoped that the explanations provided below are clear, understandable, and useful.

The Paleolithic Period The Paleolithic is the time period that began about 2.5 million years ago, when the first stone tools were found in what is called the Oldowan Culture associated with *Homo habilis*. It lasted to about 15,000 years ago, when the Cro-Magnon version of *Homo sapiens sapiens* painted bisons on cave walls during the Magdalenian Culture. Throughout most of this time period, Ice Ages came and went. Throughout this time period, mankind was a food gatherer, scavenger, and hunter.

At the end of the last Ice Age, the Wuerm glaciation, profound cultural changes occurred and transformed human life. Stone tools, the archeological record shows, became much more diverse and sophisticated so that scientists labeled this post-Ice Age period as the Neolithic. Some scientists put in a transitional phase between the Paleolithic and the Neolithic, which they called the Mesolithic Period.

Mesolithic Period It is during the Mesolithic that human cultures learned to domesticate animals and grow food. The agricultural revolution is one of the most important turning points of human history. It is during the Mesolithic that this profound transformation took place. The Mesolithic is variously dated from 15,000 to 6,000 years ago.

The Neolithic Period The Neolithic or New Stone Age is identical with the Age of Agriculture. There is strong evidence that the first deliberate growing of seeds took place near the highland plains of Persia in Western Asia some 11,000 years ago. Grass seeds, which grow wild in

Distinguish the different stone ages by time periods and human activities.

Describe the likely progression of agricultural techniques.

this area even today, are very similar to some of the earliest grains which humans grew then. It is also possible that they simply harvested wild grasses with flint-edged wooden sickles. The next step may have been a simple burning of the existing vegetation, sowing the seeds by throwing them on the ground, and hoping that they would germinate. At the appropriate time, these early agriculturalists would return to their field and see what could be reaped. From 11,000 B.C. to 7,000 B.C. is a long time to experiment, but by the end of this period agricultural village communities had sprung up throughout Anatolia (modern Turkey), the Middle East, and Western Asia. Dogs, goats, sheep, pigs, and cattle had been domesticated. Flax, wheat, barley, and other cereal grains were cultivated. Quite early on, a beer mash may have been consumed.

The development of agriculture had a profound impact on human societies and cultures. The agricultural or Neolithic revolution spread gradually throughout the entire world. Neolithic societies supplanted the older hunting/gathering style of life wherever farming was possible. Hunting societies were pushed into inhospitable regions of the globe, where some survived until the twentieth century.

Do you think the term "agricultural revolution" is justified? Explain.

It is not that agricultural people (Neolithic societies) had a better life-style. Their diet may, indeed, have been blander and less nutritious. But farmers have a steady food supply whereas hunters are often on a feast or famine cycle. If you cannot find and hunt an animal, then you starve. Farming produced a significant increase in population. Village life was born. Villagers are sedentary, not nomadic. By 3,500 B.C., farming had reached Northern Europe, India, and China. At first farmers may have lived side by side with hunters. Perhaps some hunters even lived within agricultural villages and supplemented the available food supply. The point, however, is that agriculture and village communities were spread throughout Eurasia long before the development of what are called civilizations.

Some of these early villages of one or two hundred people grew to be substantial towns as early as 6000 B.C. At the excavations site of ancient JERICHO, six miles north of the Dead Sea in Palestine, archeologists have discovered one of the earliest towns in history. Permanent settlement dates back to 9,000 B.C. By about 7000 B.C., in what archeologists have called Prepottery Neolithic A Culture, a 17-foot high wall surrounded a town of perhaps as many as 1,000 people. A 23-foot high tower with an internal flight of steps has also been excavated. This was long before Sumer and the rise of what is called civilization.

The Bronze Age: 3000 B.C. - 1200 B.C.

Neolithic people, with their extensive knowledge of rocks needed for making stone tools, also discovered metals. Copper was the first metal to be used on a regular basis. At first, it was simply beaten into shape in the same way that stone was shaped. The Chalcolithic Period or Copper-Stone Age began in eastern Anatolia, where a lot of different ores are found, as early as 10,000 years ago. But the earliest find of SMELTED copper dates from about 3800 B.C. at a site in Iran.

Copper is a very soft metal and not very useful for making tools. But when copper is smelted together with tin, it makes BRONZE. By 3000 B.C., bronze was in common use throughout the ancient Near East. While not invented by the first civilizations, it was highly prized and used by them.

What discoveries did archeologists make at Jericho?

What advantages does bronze have over copper or stone?

Who first developed iron smelting?

Hittites smelt Iron For weapons.

What is civilization?

Where were the earliest civilizations located?

Bronze is much harder than copper, can be easily cast, and when bronze objects get dented or dull, they can be reshaped and resharpened. At the hands of skilled artisans, they revolutionized many crafts. Together with gold, silver, and copper, bronze can also be used to make jewelry and other objects of art.

> **The Iron Age: From 1400 B.C.**

The Hittites of eastern Anatolia developed iron smelting before 1400 B.C. They were the first to use iron weapons and conquered an empire with them. Gradually other people learned how to smelt iron and the age of iron had begun.

> **The Rise of Civilization**

Civilizations are human societies which have reached a level of complexity qualitatively different from agricultural village societies and hunter/gatherer societies. Through the use of irrigation agriculture, they are able to feed and control much larger numbers of human beings than ever before in history. About 3100 B.C., the two earliest civilizations developed in Mesopotamia and Egypt. Both are located on rivers and depended on irrigation agriculture for their prosperity. They are discussed in the next sections of this book.

The earliest civilizations share ten characteristics which differentiate them from less developed cultures. These are:

1. IRRIGATION AGRICULTURE. Primitive, neolithic agriculture depended on natural rainfall to water the crops. Harnessing the waters of a river through a system of irrigation canals increased agricultural yields tremendously. The prosperity of ancient civilizations depended on irrigation agriculture.

In Mesopotamia, the Sumerians learned to irrigate the swamplands of the Tigris and Euphrates Rivers. The Egyptians utilized the Nile River flowing out of Africa.

2. DEVELOPMENT OF CITY-STATES, KINGDOMS, AND EMPIRES. The Sumerian city-states were the earliest urban communities in history. A village, however large, is not a city. City-states were independent, self-governing, and self-sufficient political organizations. Each city-state had an urban center and the surrounding countryside with the agricultural fields and villages which provided food for the entire community. At the center, the temple, citadel, palace, and market place provided the urban core. Often the center was fortified with impressive walls. City-states could grow into kingdoms and empires.

How did city-states differ from villages or empires?

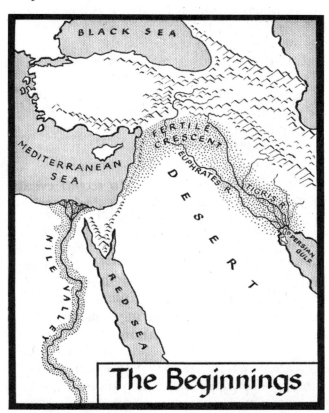

Why are temple worship and writing connected with civilization?

Is organized warfare uncivilized? Explain.

3. ORGANIZED TEMPLE WORSHIP. Civilizations are characterized by an organized religion centered around a temple. Religious beliefs date back to the Paleolithic. The belief in spirits, animism, ancestor worship, and various fertility cults long predate civilization. But the building of temples served by a professional priesthood is a new development which characterizes the establishment of civilization.

4. A WRITING SYSTEM. In Sumeria, this writing system is called cuneiform; in Egypt, it is called hieroglyphics. Writing was probably developed by priestly scribes as an aid to their record keeping chores.

5. BUREAUCRATIC KINGSHIP. Civilizations developed formal governments which were centered around a citadel and palace, ruled by a king who had both religious and military functions. In Egypt, these rulers were god-kings, to whom the Hebrews gave the name of "pharaoh." In Sumer, the kings developed after the temple priesthoods and were viewed as the stewards for the gods.

6. ORGANIZED WARFARE. Primitive man may have had fights and even gone on raiding parties, but organized warfare was an invention of civilization. To be called an army, a military force must have a certain organization, discipline, and size. Only the population increases, made possible by irrigation agriculture, made it possible to have organized warfare between rival city-states and empires. Organized warfare enhanced the power of the king as military leader. It made possible the conquest of other city-states and the formation of empires. And it had the unfortunate effect of producing slavery for those who lost the war.

7. SOCIAL STRATIFICATION. Before the creation of civilizations, there were only minimal differences between people. There were differences based on sex, age, and

strength. Clan affiliations were important. But the division of society into royal family, priests, bureaucrats, aristocrats, merchants, soldiers, artisans, peasants, and slaves is a development linked to the rise of civilization.

8. AN EXTENSIVE SYSTEM OF COMMERCE. Trade and barter date back to the Paleolithic, but the volume of trade took a qualitative leap with the rise of civilization. Sumer with few natural resources besides the plentiful food it grew had to trade for almost everything it wanted. Trading for raw materials, whether it be metals or precious woods, produced better craftsmanship in the cities.

9. METALLURGY. The production of metals was not pioneered by the Sumerians or the Egyptians. The earliest people who knew how to extract metals from various ores were Neolithic people living in near Russia, eastern Europe and modern-day Turkey. But the terms Bronze Age and Civilization are almost synonymous. Civilizations quickly learned about the advantages of metals over stone and copied the new technologies. They could trade food for ores and learn to smelt and craft swords.

10. COLOSSAL ARCHITECTURE. Again, the issue is one of quantity and quality. Preliterate cultures have produced massive structures, such as Stonehenge, but what is exceptional for them is typical for civilizations. The pyramids of Egypt and the ziggurat temples of the Sumerians typify those cultures. The fortifications surrounding a city-state and the city-state itself can also be viewed as tremendous architectural achievements.

These ten characteristics taken together mark off civilizations from other types of human societies. And since about 3000 B.C., civilizations have largely shaped the course of human history. Cultural evolution within

Why is a rise in the volume of trade connected with the rise of civilization?

List the ten characteristics shared by the earliest civilizations.

Exactly where is Mesopotamia located?

Where is Sumer?

How long did Sumerian cultural influence predominate?

civilizations has largely replaced biological evolution in shaping our human destiny.

Mesopotamian Civilization

The earliest civilization was that of the Sumerians, who settled in the swamplands at the mouth of the Tigris and Euphrates Rivers about 3,500 B.C. The Greeks, several thousand years later, called this "the land between the rivers" or Mesopotamia. It is the southeastern part of modern-day Iraq. The Sumerian culture was imitated and adapted by many peoples throughout the Fertile Crescent, underwent many internal changes, and finally ended when the Persians conquered the entire area after 550 B.C. Two thousand and five hundred years of continuous development is about the same time span as that which separates us from the Persian and Greek civilizations.

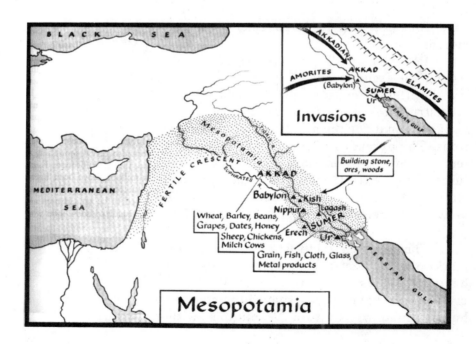

The Sumerians were the first to use irrigation to drain the swampland at the mouth of the Tigris and Euphrates rivers. Irrigation increased tremendously agricultural yields over slash and hoe agriculture. It has been estimated that one square mile of land can support one human being if that person is living off the land. One square mile of slash and hoe agricultural land can feed three persons. But one square mile of irrigated farmland can feed 750 persons. It is this increase in agricultural productivity, along with the resultant population increase, which made civilization both possible and necessary.

New forms of centralized administration were needed to maintain the irrigation system and to control the increased population. The Sumerians were the first to develop the CITY-STATE, which included a city center where the temples of the gods and the palace of the king were located and the surrounding countryside.

> Early Dynastic Period of Sumer:
> 3100 - 2500 B.C.

By 3,100 B.C., the Sumerians had reached the level of social complexity which we have described as a civilization. A dozen or so small city-states, including Eridu, Ur, and Lagash were created. Each city-state was dominated by a temple priesthood that regulated and controlled the irrigation system on which the city's agricultural abundance depended. These temple priests had developed a writing system, called CUNEIFORM, probably as an aid to their extensive record keeping. Each city-state belonged to a dominant god in whose name the city functioned. Many other gods, besides the dominant one, were worshipped. The primary god's temple was built on a raised earth platform called a

Illustrate the dramatic increase in food supplies possible with irrigation agriculture.

What were the names of some Sumerian city-states?

What is cuneiform?

What is a ziggurat?

Speculate on the relative power of the priests and kings in early Sumer.

Distinguish a dynasty from a theocracy.

ZIGGURAT. The Sumerians and nearly all other peoples throughout the ancient period of history were polytheistic. The one exception were the Hebrews, who will be discussed later.

These city-states engaged in an extensive trade with each other and other peoples. Since Sumer had almost no natural resources—no rocks, minerals, precious stones, or even wood—everything had to be traded for with grain. Through this trade, Sumerian ideas of irrigation, religion, and government spread to neighboring peoples, who developed their own city-states, upriver and throughout the region.

Though most of the people in the Middle East (as they do today) spoke in Semitic languages, the Sumerians did not. Their language is unrelated to any other known language group. While we do not know where the Sumerians originated, we do know that they were not native to the Middle East.

From early times, the Sumerians may have had a king. Such a king could have been a war leader chosen from a royal clan by the tribal assembly. The Sumerians may have had a democratic element in their early forms of government, a tribal assembly of citizen-warriors. In historic times (when we have written records) these kings were referred to as the stewards of the god of the city-state. This probably meant that the kings were initially less important than the high priest and the priesthood of the temples. But as the need for soldiers in a society increases, the importance of a war leader or a king increases. When kings can secure their positions and pass them on to their sons, then they create a dynastic system. A DYNASTY is a line of kings descended from within the same family through several generations. There may have been a shift from priestly rule, called THEOCRACY, to the rule by kings.

This is called the Early Dynastic Period.

Distinguish among the different periods of Sumerian history before the coming of the Amorites.

> Proto-Imperial Period of Sumer:
> Akkad - 2500 - 2350 B.C.
> Period.

By 2500 B.C., these Sumerian cities were beginning to encroach on each other's territory. Warfare began between these cities, and the victor attempted to rule the city that had been defeated. This Proto-Imperial Period lasted until 2350 B.C., when Sargon I of Akkad conquered the Sumerians.

> Sargonid Empire of Sumer and Akkad:
> 2350 - 2200 B.C.

SARGON I of Akkad is considered to be the first great empire builder in history. Akkad is upriver from Sumer. The people of Akkad spoke a Semitic language, but adopted and further developed the culture of the Sumerians.

Who was Sargon I?

> Sumerian Revival Under Ur III:
> 2150 - 2000 B.C.

About 2200 B.C., a people simply known as the Guti defeated the Sargonid Empire. In the aftermath of that defeat, the Sumerians were able to regain their independence. The Third Dynasty of the Sumerian city-state of Ur was able to turn the tables. Ur III, as it is abbreviated, conquered not only the other Sumerian city-states but also those of Akkad.

What was Ur III?

What did the Amorites or the Old Babylonians achieve?

(now Bagdad)

The Amorite Kingdom of Old Babylonia: 1900 - 1550 B.C.

IRAK now

About 2000 B.C., new invaders moved into Mesopotamia. These were Semitic peoples known as the Amorites and the Assyrians.

The Amorites settled upriver from Akkad and founded their capitol city of Babylon about 1900 B.C. They conquered Sumer and Akkad to form the largest empire to that date. The Sumerians were absorbed into the larger population and disappeared as a distinct population, although Sumerian remained as a sacred language used in religious ceremonies and was taught to the children of the educated as a classical language. The greatest king of the Amorites was HAMMURABI, who ruled from 1792 to 1750 B.C. Hammurabi promulgated a law code based on earlier codes dating back to the Sumerians.

Who was Hammurabi?

Compare the laws of Hammurabi with the laws of your area.

Law The CODE OF HAMMURABI categorized criminal behavior based on social class. If a nobleman committed a murder of a peasant, the punishment for the crime was treated more leniently than if a peasant murdered a nobleman. The code reflected the principle of an eye for an eye, or retribution. The death penalty was used extensively, eyes were put out, arms were cut off. For many crimes, compensation could be paid. There were no prisons in Babylon. But this was not a primitive law; the Code of Hammurabi regulated weights and measures, contracts, and all sorts of domestic relations.

This Old Babylonian Kingdom synthesized many diverse traditions of the Sumerians, Akkadians, and Amorites. Governing an empire is different from running a single city-state. Military conquests must be consolidated if they are to become permanent. Hammurabi's law code was obviously one of the methods used to try to create a common bond within the empire. But even more effective than military might and a legal system are the bonds of religion.

Religion The ancient civilizations believed that human affairs are linked to the actions of the gods. Thus if Babylon conquered another city, that triumph must mean that the chief god of Babylon, MARDUK, had conquered the god of the other city. Erecting temples to Marduk in the conquered cities reinforced this sense of supremacy.

That the Babylonian rulers were successful in having their religion accepted by the conquered peoples is reflected in the fact that great mythological stories were told about MARDUK. Human opinions about the origin of the gods, universe, and man are generally expressed in what are called, by us moderns, as their MYTHOLOGIES. That part of mythology which deals with the origin of the gods is called COSMOLOGY. The Babylonian myth epic called ENUMA ELISH tells the story of the birth of the gods and how human societies relate to this divine order. The hero of the story was Marduk. Beyond the origins of things, the story shows a struggle between an older generation of gods and a younger generation, led by Marduk. It is obvious that this mythology legitimized the rule of Babylon and its god.

The EPIC OF GILGAMESH is the most famous piece of literature and myth of the Mesopotamian civilization. It contained a story of The Flood, quite similar to that of Noah's in the Bible. The main theme of this epic concerns man's quest for eternal life: man's desire to live forever like the gods. Gilgamesh, the mythological king of Uruk, is

Was religion important in ancient civilizations?

What is mythology?

What function might the Babylonian myth, *Enuma Elish*, have served?

Summarize the epic of Gilgamesh.

so superior to his fellow men in Uruk that he demands too much and disturbs their peace. They ask the gods to create someone of equal strength and intelligence so that Gilgamesh can have some companionship. The gods create Enkidu, who is Gilgamesh's equal, but wild. The two engage in combat, then become great friends, and share adventures together. Finally Enkidu falls ill from a disease and dies. Gilgamesh, who has conquered all sorts of dangers, is helpless in the face of death.

Gilgamesh learns that a thorny plant growing in the sweet waters beneath the earth can give eternal life. After many adventures he finds it, but on his return home a snake eats the plant. The ultimate moral of the story is that eternal life is not for humankind. Note how different this conclusion is from that of the Egyptians.

What purpose did the Gilgamesh story serve?

These myths became part of the common culture of Mesopotamian civilization. Babylon remained an important religious center even after its political dominance was lost to other peoples.

The Migrations of the Hittites, Kassites, and Mitanni

What was the "Voelkerwanderung?"

Paleolithic and, to a lesser degree, Neolithic people are migratory. Hunters follow the animals they hunt and farmers may move due to soil erosion, overpopulation, or military defeats inflicted on them by others. Periodically in history, there have been migrations of peoples or, to use the German term, "Voelkerwanderung." One of these folk-wanderings began about 1800 B.C. What many historians have called the primary stage in the development of civilization came to an end as a result of the widespread disruptions which these roving movements caused.

The Hittites, Kassites, and Mitanni

migrated and settled in various parts of the Fertile Crescent. The Kassites brought an end to the Old Babylonian Empire. The Mitanni defeated the Assyrians and took over their kingdom. The Hittites settled down in Anatolia. All three groups spoke Indo-European languages and ruled as a minority over a conquered majority population.

The Mitanni kingdom, which ruled over Assyrian and Hurrian populations, reached the height of its power between 1550 and 1350 B.C. Its expansion brought it into conflict with the New Kingdom of Egypt, which resulted in a stalemate. A successful Assyrian uprising against the Mitannian rule reduced their kingdom; later the Hittites brought the Mitanni kingdom to an end. The Kassites ruled in Babylonia from 1550 to about 1200 B.C., when they were overthrown by native Babylonian rulers.

The Hittite Empire: 1380 - 1200 B.C.

By 1750 B.C., the Hittites had created a kingdom in Anatolia. Beginning after 1460 B.C., the Hittites succeeded in conquering other peoples and creating an empire. The height of this empire was between 1380 and 1250 B.C., when it defeated the Mitanni kingdom, reached the Euphrates River, and expanded into Syria-Palestine.

This latter expansion brought the Hittites into conflict with the New Kingdom of Egypt. At Kadesh on the Orontes River, about 1300 B.C., the Hittites won a major victory over the Egyptians. But both Hittites and Egyptians were weakened by these wars, which neither side could win decisively. Ramses II of Egypt and Hattusilis III of the Hittites finally negotiated a peace treaty (about 1271 B.C.) to end the fighting. The Hittites were the first people to use iron weapons in

Who were the Kassites and the Mitanni?

When were the Hittites dominant?

What technological advance did the Hittites introduce?

Judging from this chapter, what long-term chances does your nation have to maintain its independence or dominance?

warfare. The long wars, internal dissension, and the attacks of the Sea Peoples brought the Hittite Empire to an end about 1200 B.C.

The Period of the Small Kingdoms 1200 - 800 B.C.

The period after 1200 B.C. is a time of small kingdoms and renewed invasions. The People of the Sea, Medes, Persians, Dorian Greeks, and others disrupted the existing independent city-states, kingdoms, and empires. The New Kingdom of Egypt (see below) and the Hittite Empire went into decline or were destroyed. Temporarily, without large empires to challenge them, smaller nations such as the Hebrews (see below) and Phoenicians gained their independence and added their contributions to the flow of history. A new period of ever larger empires began again after 750 B.C. The Assyrian, Persian, Macedonian, and Roman Empires marched into history.

Where was Assyria located?

The Assyrians: 900 - 612 B.C.

Ancient Assyria was located on the upper region of the Tigris-Euphrates rivers and extended to the Zagros mountains and parts of Armenia. The Assyrians spoke a Semitic language and settled in the area that bears their name about 2000 B.C., at about the same time that the Amorites settled Babylon. There was an Old Assyrian Period from about 1900 to 1550 B.C. In 1550, the Assyrians became part of the kingdom of the Mitanni. They regained their independence in 1365 B.C. and retained it even after the Hittites defeated the remainder of the Mitanni kingdom. They bid their time during the period of Hittite power, but succeeded in building their own empire after 900 B.C.

Was Assyria always independent?

Figure 1.2. Winged Lion: Guardian of the Palace Gate; from the Palace of Ashurnasirapal II. Mesopotamian. 9th Century B. C. The gates of the Assyrian palaces were protected by stone lions alleged to have supernatural powers and designed to awe visitors. Assyrian kings would boast of their hideous atrocities in order to frighten their enemies. *Courtesy of The Metropolitan Museum of Art, Gift of John D. Rockefeller, Jr., 1932. (32.143.2)*

How extensive was the Assyrian Empire?

The period of greatest Assyrian might is from 745 to 612 B.C. Under rulers like Tiglath-Pileser III, Sargon II, Sennaherib, and Esarhaddon, the Assyrians conquered Elam, Media, Persia, Babylonia, Syria, Palestine, and even part of Egypt. The kingdom of Israel was destroyed by Sargon II in 722 B.C. The Assyrians prided themselves on their military prowess and, on their monuments, bragged about their cruelty to their enemies. Recent scholarship has shown that the Assyrians were not significantly crueler than other Mesopotamian peoples, but they emphasized their fierceness as a propaganda device to discourage uprisings.

When did it fall?

Under king Ashurbanipal the power of the Assyrians declined. Their conquered peoples rose up against them and, in 612 B.C., their capital city of Nineveh was destroyed.

The Chaldeans or Neo-Babylonian Empire: 626 - 539 B.C.

Why are the Chaldeans sometimes called the Neo-Babylonians (New Babylonians)?

In 626 B.C., Babylon rebelled against its Assyrian rulers and regained its independence under what is called the Chaldean dynasty. A last revival of Mesopotamian culture took place. In particular, the Chaldeans developed an astral religion, remnants of which are still found in what we today call astrology. Astronomy—observing the planets as they moved through the constellations—provided an empirical basis for the magical influence the stars were supposed to have on human affairs. In their astronomy, the Chaldeans built upon the mathematics that had been developed as long ago as the Sumerians.

The Sumerians had developed a Base-12 Numbering System. Our modern calendars still reflect their work. The hour has sixty minutes, twelve hours to the day and another twelve for the night, and twelve months for the year.

The greatest of the Chaldean kings, Nebuchadnezzar (605 - 562 B.C.), expanded his rule to the Mediterranean and destroyed the city of Jerusalem in 586 B.C. Babylon became the largest city in the Near East. Its walls, gates, temples, ziggurat, and hanging gardens were marvels of the ancient world.

In 539 B.C., Cyrus the Great of Persia conquered Babylon and incorporated Mesopotamia into his vast empire.

The End of the Mesopotamian Civilization

The Persian conquest marked the end of Mesopotamian civilization. Thereafter, the land between the rivers was a component of larger empires established by outsiders: the Persians, the Hellenistic Kingdom of the Seleucid Dynasty, the Parthian Empire, the Sassanian Empire, the Islamic Empire of the Arabs, the Ottoman Turks, and, in 1921 after World War I, the British Empire. Iraq become finally an independent state in 1932. But the end of independence did not mean, the end of Mesopotamian cultural influence. The mythology and religion of the Mesopotamians, their legal tradition, their calendar and mathematics live on even today.

What were the accomplishments of the Neo-Babylonians?

ANCIENT EGYPT

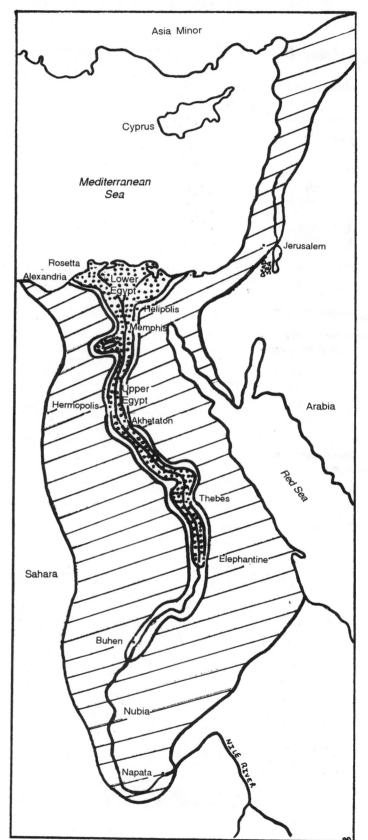

Old Kingdom
(2686 to 2181 B.C.)

Middle Kingdom
(1991 to 1786 B.C.)

New Kingdom
(1570 to 1070 B.C.)

Map 1.3. This map is reproduced, with permission, from a drawing made in December of 1995 by Branislav Bogdanovic.

2

Egyptians, Hebrews, and Persians

Egyptian Civilization

Compared to the perennial warfare and succession of empires in Mesopotamia, the history of ancient Egypt is one of relative tranquility. Egypt is the gift of the NILE River, which floods annually and predictably in September. The Nile River's fertile flood plain is surrounded by deserts, which protected Egypt from foreign invasions for much of its history. More homogeneous than other civilizations, the same Egyptian people developed for millennia without foreign invaders supplanting the original inhabitants.

Long before 5000 B.C., Paleolithic hunters and food gatherers lived in the Nile valley. As the climate became hotter and the deserts grew, claiming more fertile land, the animals retreated further south into the African continent. The stimulus to develop farming methods may have come with traders from the outside about 5000 B.C. By 4000 B.C., farming villages existed in both Upper (Southern) and Lower (Northern) Egypt.

Late Predynastic Period: 3300 - 2900 B.C.

Large villages and competing tribal kingdoms seem to have formed during what is called the Late Pre-Dynastic Period. Many of the cultural patterns that came to define Egyptian civilization can be noted in their

Look at the Nile River on a map of Egypt. Why do you suppose Upper Egypt is in the south and Lower Egypt in the north?

From south to North.

Why are the Nile River and the surrounding deserts so important in Egyptian history?

What are some of the features of the Late Predynastic Period?

formative stages, including the burial mounds for chieftains. The concern with the dead and some ideas about an afterlife appear to have animated this culture from its beginnings. Competition and warfare between different chieftains/kings produced at first two competing kingdoms and then the unification of Egypt during what is called the Early Dynastic Period.

An Egyptian historian named Manetho, writing in the third century B.C., organized Egyptian history on the basis of thirty dynasties and gave a list of pharaohs in each dynasty. Manetho wanted to demonstrate the unchanging stability of Egyptian civilization over thousands of years. Modern Egyptologists have accepted this system of classifying dynasties, but have refined it somewhat. They have also discovered that Egypt was not quite as stable and peaceful as the official accounts would have you believe. The absolute monarchical system, with the pharaoh as a god-king, did not spring into existence full-blown. It took time to develop and during the first two dynasties, which at one time were believed to be mythological, the central authority of the government was still developing.

What happened in the Early Dynastic Period?

Early Dynastic Period: 2900 - 2686 B.C.

King Narmer (also called Menes or Meni) who is now believed to have lived around 2850 B.C., is alleged to have united the two kingdoms of Upper and Lower Egypt. His successors form the First and Second Dynasty of Egyptian rulers. The degree of power that these early rulers exercised is still debated, but it undoubtedly grew over time.

Figure 1.3. The God Anubis on a Funerary Chest. Egyptian. XVIII Dynasty. This Egyptian jackal god of the dead was associated with mummification. In 1922, Howard Carter and his archaeological expedition found this chest in the untouched tomb of King Tutankhamun in the Valley of the Kings at Thebes. *Photography by Egyptian Expedition. The Metropolitan Museum of Art.*

For what is the Old Kingdom of Egypt most famous?

3rd - 6th Dynasty

Who was Imhotep and what did he do?

Provide some statistics on the Great Pyramid of Cheops.

The Old Kingdom: 2686 - 2181 B.C.

It is during the third through sixth dynasties that the traditional characteristics of Egyptian civilization were firmly in place. This is the period of the Old Kingdom.

The pharaoh was an absolute ruler, who was viewed as a living god. The amazing pyramids were built as tombs for these kings. Zoser, the founder of the third dynasty, had his great architect, Imhotep, plan and construct the first STEP PYRAMID at Saqqara. This step pyramid, a series of platforms one on top of another, much like the Mesopotamian ziggurats, reached a height of 200 feet.

During the fourth dynasty, these royal graves and displays of royal power became true pyramids and took on colossal size. The Great Pyramid of Cheops or Khufu (2590 - 2567 B.C.) covered 13 acres at its base and reached a height of 500 feet. Temples connected with the cult of the dead surrounded the pyramid. Construction may have occupied more than 10,000 workers over twenty years. It was a measure of the pharaohs' wealth and power that they could afford to undertake such public works. Even so, it must have been a drain on Egypt's resources, particularly if one considers the interior luxuries placed inside the burial chambers. Giant pyramid building ended with the Old Kingdom. However, the cult of the dead, along with the construction of elaborate tombs, remained a characteristic of Egyptian civilization until its end.

The rationale, or mythology, for building these pyramids was also developed during the period of the Old Kingdom. THE MEMPHIS THEOLOGY, which comes to us from an eighth century inscription, refers back to the alleged teachings of Menes and presents the Egyptian creation myths. Ptah, the main god of Memphis, creates all of existence out of notions in his heart which take shape as he speaks their names. The gods, nature, man, and human society are all created in this manner. His first words are the gods which take shape in material things.

Another part of this mythology sees the world being formed out of eight beings of disorder living in a primordial slime. They give rise to the sun god Atun (Aton), who gives order to the primordial disorder or chaos. In the Memphite theology, Ptah is postulated as the original creator of all.

Yet another creation myth starts with the sun god Atun or Aton. In later times, this god becomes Aton-Re. He makes Shu and Tenut (air and moisture) out of himself and they produce Geb and Nut (earth and sky). Geb and Nut's children are Osiris, Isis, Seth, and Nephthys. The first four constitute the natural order. The second four mediate between mankind and the cosmos.

The most famous of all Egyptian myths is the story of OSIRIS, the chief of the gods ruling Egypt. He was married to his sister Isis and had a son Horus. Seth, the brother of Osiris, becomes jealous of him; he murders Osiris and scatters the remains all over the earth. Upon Osiris' death, the earth becomes barren, but Isis ultimately collects Osiris' remains and brings him back to life. Half the year Osiris is lord of the underworld, the other half he lives on earth. This is obviously a fertility myth. Horus, after bitter combat with Seth, defeats him and rules Egypt. In later times, Osiris becomes the judge who determines whether humans will be given eternal life. The Osiris cult becomes an important mystery religion during Roman times.

Another myth describes the unification of Egypt as a struggle between Horus, the god

Can you make any comparisons between the Egyptian creation myths and the creation story found in Genesis?

Tell the story of Osiris.

Describe the central role of the Pharaoh in Egyptian society.

of Upper Egypt, and Seth, the god of Lower Egypt. The god Geb plays a mediating role in this struggle that is functionally similar to the role played by Ptah. Horus ultimately wins this struggle and unites Egypt. Menes and all pharaohs after him are identified with Horus.

It must be emphasized that **THE PHARAOH, AS HORUS, WAS A LIVING GOD.** His function was to maintain the cosmic order on earth. Upon his death, he became (merged with) Osiris, or later the sun god Amon-Re. The Egyptians were one of the first peoples to develop a religion that believed in life after death. At first, only the pharaoh and those of his retainers whom he took with him shared in this eternal life. Ultimately, anyone who could afford the embalming and funeral rites to preserve the physical body could share in this eternal happiness. The pyramids were symbols that linked heaven and earth. They were stairways to heaven. While the pharaoh was on his voyage to heaven, he needed to eat and drink and enjoy the comforts of life. Hence, the rich burial chambers and treasure which accompanied the pharaohs on this voyage.

Explain Ma'at.

Underneath these myths and religious practices was the concept of MA'AT: that there was a fundamental harmony within the universe of gods, nature, and man. The cycle of birth, death, and rebirth, which could be seen in the annual flooding of the Nile, the growing of vegetation, and the life of man, covered an underlying unity. It was the Pharaoh's job to maintain the harmony among the divine, natural, and social orders. Truth, justice, and order combined to form Ma'at. There was no rigid division between life and death. Each person had an eternal spirit or KA. The Egyptians envisioned life after death to be very similar to life in Egypt. Life was good, food and physical pleasures were good, the natural harmony of nature, which included the living and the dead, was good. Harmony and order had to be maintained.

The First Intermediate Period: 2181 - 2040 B.C.

7th dynasty

What are nomes?

The underlying reasons for the end of the Old Kingdom are still understood poorly. Within all human societies, there are pressures that make for centralization and decentralization: unity, and division. The Old Kingdom had seen a tremendous growth of centralization in the hands of the pharaohs. Egypt had been administered centrally through an effective bureaucracy. Egypt was divided into 42 provinces or NOMES (20 in Lower and 22 in Upper Egypt) and governed by officials from the nobility appointed by the pharaoh. Each nome also had its temples and associated priesthoods. Over time, these local officials sought to make their offices hereditary and to increase their local autonomy.

During the seventh dynasty, Egypt may have experienced several years of relative drought, and under relatively weak pharaohs, the priests and local nobility increased their opposition. Disharmony set in and the result was a period of feudalism. Central power broke down with Egypt dividing into many warring regions. This period of instability lasted for about two centuries. What is interesting to note is that even without foreign invasions, there may be a life cycle of civilizations. Even the mightiest god-kings are challenged ultimately and brought back down into chaos.

What happened in Egypt in the First Intermediate Period?

The Middle Kingdom: 2040 - 1786 B.C.

11 - 12th dynasty

Nebhepetre Mentuhotem, the founder of the 11th dynasty, conquered the north (Lower

Mention some notable rulers of the Middle Kingdom.

What was the most important religious development?

Who were the Hyksos?

Egypt) and began the rebuilding of a centralized state.

Amenemhet I (1991 B.C.) founded the 12th dynasty and made his capital near Memphis. During the Middle Kingdom, Egyptian religious practices, once reserved for the pharaoh, spread to the masses. Everyone, who could afford it, sought to have themselves embalmed and thereby gain immortality for their bodies and souls. A significant middle class developed during this time. Literature moved beyond religious themes and what may be called the first book of fiction, the story of *Sunuhet the Egyptian*, is written. In general, this is a much more complex and sophisticated society than was the Old Kingdom. Many power centers had developed which could not be reduced to one, hard as the pharaohs tried.

The Second Intermediate Period: 1786 - 1567 B.C.

The 13th through the 17th dynasties marked another period of turmoil. Dissension during the 13th and 14th dynasties weakened Egypt militarily and opened the door to foreign invasion and the establishment of two foreign dynasties (15th and 16th) beginning about 1680 B.C. HYKSOS, meaning "rulers of countries" in Egyptian, was the name given to a mixed group of mainly Semites and Hurrians from Palestine, Syria, and farther north. Some Hebrew tribes may have been part of this invading force. The Hyksos introduced horse and chariot warfare to the Egyptians, which may have given them a temporary military advantage. Once more central authority weakened and local particularism reasserted itself.

The New Kingdom or Empire: 1567 - 1085 B.C.

The Princes of Thebes led a national uprising to expel the Hyksos and founded the 18th dynasty. The pharaohs of the New Kingdom were warriors. Having experienced the pains of conquest, these Egyptian rulers sought security through expansion. Egypt became forcefully imperialistic. It expanded south into the Nubia (modern Sudan), west into Libya, and east into Palestine and Syria. Tremendous treasures flowed into Egypt from these conquests. Their eastern advances led them into conflict first with the Kingdom of the Mitanni and later the Hittites.

Not only the pharaoh but also the various temple priesthoods acquired tremendous wealth and control over agricultural lands. The same forces of internal dissension which had brought down the Old and Middle Kingdoms remained. But as long as the armies of the pharaoh were victorious and brought home rich treasures, these internal rivals could be cowed into obedience.

The 18th dynasty reached the height of its prestige under Amenhotep III (1411 - 1375), who negotiated a peace treaty with the Kingdom of the Mitanni. Kassite kings sent their daughters to the pharaoh's harem to ingratiate themselves. Even the Hittites sent letters of friendship. It seemed that an age of peace, security, and prosperity had begun. But then, as we have seen, the Assyrians rebelled successfully against the Kingdom of the Mitanni and the Hittites decided to expand into the Syria and Palestine. The pharaoh who faced these new conditions was Amenhotep IV (c.1375 - 1358 B.C.).

A great deal has been written about Amenhotep IV, who changed his name to

Discuss imperialism during the Middle Kingdom.

Was Amenhotep III a successful ruler?

Describe the religious reforms of Ikhnaton (Amenhotep IV).

IKHNATON and sought to impose a religious revolution on Egypt. Ikhnaton has been romanticized as the first "monotheist" in history. He closed down the temples of the dominant religious cult, that of Amon-Re, and demanded that henceforth Egypt worship the god Aton. Aton was symbolized by the sun disk and Ikhnaton was the living embodiment of Aton. So there were at least two gods—the pharaoh and Aton.

Ikhnaton moved his capital from Thebes and built a new city called Akhetaton. Halfway between Thebes and Memphis, near modern-day Tell el-Amarna, excavations at Akhetaton have provided us with most of the information which we have about Ikhnaton. A great deal of the diplomatic correspondence of Ikhnaton (Amenhotep IV) was recovered. We have the incoming letters from rulers and officials in Palestine, Syria, Mesopotamia, and Anatolia. They are full of pleas for help concerning the Assyrians and Hittites. We do not have the pharaoh's responses to these letters and so historians may have a very distorted picture of the pharaoh. He has been described as so absorbed in religious reforms that he neglected practical matters.

Why didn't his reforms last?

Certainly, military reverses strengthened the hands of his political enemies at home. The priesthoods of Amon-Re and other cults fought to preserve their privileges. The cult of Aton appears never to have captured popular support. If this cult was a kind of monotheism, it was imposed from the top and ended with Ikhnaton's death. While the Aton cult lasted, however, there was a tremendous release of artistic energy and creativity. A much more life-like and naturalistic style of painting and sculpture was practiced under Ikhnaton, as found at Tell el-Amarna. There is a famous sculpture of the pharaoh's queen, NEFERTITI, which exemplifies this style.

The heirs of Ikhnaton restored the cult

of Amon-Re and sought to make their peace with the powerful priesthoods. One of them, a boy who became pharaoh at the age of nine and died about age 18, was named Tutankhamen. King Tut's largely unplundered grave was found in November 1922 by Howard Carter. The beauty and richness of the objects found in this grave of an obviously minor pharaoh are astounding and cast a bright light on the wealth of the New Kingdom.

A new dynasty, the 19th, seized power about 1350 B.C. Fighting the Hittites became the major purpose of the pharaohs. The great warrior pharaoh, Ramses II (1304 - 1237) stopped the advance of the Hittites and negotiated a peace treaty which left Palestine to the Egyptians. Syria was lost to the Hittites.

Internally, Egyptian society seems to have become frozen. Art returns to the stylized conventions preceding the changes made by Ikhnaton. All change from the glorious past is viewed with suspicion and suppressed. While the high priest of Amon-Re rivals the pharaoh in power and wealth, class divisions are frozen and can no longer be resolved within the existing political structures. The iron hand of tradition weighs ever more heavily on the land. Egypt has reached stasis.

Militarily, Egypt is challenged by new enemies. The People of the Sea attack and almost defeat the Egyptians. The New Kingdom comes to an end with the 20th dynasty, when civil war divides Egypt into rival states.

For what is Tutankhamen noted?

What did Ramses II achieve?

How did the New Kingdom end?

The Decline of Egyptian Civilization: 1085 - 30 B.C.

After 1085 B.C., the Egyptians never again reach the heights of their earlier achievements. It is as if the steam had run out of their society. Egypt becomes a province of

The Egyptians are known for their pyramids and the Hebrews for their religion. Which of these cultural creations do you think will last longer? Why?

someone else's empire, as they are conquered by the Assyrians, the Persians, Macedonian Greeks, and finally, in 30 B.C., by the Romans. Egypt remains prosperous, the Nile still floods, Egyptian peasants and their traditional village lifestyle persists over the ages, until our own day. Egypt remains a cultural center throughout this period, in whatever empire it finds itself as a province. It lives off the memories of its past. As long as the pyramids remain standing, new ages are visibly reminded and brought back to the Old Kingdom of ancient Egypt so many millennia ago.

The Hebrews: The People of the Bible

The Hebrews, Jews, or Israelis, as they are variously called, are important to history because they were the first people to develop a truly monotheistic religion. Their religion directly influenced the development of Christianity and, less directly, Islam, the other two of the three great monotheistic religions of the world. It is also remarkable that this small group of people has survived, whereas the civilizations of mighty Babylon and Egypt have perished long ago. Below, we shall briefly try to present the political history of the Hebrew nation.

Name three world-wide monotheistic religions.

Prehistoric Period of the Patriarchs: 2000 - 1300 B.C.

But first it should be noted again that prehistory is the period of time in a people's past before they create or adopt a system of writing and leave written records. The prehistory of the Hebrews extends from their beginnings to the formation of the Kingdom of David about 1000 B.C. People without a written history have an oral tradition which they write down after they have become literate. By the time of King David, the Hebrew's religion was already well developed, for they believed that their worship of the one God extended back to the times of their patriarch Abraham.

We can reconstruct their prehistory by utilizing the account presented in the Bible, which refers back to those preliterate times. We can then try to fit the Biblical account into the known histories of other people and the archeological record as we now know it.

The Biblical retrospective of the Hebrews' history tells the story of Abram, living near ancient Ur in Sumeria, who moved from there to Haran, settled down awhile, and later traveled into Canaan (modern Palestine). From Canaan, Abram moved to Egypt and later back to Canaan (Genesis, Chapters 12 through 14). What is told there, in very condensed form, is the migration of the Hebrew people from southern Mesopotamia, probably after the fall of Ur III about 2000 B.C., to the city of Haran in the Kingdom of the Mitanni about 1500 B.C. After 1300 B.C., these people have established themselves in Palestine as a subgroup within the larger category of Canaanites.

From their very beginnings, the Hebrews probably were a mixture of Semitic and non-Semitic (probably Hurrian) peoples. They were related to the Canaanites, who had moved into the Syria-Palestine area beginning about 1800 B.C. They may well have been the Khapiru, who are mentioned in Mesopotamian, Hittite, and Egyptian sources as raiders, wanderers, and captives. These caravan traders who traveled between Egypt and the Euphrates River are also called Habiru. Later

From where did Abram or Abraham come?

What do we know about the origins of the Hebrews?

Who are the patriarchs?

they may well have been part of the Hyksos, who invaded Egypt.[3]

In any case, the Biblical account is largely confirmed by other sources. Later in the Biblical narrative, after he makes his covenant with God, Abram becomes Abraham. Abraham, Isaac (his son), and Jacob or Israel (the son of Isaac) are the patriarchs. According to the Bible, Joseph, the son of Jacob, was sold by his brothers as a slave in Egypt, where he rose to high office in the court of the Pharaohs. He was able to bring his brothers and father to Egypt to avoid starvation in Canaan.

Why is Moses important to the Hebrews?

> Moses and the Conquest of Canaan:
> 1300 - 1025 B.C.

About 1300 B.C., Moses led the descendants of the sons of Israel out of Egypt. This is during the period of the New Kingdom, after the Hyksos had been expelled. Ikhnaton had briefly revolutionized Egypt's religion and one can speculate whether Ikhnaton's ideas influenced the Israelites or vice versa.

Moses is held by many to have been an historical figure who received the Ten Commandments from God on Mount Sinai. These religious principles, while clearly building on existing beliefs, created the basis for a true monotheistic religion. When accepted by the entire community, Moses was able to transform the tribes of Israel (Jacob) into one nation under their God, Yahweh or Jehovah. God made the covenant with Moses and gave the Law (Torah), including the Ten Commandments, to the people. The first commandment clearly stated that the Lord is God and there are no other gods.

Under Joshua the conquest of Canaan begins and. Jericho falls. The Israelites fleeing from Egypt are joined by other Hebrew tribes who had not been in Egypt This is the Biblical period of the Judges.

About 1100 B.C., the People of the Sea attack Egypt, Palestine, and Anatolia. The Philistines belong to the People of the Sea. They conquer the coast of Palestine and threaten the Hebrews. Under these pressures for stronger military leadership, a king was chosen.

Name the first Hebrew kings and tell what they accomplished.

The Period of the Kings: 1025 - 586 B.C.

Saul (1025 - 1000 B.C.) is the first king, followed by David (1000 - 960 B.C., and Solomon (960 - 933 B.C.) King David conquers Jerusalem and makes it his capital city. King Solomon builds the Temple. Under Solomon, the Hebrew kingdom reached the height of its power. But heavy taxation and autocratic central authority led to the split of the Kingdom after Solomon's death.

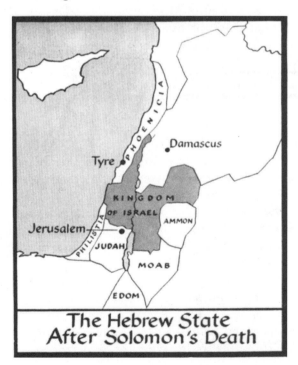

The Hebrew State
After Solomon's Death

How did each of the Hebrew kingdoms fall?

Ten tribes formed the northern Kingdom of Israel with its capital city at Samaria. Two tribes form the weaker, southern Kingdom of Judah, but retained Jerusalem, with the Temple, as their capital city. This was the time of the prophets who spoke in the name of God and warn about impending disaster unless the Covenant and the Law were obeyed. The prophets also preached against growing injustice and inequality. In 722 B.C., the Assyrians destroyed the Kingdom of Israel and disperse the population. These are the ten lost tribes of Israel. In 586 B.C., the Chaldeans destroyed the Temple in Jerusalem and forced the leading families of the Kingdom of Judah (king, high priest, and aristocrats) to live in exile near Babylon. Political independence had come to an end. Independent Hebrew kingdoms lasted only from 1025 to 586 B.C. and were never very powerful compared to some of the empires which we have discussed. But the story of the people of Abraham, Isaac, Israel, Joseph, Moses, Joshua, David, and Solomon was not over. A new chapter in the history of The Chosen People had begun.

What were the religious consequences of the loss of political independence and of the Temple?

The Babylonian Exile: 586 - 538 B.C.

The destruction of the Temple in 586 B.C. produced a major religious crisis within Judaism. Did the destruction of the Temple mean the end of the Covenant, the end of Judaism? How could God be worshipped without the Temple? The synagogue may well have developed during this period. While in exile, Jewish thinkers developed a deeper understanding of God. God works the divine will in history not only through the Jewish people, but through all peoples. Even Assyrians, Babylonians, and Persians have their divinely ordained roles to play. There is only One God for all people, whether they recognize the Deity or not. There is also a greater emphasis on an individual relationship with God and on the moral as opposed to the cultic dimension of religion. The prophets Jeremiah and Ezekiel predicted the ultimate restoration of Israel.

In 539 B.C., Cyrus the Great of Persia conquered Babylon and allowed the Jews to return to Jerusalem. The Book of Esther describes the plight and triumph of the Jews within the Persian Empire. The Babylonian Exile (586 - 538 B.C.) came to an end when the Scribe Ezra and Governor Nehemiah led some of the Jews back to Jerusalem. They wrote two books of the Old Testament that deal with the return of the exiles to Jerusalem, the building of the wall around Jerusalem, and the rebuilding of the Second Temple. It should be noted that not all the Jews returned from the exile; there remained a vibrant Jewish community outside the Holy Land. The Old Testament story closes shortly after the return to Jerusalem.

How did the Babylonian exile end?

> **The Persian Period of Jewish History:**
> **538 - 332 B.C.**

Did the Persians favor Judaism? Explain.

The Persians did not allow the Jews to create an independent state, but they permitted the existence of a vassal province where Judaism was the official religion. The High Priest and the Temple governed the religious life of the Jewish community in Israel. At best, this could be described as a theocracy.

> **The Hellenistic Period of Jewish History:**
> **332 - 160 B.C.**

In 332, the Macedonian King Alexander the Great conquered Jerusalem. His conquests brought an end to the Persian empire, but the theocratic Temple government continued

What prompted the revolt of Judas Maccabaeus?

under the Ptolemaic rulers of Egypt (323 - 200 B.C.), and then, under the Seleucid kings of Syria (200 - 163 B.C.). This tolerant treatment of Jews ended with King Antiochus Epiphanes (175 - 163 B.C.), who sought to forcibly make the Jews adopt the Hellenistic culture and forbade the Jewish ritual at the Temple. He set up a statue of Zeus in the Temple, whereupon the Jews rebelled. Under the leadership of Judas Maccabaeus, the Jews fought and defeated the Syrian forces. Three years to the day after pagan rites had been performed in the Temple, a proper Jewish sacrifice was made on 25 Kislev, 164 B.C.E.,* after Jerusalem had been captured. This victory has since been celebrated during the festival of Chanukah.

> The Hasmonaean or Maccabaean Period
> of Jewish History: 164 - 37 B.C.

What were the results of the revolt?

Eight Hasmonaean kingly High Priests ruled an independent state for 126 years till 37 B.C. But even during this period, Judaea was gradually drawn into the orbit of Rome. Divisions within Judaism between the Sadducee (accepting only the written Mosaic law) and the Pharisee (emphasizing strict observation of both written and oral forms of the Mosaic law) began. Most of the Dead Sea Scrolls, found in a cave in 1947, date from this time period.

> Judaea under Roman Domination:
> 37 B.C. - 70 A.D.

From 37 - 4 B.C., King Herod the Great ruled Judaea as a client king of the Romans. While he was Jewish, many of his policies,

---

* B.C.E. stands for before the common era. it means the same as B.C.

especially those designed to ingratiate himself to the Romans, offended religious sensibilities. After his death, the Romans assumed ever greater control over Judaea and religious tensions increased. During this period of time, Jesus of Nazareth was born, taught, and was crucified by the Romans. We will deal with this time period again when we discuss the Roman Empire and the rise of Christianity. In 66 A.D.,* that is of the Common Era which Jews share with Christians, the Jews rose up against the Roman rule. In 70 A.D., the Temple was stormed by the Romans, Temple worship was abolished, and Jews were exiled from Judaea. Any semblance of Jewish independence was eradicated.

Who was Herod?

Why did the Jews revolt against the Romans?

> Diaspora, Holocaust, and Return:
> 70 A.D. - 1948 A.D.

From the Destruction of the Second Temple in 70 to 1948, there was no independent Jewish state. This is the period of the DIASPORA. But despite the destruction of the Temple, Judaism survived and flourished, in part because ever since the Babylonian Exile a Jewish community continued to live outside of Judaea. Those who fled Jerusalem after the destruction of the Temple could join others living in most of the cities of the Roman Empire. The Rabbis, between 70 and 500 of the Common Era, radically transformed the Jewish religion and created the basis for contemporary Judaism.

There is a rich and extensive Jewish history throughout the Middle Ages and the

What was the result?

---

*A.D. stands for Anno Domini, in the Year of the Lord. Those of the Jewish faith use the designation C.E., that is Common Era, to designate the historical time which Jews and Christians share in common.

When did the Jews again attain independence?

Modern Period. Elements of that history are covered in other sections of this book. In the twentieth century, this history reached a crescendo with the Holocaust. After the Holocaust, during which Nazi Germany murdered as many as six million Jews, and at the end of World War II, a new State of Israel arose, almost miraculously, in 1948.

Judaism as the Religion of the One God

How was the God of the Jews different from the gods worshipped by other ancient peoples?

For a small nation, the descendants of Abraham have had a major impact on world history and, particularly, on European Civilization. That impact has been due, largely, to the religious beliefs which the Jewish people were the first to develop. Judaism, as a religion, is monotheistic. There is only one God and no other gods may be worshipped. Living in a polytheistic world, this command was, at first, hard to obey and there was much backsliding as the Bible records. But the belief in the one God always prevailed.

This God of Israel created Heaven and Earth, but was not a nature god or a god of nature. The one God is transcendental: outside of time and space. God works within the physical and human worlds, but is not a physical force like the sun-god or the wind-god or a fertile mother-earth goddess. God works within a historical setting.

This God first made a covenant with Abraham, and later with Moses. The Covenant, a central idea within Judaism, included the requirement of obedience to God's law, the Torah. In addition to the prime command of worshipping only the one God, the Torah required ritual and moral behavior. Ritual requirements included circumcision, sacrifices, and various dietary regulations. The moral requirements demanded righteousness, fair dealings with others, and help for those less fortunate than oneself: widows, orphans, and strangers. The prophets, in particular, exposed social injustices and the abuse of power by the strong. The ideas of freedom and justice are fundamental to Judaism, since they date back to Moses leading the children of Israel out of oppression and slavery in Egypt.

The God of Israel is not only the God of Power and Might, but also the God of Love and Forgiveness. Individuals can have a personal relationship with God, conceived not as some abstract, logical category, some Prime Mover or First Cause, but as a living God. God expects each individual's worship and God cares for each individual's welfare.

Since Judaism is the record of this special relationship between God and The People of the Covenant, the Jews were the first people to develop a sense of history. Their history was important because it contained lessons from God. Temple scribes wrote down this history from generation to generation. The oral tradition, various writings from the period of the Kings, prophetic sayings, and songs were compiled into what became the Hebrew Bible or the Old Testament. By 100 A.D., the Hebrew Bible had reached its current form. Some written parts date back to the days of King David. Ezra, after the return from Babylonian Exile, had the five Books of Moses, the Pentateuch, published.

Judaism was the first religion to put all these ideas together and the Jewish people have tried to practice these beliefs. It is the impact of these beliefs and practices which make this history so important. During their long history, the Jewish people have often been subjected to prejudice and persecution on account of their religion. The reasons for this prejudice are hard to fathom, but the Jewish people have kept to their faith and

Was the God of Israel a god of righteousness? Explain.

Why is the idea of a Covenant important?

Why do you think the Jews have suffered continuing persecution?

Name some of the ancient peoples who occupied Iran.

believe God has kept the Covenant.

The Persian Empire

Persia was the name which the Greeks gave to the Iranian peoples and to the territory where these people lived. The Iranian plateau was occupied during the Paleolithic and Neolithic periods. By the second millennium, the Elamites, mentioned in the Bible, lived in the southern portion of the plateau near Mesopotamia, and the Kassites lived to the north in the mountains. The Kassites, as we have seen, later occupied Mesopotamia and Babylon. During the Voelkerwanderungen after 1800 B.C., Indo-European peoples, who called themselves Aryans, conquered both the Indian subcontinent and the Iranian plateau.

When did the Parsa or Persians gain their independence?

A second wave of migratory invasions took place after 1200 B.C. The Medes, one of the Iranian tribes, created a kingdom in Western Iran by 700 B.C. In 612 B.C., in alliance with Chaldean Babylon, they destroyed the capital city of the Assyrian Empire. In 549 B.C., the last king of the Medes was defeated by Cyrus the Great of the Parsa, who until then had been a vassal ruler.

Were the Persians influenced by the Sumerians? Explain.

The Parsa or Persians had migrated into Persia at about the same time that the Dorian Greeks moved into Greece, that is after 1200 B.C. Persians and Greeks were related peoples and both spoke Indo-European languages. Since the Persians were in closer physical proximity to the ancient centers of civilization, their acculturation was faster and they borrowed more heavily from Mesopotamian civilization than did the Greeks. While adopting and continuing many elements of Mesopotamian civilization, the Persian Empire marked the end of that tradition, which had begun with the Sumerians.

The Achaemenid Dynasty of Persia: 549 - 330 B.C.

Cyrus the Great, who ruled from 549 to 530 B.C., belonged to the ACHAEMENID dynasty of rulers and was the founder of the Persian Empire. He conquered and governed Iran, Mesopotamia, Anatolia, Syria, and Canaan. His son Cambyses II, who ruled from 530 to 522 B.C., added Egypt to the empire. After a year of battling a rival to the throne, Darius I (c.521 - 486 B.C.) gained control of the empire, consolidated power, and further expanded its size. It is under Darius that the wars against Greece began, which the Greeks called the Persian Wars. Darius' son Xerxes I (c.486 - 465 B.C.) launched a major invasion against Greece in 480 B.C., and was defeated. This defeat marked the end of further expansion and the beginning of decline. But the largest empire created up to this time continued under Artaxerxes I (c.465 - 424 B.C.), Xerxes II (c.424 - 423 B.C.), Darius II (c. 423 - 404) B.C., Artaxerxes II (c. 404 - 359 B.C.), Artaxerxes III (c.359 - 338 B.C.), the usurper Arses (c.338 - 336 B.C.), and, the last of the Achaemenid family, Darius III (c.336 - 330 B.C.). Darius III was defeated in battles by Alexander the Great and was murdered by his own followers in 330 B.C.

Zoroastrianism

The Iranian peoples produced a rich civilization. Their mythologies were similar to those of the Aryans who settled in India and to those of the Greeks. Based on these traditional beliefs, the prophet ZOROASTER (also called Zarathustra), who lived about 628 to

Summarize the political development of Persia from Cyrus the Great to Darius III.

Who was Zoroaster?

Describe the main tenets of Zoroastrianism.

551 B.C., developed a dualistic religion. Ahura Mazda, the god of creation and goodness, is opposed by Ahriman, the god of destruction and evil. The physical world is a battleground for these two forces. Human beings have elements of both and must chose which side to take in the struggle. There will be, ultimately, a great battle between good and evil: the earth will perish, evil will be destroyed, and a new creation will usher in a perfect world.

Zoroastrianism was the official religion of the Achaemenids and remained important until the triumph of Islam. The priests of Zoroastrianism were known as the Magi. Zoroaster appeared to have emphasized the ethical dimension of this religion. His ideas, in turn, influenced Judaism, Christianity, and Islam. While dualistic, Zoroastrianism tended to decay into polytheism, since both Ahura Mazda and Ahriman headed subordinate groups of good and evil gods, respectively. The ahuras were good and the daevas were evil. The idea of angels and devils within the main monotheistic religions is clearly dualistic.

What is dualism?

The Subsequent History of Iran

What happened to Persia after Alexander the Great's conquest?

With the Persian conquest by Alexander the Great, Iran became part of Hellenistic civilization. After Alexander's death, Seleucus, one of his generals, gained control of Babylon in 312 BC. He established the SELEUCID EMPIRE, which included most of Iran. The Seleucid dynasty ruled Iran until 187 B.C.

The PARTHIAN KINGDOM under the Arsacid dynasty ruled Iran from about 187 B.C. until 224 A.D. They were followed by the SASSANIAN dynasty of the Persians, who reigned from 224 A.D. to 651 A.D.

Thereafter, the Arabs ruled Iran, bringing
with them the new religion of Islam.

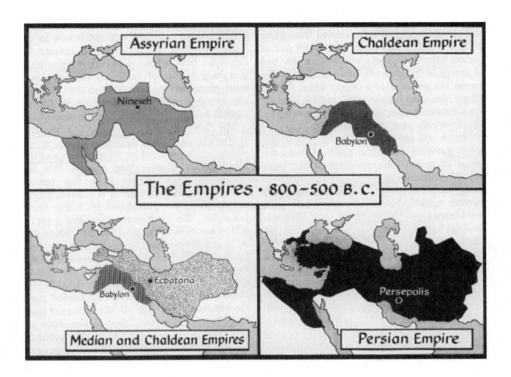

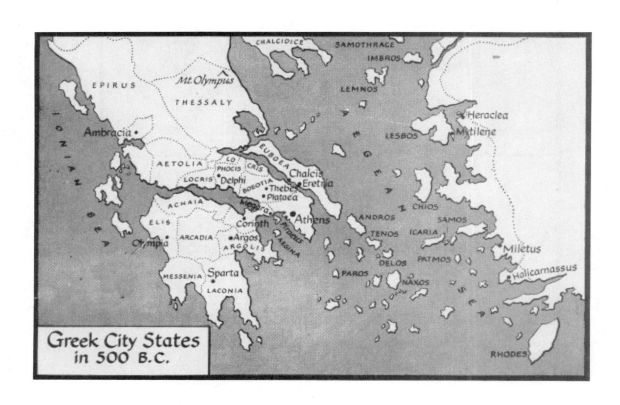

Greek City States in 500 B.C.

3

The Greek City-States

The Aegean region includes Greece, Macedonia, and the many islands that lie offshore, including Crete and Cyprus. Neolithic peoples moved into this area between 5000 and 4000 B.C. either from Anatolia or southern Russia. By 3000 B.C. an early Bronze Age culture had developed that was subjected to waves of migration, including several by Greek-speaking Indo-Europeans.

What is the Aegean region?

Three successive, but related, civilizations developed in this area between 2000 and 300 B.C. These were the Minoan, the Mycenaean, and the Hellenic civilizations. Each will be discussed in turn in the following pages. The Hellenic civilization came to be partially incorporated into the Hellenistic civilization, which developed after the death of Alexander the Great in 323 B.C. and lasted until 30 B.C., the time of the first Roman emperor, Caesar Augustus.

What civilizations developed in the area?

Minoan Civilization: 2000 - 1450 B.C.

The Minoan civilization was centered on the island of Crete. By 2500 B.C., a Bronze Age culture of peoples from the Eastern shores of the Mediterranean, who were not of Indo-European stock, had settled Crete and had developed a writing system called Linear A. Large palaces were built on the island, which had become the center of this burgeon-

Where was the Minoan civilization centered?

Was the Minoan civilization very advanced? Explain.

Why is the term "Minoan" used to describe this culture?

ing civilization. Several palace complexes have been excavated at Knossos, Phaistos, Mallia, and Zakros. The largest, at KNOSSOS, had more than 1500 rooms arranged around a central courtyard. Their staterooms had parquet floors and were decorated with wall paintings showing naturalistic pictures of dolphins, other fish, birds, butterflies, and flowers in vivid colors. Their storerooms contained large jars, as tall as six feet, for storing wine, olive oil, and grain. Workshops for making various handicrafts were also found within these palace complexes. Knossos had a plumbing system that included flush toilets. It was also remarkable that no fortifications surrounded these palaces and their frescoes did not include scenes of war. The Minoans seem to have been a mercantile people whose ships protected them from attack. Their civilization reached the height of its development during the Middle Bronze Age from about 1700 - 1450 B.C.

The civilization centered on Crete was called MINOAN after a legendary King Minos, whose name appeared in Greek legends of the classical age. Athens, the legend went, had to send ten young men and ten maidens as tribute to Crete. The Athenian hero Theseus went to the island, slew the minotaur, a beast half-bull and half-man, and escaped from a labyrinth. When Sir Arthur Evans began excavations at Knossos in 1899, he named his finds Minoan in memory of the legend.

The Minoan civilization was a very sophisticated, commercial society that had extensive trade with other civilizations. The Minoans also founded settlements on other Aegean islands and on the Greek mainland. Several palace centers have now been excavated. Each palace appears to have been independent of the others. Each may have been ruled by a priest-king since no temples separate from the palaces have been found.

Their religion may have been based on a fertility cult, including a mother goddess often depicted bare chested and holding two snakes in her hands. A bull, perhaps the legendary minotaur, played an obvious function. Their wall paintings included pictures of bull leaping, where young athletes sought to leap over the back of a charging bull. Both young men and women participated in these practices, which may have had both athletic and religious significance. The double axe appears to have been a symbol of this culture. The palace at Knossos was destroyed about 1450 B.C. by a mainland, Greek-speaking people who have been called the Mycenaeans.

Mycenaean Civilization: 1450 - 1100 B.C.

About 1800 B.C. or so, an Indo-European people conquered and settled the mainland of Greece. They may have intermarried with the indigenous population. These people developed their own Bronze Age culture, which has been called MYCENAEAN, traded with the Minoans for over one hundred years from about 1600 - 1500 B.C., and adopted many cultural characteristics from the Minoans. They also seem to have copied the Minoan writing system, Linear A, and modified it for their own Greek language, thereby creating Linear B. The fact that Linear B is an early version of Greek came as a considerable surprise to scholars when Michael Ventris succeeded in deciphering that script in the 1950s. Linear A has not yet been decoded. Whether Linear B was first developed on the mainland or on Crete is also still debated. The Linear B writing has been found

Do you see any features that differentiate Minoan civilization from those previously discussed?

Who were the Mycenaeans?

Distinguish Linear A from Linear B.

Against what peoples did the Mycenaeans make war?

Do you think the *Iliad* is purely a legend? Explain.

What was a "wanax"?

at Knossos after 1450 B.C., giving evidence of an invasion.

At first the Mycenaeans may have paid tribute to the Minoans, but later they turned tables. About 1450 B.C., these mainlanders conquered Crete itself and installed themselves in the palaces. A final destruction of the palaces on Crete took place about 1400 B.C., by whom is still unclear.

Mycenaeans, too, were named after the legends of classical Greece. Homer's *Iliad* tells the story of how Paris, the ill-fated son of Priam, king of Ilium or Troy, captured fair Helen, wife of Menelaus, king of Sparta and brother of Agamemnon, king of Mycenae. Agamemnon raised a mighty fleet and army to make war on Troy to punish the raiders. The siege of Troy lasted ten years until the mighty city, on the Asiatic side of the Hellespont, fell to the mainland Greeks.

Homer's poem of 16,000 lines of dactylic hexameter was probably written in the eighth century B.C. in Ionia. Its descriptions of war, armor, banquets, and other events makes it clear that this poem referred back to an earlier age than the lifetime of the poet. A German amateur archeologist, Heinrich Schliemann, who took his Homer seriously, began excavations at the ancient site of Mycenae and in 1876 found unplundered shaft graves that contained a large gold treasure. The objects found there were similar to objects described by Homer and this entire civilization has been called Mycenaean.

The Mycenaeans were a war-like people who built fortress palaces on top of mountains. Besides Mycenae, major palaces also existed at Athens, Tiryns, and Pylos. Each of these states was ruled by a king called a "wanax," who acted like an absolute despot and controlled the economy and all aspects of social life through his bureaucracy. The king of Mycenae may have had an overlordship over the other states. Their war against Troy took place about 1250 B.C.

For reasons still unclear—whether it was the long struggle with Troy, growing conflict among themselves, or new invaders after about 1200 B.C.—the Mycenaean civilization came to an end by 1100 B.C. Memories of its glories are recalled only in legend.

When did Mycenaean civilization end?

Ancient Greece: 1200 - 323 B.C.

end of mycereans.

The Greek Dark Ages: 1200 - 800 B.C.

Who were the invaders of the Greek Dark Ages?

Ionion the largest group that enter Greece.

During this period, the Mycenaean civilization's highly centralized, bureaucratically-run governments and economy collapsed. The hilltop citadels were destroyed, population declined, and literacy came to an end. Some Mycenaeans fled from the mainland and settled in Anatolia, in modern Turkey, where they created a Greek-speaking region called IONIA. On the mainland, Dorian Greek invaders established themselves in parts of Greece and may have merged gradually with the resident population. It was a time of turmoil, decline, and new beginnings.

Where is Ionia located?

The Formative Period of Classical Greek Civilization: 800 - 500 B.C.

When did Hellenic civilization begin?

By 800 B.C., a new civilization was forming. This was the Classical Greek or *Ionians →* HELLENIC CIVILIZATION that is at the root of our own Western Civilization. First in Ionia and then on the mainland, the Greeks

What was the polis?

developed a new political organization, the POLIS, which came to define them. Polis is the Greek name for city-state, which included an agricultural territory controlled from a walled inner city. The center included a citadel, shrines and temples to the gods, a market place or agora, and a residential quarter, all protected by walled fortifications. Each polis was economically and politically independent of other city-states. Despite their independence, these poleis recognized a common bond of language, culture, and religion.

Population Growth

Name some poleis on the Greek mainland.

From the Greek city-states of Ionia, new cultural ideas were transmitted to the Greeks on the mainland. There, too, the polis became the basic organizational structure. Many poleis were formed, not only Athens and Sparta, but also Thebes, Argos, Corinth, Pylos, Chalcis, Megara, Samos, and many more. Each polis had its own distinct history, but all of them shared in certain common patterns.

What was the effect of population increases on the poleis?

Originally each polis was largely self-sufficient and depended on farming to feed itself. But over time, stable communities tended to increase in population, to grow in social complexity, and to become more differentiated economically. Since the amount of agricultural land was fixed, population increases created serious problems for agricultural societies. They tended to increase the divisions between social classes and harden the lines between the rich and the poor. When a population grew beyond the available supply of food that the land could supply, there were three distinct solutions to the crisis. The community might split and one part could seek new land to colonize. A second solution was to go to war and conquer the land of one's neighbor. A third solution was to transform one's social and economic system in such a way that the same land and resources could feed a much larger population. All three methods were tried by the ancient Greeks, as we shall see in the following three sections.

How did the Greek city-states deal with the problem of over-population?

Greek Colonization Between 750 and 500 B.C., many Greek city-states formed colonies. New poleis were formed all around the Black Sea, in southern Italy and Sicily, southern France, parts of Spain, Libya, and even one in the delta of Egypt. What is interesting from a modern perspective is that each colony was totally independent from the original polis from where the settlers had come. An old city-state simply split in two and a substantial part of the population settled in a new location. There were, of course, ties of kinship which fostered trade, but politically each new colony was totally independent from its very beginning. This was very different from the method of colonization employed by the Spaniards and other European colonial powers in our period of history. Ultimately, the Greeks ran out of new lands where poleis could be founded and were confronted with population pressures once again.

How were Greek colonies different from European colonies of modern times?

The Garrison State of Sparta

Sparta is located in the region of LACONIA, which is the southeastern quarter of the PELOPONNESUS in Greece. The Peloponnesus region has more fertile farmland than most of mountainous Greece. Sparta was allegedly formed out of four villages. The

What was the relationship between the Spartans and the Messenians?

Dorian Greeks, who conquered this region in the eleventh century, seem to have dominated the earlier inhabitants from the very beginning. But until the seventh century, Sparta was a typical Greek polis and participated in the wave of Greek colonization.

But Sparta also used the second option of increasing the supply of land by conquering the land of others. Between 735 and 715 B.C., in the First Messenian War, the polis of Sparta had conquered the neighboring polis of MESSENIA and proceeded to make the Messenians into a subject population. Not surprisingly, the Messenians revolted several times. The Messenians, who were also Dorian Greeks, almost turned the tables on the Spartans during the Second Messenian War from about 650 to 630 B.C. Only with the greatest effort did the Spartans finally succeed in defeating the Messenians.

Describe the class structure of Sparta.

In the aftermath of this war, the Spartans reorganized their government to create what came to be called the typically Spartan GARRISON state. They attributed these changes to the legendary law-giver LYCURGUS, who may have lived during the ninth century. Based on existing class divisions, Sparta came to be divided into three rigid classes. The conquered people, including the Messenians, were turned into HELOTS, who performed forced agricultural labor. A middle class of free merchants and traders received the status of PERIOIKOI. Only the SPARTANS, perhaps ten percent of the total population, were citizens and ran the polis.

These Spartans formed a permanent standing army because they were always afraid of another helot uprising. At the age of seven, young boys were taken away from their mothers and lived communally in barracks. They began their life-long training as soldiers. Men could marry at age eighteen, but continued to live in the barracks until age thirty. To meet their wives, they had to go AWOL and if caught were severely disciplined. Meals were taken communally in a mess hall until the age of sixty. The Spartan women had control over the family farm, which was worked by the helots. Once a year, the Spartans formally declared war on the helots and, during this special period, any Spartan could legally kill any helot with whom he had a grievance.

The Spartan government was also strange. They had two kings who served mainly ceremonial functions and as war leaders. Real power was exercised by the five EPHORS, elders who were sixty years or older. The ephors would inspect every newborn child and if they found any defects, the child was exposed on the mountainside to die. This regimented society did produce one of the largest and best disciplined armies in all of Greece. Their military power was gained at the price of stifling all creative impulses and individuality. There are no Spartan painters, sculptors, dramatists, or philosophers. The Spartans discouraged trade, because they knew that commerce brings change and new ideas. Their economy remained agricultural and stagnated.

In the early sixth century, Sparta seized additional lands from Argos, their chief rival, and became the dominant power in the Peloponnesus. They made alliances with lesser poleis, except Argos, to form the PELOPONNESIAN LEAGUE.

The Evolution of Government Elsewhere in Greece: From Tribal Monarchy to Aristocracy

The Dorian Greeks during the Dark Ages appear to have had a tribal monarchy. All the warriors of a tribe belonged to a popular assembly called the ECCLESIA.

Demonstrate the militarism of Spartan society.

What was the Peloponnesian League?

Describe the structure of early tribal monarchy.

These warriors were led by a king, who came from a royal clan. This tribal king was advised by a council of elders, representing the other clans of the tribe, called the GEROUSIA.

As the Greeks established themselves in their valleys, became settled farmers, and formed poleis, this system of government gradually became aristocratic. The largest landowners replaced the elders of the tribe as the dominant social class. Kingship was abolished and the gerousia became an aristocratic council. The ecclesia became dominated by the retainers of the large landowners and many poorer farmers lost their standing in the ecclesia, since they could no longer afford the military equipment required of a warrior.

What replaced the monarchy?

The Challenge to and Transformation of the Aristocratic Form of Government

While colonization had alleviated these population pressures, it did not permanently resolve the problem. The Greeks soon ran out of suitable land for further colonies. Except for Sparta, conquering neighboring poleis proved impossible since each polis was able to defend itself and maintain a balance of power within Greece.

Discuss the fate of many small farmers.

The Challenge from the Small Farmers

By 650 B.C., aristocratic rule was being challenged in most Greek poleis. Small farmers with too many sons could not provide each with a plot of land large enough to feed a family. Cutting of trees and soil erosion were reducing the yields from mountain plots. Many small farmers went into debt and when they could not repay, they were forced to sell their children, and finally themselves, into debt slavery. In most poleis, these small farmers had had citizen status and they became increasingly resentful of aristocratic rule.

| The Transforma-
tion of Warfare | There was also a change in the conduct of warfare. During the Mycenaean Period and the early Dark Ages, as described by Homer, warfare was waged by warriors on horses and even in chariots. Keeping a horse has always been extremely expensive. As Greek society divided into wealthy and poor farmers, only the aristocracy could afford to keep horses and other military equipment. The small farmers were increasingly disenfranchised and lost their status in the ecclesia.

But at the same time that the poleis were dividing into distinct social classes, they were also growing in population. This growing population made possible a new form of military organization: HOPLITE infantry replaced the earlier knights. While hoplite armor was still expensive, it was less so than maintaining a horse. The hoplites were organized into a PHALANX formation, in which several rows of men, protecting each other with their shields, marched in unison with their spears stretched out. If a man in the front row fell, those in the back rows would take his place. A phalanx could easily take on a knight. Manpower became decisive in fighting wars. Even some of the aristocrats recognized that they must make concessions if the polis itself was to survive.

| The Challenge
from the New
Middle Class | Colonization had stimulated trade and Greek poleis developed a new middle class of merchants, craftsmen, and sailors. Someone who has traveled has a broader vision than a village peasant or even some tradition-bound aristocrat. Liter-

Describe the hoplite infantry organization.

How did this development help the small farmers?

Why did the Greek merchants favor the small farmers over the aristocrats?

Who were the tyrants?

acy itself is a sign that a given community has reached new levels of complexity.

The Greek merchants adopted the Lydian practice of minting coins of gold and silver. Lydia was a rich kingdom in Western Anatolia where the idea of coins and money appear to have originated in the seventh century. King Croesus of Lydia was legendary for his wealth until he was conquered by King Cyrus the Great of Persia in 547 B.C. Money served as a new source of wealth in addition to land. While some of the new merchants came from the ranks of the aristocracy, most did not. Merchants resented the special status of the nobility and made common cause with the poor farmers.

The rising merchant class of Greece provided a counter-elite to the dominant aristocracy. By becoming the champions of the poor farmers, leaders of this new class could develop a mass following and challenge the traditional ways. Unscrupulous leaders, called TYRANTS, seized power and pushed through needed reforms while enriching themselves. When the many got wise to the tyrants, they took power into their own hands and developed the form of government known as DEMOCRACY. This trend toward rule by the many went furthest in Athens, which will be used to illustrate this pattern.

The Athenian Experiment in Democracy

Athens is located in the region of Greece called Attica. Athens dates back to the Minoan and Mycenaean Ages. Mycenaean refugees used it as a debarkation point when they established themselves in Ionia. Throughout its history, Athens continued to have strong ties to the coast of Anatolia.

During the Dark Ages, Athens moved from tribal monarchy to aristocracy. By 650

B.C., aristocratic dominance was increasingly challenged by the demands of the small farmers and the newly developing merchant class. Athenian politics became a struggle between the aristocratic faction and the popular faction. After more than a hundred years of struggle, the popular faction gradually gained power. The first step toward democracy was taken under Draco.

Draco In 621 B.C., Draco codified and put in writing the previously customary law of Athens. While he abolished blood feuds and created courts to settle crimes, so many offenses were punished by death that the word "draconian" is still used to describe harsh penalties.

Before Draco, the Athenians had a customary, unwritten law which was applied exclusively by aristocratic judges. Writing down the law is a first step toward curbing the power of the traditional nobility. It also presupposes a literate society, which in itself is a sign of social advancement.

Solon Solon, who lived from about 639 to 559 B.C., was an aristocrat and a reformer. In 594 B.C., he was appointed sole ARCHON and given the supreme legislative power to reorganize Athenian society. There usually were nine archons in Athens who were the chief magistrates of the polis.

Solon understood that the traditional form of agriculture, where each farm family produced the food for its own survival, needed to be transformed. He believed Athens should develop a commercial economy and an export-oriented agriculture in order to alleviate the growing poverty of the small farmers.

Solon passed laws canceling the debts and prohibiting debt slavery. State money was used to buy the freedom of some who had been sold into slavery outside of Athens. That

What did Draco accomplish?

What did Solon do?

Was Solon a success?

was certainly popular with small farmers.

Solon realized that the soil and climate of Greece were much more suitable for growing grapes and olives than cereals. He encouraged the transformation of family farms into vineyards and olive groves. Olive oil and wine could be exported to buy more grain than Athens could produce.

Solon's reforms were far-reaching, but they did not solve the immediate problems. Conversion of farms to vineyards and olive groves takes time; what are people to eat in the meantime? Farmers freed of debt on their persons still lacked adequate land to feed their families. The aristocrats thought Solon had gone too far in his reforms while the small farmers thought that he had not gone far enough. Turmoil continued until Peisistratus, after two unsuccessful tries, established himself as tyrant.

Why was Peisistratus popular?

| Peisistratus | Peisistratus lived from about 605 to 527 B.C. He was the commanding general who conquered SALAMIS for the Athenians in about 565 B.C. His popularity led him to seek dictatorial power in 561 and again from 560 to 556 B.C. He finally succeeded in 546 when he was made TYRANT of Athens, a position he continued to hold until his death. Those who opposed him had their lands confiscated and some lands were redistributed to the poor farmers.

Tyranny arose in most Greek poleis and imposed a crude stability on the turbulence of politics. Since the tyrants were usually opposed by the aristocrats, their policies tended to benefit the poor. Dictators usually encourage massive public works projects, in this case temples and roads, that also benefit the poor and middle classes. Peisistratus began the beautification of Athens by building new stone temples, to replace the wooden ones, on the Acropolis.

All factions tired gradually of the oppression and arbitrariness of the tyrant. When Peisistratus died in 527 B.C., his sons Hipparchus and Hippias took over. Hipparchus was killed in an uprising against the tyranny in 514; subsequently Hippias was forced into exile, with foreign help, in 510 B.C. After renewed factional strife, Cleisthenes became the leader of Athens.

| Cleisthenes | Cleisthenes is known as the father of Athenian democracy. He lived from about 570 to 508 B.C. and gained power after the overthrow of the tyranny. He placed Athenian government on a territorial basis. The four old traditional tribes based on blood relationships were replaced with ten new tribes based on a territorial subdivision of Athens. Athens was divided into regions: the coast, the city proper, and the hill country. Each region was divided into ten districts or DEMES. Each of the ten new tribes was allocated one district in the hill country, the city proper, and the coastal area. Anyone living in a district belonged to the tribe to whom the district had been allocated. Thus each of the ten tribes represented a microcosm of Athens.

From their citizenship rolls, each tribe selected fifty persons each year by lot to serve on a newly formed COUNCIL OF FIVE HUNDRED. The Council of Five Hundred prepared legislation to be proposed to the Assembly of all Athenian citizens, the ECCLESIA. The Ecclesia could only approve or disapprove legislation, but not initiate it. Fifty persons from the Council of the Five Hundred served as a steering committee which was always on duty. These fifty, who rotated every month among the ten tribes of the Council, conducted the day-to-day business of the city-state.

Each of the ten tribes was also respon-

Who was Cleisthenes?

was a political economist.
Try to make everybody responsible.

What were the demes?

10 tribes district → the coast
→ the city
→ the hill country

each region divide into 10 districts.
or demes.

What was the role of the Council of the Five Hundred?

Who were the strategos?

sible for providing a military contingent. The leader of the tribe's militia was called the STRATEGOS. The ten *strategoi* were elected rather than chosen by lot.

The old aristocratic Areopagus lost most of its powers, but was retained as a court of appeal and for some religious functions. There was also a jury system, the HELIEIA.

The system created by Cleisthenes made Athens highly democratic while providing it with effective government. Class conflict appears to have declined as Athens in general grew more prosperous. This new stability came just in time because the rise of the Persian Empire threatened the survival of Athens and the other Greek poleis.

When was the Golden Age of Classical Greece?

The Golden Age of Classical Greece

The Fifth Century, from 499 to 400 B.C., is the Golden Age of Hellenic Civilization. It is bounded by two wars. At the beginning of the century are the Persian Wars, which represented the Greek's finest hour. At the end is the Peloponnesian War between Athens and Sparta, a civil war among the Greeks, which led to the decline of their civilization.

What were the causes of the Persian Wars?

The Persian Wars

Cyrus the Great lived from about 599 to 530 B.C. and was the founder of the Persian Empire of the Achaemenid dynasty, which he ruled from 549 B.C. to his death. He defeated King Croesus in 547 B.C. and conquered his Kingdom of Lydia. The Greek city-states of Ionia which had been vassals of King Croesus now fell under Persian domination. About 499 B.C., the Ionian Greeks rebelled against the Persians and received help from Athens and Eretria.

The Persians quelled the rebellion by 493 B.C., but Darius I, the grandson of Cyrus, determined to punish the meddling mainland Greeks. Darius sent a fleet with an invasion force to punish Athens and Eretria. The Persians invaders destroyed Eretria, but were defeated at the Battle of MARATHON in 490 B.C. The Athenians, after the battle, marched all night from Marathon to Athens, 22.5 miles away, and were ready to fight the Persians again next morning when the Persian navy entered the Athenian harbor of Piraeus. The Persians decided to withdraw. Miltiades was the Athenian strategos who won the Battle of Marathon. The march of the Athenians is still remembered with today's marathon run, whose distance has, however, been fixed at 26 miles and 385 yards.

It was clear to the Greeks and the Persians that this Greek victory was only a temporary respite before a full-scale invasion would take place. It took the Persians ten years to get ready due to dynastic and internal problems. But in 480 B.C., XERXES, the new ruler, was ready. He had a bridge of ships built across the Hellespont so that his army of 100,000 men could march from Asia to Europe. This army was supported by the Persian navy, which supplied the logistics for the army.

In this war against a Persian invasion, the Athenians and the Spartans were on the same side. The Spartans had the largest Greek army. The Athenians had used the time after Marathon to build a significant navy. The Athenian leader THEMISTOCLES had persuaded his fellow citizens that their only chance against the superior manpower of the Persians was through the building of a NAVY. He reasoned, correctly, that if the Athenians could defeat the Persian navy, then the large army would be deprived of its supplies and would retreat. The discovery of a

What was notable about the Battle of Marathon?

What was Xerxes's strategy?

Who was Themistocles?

Why is Thermopylae famous?

What was the consequence of the Battle of Salamis?

new vein of silver at the Athenian mines eased the expenses of building a navy.

On their way to Attica, the Persian army was briefly stopped by the Spartans at the mountain pass of THERMOPYLAE (480 B.C.). King Leonidas and his 300 Spartan warriors stopped the entire Persian army for three days until betrayed by a Greek traitor, who showed the Persians a second mountain pass to the rear of the Spartans. Attacked from both sides, the Spartans fought to the last man, sending only a messenger back to Sparta to tell the story. Thermopylae was one of the greatest and most heroic battles of the Spartans, worthy indeed of the heroes of old.

From the Persian perspective, it had been a nuisance which barely delayed their advance on Attica. They took and destroyed the city of Athens, which had, however, been evacuated by its women and children. The men were aboard their ships and at the naval Battle of SALAMIS in 480 B.C., the Athenian navy destroyed the Persian navy while Xerxes watched furiously from the shore.

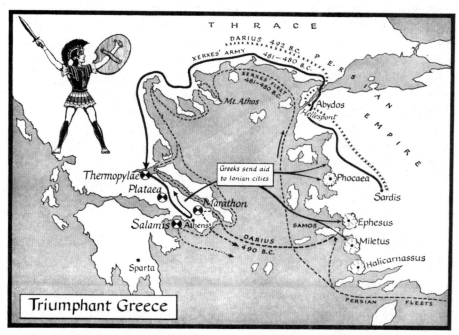

Triumphant Greece

Having destroyed the buildings of Athens, bringing victory of sorts, the Persians retreated from Greece as Themistocles had predicted. The following year (479 B.C.), the Greeks under Spartan leadership defeated the Persian army at the Battle of PLATAEA. This ended the threat of a Persian invasion that might have turned Greece into another Persian province. It did not mean the end of the Persian empire which remained powerful until finally conquered by Alexander the Great.

After Plataea on their way back to their polis, the Spartan army stopped in Athens. Their leaders suggested that the Athenians keep their fortifications, destroyed by the Persians, as a war memorial. The Athenians heartily agreed. As soon as the Spartans went home, they rebuilt their walls stronger than ever.

Once the threat of invasion was over, the Spartans were not interested in continuing and bringing the war to Persia. The Athenians, however, wanted to liberate the Greek city-states of Ionia. Since the Spartans, as ever, were worried about their helots, leadership of the Greeks fell to the Athenians. The Athenians and other like-minded Greek city-states formed the DELIAN LEAGUE to liberate the Ionian poleis.

Themistocles played an active role in Athenian politics until 471 B.C. when his enemies succeeded in having him ostracized. OSTRACISM was a unique feature of Athenian democracy whereby an unpopularity contest was held. The ecclesia voted among rival political leaders as to who should be expelled from Athens for ten years. The person who remained in Athens, obviously, became the popular leader and was allowed to pursue his policies.

CIMON, the son of Miltiades, the hero of the Battle of Marathon, emerged as the dominant leader of Athens. He was a moder-

Who won the Battle of Plataea?

Was Athens or Sparta most aggressive towards Persia?

What was ostracism?

Why was Athens able to dominate the Delian League?

ate democrat, who strongly pursued the war against Persia but sought to retain friendship with Sparta. Cimon was ostracized in 461 B.C. when his pro-Spartan policies became unpopular in Athens.

The Delian League The League began in the winter of 477 B.C. as a voluntary association of like-minded city-states, but Athens was always the predominant member. Athens provided the largest navy, whereas most other poleis provided money, rather than ships, for the common cause. The treasury of the League was kept on the island of DELOS, hence the name. By 467 B.C., the League succeeded in liberating the Ionian cities and driving the Persian fleet out of the Eastern Mediterranean. Cimon won a great naval battle against the Persians at the EURYMEDON RIVER in 467 B.C. Having achieved its aims, the Delian League's triumphs led the membership to demand that the League be disbanded, and that the treasury be divided among the members.

How did the League become an Athenian Empire?

Athens refused and forced the other members to continue to make their contributions, thereby transforming the League into the Athenian Empire. After Cimon's ostracism, EPHIALTES became the leader of the radical democrats. Ephialtes further reduced the remaining powers of the old aristocratic assembly, the Areopagus, to that of a homicide court. He also restructured the Athenian court system. After Ephialtes was murdered in 462 B.C., PERICLES (d. 429 B.C.) emerged as the popular leader of Athens.

The Athenian Empire The period from 467 to 431 B.C. saw the development of the Athenian Empire. The tribute which the empire produced helped to finance Athenian democracy. During most of this time Pericles was the great, democratic leader of Athens. He sponsored legislation which provided pay for jury service. This was popular with the poor because it allowed them to actively participate in government service. The empire also created opportunities for new Athenian settlements, which helped to relieve population pressures. The large Athenian navy provided additional job opportunities for Athenian citizens. Trade and commerce was stimulated by the expansion of Athenian power. Because imperialism profited Athens, it was popular with the people.

Within Greece, only Sparta rivaled Athenian might and was the leader of a league of city-states called the PELOPONNESIAN LEAGUE. A delicate balance of power between the Athenian Empire and the Peloponnesian League emerged, which even minor shifts might upset. After the fall of Cimon, Sparta and Athens were on a collision course. Several small wars were fought between Athens and Sparta between 460 and 445 B.C. in what is often called the First Peloponnesian War. A Thirty Years' Peace was signed in 445 B.C., which lasted only until 431 B.C. when the Great Peloponnesian War began.

> The Great Peloponnesian War: 431 - 404 B.C.

The war was a complex conflict involving many poleis of the two competing alliance systems. It was not simply Sparta fighting Athens, but that was what it ultimately became.

Sparta began the war with the strongest army in Greece and Athens depended on its navy. Armies cannot fight navies or vice versa. Neither side, therefore, had the necessary forces to defeat the other side as long as each side played to their strength.

The war began with Sparta invading Attica and laying siege to Athens. The Athenians took refuge behind their great walls

How did Pericles contribute to the development of Athenian democracy?

Why do you think Sparta became involved in wars against Athens?

What were the relative strengths of Athens and Sparta?

What was Pericles's strategy?

while their navy supplied them with food, raided the coasts of the Peloponnese, and disrupted the commerce of their enemies.

Pericles had devised this defensive strategy. He refused to fight a major land battle, which the Athenians would probably have lost; he surrendered the Athenian countryside to Spartan invasion, and at the same time fought a war of attrition against his enemies. He hoped that the Spartans would tire of the war, turn their back on their allies, and make peace with Athens.

Why did it fail?

For several years, the Spartans annually ravaged the Athenian countryside. The Athenians, cooped up in their city, lived under horrible hygienic conditions and in 430 B.C. a great plague broke out. When Pericles died of the plague in 429 B.C., CLEON (d. 422 B.C.) became the leader of the democratic war party, while NICIAS led the conservative peace party. The war see-sawed back and forth until 421 B.C. when the Peace of Nicias was signed. Though this peace agreement was to last for 50 years, its terms were never carried out completely by either side.

Who was Alcibiades?

In 415 B.C., the war party led by ALCIBIADES (c.450 - 404 B.C.)persuaded the Athenian ecclesia to authorize a high-risk military mission to involve the Athenians in the complex politics of the Greek city-states on Sicily. The aim was to gain control of the rich and powerful city-state of Syracuse. The Athenian forces were placed under the divided command of Alcibiades and Nicias. By 413 B.C., this entire expedition had been decisively defeated. Athens lost more than 200 ships.

This major defeat triggered rebellion within the Athenian empire and led the Persians to provide financial aid to the Spartans. Athens was able to raise another navy, but after that too was defeated in 405 B.C., the Athenians could no longer feed themselves by sea and were starved into surrender by the Spartans in 404 B.C. Athens had lost the Peloponnesian War. Though it survived as a polis, it had to give up its empire.

Who won the Peloponnesian War?

The Twilight of the Greek City-States

The defeat of Athens in the Peloponnesian War ushered in a period of incessant warfare. None of the great poleis of Greece could establish its dominance. The civil wars among the Greeks sapped their strength and opened the door to King Philip II of Macedonia's conquest.

The Rise of Macedon

Macedonia was the northernmost of the Greek states. It was a kingdom rather than a city-state. Until its rise to power under their king PHILIP II, who ruled from 359 to 336 B.C., the Macedonians had been a backward kingdom. The Hellenes had considered Macedonians to be semi-barbarians. Philip, who had spent three years in Thebes as a hostage during his youth, had learned much about Greek politics and warfare. He applied these lessons in building up his kingdom, steadily increased his influence in Greece until, at the Battle of CHAERONEA in 338 B.C., he defeated them and ended the independence of the poleis.

Who was Philip II of Macedon?

Macedonian troops were stationed in Greek cities. A congress was held at Corinth and an HELLENIC LEAGUE was proclaimed with Philip as HEGEMON. Philip announced a crusade against Persia, but was assassinated while preparations for it were under way. His twenty-year old son became king as Alexander III of Macedonia. This was Alexander the Great, who would conqueror the mighty Persian Empire.

What happened at Chaeronea?

While the defeat at Chaeronea brought an end to the political independence of the

Was Alexander the Great anti-Greek? Explain.

Greek city-states, it did not mean an end to Greek influence. As will be seen in the next section, Greek cultural influence was actually diffused over a wider area thanks to the conquests of Alexander and subsequent establishment of Greek-speaking Hellenistic kingdoms over much of the Middle East.

Figure 1.4. Stone Inscriptions. Mesopotamian-Babylonian, Sumerian, c. 2000 B. C. Cuneiform, the earliest form of writing, is found chiseled on this fragment of black marble. Writing initially started with pictographs. Some, found at Uruk, date to 3100 B.C. Pictographs later evolved into these inscriptions that you see before you. The main purpose of the ancient writing was to record business transactions, construction records, and data on water usage. *Courtesy of The Metropolitan Museum of Art, Bequest of W. Gedney Beatty, 1941. (41.160.185)*

NOTES

[1] Donald C. Johanson and Maitland A. Edey, <u>Lucy: The Beginnings of Humankind</u> (New York: Simon and Schuster, 1981), pp.16-21.

[2] Rick Gore, "Neanderthals," <u>National Geographic</u> (January 1996): 2-35.

[3] William F. Albright, "Judaism, the Ancient Near East, and the Origins of Christianity" in Norman F. Cantor, ed. <u>Perspectives on the European Past: Conversations with Historians</u>, Part I (New York: The Macmillan Company, 1971), pp. 38-62.

Figure 1.5. Seated Figure of Gudea. Mesopotamian Sculpture, c. 2100 B. C. King Gudea ruled the Sumerian city-state of Lagash around 2150 B. C. Celebrated for his construction of temples, he was also honored as a patron of the arts. Notice the round, naturalistic face and large eyes of the statue. *Courtesy of The Metropolitan Museum of Art, Harris Brisbane Dick Fund, 1959. (59.2)*

HAMMURABI

Code of Laws

Hammurabi was a Babylonian king who ruled from 1792 to about 1750 B. C. His accomplishments include completing the conquest of Mesopotamia, bringing relative peace to chaotic times, and compiling one of the oldest written code of laws. French archaeologists uncovered this Code in 1901-1902. The eight-foot stele (basalt column) they found depicts Hammurabi receiving the laws from the god of justice, Shamash. The inscriptions are engraved in cuneiform, the wedge-shaped writing of the time, and are relatively well preserved. In his prologue to the 282 laws Hammurabi states he is bringing justice to the land and is promoting the welfare of the people.

The Code dealt with virtually every aspect of human life: theft, arson, incest, kidnapping, medical and construction malpractice, business transactions, debt, divorce, adultery, land use, irrigation practices, tenancy, and false testimony. The laws were in plain sight for all to see. Thus even though the punishments were physical and harsh, they were clear guidelines of what penalty or monetary payment would be imposed on an wrongdoer. Class distinctions—nobles, commoners, slaves—were incorporated into the penalties that were meted out. For example, the principle of retribution of "an eye for an eye, a tooth for a tooth" is pronounced for men of the same class. Similar harsh practices are found in the Islamic law or the Shari'ah that is in force in countries such as Saudi Arabia today. It prescribes that if someone commits a theft, he should forfeit a hand.

HAMMURABI'S CODE OF LAWS[*]

2. If any one bring an accusation against a man, and the accused go to the river and leap into the river, if he sink in the river his accuser shall take possession of his house. But if the river prove that the accused is not guilty, and he escape unhurt, then he who had brought the accusation shall be put to death, while he who leaped into the river shall take possession of the house that had belonged to his accuser.

3. If any one bring an accusation of any crime before the elders, and does not prove what he has charged, he shall, if it be a capital offense charged, be put to death.

[*] From *The Letters and Inscriptions of Hammurabi, King of Babylon, about B.C. 2200*, translated by L. W. King (London: Luzac and Co., 1898-1900).

4. If he satisfy the elders to impose a fine of grain or money, he shall receive the fine that the action produces.

5. If a judge try a case, reach a decision, and present his judgment in writing; if later error shall appear in his decision, and it be through his own fault, then he shall pay twelve times the fine set by him in the case, and he shall be publicly removed from the judge's bench, and never again shall he sit there to render judgement.

6. If any one steal the property of a temple or of the court, he shall be put to death, and also the one who receives the stolen thing from him shall be put to death.

7. If any one buy from the son or the slave of another man, without witnesses or a contract, silver or gold, a male or female slave, an ox or a sheep, an ass or anything, or if he take it in charge, he is considered a thief and shall be put to death.

8. If any one steal cattle or sheep, or an ass, or a pig or a goat if it belong to a god or to the court, the thief shall pay thirtyfold therefor; if they belonged to a freed man of the king he shall pay tenfold; if the thief has nothing with which to pay he shall be put to death.

9. If any one lose an article, and find it in the possession of another: if the person in whose possession the thing is found say "A merchant sold it to me, I paid for it before witnesses," and if the owner of the thing say, "I will bring witnesses who know my property," then shall the purchaser bring the merchant who sold it to him, and the witnesses before whom he bought it, and the owner shall bring witnesses who can identify his property. The judge shall examine their testimony—both of the witnesses before whom the price was paid, and of the witnesses who identify the lost article on oath. The merchant is then proved to be a thief and shall be put to death. The owner of the lost article receives his property, and he who bought it receives the money he paid from the estate of the merchant.

10. If the purchaser does not bring the merchant and the witnesses before whom he bought the article, but its owner bring witnesses who identify it, then the buyer is the thief and shall be put to death, and the owner receives the lost article.

11. If the owner do not bring witnesses to identify the lost article, he is an evil-doer, he has traduced, and shall be put to death.

12. If the witnesses be not at hand, then shall the judge set a limit, at the expiration of six months. If his witnesses have not appeared within the six months, he is an evil-doer, and shall bear the fine of the pending case.

[editor's note: there is no 13th law in the code, 13 being considered and unlucky and evil number]

14. If any one steal the minor son of another, he shall be put to death.

15. If any one take a male or female slave of the court, or a male or female slave of a freed man, outside the city gates, he shall be put to death.

16. If any one receive into his house a runaway male or female slave of the court, or of a freedman, and does not bring it

out at the public proclamation of the major domus [commanding officer], the master of the house shall be put to death.

17. If any one find runaway male or female slaves in the open country and bring them to their masters, the master of the slaves shall pay him two shekels of silver.

18. If the slave will not give the name of the master, the finder shall bring him to the palace; a further investigation must follow, and the slave shall be returned to his master.

19. If he hold the slaves in his house, and they are caught there, he shall be put to death.

20. If the slave that he caught run away from him, then shall he swear to the owners of the slave, and he is free of all blame.

21. If any one break a hole into a house [break in to steal], he shall be put to death before that hole and be buried.

22. If any one is committing a robbery and is caught, then he shall be put to death.

23. If the robber is not caught, then shall he who was robbed claim under oath the amount of his loss; then shall the community, and . . .[the governor] on whose ground and territory and in whose domain it was, compensate him for the goods stolen.

25. If fire break out in a house, and some one who comes to put it out cast his eye upon the property of the owner of the house, and take the property of the master of the house, he shall be thrown into that self-same fire.

45. If a man rent his field for tillage for a fixed rental, and receive the rent of his field, but bad weather come and destroy the harvest, the injury falls upon the tiller of the soil.

46. If he do not receive a fixed rental for his field, but lets it on half or third shares of the harvest, the grain on the field shall be divided proportionately between the tiller and the owner.

47. If the tiller, because he did not succeed in the first year, has had the soil tilled by others, the owner may raise no objection; the field has been cultivated and he receives the harvest according to agreement.

53. If any one be too lazy to keep his dam in proper condition, and does not so keep it; if then the dam break and all the fields be flooded, then shall he in whose dam the break occurred be sold for money, and the money shall replace the corn which he has caused to be ruined.

54. If he be not able to replace the corn, then he and his possessions shall be divided among the farmers whose corn he has flooded.

55. If any one open his ditches to water his crop, but is careless, and the water flood the field of his neighbor, then he shall pay his neighbor corn for his loss.

56. If a man let in the water, and the water overflow the plantation of his neighbor, he shall pay ten gur of corn for every ten gan of land.

64. If any one hand over his garden to a gardener to work, the gardener shall pay to its owner two-thirds of the produce of the garden, for so long as he has it in possession, and the other third shall he keep.

65. If the gardener do not work in the garden and the product fall off, the gardener shall pay in proportion to other neighboring gardens.

102. If a merchant entrust money to an agent [broker] for some investment, and the broker suffer a loss in the place to which he goes, he shall make good the capital to the merchant.

103. If, while on the journey, an enemy take away from him anything that he had, the broker shall swear by God and be free of obligation.

104. If a merchant give an agent corn, wool, oil, or any other goods to transport, the agent shall give a receipt for the amount, and compensate the merchant therefor. Then he shall obtain a receipt form the merchant for the money that he gives the merchant.

105. If the agent is careless, and does not take a receipt for the money which he gave the merchant, he can not consider the unreceipted money as his own.

106. If the agent accept money from the merchant, but have a quarrel with the merchant [denying the receipt], then shall the merchant swear before God and witnesses that he has given this money to the agent, and the agent shall pay him three times the sum.

107. If the merchant cheat the agent, in that as the latter has returned to him all that had been given him, but the merchant denies the receipt of what had been returned to him, then shall this agent convict the merchant before God and the judges, and if he still deny receiving what the agent had given him shall pay six times the sum to the agent.

109. If conspirators meet in the house of a tavern-keeper, and these conspirators are not captured and delivered to the court, the tavern-keeper shall be put to death.

110. If a "sister of a god" [nun] open a tavern, or enter a tavern to drink, then shall this woman be burned to death.

115. If any one have a claim for corn or money upon another and imprison him; if the prisoner die in prison a natural death, the case shall go no further.

116. If the prisoner die in prison from blows or maltreatment, the master of the prisoner shall convict the merchant before the judge. If he was a free-born man, the son of the merchant shall be put to death; if it was a slave, he shall pay one-third of a mina of gold, and all that the master of the prisoner gave he shall forfeit.

117. If any one fail to meet a claim for debt, and sell himself, his wife, his son, and daughter for money or give them away to forced labor: they shall work for three years in the house of the man who bought them, or the proprietor, and in the fourth year they shall be set free.

118. If he give a male or female slave away for forced labor, and the merchant sublease them, or sell them for money, no objection can be raised.

119. If any one fail to meet a claim for debt, and he sell the maid servant who has borne him children, for money, the money which the merchant has paid shall be repaid to him by the owner of the slave and she shall be freed.

120. If any one store corn for safe keeping in another person's house, and any harm happen to the corn in storage, or if the owner of the house open the granary and take some of the corn, or if especially he deny that the corn was stored in his house: then the owner of the corn shall claim his corn before God [on oath], and the owner of the house shall pay its owner for all of the corn that he took.

121. If any one store corn in another man's house he shall pay him storage at the rate of one gur for every five ka of corn per year.

122. If any one give another silver, gold, or anything else to keep, he shall show everything to some witness, draw up a contract, and then hand it over for safe keeping.

123. If he turn it over for safe keeping without witness or contract, and if he to whom it was given deny it, then he has no legitimate claim.

124. If any one deliver silver, gold, or anything else to another for safe keeping, before a witness, but he deny it, he shall be brought before a judge, and all that he has denied he shall pay in full.

125. If any one place his property with another for safe keeping, and there, either through thieves or robbers, his property and the property of the other man be lost, the owner of the house, through whose neglect the loss took place, shall compensate the owner for all that was given to him in charge. But the owner of the house shall try to follow up and recover his property, and take it away from the thief.

126. If any one who has not lost his goods state that they have been lost, and make false claims: if he claim his goods and amount of injury before God, even though he has not lost them, he shall be fully compensated for all his loss claimed. [i.e., the oath is all that is needed.]

127. If any one "point the finger" [slander] at a sister of a god or the wife of any one, and can not prove it, this man shall be taken before the judges and his brow shall be marked. [by cutting the skin, or perhaps hair.]

128. If a man take a woman to wife, but have no intercourse with her, this woman is no wife to him.

129. If a man's wife be surprised [*in flagrante delicto*] with another man, both shall be tied and thrown into the water, but the husband may pardon his wife and the king his slaves.

130. If a man violate the wife [betrothed or child-wife] of another man, who has never known a man, and still lives in her father's house, and sleep with her and be surprised, this man shall be put to death, but the wife is blameless.

131. If a man bring a charge against ...[his] wife, but she is not surprised with another man, she must take an oath and then may return to her house.

132. If the "finger is pointed" at a man's wife about another man, but she is not caught sleeping with the other man, she shall jump into the river for her husband.

133. If a man is taken prisoner in war, and there is a sustenance in his house, but his wife

leave house and court, and go to another house: because this wife did not keep her court, and went to another house, she shall be judicially condemned and thrown into the water.

134. If any one be captured in war and there is not sustenance in his house, if then his wife go to another house this woman shall be held blameless.

135. If a man be taken prisoner in war and there be no sustenance in his house and his wife go to another house and bear children; and if later her husband return and come to his home: then this wife shall return to her husband, but the children follow their father.

136. If any one leave his house, run away, and then his wife go to another house, if then he return, and wishes to take his wife back: because he fled from his home and ran away, the wife of this runaway shall not return to her husband.

137. If a man wish to separate from a woman who has borne him children, or from his wife who has borne him children: then he shall give that wife her dowry, and a part of the usufruct [right to use and profit from] of field, garden, and property, so that she can rear her children. When she has brought up her children, a portion of all that is given to the children, equal as that of one son, shall be given to her. She may then marry the man of her heart.

138. If a man wishes to separate from his wife who has borne him no children, he shall give her the amount of her purchase money and the dowry which she brought from her father's house, and let her go.

139. If there was no purchase price he shall give her one mina of gold as a gift of release.

140. If he be a freed man he shall give her one-third of a mina of gold.

141. If a man's wife, who lives in his house, wishes to leave it, plunges into debt, tries to ruin her house, neglects her husband, and is judicially convicted: if her husband offer her release, she may go on her way, and he gives her nothing as a gift of release. If her husband does not wish to release her, and if he take another wife, she shall remain as servant in her husband's house.

142. If a woman quarrel with her husband, and say: "You are not congenial to me," the reasons for her prejudice must be presented. If she is guiltless, and there is no fault on her part, but he leaves and neglects her, then no guilt attaches to this woman, she shall take her dowry and go back to her father's house.

143. If she is not innocent, but leaves her husband, and ruins her house, neglecting her husband, this woman shall be cast into the water.

152. If after the woman had entered the man's house, both contracted a debt, both must pay the merchant.

153. If the wife of one man on account of another man has their mates [her husband and the other man's wife] murdered, both of them shall be impaled.

154. If a man be guilty of incest with his daughter, he shall be driven from the place [exiled].

155. If a man betroth a girl to his son, and his son have intercourse with her, but he [the father] afterward defile her, and be surprised, then he shall be bound and cast into the water [drowned].

156. If a man betroth a girl to his son, but his son has not known her, and if then he defile her, he shall pay her half a gold mina, and compensate her for all that she brought out of her father's house. She may marry the man of her heart.

157. If any one be guilty of incest with his mother after his father, both shall be burned.

158. If any one be surprised after his father with his chief wife, who has borne children, he shall be driven out of his father's house.

159. If any one, who has brought chattels [moveable property] into his father-in-law's house, and has paid the purchase-money, looks for another wife, and says to his father-in-law: "I do not want your daughter," the girl's father may keep all that he had brought.

168. If a man wish to put his son out of his house, and declare before the judge: "I want to put my son out," then the judge shall examine into his reasons. If the son be guilty of no great fault, for which he can be rightfully put out, the father shall not put him out.

169. If he be guilty of a grave fault, which should rightfully deprive him of the filial relationship, the father shall forgive him the first time; but if he be guilty of a grave fault a second time the father may deprive his son of all filial relation.

170. If his wife bear sons to a man, ...[and] his maid-servant have borne sons, and the father while still living says to the children whom his maid-servant has borne: "My sons," and he count them with the sons of his wife; if then the father die, then the sons of the wife and of the maid-servant shall divide the paternal property in common. The son of the wife is to partition and choose.

171. If, however, the father while still living did not say to the sons of the maid-servant: "My sons," and then the father dies, then the sons of the maid-servant shall not share with the sons of the wife, but the freedom of the maid and her sons shall be granted...

195. If a son strike his father, his hands shall be hewn off.

196. If a man put out the eye of another man, his eye shall be put out.

197. If he break another man's bone, his bone shall be broken.

198. If he put out the eye of a freed [poor] man, or break the bone of a freed man, he shall pay one gold mina.

199. If he put out the eye of a man's slave, or break the bone of a man's slave, he shall pay one-half of its value.

200. If a man knock out the teeth of his equal, his teeth shall be knocked out.

201. If he knock out the teeth of a freed man, he shall pay one-third of a gold mina.

202. If any one strike the body of a man higher in rank than he, he shall receive sixty blows with an ox-whip in public.

203. If a free-born man strike the body of another free-born man or equal rank, he shall pay one gold mina.

204. If a freed man strike the body of another freed man, he shall pay ten shekels in money.

205. If the slave of a freed man strike the body of a freed man, his ear shall be cut off.

206. If during a quarrel one man strike another and wound him, then he shall swear, "I did not injure him wittingly," and pay the physicians.

207. If the man die of his wound, he shall swear similarly, and if he [the deceased] was a free-born man, he shall pay half a mina in money.

208. If he was a freed man, he shall pay one-third of a mina.

209. If a man strike a free-born woman so that she lose her unborn child, he shall pay ten shekels for her loss.

210. If the woman die, his daughter shall be put to death.

211. If a woman of the... [poor] class lose her child by a blow, he shall pay five shekels in money.

212. If this woman die, he shall pay half a mina.

213. If he strike the maid-servant of a man, and she lose her child, he shall pay two shekels in money.

214. If this maid-servant die, he shall pay one-third of a mina.

215. If a physician make a large incision with an operating knife and cure it, or if he open a tumor [over the eye] with an operating knife, and saves the eye, he shall receive ten shekels in money.

216. If the patient be a freed man, he receives five shekels.

217. If he be the slave of some one, his owner shall give the physician two shekels.

218. If a physician make a large incision with the operating knife, and kill him, or open a tumor with the operating knife, and cut out the eye, his hands shall be cut off.

219. If a physician make a large incision in the slave of a freedman, and kill him, he shall replace the slave with another slave.

220. If he had opened a tumor with the operating knife, and put out his eye, he shall pay half his value.

221. If a physician heal the broken bone or diseased soft part of a man, the patient shall pay the physician five shekels in money.

222. If he were a freed man he shall pay three shekels.

223. If he were a slave his owner shall pay the physician two shekels.

224. If a veterinary surgeon perform a serious operation on an ass or an ox, and cure it, the owner shall pay the surgeon one-sixth of a shekel as a fee.

225. If he perform a serious operation on an ass or ox, and kill it, he shall pay the owner one-fourth of its value.

228. If a builder build a house for some one and complete it, he shall give him a fee of two shekels in money for each sar of surface.

229 If a builder build a house for some one, and does not construct it properly, and the house which he built fall in and

kill its owner, then that builder shall be put to death.

230. If it kill the son of the owner, the son of that builder shall be put to death.

231. If it kill a slave of the owner, then he shall pay slave for slave to the owner of the house.

234. If a shipbuilder build a boat of sixty gur for a man, he shall pay him a fee of two shekels in money.

235. If a shipbuilder build a boat for some one, and do not make it tight, if during that same year that boat is sent away and suffers injury, the shipbuilder shall take the boat apart and put it together tight at his own expense. The tight boat he shall give to the boat owner.

236. If a man rent his boat to a sailor, and the sailor is careless, and the boat is wrecked or goes aground, the sailor shall give the owner of the boat another boat as compensation.

249. If any one hire an ox, and God strike it that it die, the man who hired it shall swear by God and be considered guiltless.

250. If while an ox is passing on the street [market] some one push it, and kill it, the owner can set up no claim in the suit [against the hirer].

251. If an ox be a goring ox,

and it shown that he is a gorer, and he do not bind his horns, or fasten the ox up, and the ox gore a free-born man and kill him, the owner shall pay one-half a mina in money.

252. If he kill a man's slave, he shall pay one-third of a mina.

278. If any one buy a male or female slave, and before a month has elapsed the benu-disease be developed, he shall return the slave to the seller, and receive the money which he had paid.

279. If any one buy a male or female slave, and a third party claim it, the seller is liable for the claim.

280. If while in a foreign country a man buy a male or female slave belonging to another of his own country; if when he return home the owner of the male or female slave recognize it: if the male or female slave be a native of the country, he shall give them back without any money.

281. If they are from another country, the buyer shall declare the amount of money paid therefor to the merchant, and keep the male or female slave.

282. If a slave say to his master: "You are not my master," if they convict him his master shall cut off his ear.

Questions for Critical Thinking and Discussion

1. Explain in detail what the Code of Hammurabi tells about the type of society and culture for which the Code was framed. Refer to specific articles to support your hypotheses.

2. Give two to three possible explanations for the long-term historical importance of the Code to Western civilization. (Look at Exodus in the Old Testament. Are there any similarities or differences?) Why is this document considered valuable for studying ancient Babylon? Do you think this Code influenced other civilizations?

3. Discuss the differences in the penalties now in force and those in the time of Hammurabi (c.1750 B.C.) for the following offenses: incest, robbery from a house, divorce.

4. Discuss the differences in the penalties now in force and those in the time of Hammurabi (c.1750 B.C.) for the following offenses: adultery, indebtedness, a nun drinking at a bar. Refer to specific articles.

5. Discuss the differences in the penalties now in force and those in the time of Hammurabi (c.1750 B.C.) for the following offenses: medical malpractice, kidnapping, building collapse due to shoddy construction. Refer to specific articles.

6. Explain with specific examples from the Code why it is said to be based on the principle of retribution; that is, "an eye for an eye." Do you feel severe punishments would change the number of criminals incarcerated today? Why or why not?

7. Give examples of differences in monetary payment penalties for the same offense among the three social classes. Refer to specific articles.

8. Does this society value women, children, unborn children? Provide evidence to support your opinion.

Self-Test

Part I: Identification

Can you identify each of the following? Tell who, what, when, where, why, and/or how for each term.

1. Big Bang Theory
2. Hominid
3. Australopithecus
4. *Homo habilis*
5. *Homo erectus*
6. *Homo sapiens*
7. Neanderthal Man
8. Cro-Magnon Man
9. Paleolithic Age
10. Neolithic Revolution
11. Prehistory
12. Jericho
13. Bronze Age
14. Hittites
15. City-state
16. Cuneiform
17. Hieroglyphics
18. Ziggurat
19. Fertile Crescent
20. Theocracy
21. Sargon I of Akkad
22. Code of Hammurabi
23. *Epic of Gilgamesh*
24. Assyrians
25. The Old Kingdom
26. Osiris
27. Isis
28. Ma'at
29. Nomes
30. Ikhnaton
31. Yahweh
32. Covenant
33. Xerxes
34. Zoroastrianism
35. Minoan Civilization
36. Mycenaean Civilization
37. *Iliad*
38. Hellenic Civilization
39. Polis
40. Helots
41. Peloponnesian League
42. Hoplite
43. Phalanx
44. Draco
45. Solon
46. Peisistratus
47. Cleisthenes
48. Ecclesia
49. Marathon
50. Salamis
51. Thermopylae
52. Delian League
53. Great Peloponnesian War
54. Philip II of Macedon

Part II: Multiple Choice Questions

Circle the best response from the choices available.

1. The Big Bang is assumed to have occurred
   a. 12 to 15 billion years ago.
   b. 4.6 billion years ago.
   c. 3 million years ago.
   d. 50,000 years ago.

2. Once large amounts of historical data have been collected, there is still a problem of
   a. unraveling the single chain of cause and effect.
   b. the non-Christian bias of most ancient records.
   c. the culture bias of the historian and the problem of interpretation.
   d. There are no other problems. The data speak for themselves.

3. The earliest fossils of bipedal hominids, such as "Lucy," are:
   a. at least 10 million years old.
   b. 3.5 million years old.
   c. 1 million years
   d. 500,000 years old.

4. Cro-Magnon Man
   a. was a great hunter.
   b. painted naturalistic scenes of animals deep inside caves.
   c. seems to have practiced a definite religion.
   d. all of the above.

5. A characteristic which differentiated Cro-Magnon Man from his predecessors was
   a. a writing system.
   b. the use of tools
   c. walking on two legs and an upright posture.
   d. wall paintings.

6. The Neolithic Revolution is best represented by
   a. the manufacture of stone tools and weapons by grinding and polishing as well as the discovery of new technical skills.
   b. the domestication of plants and animals, and the start of agriculture.
   c. the origin of religion and art.
   d. all of the above.

7. One of the oldest agricultural towns was excavated at
    a. Jericho.
    b. Ur.
    c. Thebes.
    d. Paris.

8. The age of agriculture was a necessary but not sufficient precondition for the development of
    a. human language.
    b. sailboats.
    c. technological change.
    d. city culture and civilization.

9. The earliest civilizations all developed near rivers which provided the bases for
    a. trade and commerce.
    b. irrigation agriculture.
    c. plentiful fish and wildlife.
    d. symbols of divinity.

10. Among the principal features of ancient Babylonian law was the practice of
    a. excusing first offenders.
    b. confining hardened criminals in far-off prisons.
    c. revising the law at regular intervals.
    d. punishing convicted persons by physical mutilation.

11. The *Epic of Gilgamesh*
    a. is an old Babylonian poem.
    b. includes accounts similar to the Biblical story of creation and the flood.
    c. has Gilgamesh, the hero, search for immortality.
    d. all of the above.

12. The main cultural traits of Egyptian civilization were
    a. war, strife, and uncertainty.
    b. optimism, stability, and timelessness.
    c. commerce, manufacture, and competition.
    d. other worldliness, mysticism, and self-sacrifice.

13. The pyramids were built
    a. to show off the wealth of the Egyptian middle class.
    b. to secure immortality for those buried within.
    c. to store excess grains for lean years.
    d. to appease the wrath of the gods and thus to secure fertility to Egypt.

14. All of the following were important Egyptian gods <u>except</u>
    a. Osiris.
    b. Amon-Re.
    c. Horus.
    d. Marduk.

15. Ikhnaton's "monotheism"
    a. had little impact on the masses of Egyptians.
    b. was destroyed by his successors.
    c. was opposed by the priests.
    d. all of the above.

16. The imminent cause of the Old Kingdom's collapse was
    a. the exhaustion of the soil due to the repeated flooding of the Nile.
    b. universal poverty and demoralization among pharaoh's subjects.
    c. attack by foreign tribes against whom local militias were powerless.
    d. internecine wars between the civil governors of local areas, against whom the pharaohs were powerless.

17. The ancient Hebrews are historically most important because of
    a. their Exodus from Egypt.
    b. the empire created by Solomon.
    c. their monotheistic religion.
    d. the Kingdoms of Israel and Judah.

18. The Hebrew prophets insisted that Yahweh's chief demand on men was
    a. sacrificial offerings.
    b. upright moral conduct.
    c. loyalty to the king.
    d. strict observance of the Sabbath.

19. The Hebrew view of nature held that
    a. it was filled with God-like spirits.
    b. it was God's dwelling place.
    c. it was God's creation but was not itself divine.
    d. it should be examined in a logical fashion.

20. The Minoans
    a. were a Greek-speaking people.
    b. lived in temple palaces that provided indoor plumbing, such as the one at Knossos.
    c. practiced an exquisite naturalistic art of birds, flowers, and sea creatures.
    d. b and c.

21. Which statement best explains the impact of geography on Greek history?
    a. rugged mountains and good harbors promoted seafaring and commerce among many small, independent city-states.
    b. rich agricultural lands gave control to the peasants.
    c. vast plains and good land transportation unified the Greek people.
    d. there were few good harbors in Greece.

22. In contrast with most other important Greek city-states, Sparta sought to resolve its economic problems by
    a. expanding overseas.
    b. giving freedom to the peasants.
    c. enslaving its neighbors.
    d. developing skilled industries.

23. In general, the tyrants in Greek history led revolutions against
    a. monarchs.
    b. aristocrats.
    c. democrats.
    d. priests.

24. The Classical or Golden Age of Hellenic Greece is marked by two wars:
    a. 1st and 2nd Punic War.
    b. Persian Wars and Peloponnesian Wars.
    c. Persian and 1st Punic War.
    d. Peloponnesian War and Alexander the Great's wars.

25. The original purpose of the Delian League was to
    a. continue the war against Persia.
    b. expand Athenian commerce.
    c. defend Delos against Sparta.
    d. unify Greece politically.

Part III: Review and Thought Questions

1. How did the Egyptian concern for the dead and the belief in an afterlife influence Egyptian society? Explain fully.

2. Describe Ikhnaton's religious revolution in Egypt. Why couldn't he carry it forward?

3. Herodotus, a 5th century B.C. historian, has called Egypt "the gift of the Nile." Is his description appropriate? Explain your response.

4. How did the Hyksos invasion affect ancient Egyptian history?

5. Describe the Osiris myth. Is there any commonality with the *Epic of Gilgamesh*?

6. How did geography influence the historical development of the city-states of the Fertile Crescent?

7. Define the term "theocracy." Can your definition be applied to ancient Egypt? Why or why not?

8. From your reading, what can you deduce about the extinction of the Neanderthals?

9. Explain the concept of the Covenant. What did it involve?

10. Despite many dire happenings, such as the Diaspora and the Holocaust, the Hebrews have over 5,000 continuous years of history as a people. What explanation would you hypothesize to explain this success.

11. Compare and contrast the Minoan and Mycenaean civilizations.

12. What did Cleisthenes do to become the "father of democracy"?

13. What was the Delian League? How do you account for Athenian imperialism?

14. Explain how the Greek concept of their polis eventually led to the decline of their civilization.

15. Describe the Zoroastrian religion. How did it possibly influence Christianity?

16. Why did the phalanx formation, incorporating the hoplite infantry, cause a change in warfare among the early Greeks?

17. Why was it possible for the Athenians to develop a high culture while the Spartans did not?

Part IV: Full-Length Essays

1. Describe eight of the ten characteristics that differentiate a civilization from a less developed culture. Apply four of these characteristics to ancient Egypt.

2. Explain how the mythology, religion, legal tradition, calendar, and the mathematics of the ancient Mesopotamians have influenced Western civilization.

3. Compare and contrast the mythology and the religious beliefs of the ancient Greeks with the Hebrews.

4. Describe the distinguishing characteristics of the Paleolithic Age compared to the Neolithic Revolution. Did the two ages have any commonalties or were there only differences?

5. Trace the evolution of *Homo sapiens* beginning with *Homo habilis* and ending with *Homo sapiens sapiens*.

6. Compare and contrast the causes, events, and outcomes of the Persian with the Peloponnesian Wars.

7. If you had access to a time machine, would you prefer to visit ancient Crete, ancient Athens, or ancient Sparta? Give reasons for your selection.

8. Compare and contrast the political, social, economic, and military systems of the city-states of Athens and Sparta.

9. Describe the development of democracy in ancient Athens. How is it different from the democracy practiced today in the United States?

10. Describe how religion was intertwined with politics in ancient Egypt and in ancient Israel.

Figure 2.1. Statue of a Kouros. Island Marble. Greek, c. 600 B.C. This archaic statue of an unclad youth exemplifies the ideal of physical perfection of ancient Greece. The left leg is advancing forward and the fists are clenched at the sides. Notice the perfection and intricacy of the plaited hair, which was very typical of these sculptures. *Courtesy of The Metropolitan Museum of Art, Fletcher Fund, 1932. (32.11.1)*

Chapter II

GREEK CULTURE

AND THE ROMAN

REPUBLIC

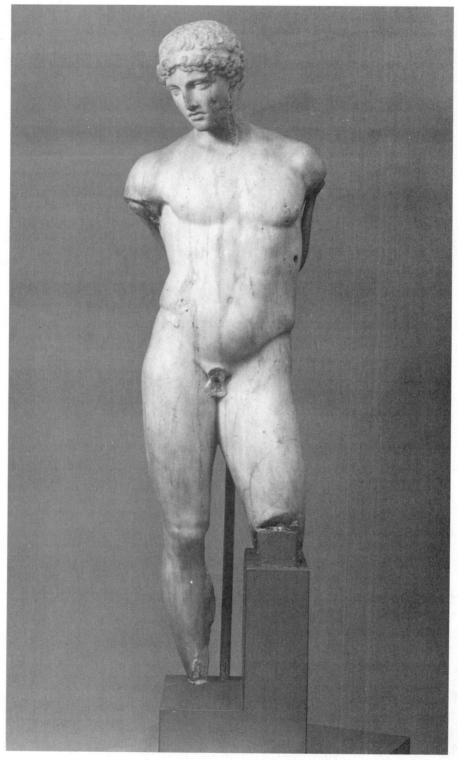

Figure 2.2. Statue of a Youth. Roman Copy of a Greek Work of the Fifth Century. Marble (450-425 B.C.). Although this marble statue has been damaged over the centuries, it was sculpted originally to convey the idealized form of classical Greek male perfection. The youth displays serenity and timelessness through the use of balance, symmetry, and mathematical proportion. *Courtesy of The Metropolitan Museum of Art, Fletcher Fund, 1926. (26.60.2)*

4

Religion and Philosophy in Classical Greece

Hellenic Culture

Hellenic culture has had a fundamental impact on the development of Western civilization. It may be said to have had a similarly profound influence on some non-Western civilizations, Islam for example, since Greek ideals and ideas were spread by Alexander the Great and his successors throughout the Mediterranean, the Near East, and as far as India. Different civilizations and historical periods have emphasized different aspects of Hellenic culture. What was it about the Greeks that draws us back to their legacy and civilization?

As we have already indicated, the Greeks, particularly the Athenians, were the first people to develop democracy as a form of government. They were the first to allow the "many," the majority, the common people to make the important decisions about society's future: Should there be war or not? Who should the magistrates be? Should taxes be raised?

For about a century, the Athenians practiced a form of direct democracy even more democratic for male citizens than what exists in our American representative democracy. The Athenian majority made decisions during the Peloponnesian War that directly contributed to their defeat. Ever since, these fateful decisions have been used by the well-

Our culture is indebted to many ancient peoples. What do you think we owe to the Greeks?

What do we owe to other ancient peoples?

What are some of the values presupposed by democracy?

Who were Zeus, Hera, Poseidon, and Hades?

to-do and educated elites as proof that the many's judgment cannot be trusted, that the people are easily turned into a mob when stirred up by a demagogue. Maybe, but the Athenians might have lost the war even if Pericles had not died of the plague at a critical moment in the war. Many wars have been lost by kings and aristocrats without popular input, and yet it was the common people who have always paid the price of defeat. At least the Athenian people chose their own destiny.

There is another, perhaps more important, principle which must be addressed. Democracy presupposes certain attitudes about humankind. It assumes that individual human beings are important, that they have the ability to express themselves, deserve the respect of being heard, and can organize themselves into mutually advantageous enterprises. Democracy presumes individuality, personal liberty, and equality. We derive these values from Hellenic civilization.

A society which sees itself as a community of free individuals in voluntary association with each other has a value system that can be seen exemplified in many aspects of classical Greek culture, which is the Hellenic culture of the 5th and 4th centuries B.C. prior to the conquests of Alexander the Great—in its religion and mythology, its art and architecture, its literature, its philosophy, drama, historical writings, and its politics.

Greek Religion

The Greeks believed in a PANTHEON of gods. Their chief god was ZEUS, his wife HERA, and his brothers POSEIDON and HADES. Hades was the god of the underworld; Poseidon, the god of the sea; Hera, a mother goddess of the earth; and Zeus, the god of the sky and chief deity. There were twelve OLYMPIAN gods, called such because Zeus and his family lived on Mount Olympus. Zeus, the son of Kronos and Rhea, was himself the youngest son of an earlier generation of gods known as the TITANS. Greek mythology told of a ten-year war pitting Zeus and his Olympians against Kronos and the Titans, a war which Zeus won. Perhaps these legends rationalize the struggle that the Dorian Greeks waged against the Mycenaeans.

Why were Zeus and his cohorts called Olympian gods?

The Olympian gods in many ways mirror the aristocratic, warrior society that existed during the Greek Dark Ages. Honor, courage, loyalty, and physical strength were the main values among warriors. The Olympian gods fought their enemies, squabbled with each other, got drunk, and liked to seduce women. From the perspective of later times, the Olympians behaved very immorally. Zeus regularly cheated on his wife and had many illegitimate children. Hera was often angry and jealous. Many a legend dealt with the conflicts which her rage produced. The Greek gods were ANTHROPOMORPHIC, that is, they had human-like personalities and emotions. Since all the gods were also immortal, everybody somehow had to come to terms with each other in the end. Since the gods' quarrels impacted on human affairs, these divine disagreements had serious negative consequences on humankind in producing wars and other disasters.

Demonstrate the anthropomorphic qualities of the Greek gods.

APOLLO, and his twin sister ARTEMIS, the children of Zeus and the Titan goddess Leto, belong to what are known as the younger generation of gods. Apollo was widely worshipped throughout the Greek world and bonded them together almost as much as Zeus. Sometimes linked to the sun, Apollo was the patron of medicine, music, archery, and shepherds. A prophet who re-

Why was Apollo important?

Who was Athena?

What was the origin of the Olympian games?

What was the Delphic Oracle?

vealed Zeus' will to humankind, Apollo, more than any of the other gods, came to symbolize the Greek ideal.

Another goddess, ATHENA, was allegedly born, full-grown in a suit of armor, from the head of Zeus. Athena was the chief deity of Athens, who later came to be identified with wisdom. The owl was her symbol.

All these gods were worshipped throughout the Greek-speaking world, but especially important cult centers existed for Zeus at Olympia, Apollo at Delphi, Artemis at Delos, and Athena at Athens. The Greeks celebrated special festivals at these shrines with sacrifices, songs, dance, and athletic contests. For example, the festival of Zeus at Olympus gave rise to the OLYMPIAN GAMES. The first of these festivals was held in 776 B.C. Each Olympiad was held every four years and the Greeks of the classical age dated time in terms of these Olympiads. Foot races, javelin and discus throwing, wrestling, boxing, chariot racing, and other athletic events were practiced during these festivals. The winners, who were crowned with laurel wreaths as an honor from Zeus, were honored throughout the Greek world. Athletes on their way to Olympus were sacred and the Greeks suspended wars between their city-states during the Olympic Games.

At Delphi, the oracle of Apollo prophesied the future. Greek poleis would often consult the oracle before making major political decisions, such as whether or not to go to war. The oracle gave cryptic answers that often had a double meaning. Thus, whatever the outcome, the oracle was felt to have accurately predicted the future. In any case, the Greeks went to Delphi for many centuries.

At Athens, the festivals for Dionysus included the production of dramatic plays. The great Greek playwrights Aeschylus,

Sophocles, and Euripides produced their tragedies at Athens.

The worship of common gods, the festivals, and the rules whereby travelers to these festivals were allowed safe conduct bound the Greeks together, despite the independence of their city-states.

Each Greek polis had an annual cycle of festivals to the gods of particular importance in that particular city. Politics, commerce, culture, and religion were interconnected and formed what is called a CIVIC RELIGION. The gods, public festivals, and ceremonies were held to assure the welfare, security, and survival of the city-state and its citizenry. Greek religion included both an APOLLONIAN and a DIONYSIAN ELEMENT.

APOLLO was the god of moderation and law. This side of Greek religion was symbolized by its temples with their geometric symmetry, proportion, and harmony and was reflected in Greek classical art with its idealized human forms showing faces of serene contemplation. The Greeks avoided strong emotions, physical deformities, and the ravages of old age in their art of the classical period. To a very large degree, Western civilization derives its definition of beauty from this Greek tradition.

But there was another side to Greek religion. DIONYSUS, the god of fertility, ritual dance, and ecstatic experiences, supposedly invented wine making. This was the excessive, orgiastic side of the Greeks, which is often not discussed in textbooks. Both elements of their polytheistic religion were important and helped to shape this civilization so fundamental to our own development. But we, too, will overemphasize the rational, moderate element because it has more to offer us than frightening, unbridled orgasms however primordial they may be.

How was Greek drama connected to religion?

Distinguish the Apollonian from the Dionysian elements of Greek religion.

Greek Philosophy

How can philosophy be distinguished from religion?

The ancient Greeks were the first people to develop philosophy. Philosophy attempts to understand the world and ourselves through purely rational analysis. Even the gods must be rationally examined, explained, justified. Are there gods? What do gods do? Why are there gods? How do the gods originate? How do the gods impact on mankind? Philosophy differs from religion in this insistence on rational explanation.

Religion also provides answers to mankind's quest for understanding. But whenever difficult questions arise that human rationality seems not to be able to answer, religion has a ready-made solution: the gods or god want it so. All things are as the gods ordered them and if men cannot understand that order, then the failing lies with mankind.

What is the difference between philosophy and science?

That may be so, but philosophy refuses to accept that religious response as the only possible answer. "The gods did it" does not satisfy philosophers. Philosophy also differs from modern science, which tests its hypotheses through experiments. Science seeks to explain physical phenomena, the natural world of which we are a part and in which we live. We understand how nature works if we can predict, verify, and duplicate natural events.

Except for Aristotle, Greek philosophers did not understand or articulate the operations of scientific prediction, experimentation, and verification. Though it should be acknowledged that the Greek doctor, HIPPOCRATES (c.460 - 370 B.C.), often called the Father of Medicine, did recognize the importance of carefully observing his patients' responses to cures. Hippocrates emphasized

GREEK CULTURE AND THE ROMAN REPUBLIC

the rational rather than the supernatural approach to understanding medicine.

Philosophy is based on first principles which are then logically developed. Logic is related to mathematics. It is especially close to geometry, that branch of mathematics particularly linked to the Greeks. Logically analyzing right triangles has produced many important insights. Trigonometric tables are very useful for land surveying, but the validity of the tables does not depend on their usefulness. The validity of a philosophic system does not depend on its being empirically verifiable.

These differences between philosophy and both religion and science must be kept in mind when reading the following couple of pages.

The Ionian or Milesian School of Natural Philosophers

The Ionian philosophers were interested in nature. How did the physical world come into being? Was there an underlying one thing from which all other things came? How did things change from one thing into another?

THALES, considered to be the first philosopher, lived in Miletus, the Greek city-state in Asia Minor or Ionia. His traditional dates are c.636-c.546 B.C. Thales was held to have predicted an eclipse of the sun in 585 B.C. and to have traveled widely to Babylonia and Egypt. Thales thought that the earth floated on water and that all things are made of WATER.[1]

Pythagorean or Italian Philosophers

The Pythagoreans formed a quasi-religious community of believers who lived

Who was Hippocrates?

What was the major concern of the Ionian philosophers?

Who taught that all things were composed of water?

What, according to the Pythagoreans, was the basis for the universe?

What were some of the sayings of Heraclitus?

What point is he making?

Do you agree?

near the Greek colonial settlement of Croton in southern Italy from about 525 B.C. The settlement was founded by **PYTHAGORAS OF SAMOS**, c.560 - c.480 B.C., who had migrated to Croton. Again, we know about the Pythagoreans from later sources, but it appears that Pythagoras was an original thinker who made significant contributions to mathematics, astronomy, and the theory of music. The Pythagorean Theorem in geometry, that in a right triangle $A2 + B2 = C2$, is named after him.

For the Pythagoreans, NUMBER was the basic concept of their philosophy and was the basis of the universe. The number ONE formed a limit, a beginning. The opposite of limit is the unlimited. There seems to have been a strong magical and quasi-religious element to the Pythagorean numerology. The universe was created when the One or Limit "breathed" and brought order to the Unlimited.

The Pythagoreans contributed to the development of abstract thought. They may have begun the idea that there is another reality beyond that of our sense experience, a concept which is so important in the thought of Plato. Is God a great mathematician who conjures up mathematical formulas in his mind that upon being thought become our empirical world? Pythagoreans might have agreed with that idea.[2]

Heraclitus

Heraclitus was an Ionian who lived in the city of Ephesus about 505 B.C. He is most famous for saying that: "One cannot step twice into the same river." And: "All things flow; nothing abides"[3] in the physical world in which we live. Change is to be accepted and embraced, for it makes life exciting and enjoyable.

But change is not totally random or erratic. It is governed by the Logos, which term has been variously translated as "the Word," "Reason," "the Divine Fire," and hundreds of other definitions. Heraclitus was the first person to use the term 'Logos' in this philosophical sense. The Logos drives the world of change.

For Heraclitus: "This universe, the same for all, no one, either god or man, has made; but it always was, and is, and ever shall be an ever-living fire, fixed measures kindling and fixed measures dying out."[4] Things are in perpetual flux, ever changing, one thing decaying and another thing being born. Nothing ever remains the same except the Law of Change, the Logos, itself.[5]

The Atomists

The Atomists believed that since things cannot be reduced to nothingness, there must be a point when a thing can no longer be divided. At that point, you have reached the atom.

It must be noted that this atomic theory is reached by logic and not through experimental physics. And yet, this logical idea of the Greeks bore fruit more than 2400 years later.

LEUCIPPUS, who lived about 440 B.C. and DEMOCRITUS, c.460 - c.370 B.C., held that there were only atoms and the void. Atoms are invisible and irreducible. Their combining with each other in space formed the material and sensible world. These atoms have shape, mass, and motion, but not color or taste. Atoms collide with each other to form the things we see. Our perceptions are

What is the Logos?

Name some ancient Atomists.

Does their atomic theory differ from today's?

Who were the Sophists?

subjective; we do not perceive the real world of physical nature.

For the atomists, there were no gods or life after death. There was only a material universe. Morality depended on the conscience of the individual. A life of moderation was best because excesses cause pain.[6]

| The Sophists | *PrivATE toTors.* *they develop Logic* |

The Sophists turned from asking questions about nature to asking social questions about human societies. The traditional morality and religious beliefs of the Greeks were being undermined through the rapid social changes brought about in the aftermath of the Persian Wars. The Olympian gods, as described by Homer and Hesiod, could hardly be taken as role models for moral behavior. The belief that the gods punished human transgressions with thunderbolts, diseases, and war was also wearing thin.

What is rhetoric?

As the Greeks, and in particular the Athenians, came into contact with many different poleis and other peoples, they learned that human customs differed from place to place. Cultural differences between peoples gave rise to a philosophy of cultural relativism.

Relate the Sophists to Athenian democracy.

As the Athenians developed their direct democracy, the ability to speak in public and to persuade the assembly of citizens became the key to political success. The Sophists were not so much philosophers as teachers of rhetoric. Rhetoric is the art of persuasive public speaking. It requires an understanding of language, a good vocabulary, proper grammar, a broad general knowledge, and a sense of style. An applied knowledge of human motivations, passions, and prejudices is also useful so that the human psyche, or soul, can be manipulated in a propagandistic manner. Argumentation need not always be objective; nor does truth necessarily win the debate. The purpose of rhetoric is to score points and to persuade the audience.

The most famous saying of the Sophist PROTAGORAS, c. 490 - c.420 B.C., was that: "Man is the measure of all things."[7] Presumably this meant that ethical standards and laws are man-made and must serve human purposes. At its most extreme, this could mean that each person defined for themselves what was right or wrong, good or bad. Some of the Sophists apparently held that "might makes right," a doctrine still favored by realist politicians, particularly when applied to the international relations between states. Such extreme moral relativism denied that there are objective, universal standards of law and morality.

Protagoras also said: "With regard to the gods, I know not whether they exist or not, or what they are like."[8] If there may be no gods, then obviously law and morality do not derive from them. Law and morality serve human, utilitarian purposes and must be judged by human standards.

The Sophists taught a humanistic relativism. They criticized the old traditions, but had nothing new with which to replace them. They spread doubt and skepticism. The mood of our own age has much in common with the times during which the Sophists flourished.[9]

Socrates, Plato, and Aristotle

It was in reaction to this relativism of the Sophists that the three greatest Greek philosophers responded. These were Socrates, Plato, and Aristotle.

What is the most famous saying of Protagoras?

What is moral relativism?

Argue for or against absolute standards of morality.

Who was Socrates?

Socrates

Socrates was born in Athens about 470 B.C., lived in Athens for over seventy years, and died there in 399 B.C. At the order of an Athenian court, he committed suicide by drinking the deadly hemlock. He left us no writings and all that we know about him comes from the writings of others, particularly Plato.

Socrates used to go to the town square, the agora, and stop people to chat. But these conversations soon turned into dialogues on philosophical questions, such as: "What is goodness?" "What is courage?" What is justice?" Socrates questioned his friends using what has come to be called the SOCRATIC METHOD: a question and answer search for the truth. Socrates was not interested in examples of courage, but in an all-inclusive universal definition. He would often show that those who thought they knew the answers to such questions, knew very little, and contradicted themselves.

What was the Socratic Method?

Showing up the foolishness of many so-called wise men made Socrates many enemies. Socrates was not a Sophist because he believed that objective truth was possible. Socrates held that, by following logic and his Socratic Method, our reasoning abilities can lead us to discover universal standards of moral goodness.

Was Socrates a Sophist? Explain.

"Know thyself" and "The unexamined life is not worth living" were two of Socrates' maxims. The Oracle at Delphi had said that Socrates was the wisest man in all of Greece. Socrates took the Oracle very seriously. How could he, Socrates, be the wisest man of Greece when he felt that he knew almost nothing for certain. Socrates finally reached the conclusion that he was the wisest man because he *knew* he did not know and acknowledged how little he knew. So many others pretended to know, but did not.

The Socratic Method used the dialectic to arrive at the truth. Socrates developed the question-and-answer method to arrive at universal definitions. Such universals might in turn lead through deduction into practical advice on moral conduct.

Socrates lived through the Age of Pericles, the period of the Peloponnesian Wars, the Athenian defeat, the excesses of the Thirty Tyrants, and the restoration of the democracy in a spirit of vindictiveness. In 399 B.C., Socrates was accused of "impiety to the gods" and "corrupting the youth of Athens."

Many of Socrates' friends were rich aristocrats. Alcibiades, in particular, was a close friend who turned out to be an Athenian traitor and contributed significantly to the Athenian defeat in the war with Sparta. Several of the Thirty Tyrants had been Socrates' students.

Nonetheless, the charges against Socrates were patently untrue. Socrates had searched for and taught moral virtue. He had dissuaded the youths of Athens from a dissolute life. He had respected the traditional gods of Athens and his thought had deeply religious implications.

Socrates' trial and execution have been compared to that of Jesus. An innocent man is killed because he is, indeed, righteous and holds up to the community a moral standard higher than they are prepared to accept.

Plato wrote several dialogues about the trial of Socrates. The *Euthyphro* describes Socrates just before the trial. The *Apology* is Socrates' defense during the trial. Socrates is convicted of the charges by a jury vote of 281 to 220. In the *Crito*, Socrates is given the chance to escape from prison, but refuses because he will not disobey the laws of Ath-

How did the Athenians treat Socrates?

Discuss the Platonic dialogues dealing with the trial and death of Socrates.

Describe Plato's background.

ens merely to save his own life. The *Phaedo* discusses the nature of the soul and gives Socrates' account of an afterlife. It is made poignant by Socrates' impending death.

Plato

Plato was born in Athens about 428 B.C. of an aristocratic family and died there in 348 B.C. He was deeply influenced by Socrates. After Socrates' death, he left Athens and traveled widely. He lived in Syracuse for a while where he became the friend of King Dionysus the Elder. In 387 B.C., Plato returned to Athens and founded the ACADEMY.

What was the Academy?

The Academy was the world's first institution of higher learning, where Plato thought, wrote, and lectured to students, including his greatest disciple Aristotle. Plato gave up participation in the public life of Athens and made it his life's mission to present and develop the implications of Socrates' thought.

Who is Plato's most famous pupil?

Plato wrote 26 dialogues and other philosophic works, all of which appear to have survived. These dialogues are divided into an early, middle, and late period. In the early dialogues, which date from the death of Socrates to the founding of the Academy, Socrates is the main figure. Also, these dialogues seem to present Socrates' teachings.

What was Plato's best-known work?

The Middle Dialogues date from about 387, the founding of the Academy, to about 367 B.C., when Plato made another visit to Syracuse after Dionysus the Elder had died. In the Middle Dialogues, Plato developed his own ideas and wrote his greatest masterwork, *The Republic*. The visit to Syracuse from 367 to 366, and another from 361 to 360 B.C., ended in failures. During those visits, Plato may have been seeking to establish the rule of a philosopher-king in Syracuse.

Platonic Dialogues[10]

Early Socratic Dialogues

Protagoras	*Charmides*
Ion	*Laches*
Apology	*Republic* Book I
Crito	*Hippias* I and II
Euthyphro	

Middle Dialogues—Plato Expounds Own Views

Gorgias	*Symposium*
Meno	*Phaedrus*
Menexenus	*Republic* Books II to X
Euthydemus	*Cratylus*
Phaedo	

Later Dialogues

First Group:	Second Group:
Parmenides	*Timaeus*
Theaetetus	*Critias* (unfinished)
Sophist	*Philebus*
Statesman	*Laws*
	Epinomis (Appendix to the *Laws*)

What distinguishes Plato's early, middle, and later dialogues?

In the later dialogues, Socrates receded into the background. The lively dialogues become mainly monologues and the mature philosophy of Plato is expounded.

Plato, though not a systematic thinker, can be viewed as the greatest philosopher of all time. His thought is as much evocative, literary, and mystical as it is strictly rational. And yet, all subsequent thinkers have been influenced by him, even those who disagree. Plato was the first person to develop metaphysics. He argued clearly that beyond our physical world of sense experience, there is another non-physical, transcendental world. This other world is unchanging, eternal. It is the realm of the Forms or Ideas.

Around what did Plato's metaphysics center?

Explain Plato's theory of forms or ideas.

For Plato, the world in which humans live is that of Heraclitus, where all things are in a continual state of flux. But there is another realm, that of the Forms, which are unchanging, forever. Plato reconciled the problem of the one and the many by holding that things that change on earth are merely the pale reflections of the unchanging forms of things in this other realm. There is a Form of Absolute Courage, Honor, Beauty, Friendship, Truth, Justice, and Goodness. Things are beautiful on earth because they partake of the Form of Beauty.

What is the highest of these ideas?

Plato was deeply influenced by the Pythagoreans and their discovery of the abstractness of mathematics. He also incorporated earlier conceptions of the Logos, Mind, and Soul. The ultimate form, the ultimate value, which all things seek, is Goodness. To reach the Good, human beings require knowledge. Once you have knowledge of the Good, according to Plato, you will never give up on it. Error and badness arise from inadequate knowledge.

What does Plato understand by justice? Does our society have the same understanding of justice?

In *The Republic*, Plato is concerned with Justice. What would a just society be like and what would be the ideal form of government for such a state? Justice is when everyone is in their proper place within society, when equals are treated equally and unequals unequally. In a just society, the role of the good citizen and the role of the good man would be in harmony with each other.

Based on his analysis of human psychology, that is the human psyche or soul, he identifies three types of persons: those with souls of bronze, silver, and gold. Each person's personality, soul, has three components: our drives or appetites, our spirited or passionate part, and our rational part. Plato compares the soul to a chariot. Only if the human driver, our rational part, has control over the two horses pulling the chariot will it avoid a crash. If the black horse, our drives, predominates, the chariot will veer to one side; and if the white horse, our spirit for adventure, predominates, the chariot will go to the other side. For Plato, humans who are most concerned for their well being—eating, drinking, and fun—have souls of bronze. They make good farmers and artisans. This is the average guy who wants a job, a wife, and a home. But there are some who seek adventure, whose spirited part predominates. They have souls of silver and make good warriors. Only in a few does reason control both the appetite for adventure and the needs of comfort. These few have souls of gold, and should be the rulers of society, the Guardians.

If a king has a soul of silver, he will forever seek war and conquest until his state is finally defeated by someone stronger. If the king has a soul of bronze, his primary concern will be to accumulate wealth until his riches attract the envy of others and lead to war. Only a ruler with a soul of gold will keep the kingdom prosperous and strong without permitting excesses that lead to war. Moreover, the citizens in such a kingdom will be content because those with souls of bronze will enjoy their commerce and comforts, those with souls of silver will enjoy the adventure that an army life can provide, and those with souls of gold will serve as the guardians of all.

The ideal state, therefore, was one in which Platonic philosophers were kings and kings philosophers. For those with souls of gold, Plato prescribed an unusual education. Both girls and boys would be educated in common. Guardians would own no property. All things would be held in common. Even personal relationships would be freely chosen and changed without regard to marriage.

As long as each type of soul was in its proper place, justice would be maintained

Describe the three types of persons according to Plato.

Who should rule?

Did Plato believe in education? Explain.

Are Platonic ideals compatible with democracy?

What strengths or weaknesses do you perceive in Platonic thought?

within the state. Plato recognized that parents with souls of bronze might have a child with a soul of gold and vice versa. Identifying and placing children properly was an important function of the Guardians.

Plato was not a friend of popular government. He was an aristocrat who blamed the Athenian people for the death of Socrates. Twentieth-century critics of Plato have called him a proponent of totalitarianism. Some would answer that such views retroactively and invalidly apply current ideas into an entirely different social setting.

During his later life, Plato became aware that his dualistic philosophy entailed logical problems. How did the world of the Forms interact with the world of ordinary sense experience? To say that it does without establishing some logical link of how, is to enter the realm of religion and to leave that of philosophy. In the Myth of the Cave, Plato attempts to give an allegorical explanation of the relationship between the Forms and sense experience.

In the *Timaeus*, Plato goes beyond rational philosophy and develops a quasi-religious cosmology. Plato postulates a Divine Craftsman who creates the physical universe, including bodies and souls, out of a pre-existing material stuff. This Divine Craftsman merely applies the pattern of the Eternal Forms to the material stuff as best as he can. The stuff of the material universe is chaotically in motion and resists the patterns imposed on it. The Eternal Forms, particularly the Form of the Good, and the Divine Craftsman are themselves perfect and good. The Divine Craftsman makes the material universe as good as he can, but the stuff of which it is made resists perfection. This is why disease, catastrophes, and war mar human societies.

This universe is diffused by the World-Soul. Human souls leave their physical bodies upon death gladly. They seek to be reunited with the Ideal Forms. But human souls contain various parts; only reason is pure. The unruly parts of the human soul have their counterpart in the World-Soul. The disorder in the universe is due to the fact that the World-Soul, too, has disorderly parts that resist divine law and reason. Plato differentiates necessity from law. Law, rationality, and human reason partake of the Divine Soul of the Divine Craftsman, who Himself works according to the unchanging patterns of the Form of the Good.

This speculative philosophy goes way beyond what can be learned through logic, the Socratic method, or the dialectic. It is a grand vision that belongs to mystics. Nonetheless, this aspect of Plato had a profound impact on later Neoplatonists, particularly Plotinus, and on Christian thinkers.

Why do you think some early Christian thinkers were attracted to Plato?

Aristotle

Aristotle brings us back from these metaphysical fancies to the physical world in which we humans must live. Aristotle was a great scientist, in addition to being one of the few greatest philosophers of all time. He was born in 384 B.C., in Stagira in Chalcidice on the North Coast of the Aegean at the edge of the Greek world and within the sphere of influence of the rising Macedonian kingdom. He came from a family of physicians; his father was Court Physician to the Macedonian king Amyntas II.

At age 18, he joined Plato at his Academy in Athens and remained as Plato's student until Plato's death in 348 B.C., almost eighteen years later. When Plato's nephew

Describe the background of Aristotle.

Who was Aristotle's most famous pupil?

went to macedonia

What was the Lyceum?

Would you describe Aristotle as a generalist or a specialist? Why?

Is Aristotle always faithful to his mentor, Plato?

Speusippus was chosen to head the Academy, Aristotle and several other students left. From 343 to 340 B.C. Aristotle was the tutor of the young Alexander the Great. One can only speculate on what impression the great philosopher made on the greatest world conqueror. Apparently relatively little, but it is interesting to note that Alexander sent Aristotle strange specimens of plants and animals from wherever Alexander found them on his conquests. So the two men remained in touch with each other even after the tutorial relationship ended.

In 335 B.C., Aristotle returned to Athens and founded his own school or research center which came to be called the LYCEUM or PERIPATUS. He worked there until 323 B.C., the year Alexander died and growing anti-Macedonian sentiment made it unsafe for Aristotle to remain in Athens. He died in 322 B.C. in Chalcis.

Aristotle's philosophy was deeply influenced by the science of biology. Aristotle's thought is analytical. He is the great classifier. Aristotle made original contributions to the major fields of philosophy: Logic, Natural Philosophy, Metaphysics, Politics, Ethics, Rhetoric, and Aesthetics. Aristotle's works were compiled in the 2nd century A.D. into what is called the *Corpus Aristotelicum*. The table at the end of this discussion presents a list of his known writings.

Aristotle's thought cannot be summarized in a couple of paragraphs. But a few observations must be made to give a flavor of his philosophy.

1. Aristotle agrees with Plato that objective knowledge and universal truths are possible.

2. Aristotle rejects the Platonic Theory of the Forms. Platonic dualism is rejected. There is only one world; not a world of

changing sense impressions and a world of unchanging forms.

3. Aristotle begins his philosophy with our sense experiences. His analysis of objects of sense, things, leads him to develop the concept of substances. SUBSTANCES, things, are made up of FORM and MATTER. The matter is the changing or indeterminate part of a thing. The form is the pattern of a thing—that which delimits it or gives it specificity. Both form and matter go together and make a thing what it is: a particular substance. This doctrine that forms are within a thing is very different from Plato's teaching that forms exist apart from the material world. For Aristotle, forms are found only embedded in things, though the intellect is capable of separating form from matter for the purpose of analysis.

4. Aristotle classified different substances by various characteristics. For example, rocks are substances without life; plants are substances with life but without locomotion; animals are substances with life and the ability to move but without rationality. Humans are substances with life, locomotion, and rationality but without immortality. There is implicit in Aristotle the conception of "A GREAT CHAIN OF BEING." Beyond humans, there may be Angels, Powers, and God, the Unmoved Mover.

5. Aristotle's thought is TELEOLOGICAL. Each substance has a purpose. In achieving their purposes, substances become actualized. They move from a POTENTIAL stage to their ACTUAL stage. The purpose of the acorn is to become an oak tree. Growth and change is the actualization of the potential which substances have. The purpose of man is the actualization of his rational self or soul. The highest form of human activity is to be engaged in intellectual contemplation.

Explain Aristotle's theory of matter and form.

What is a chain of being?

What does it mean for a substance to change from potency to actuality?

Explain the different kinds of causation according to Aristotle.

6. Aristotle is most important for the development of logic. Aristotelian logic recognizes four kinds of causation: efficient cause, formal cause, material cause, and final cause. With regard to shoes, the efficient cause would be the shoemaker who made the shoes; the formal cause is the form or design which makes a shoe a shoe; the material cause is the stuff which went into the making of the shoe; and the final cause is the purpose for which shoes are made. Only if we know these four causes do we fully understand a particular substance.

One of the great achievements of Aristotle was the development of the logical SYLLOGISM. In a syllogism, there is a major premise, followed by a minor premise that links to the major premise, and then there is the inevitable conclusion. For example:

Major premise

All humans are mortal.

Minor Premise

"X" is a human.

Conclusion

Therefore, X is mortal.

What is a syllogism?

This statement is absolutely true. Logically. Unfortunately, it does not tell us anything new about Mr. or Ms. X. Syllogistic reasoning is best used for the clarification of thought processes and arguments.

7. Aristotelian Ethics, as presented in the *Nicomachean Ethics*, is that of the Golden Mean. The avoidance of extremes is the recommended course of moral behavior. Thus virtue lies in the middle between two extremes or vices. For example, courage is the mean between cowardice and rashness and modesty is the mean between shamelessness and bashfulness. Since man is a social animal with reason, according to Aristotle, community life and law are essential to the development of the individual. While rational contemplation

is the ideal of human life, the perfection of human character is the aim of morality.

8. It must be noted that both Plato and Aristotle limited their analysis of governments to that of the city-state, the polis. Even though both philosophers lived when the polis was failing as an institution and was on the verge of being replaced by larger kingdoms, these great philosophers never addressed the question of how larger kingdoms or empires might be governed democratically.

Aristotle classified existing states into a six-fold classification based on who ruled and for whose benefit. The following table shows this six-fold classification. The best practical form of government was polity, where the many ruled but were limited by a constitution or system of laws. He expected the middle class to take the lead in the administration of such a government.

How can humans be virtuous?

Examine Aristotle's classification of governments. How do his values appear to differ from those of your political culture?

Types of Government

RULE BY:	LEGITIMATE GOVERNMENTS: (benefits for all)	ILLEGITIMATE GOVERNMENTS: (benefits for rulers)
ONE	MONARCHY	TYRANNY (Dictatorship)
FEW	ARISTOCRACY	OLIGARCHY
MANY	POLITY	DEMOCRACY

Aristotle is not as soaring and mystical as Plato. But his philosophy, which complements Plato, is a healthy corrective against the latter Plato whose metaphysics entered the realms of religious visions.

What strengths or weaknesses do you perceive in Aristotelian thought?

Corpus Aristotelicum[11]

(1) Logical writings—*Categories, On Interpretation, Prior and Posterior Analytics, Topics, Sophistical Refutations;*
(2) Physical and psychological writings—*Physics, On Generation and Corruption, On the Heavens, Meteorologica, On the Soul, Parva Naturalia, History of Animals, Parts of Animals, Generation of Animals, Motion of Animals;*
(3) *Metaphysics;*
(4) Ethical writings—*Nicomachean Ethics, Eudemian Ethics, Magna Moralia, Politics;*
(5) *Rhetoric, Poetics.*

It has often been said that subsequent Western philosophy is merely a long series of footnotes on Plato and Aristotle. While exaggerated, there is considerable truth in that statement.

Plato and Aristotle both founded schools, the Academy and the Lyceum respectively, which flourished after their founders' deaths They were finally shut down by order of the Emperor Justinian in 529 A.D., when the rising tide of Christianity had become inhospitable to philosophical speculation.

After Aristotle's death, several major schools of philosophy developed. These included the Neoplatonists, the Peripatetics (that is the followers of Aristotle), the Cynics, the Epicureans, and the Stoics.

5

From the Greeks to the Romans

Literature, History, and Art in Classical Greece

Greek Literature

Why was Homer so important to the Greeks?

Poetry

The best known works of poetry were the *Iliad* and *Odyssey* by HOMER. Homer is believed to have lived in Ionia, possibly Miletus, during the eighth century B.C. His story of the Trojan War, read by all Greeks, came to serve the function of a Bible. All literate Greeks knew their Homer, and much of their later literature used some episode from Homer as its starting point.

The great poet HESIOD, who may have been a contemporary of Homer, wrote the *Theogony*, in which he gave an account of the origins of the gods and their relationships to each other. Hesiod also wrote the poem *Works and Days*, which praised the virtues of the small farmer making an honest living from the barren soil of Greece.

Other well known Hellenic poets include SAPPHO and PINDAR. Sappho was

Who was Hesiod?

What were the poetic accomplishments of Sappho and Pindar?

born sometime between 630 and 612 B.C. on the island of Lesbos, where she ran a school for girls. Her love poetry revealed her erotic feelings for several of her pupils. Greek culture of the time was much more accepting of homosexuality than contemporary American culture. Pindar, who wrote in the period 498-446 B.C., is famed for his verses celebrating athletic victories.

Drama: Tragedies and Comedies

Attic drama had its origins in the annual festivals to the god Dionysus. For six days toward the end of March, the Greater Dionysia was held in Athens to celebrate the beginning of spring with revelry. Part of the celebrations was the performance in the great theater of Dionysus of tragedies, satyr plays, and comedies. Playwrights competed with each other for the honor of first prize. For the festival, each dramatist apparently produced three tragedies and a satyr play, which were staged on the same day. According to Aristotle, the viewer of tragedies experienced a purification or CATHARSIS of his/her senses through the emotions of fear and pity excited by the plays. Comedies, written and produced separately, were extremely raunchy, sexually explicit, and mocked even the highest authorities with slapstick humor.

What was catharsis?

The three great tragedians were Aeschylus, Sophocles, and Euripides. Aristophanes was the great playwright of the Old Comedy style just described. The poet THESPIS (6th century B.C.), considered to have been the first dramatist, added an actor to the traditional chorus, which sang religious chants. This innovation created a dialogue between the actor and the chorus. Thespis was also the first actor since he performed in

Who was the first dramatist?

his own plays. The first dramatic contest was held in Athens in 534 B.C.

AESCHYLUS, 525 - 456 B.C., wrote some 90 plays, of which only seven survive. His *Oresteia*, first performed in 458 B.C., is the only complete surviving trilogy. Composed of *Agamemnon*, *Choephoroe*, and *Eumenides*, this tragedy tells the story of the curse of the House of Atreus. Clytemnestra conspired with her lover to murder her husband, King Agamemnon, the leader of the Greeks during the Trojan War. Agamemnon had earlier sacrificed his daughter Iphigenia to propitiate the gods. Clytemnestra had never forgiven her husband for what she considered the murder of their daughter.

After Agamemnon's murder, the couple's son, Orestes, avenges his father's death, as he must. When Orestes realizes that he has killed his mother, he goes mad with despair caused by the Furies. Finally, Athena intervenes, a trial is held, and Orestes is forgiven. The curse on the House of Atreus is lifted.

What is important here, and what makes for tragedy, is that human beings are subjected by Fate, the gods, and their own passions to impossible demands. A father should never have to choose between his duties as a military commander to ensure the success of a war and his love for his daughter. A wife should never have to choose between the duty and love due her husband and the love and revenge owed her daughter. And a son should certainly never have to choose between avenging the murder of his father and killing his murderous mother. The Greek tragedies are not morality plays between good and evil. In such a conflict, the choice is easy. Of course, good should prevail. But real life, and real tragedy, forces us to choose between conflicting principles when there is no right choice. The only moral, perhaps, is that we should never allow ourselves to be

Chorus

Discuss the tragedies of Aeschylus.

What choices confronted to the heroes or heroines in Greek tragedy?

Describe the plot of the *Antigone* by Sophocles.

done

How did Euripides differ from Sophocles?

done

driven to extremes. Any passion carried to excess will be self-destructive. That is the fate and tragedy of mankind.

SOPHOCLES, c.497 - 406 B.C., is believed to have written some 123 plays and won 24 victories. Only seven of his plays have survived. Whereas Aeschylus had pioneered in adding a second actor, Sophocles added a third actor and thereby increased the dramatic interactions between characters. Sophocles is often considered to be the greatest of the great dramatists.

His *Antigone* told the story of the heroine who must choose between her familial obligation to bury her brother Polynices and the command of the King of Thebes, Creon, that those who warred illegally against their own city be left unburied to be eaten by the crows. Polynices had engaged in civil war against his city. Antigone buried her brother and the king has Antigone executed for defying his will. Could, should these tragedies have been avoided?

EURIPIDES, c.485 - 406 B.C., died just before Sophocles and was eulogized by the older man. Despite the closeness in ages, Euripides expressed the outlook of an entirely different generation, one that was increasingly skeptical of the old values. Euripides produced some 92 plays, of which 19 survive. The tragedies of Euripides that we have were all written during the Peloponnesian War, that disastrous conflict marking the end of the Golden Age of Greece. In several of his plays he criticized that war.

Euripides was more psychological than his predecessors. Human passions, rather than cosmic conflicts or divine interventions, often provided the motives for disastrous human actions. His earlier surviving plays all dealt with the tension between love and revenge. In *Medea* (first produced in 431 B.C.), when Jason deserts his wife for another woman,

Medea in revenge kills their children, whom Jason also loves. Several of Euripides's plays were psychological studies of women. They were misinterpreted by the ancients who thought Euripides was a women hater.

The later plays, written toward the end of the Peloponnesian war, were much more somber and fit more into the earlier tradition. *Iphigenia in Aulis* dealt with Agamemnon's decision to sacrifice his daughter to the gods. The Greek fleet was ready to set sail for Troy, but no wind had blown for three days, which was very unusual for the Aegean Sea. Agamemnon consults a soothsayer who tells the king that the gods want a sacrifice: Agamemnon's daughter Iphigenia. The story of the Trojan War was familiar to all Greeks from Homer. All three tragedians dealt with the House of Atreus. Tragedy dealt with known stories, but the playwrights presented new moral insights from fresh perspectives.

The counterpoint to tragedy is comedy. ARISTOPHANES, c.445 - c.385 B.C., was the greatest comic playwright of classical Greece. He is held to have written about 40 comedies, of which eleven have survived. To understand his Old Comedy style, it must be remembered that these plays started as part of religious celebrations to the god of wine. Imagine a New Orleans carnival that included not only street demonstrations and parties but also a public play on the order of *Animal House*.

The Old Comedy of Athens mocked public figures, philosophers, dramatists, and even war. The themes of the Old Comedy dealt with public issues rather than private matters. But these plays were still funny and ribald rather than sad and tragic.

In *The Clouds* (first produced in 423 B.C.), philosophy is mocked and Socrates is identified as a Sophist who corrupted the traditional values of Athenians. In *The Wasps*

Comedy

What were the plots of some of Euripides's plays?

How did Aristophanes differ from the playwrights previously mentioned?

What were the plots of some of Aristophanes's plays?

Satire

How did the New Comedy differ from the Old Comedy?

(422 B.C.), fun is made of lawyers, paid jury service, and the excessive degree of litigation engaged in by senior citizens. In *The Birds* (414 B.C.), Aristophanes imagined a city in the sky (Cloudcuckooland) built by the birds where not even the gods could intervene.

Perhaps his most famous play is *Lysistrata* (411 B.C.), in which the women of Greece refuse to have sex with their husbands to force them to stop going to war. Both women and men want to have sex, but the women persist until finally the men agree to end war. This was a direct appeal to end the Peloponnesian War, which was to lead to the defeat of Athens in 404 B.C.

Aristophanes also wrote two plays that dealt with Euripides. In one, Euripides is lampooned as a woman hater; in the other, Euripides is unfavorably compared to Aeschylus in a contest conducted in Hades.

After the defeat of Athens, public opinion and the Athenian government became less tolerant of the broad-gauged criticism and mockery of public figures. Old Comedy, also called high comedy, largely ended with that defeat. A transition was made toward New Comedy, or low comedy. The subject matter of comedy shifted toward, what we might call today, Sitcoms. The cheating husband, the maiden with more than one suitor, the rich man who wants a young wife, all of these personal situations formed the stock in trade of the low comedy of manners and social mores.

Even Aristophanes pointed in the new direction with a play called *Plutus*, in which private matters replaced issues of societal importance. MENANDER, 342 - 292 B.C., was the great Greek playwright of the New Comedy, which has influenced the Romans, the Renaissance, and our own made-for-TV comedies.

The Greek Historians

The same mental framework that produced philosophy and drama also generated the first historical writings. History is not simply chronology: a list of kings, their battles and great deeds, and dates. The ancient Egyptians had their lists of dynasties and kings and there are Mesopotamian chronologies. History must also not be confused with mythology. Almost all peoples, even preliterate ones, have mythologies that explain their own existence and their relationships to their gods. While mythologies provide some historical information, they are not, strictly speaking, history. Of all ancient peoples, the Hebrews, in their Bible, came closest to writing history. But, even here the motive is different. The Bible is primarily a record of the Hebrews' relationship with their God. Historical events are important only as they relate to God's message. God is the active element in the Biblical writings. They are not history *per se*.

The Greeks were the first people to be interested in human events simply as a human story. Humans make and shape their own history. Just as with philosophy, human events are not to be explained as Divine interventions either for good or ill. Human events are neither the object lessons of the gods nor their rewards and punishments. If we study human events carefully, we may be able to identify their causes and effects. Individuals and their behavior shape history. But we may also be able to discern broader ecological, economic, and social forces at work in the making of history. Fate, or chance, if it does play a role, should be used as a last resort in trying to make sense of human his-

How does history differ from myth?

Were the Greeks or the Hebrews the first historians? Explain.

What is the subject of Herodotus's *History*?

Why have historians admired the *History of the Peloponnesian War* by Thucydides?

tory. It is only with fate that the intervention of the gods may play a role.

HERODOTUS, c.484 - c.420, has been called the Father of History. While indebted to predecessors, particularly Hecataeus (c.500 B.C.), Herodotus omitted mythology as his starting point and went beyond a travelogue. Herodotus' *History* does contain descriptions of imaginary animals as if they were facts, but wherever possible he does differentiate what he has personally seen from fanciful tales he has heard from others. His main concern is the struggle between the Persian Empire and the Greek world from about 550 B.C. to about 479 B.C. Herodotus gives a detailed account of the Battle of Marathon. Providing a moral framework for the war, he explains the Greek victory over the much larger Persian Empire in terms of his opinion that free men, the Greek citizen-soldiers, were more willing to sacrifice themselves to protect their country from invaders than the Persian armies were prepared to die to conquer yet another province for the empire. Mercenary soldiers in the pay of a great emperor were not as motivated as the Greeks.

THUCYDIDES, c.460 - c.400 B.C., was an Athenian who wrote a contemporaneous *History of the Peloponnesian War*. He began his history in 431 B.C., when the war broke out. He was himself an Athenian general, who in 424 B.C. suffered defeat at the hands of the Spartans and was expelled from Athens for that reason. He returned to Athens in 404 B.C. after the final loss. His *History* breaks off abruptly with the year 411 B.C. Remarkably objective in his history, Thucydides blamed Athenian imperialism as the ultimate cause of the war. He was careful to weigh his sources of information and only wrote down what he considered to be established facts. His work has served as a model for the historian's craft ever since.

Greek Temples and Art

The poleis of the Hellenic Age were never very large or particularly rich. Individuals spent an extraordinary amount of time and resources on public business in Athens and the other democratically governed city-states. Only idiots did not participate in the public life of their city.

Given their relatively meager resources, it is remarkable that Greek city-states were able to build magnificent temples and other public buildings. These temples were built up on a hill, perhaps reminiscent of Mycenaean practices. The most famous of these temples was the PARTHENON, dedicated to Athena, on the ACROPOLIS above Athens.

Temples were built in what we now call the classical style of architecture, that is, colonnaded, one-story rectangular buildings with a roof. Generations of students have been exposed to the differences between Dorian, Ionian, and Corinthian columns. We shall not delve into the intricacies of Hellenic architecture, but it is recommended that students consider taking an art history or history of architecture course sometime during their college career.

Greek sculpture was produced mainly as statues for the temples. Each temple was dedicated to a god and the god's image stood at one end of the temple. Most of these sculptures, often clad in gold and ivory, have long since disappeared. We know about the work of famous sculptors like PHIDIAS, c.490 - 430 B.C., and PRAXITELES, c370 - 330 B.C., from descriptions of their work and sometimes from copies. The Romans were prolific in copying Greek sculpture and most

Why do you suppose the Greeks lavished so much of their resources on public buildings?

What was the Parthenon?

Hellenistic Period
Doric. Ionian Corinthian Bush
Roman use this

Who were Phidias and Praxiteles?

Athenos 30' high; zeus (at olympia) (Sat)

What were some features of Greek sculpture in the classical period?

other things Greek. Many of these Roman copies have survived. It is largely from Greek sculpture that Western Civilization has derived its sense of the beautiful. Greek sculpture idealized human nature, and the Greek gods were depicted as naked men and women in their most youthful bloom, perfect without blemishes. Marble was cut and bronze was cast into these idealized, anthropomorphic gods. The Elgin Marbles, now in the British Museum in London, once decorated the Parthenon.

Classical Greek painting has largely survived through pottery. The Greeks used large jars, called kraters, to store their wine and olive oil. These kraters came to be decorated first with geometric designs and later with pictures from Greek mythology. The Metropolitan Museum of Art in New York City has an extensive collection of kraters and Greek art.

The Hellenistic Period

Did Alexander the Great enjoy a long life?

Alexander the Great

Why do you suppose he conquered the Persian Empire?

Alexander was born in 356 B.C. During his youth, he was tutored by the great philosopher Aristotle. At Chaeronea, Alexander led a cavalry charge that may have been decisive in winning that battle. He became king in 336 after the murder of his father, Philip II of Macedon, and ruled until his death in 323 B.C. Alexander was a military genius who claimed that he was a living god, the son of Zeus Amon.

Between 334 and 330, Alexander attacked and conquered the Persian Empire.

His conquests began the HELLENISTIC PERIOD of history, during which Greek and Oriental cultures interrelated with each other.

Alexander's first victory against the Persians came at the Granicus River on the coast of Asia Minor in 334 B.C. This was followed by the Battle of Issus in Syria in 333 B.C., where he defeated the main Persian army under Darius. Alexander next laid siege to Tyre in Phoenicia, which fell after seven months in 332 B.C. He then moved on and was welcomed in Jerusalem. He invaded Egypt and was crowned pharaoh as the son of Amon, who has often been linked to the Greek god Zeus. While in Egypt, he founded the city of Alexandria.

In the spring of 331 B.C., Alexander was on the move again, marching to Mesopotamia and defeating Darius at the Battle of Gaugamela in October. Darius fled in terror and was murdered later in 330 B.C. by his own followers. Babylon and Susa surrendered; Persepolis offered resistance and was taken in January 330 B.C. Tremendous treasure was looted by Alexander with these victories. The wealth liberated from the royal treasure vaults of the Persian kings helped to fuel economic prosperity for the next century.

Alexander was not content with these tremendous achievements, which made him master of both the Greek and the Persian worlds. He moved his army into modern-day Pakistan and reached the Indus River. He conquered a considerable part of India and was ready to move on toward unknown lands, including the legendary land of China. Alexander encountered war elephants in India; beasts that his Macedonian soldiers had never dreamed existed. He was finally forced to turn back when his troops mutinied in 326 B.C. and refused to fight on the other side of the Indus River.

Describe the progress of Alexander's conquests.

Why did he stop his eastward advance?

Was Alexander arrogant?

He was back in the Persian city of Susa in 324 B.C. where he celebrated his achievements in typical Macedonian fashion: with a drunken orgy. In a drunken rage, he put a spear through one of his long time companions, Cleitus, who dared criticize Alexander for his increasingly arrogant assertions that he was a god.

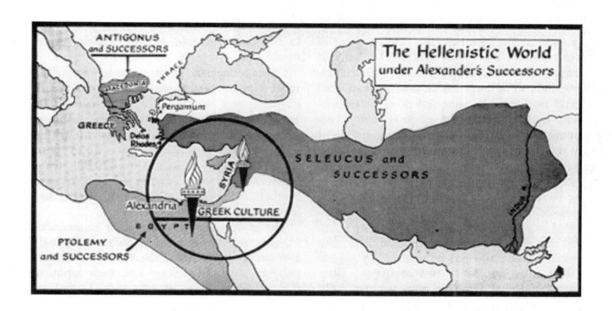

Alexander sought to fuse Macedonians, Greeks, and Persians into a single ruling class. To that end, Alexander married a Bactrian princess, Roxane, and had many of his officers and soldiers marry similarly. Thirty-thousand Persian men were trained to become soldiers in his army. Since his days in Egypt, Alexander encouraged the belief that he was a god. Such beliefs were common to the East, but rare in Greece. Clearly, Alexander was adopting the monarchical principles of the East.

In 323 B.C., while in Babylon full of plans for the future, Alexander unexpectedly died of swamp fever on June 12. His wife was pregnant. On his deathbed, Alexander was asked who should succeed him. In his typical fashion he was supposed to have answered: "the strongest."

What was Alexander's attitude towards the conquered Persians?

The Hellenistic Kingdoms

What happened following Alexander's death?

The Diadochi

Even if Alexander had lived to a ripe old age, it would have been difficult to maintain the unity of this vast empire. He died leaving his pregnant widow, Roxane, his illegitimate and retarded stepbrother, and his always dangerous mother, Olympia. There was no heir capable of stepping in his shoes. Almost immediately, the generals who had served Alexander began jockeying for power. These "successors" were later called the DIADOCHI.

Three regents were chosen by the Macedonian nobility to rule the huge empire in the name of his half brother, who was

Who were the Diadochi?

Describe the major Hellenistic kingdoms established after Alexander's death.

called Philip III, and his posthumously born son, known as Alexander IV. Olympia had Philip III murdered in 317 B.C. Olympia was murdered in 316; Roxane and her son were murdered in 309 B.C. by Cassander, the son of the last of the regents. Any pretense that Alexander's empire was being preserved for his heir ended; the old Macedonian dynasty had come to an end.

After several decades of instability during which the Diadochi, that is the first generation of rulers after Alexander, died in battle, were assassinated, or succumbed to old age, his conquests were divided into three main kingdoms and several minor states. Macedonia was ruled by a new dynasty under Antigonus I Monophthalmus, one of Alexander's generals. In 307, Antigonus had himself and his son, Demetrius I Poliocretes, declared kings. Thus began the Antigonid dynasty of Macedonia. Alexander's vast Asian conquests were seized by Seleucus I Nicator, who in 305 assumed the title of king and founded the Seleucid dynasty of Syria and Mesopotamia. Ptolemy I, another of Alexander's generals, entrenched himself in Egypt, assumed the title of king in 304, and became the first ruler of the Ptolemaic dynasty.

Antigonid Macedonia and the Greeks

Macedonia and Greece were at the center of the wars of succession that erupted after Alexander's death. Antigonus I's failure to gain control over all of Alexander's conquests and his death at the Battle of Ipsus in 301, plunged Macedonia into turmoil. In 279 B.C., the Celtic tribe of the Gauls invaded Macedonia. The victory of Antigonus II Gonatas, grandson of the great Antigonus, over the Gauls led to his appointment as Macedonian king in 276 B.C. His heirs continued to rule Macedonia and most of Greece until 168 B.C. when the last of the Antigonid rulers, Perseus, was defeated by the Romans. The Romans abolished the Macedonian monarchy, incorporated Macedonia into their empire, and Perseus died in Roman captivity in 165 B.C.

Although Philip II had brought Greece under Macedonian hegemony after the Battle of Chaeronea in 338 B.C., the poleis of Greece continued to enjoy considerable autonomy and rebelled periodically when Macedonian preoccupations elsewhere made it possible. Athens, Sparta, the Aetolian League, the Achaean League, Rhodes, Delos, and Pergamum had their distinct histories during the Hellenistic age.

Athens developed a special relationship with Macedonia, perhaps because of the linkage between Alexander and Aristotle. It came to occupy a privileged position within the Hellenistic world, and even the Romans later honored Athens as the cradle of Hellenic civilization. Athens became a university town. Various schools of philosophy flourished there and taught generations of scholars.

Sparta, although greatly reduced in power, particularly after Messenia was restored to independence, had never made peace or joined Philip's Hellenic League. During the third century, there were several efforts to restore the old military tradition, which ultimately failed.

Scattered villages in northwestern Greece, which had been backward during the Classical age, joined together and formed the Aetolian League during the Hellenistic period. This league was a true federation and exercised considerable power.

It was opposed by another federation, the Achaean League. The Achaean League was made up of the lesser towns of the Peloponnese, particularly those on the southern

What was the relationship between Macedonia and Greece during the Hellenistic age?

What leagues formed on the Grecian peninsula?

What contributed to the independent survival of Rhodes, Delos, and Pergamum?

shore of the Gulf of Corinth. Any perceived increase in the power of Sparta was seen as a threat by the Achaean League. Once again, an unstable balance of power prevailed in Greece, which the Macedonian kings were usually able to exploit to their advantage.

Rhodes and Delos benefited from the fact that they were islands, which protected them from land-based armies. They became important centers of the Mediterranean-Sea trade. Their safe harbors and neutrality served the interests of all the major protagonists. Pergamum in western Anatolia survived by playing off Antigonid and Seleucid power against each other, usually in alliance with Ptolemaic Egypt.

Seleucid Mesopotamia and Persia

Describe the fortunes of the Seleucid Empire.

After 301 B.C., the bulk of Alexander's conquests fell to Seleucus and his heirs. The Seleucid Empire included parts of India, Afghanistan, Persia, Mesopotamia, and Syria. Palestine was contested with Ptolemaic Egypt and Asia Minor (Anatolia) with Antigonid Macedonia. It was too large a territory to be effectively governed. Moreover, Greeks and Macedonians formed a tiny minority within these vast lands. The history of the Seleucid Empire is a tale of progressive defeats as indigenous peoples one by one reestablished their independence. India fell away almost immediately. The Parthians regained control of Iran and later control of Mesopotamia. Ultimately only a greater Syria remained to the Seleucids. Perpetual warfare with Macedonia and Egypt weakened all the great Hellenistic kingdoms. In 63 B.C., the Romans incorporated the last remaining Seleucid lands into the Roman province of Syria.

Ptolemaic Egypt

Who were the Ptolemies?

Ptolemy I, c.367 - 283 B.C., was appointed governor (satrap) of Egypt in 323 B.C. and became the founder of the Macedonian dynasty that ruled Egypt until 30 B.C. Ptolemy and his successors were recognized by the Egyptians as legitimate pharaohs, that is as god-kings. Until 200 B.C., the Egyptians controlled much of Palestine and Syria. They had a large navy with which they played an important role in the Aegean. They were the wealthiest and most important of the Hellenistic kingdoms. After 200 B.C., they lost Palestine to the Seleucids and declined in power. Rome began to play an increasing role in the dynastic politics of Egypt beginning with Ptolemy VI, who ruled from 180 to 145 B.C. As a Roman ally, Egypt remained nominally independent until 30 B.C. Under the last Ptolemaic ruler, Cleopatra VII, who was born in 69 B.C. and became queen and co-ruler of Egypt in 51 B.C., Egypt played an important role in the Roman civil wars that ended the Republican era of Roman history.

Were their experiences with Rome entirely happy? Explain.

Hellenistic Culture

The conquest by Alexander the Great of most of the civilized world from India to Egypt marked an important moment in world history. Alexander may have begun his conquests as the champion of Panhellenism: the man who would unite all Greeks under one ruler and who would finally destroy the ever-looming presence of the Persian Empire. Most of his Macedonian generals and soldiers were content with this Panhellenic vision. Alexander, however, moved beyond this parochial Greco-centric vision. He may have sought to obliterate cultural differences and form a new

If Alexander had lived longer, do you think he would have succeeded in integrating the Greeks and the Persians? Why?

Were the Hellenistic states truly cosmopolitan? Explain.

cosmopolitan and universal society of all human beings. It is clear that he sought to obliterate the differences between Greeks and Persians. He married a Bactrian princess. Ten thousand of his soldiers were married to Asiatic women. While reconciliation with the Persians was clearly Alexander's intent, and led to significant opposition within his Greek-Macedonian army, it is less clear whether such cosmopolitan equality was being offered to all his subject peoples.

WORLD

Cosmopolitanism Implicitly, however, a cosmopolitan ideal was being born. Three hundred years before the rise of Christianity, we have here a hint of the brotherhood of mankind. Belonging to a group, to be an Athenian or a Spartan, or even to be a Greek, Persian, Egyptian, Jew, or Syrian, can be a comforting thought. To be a citizen of the world, without a country, equally at home everywhere and with everyone your brother, that thought was a radically new idea. Especially for the Greeks, with their traditional loyalties to their particular poleis, this was an almost unbearable idea.

After Alexander's death, most of the interracial marriages that he had encouraged were dissolved. The Hellenistic kingdoms were not truly cosmopolitan. A thin veneer of Greek culture and a small Greek-speaking minority dominated a majority of conquered peoples. Nonetheless, a new ideal had been born.

Eclecticism in Religion So many different peoples with so many different cultures were being thrown together in these large Hellenistic kingdoms. Even if they did not merge into one, some degree of learning from one another did take place. Some common denominators had to be found. Religion can offer consolations in an increasingly uncertain world.

Alexander had linked the Greek idea that a human being who performed heroic deeds could become a god with the Egyptian belief that the pharaoh was a living god. He had demanded that even his Macedonian officers prostrate themselves in his presence. The Greeks only prostrated themselves before the images of their gods; prostration before a human, they saw as degrading. Some of Alexander's most competent officers refused and were put to death. Alexander was assuming the trappings of the oriental monarchs and was attempting to make his divine person into a symbol of unity for his cosmopolitan state. His string of unprecedented military victories and the sayings of several oracles that he was the son of Amon may have truly convinced him that he was more than a mortal.

The Seleucid and Ptolemaic kings copied Alexander's model and also assumed the divine trappings of Mesopotamian and Egyptian rulers. Emperor worship was used later by the Romans as a tool for unifying their diverse empire.

Ordinary people continued to worship their household and local gods. Belief in the Olympian gods and the civic cults of particular cities declined. Belief in soothsayers, diviners, and astrologers increased. Hardly any public action was taken without consulting oracles, using spells or potions, or having one's fortune told. Local mythologies and legends became synthesized. A broad Hellenistic cosmology developed, into which Greek, Babylonian, Egyptian, and Persian myths became syncretized and amalgamated. Parallels were drawn between gods from different traditions having similar functions: sun god, sky gods, earth goddesses, fertility gods, etc.

Most spectacular was the growth of various mystery religions. Often these cults had roots in very primitive fertility rites. The

How did Alexander and his Hellenistic successors use religion?

Were the local myths preserved intact? Explain.

What did the mystery religions have in common?

Greeks had their Dionysian, Eleusinian, and Orphic Mysteries. The Egyptians provided the cults of Isis and Serapis. The Babylonians weighed in with Ishtar and from Persia came Mithraism. In most of these mysteries, the devotee sought mystical union with the god or goddess and life after death. The dualistic religion of Zoroastrianism and the monotheistic religion of Judaism must also be mentioned. In particular, the ethical monotheism of the Jews was having an intellectual impact on the broader gentile world. There was, indeed, during the Hellenistic period, a broad intellectual movement toward the belief in a single god or principle from which all things derived. Even the gods could not change FATE; and FORTUNA could smile on anyone without good reason.

Why was there greater stress on individualism in Hellenistic than in Hellenic times?

| Individualistic Philosophies | The philosophy of Plato and Aristotle had been concerned with the questions of absolute knowledge and justice. The polis had served as the unit of social life for both these great philosophers. Neither had been cosmopolitan in their outlooks. The problems of morality, ethics, and politics within the large Hellenistic monarchies rooted in Alexander's conquests were not considered, even though, as we know, Aristotle knew the great general.

Certainly the democratic participation of free citizens in the public life of their city-state became more difficult or impossible in the large multi-cultural, universal empires ruled by divine right god-kings. The more remote government became from the individual, the less the individual could define himself in terms of the state. The good citizen and the good man were no longer identical, as they were for Plato. As a life of public service became less of an option for most persons, private life became more important. Cosmopolitanism implied individualism. How could the isolated individual living in a vast sea of humanity structure his life in a meaningful way? That was the question which the Hellenistic philosophers attempted to answer.

Philosophic questions and answers are generally of interest only to a minority of the population. The majority, as we have already seen, usually take refuge in religion when daily life becomes more and more burdensome and meaningless.

Although Alexandria, Antioch, Pergamum, Rhodes, and other Hellenistic cities were more prosperous and had a higher material culture, philosophy always remained anchored in Athens. The Academy of Plato and the Lyceum of Aristotle flourished there until closed by the Eastern Roman Emperor Justinian in 529 A.D.

While Plato and Aristotle continued to influence the Hellenistic world, four new schools of philosophy developed. These were the Cynics, Skeptics, Epicureans, and Stoics. Each concerned itself with the question of how an individual could achieve happiness.

The CYNICS were the "hippies" of the Classical Age; they rejected the social conventions of normal people, rejected material possessions, and advocated "a natural life." This natural life included a refusal to wash, and some refused to wear clothes. They held that civilization and society corrupted individuals, and that stripped of clothing, possessions, and status all persons were equal in nature. The most outrageous cynic was Diogenes of Sinope (c.400 - c.325 B.C.) who carried a lighted lamp at noontime through the streets of Athens saying that he was looking for an honest man. He claimed that he never found one. He slept in a barrel, wore almost no clothes, and ate his food raw to illustrate that even houses, clothes, and fire were unnecessary conventions. Diogenes made his

Given this individualism, did the schools of Plato and Aristotle survive the Hellenistic Age?

What other philosophies arose?

Who was Diogenes of Sinope?

How did the Cynics attempt to be "natural"?

Distinguish the Skeptics from the Cynics.

living by begging. He declared himself to be a "citizen of the world," a cosmopolitan, and claimed to be seeking virtue. The Cynics admired Socrates for his self-sufficiency and indifference to possessions. Their emphasis on nature, even if at a crude, almost animal-like level, influenced the Stoics, who transformed the idea of nature into something quite different.

To be cynical is to be highly critical of all persons, institutions, and ideas. It is to suggest some corrupt motive behind all actions. Cynicism is a destructive mental attitude because it leads to passivity, negativism, pessimism, and despair.

The SKEPTICS rejected claims of certainty based on dogma and authority. They also questioned whether human minds could have absolute knowledge. The Sophists were skeptical about whether moral standards were universally true. Plato's response depended on his conception of the ideal forms. But later Academics, those teaching at Plato's Academy, questioned whether human minds could understand and know these ideal Forms. Skepticism is a philosophy of doubt. It need not be a destructive philosophy because even the statement—there are no absolute truths or certainties—is open to doubt. Since all dogmas could be wrong, skeptics advised that individuals follow the social conventions of their environment but with one's mind engaged. There was no deliberate challenge of authority, as with the cynics.

Another group of Hellenistic philosophers were the EPICUREANS. The founder of this philosophy was Epicurus (342 - 270 B.C.), who thought that human beings were most interested in happiness. The question was how this happiness might be achieved. Obviously, one way to achieve happiness was to remove those things that made for unhappiness. Chief among those, according to Epicurus, were fear of the gods and fear of death. Epicurus thought that these fears were unfounded because the gods took no interest in human affairs and death was final. There was no afterlife during which the gods either rewarded or punished the individual:

> Therefore, the most formidable of evils, death, is nothing to us, since, when we exist, death is not present to us; and when death is present, then we have no existence. It is no concern then either of the living or of the dead; since to the one it has no existence, and the other class has no existence itself.[12]

Epicurus based these views on the atomic theory of Democritus of Abdera, who held that all matter is composed of atoms, constantly colliding and recombining. The universe was conceived as being entirely materialistic. Once it is realized that this life is all there is, then happiness depends on structuring this life as pleasantly as possible. Avoiding fear, pain, and suffering became the key to happiness.

Opponents of Epicureanism from ancient times onward have deliberately misrepresented this emphasis on pleasure. Epicureanism does not advocate a life of wine, women, and song. The highest pleasures for Epicureans were intellectual. Food and drink should be taken in moderation, because excesses cause pain. The companionship of good friends and stimulating conversation in the privacy of a well-apportioned country villa, those were the pleasures of the Epicureans. So there is perhaps a modicum of truth in the modern meaning of an "epicure" as "a lover of fine food, a gourmet." But it would be wrong to call such a person a glutton.

It should be noted that the Epicureans were advocating private happiness. There was no concern about the public welfare, good government, or justice. This is an ideal of

According to Epicurus, what attitude should humans take towards death?

Did Epicureans stress physical or intellectual pleasure? Explain.

What places do detachment and natural law have in Stoic thought?

Distinguish Stoicism from Epicureanism.

withdrawal from the world at large. It is an aristocratic ideal because only rich people can afford a pleasant country estate where they can enjoy making music, painting, and cultivating their private garden.

The STOICS were another group that extolled individuality and inner peace; however, they felt the best way to live one's life was to accept his or her fate. Along with emotional detachment from life, the individual should live in harmony with nature, striving for virtue. Today we use the word STOIC to mean indifference to suffering or pain. Back then a Stoic would be indifferent to both joy and pain. The name originally came from the *Stoa Poikile* (Painted Porch) in Athens where Zeno (335 - 263 B.C.), the founder of Stoicism, taught.

Included in this philosophy was the concept of nature and natural law. The universe, for the Stoics, was ruled by rational principles. It embodied the LOGOS, or divine reason. Every human being was part of this rational order—slaves, women, foreigners. All human beings were equal and brothers under the skin, regardless of their different social positions. Within each person resided LOGOS (divine reason), making her or him capable of knowing the divinely-established law of nature. Obedience to this natural law made a person free, whether one was a slave or an emperor.

Stoic philosophy carried over to the Roman world, for it taught that duty and self-discipline were of paramount importance. The Stoics encouraged participation in public affairs. Stoicism fitted in well with the traditional Roman values of patriotism, honor, and civic duty. Cicero, the orator and statesman, Seneca, the tutor of the Emperor Nero, and Marcus Aurelius, the last of the Good Emperors, were disciples of this philosophy.

Hellenistic Science

Alexander conquered lands of which the Greeks had previously had only the vaguest knowledge. It was obvious to his officers that their maps of Afghanistan, Pakistan, and India were totally inadequate. The new knowledge acquired during his campaigns and the need for additional information greatly stimulated the scientific study of geography. Alexander's friendship with Aristotle benefited science. Rare or new, to the Greeks, specimens of plants and animals were sent to the Lyceum on orders of the great conqueror. Theophrastus, who succeeded Aristotle as head of the Lyceum, established the science of botany based on the specimens sent to him.

The most important center of Hellenistic science was Alexandria, the cosmopolitan capital of Ptolemaic Egypt at the delta of the Nile. The fantastic wealth of Egypt, increased by trade and commerce, allowed the Ptolemaic rulers to have their architects build a model city with wide avenues, magnificent palaces, a 400-foot lighthouse called the Pharos at the entrance to the harbor, and a world-famous library with an adjacent museum. Until replaced by Rome centuries later, Alexandria was the largest city in the world. Its library housed over 500,000 papyrus scrolls, the ancient equivalents of books and manuscripts. The Museum, named after the nine Muses of the Arts, served as one of the world's first "think tanks," where scholars, scientists, and mathematicians, at government expense, engaged in research. Much of their work was routine cataloging, compilations of dictionaries, and glossaries on previous works. However, science was an area where real creative work was done.

Not until the Scientific Revolution of the 16th century would science again match the achievements of the Hellenistic Age. EUCLID, who lived about 300 B.C., produced

Why did Alexandria in Egypt become an important center of learning?

Describe the resources of the library in Alexandria.

Do you think the scientific study in the Hellenistic period surpassed that of the Hellenic age?

Discuss the contributions of Euclid in geometry and Eratosthenes in geography.

rational proofs for geometric relationships involving points, lines, triangles, and circles. His *Elements of Geometry* are still used today in high school courses on plane geometry. There were other mathematicians who wrote about circles, spirals, spherical cones, and other elements of spherical geometry.

Geographical knowledge was dramatically increased by ERATOSTHENES (c. 275-194 B.C.), head of the Alexandrian library. He was the first to place lines of latitude and longitude on maps. He believed that the world's oceans were joined and was convinced that Europe, Asia, and Africa were once one single continent. Using geometry, he calculated the circumference of the earth accurately with an error of only 200 miles—quite an astonishing feat for the time.

One Alexandrian astronomer, called ARISTARCHUS OF SAMOS (310 - 230 B.C.), speculated that the sun was at the center of the universe with the planets revolving around it in circles. He also had the earth revolving on its axis. Unfortunately, his view was not supported by empirical observations (planets travel in elliptical rather than circular orbits). His version of the heliocentric theory lost out to the views of the astronomers Hipparchus of Nicaea and CLAUDIUS PTOLEMY, who held that the earth is the center of the universe. This geocentric view was also in agreement with religious dogma. The belief in an earth-centered universe was thought to be valid until the 16th century, when Copernicus revived the ideas of Aristarchus.

Contrast the views of Aristarchus and Ptolemy.

Another important mathematician and physicist was ARCHIMEDES OF SYRACUSE (c. 287 - 212 B.C.). He was the scientist who, after having thought of the displacement of water by his body, stepped out of his bath naked onto the street, exclaiming "Eureka" (I have found it!). What he had found was specific gravity and the law of buoyancy. He pioneered the science of hydrostatics. Archimedes also designed complex pulleys that could lift very heavy loads. He designed war machines that helped defend his city of Syracuse against the Romans. The Romans still took the city. Archimedes is also credited with determining the value of pi as the ratio between a circle's circumference and its diameter. Archimedes was a truly multi-faceted genius.

Hellenistic physicians made giant strides in the areas of anatomy and physiology. Some used cadavers as well as LIVE prisoners from the King's dungeons. HEROPHILUS (c.285 B.C.) and ERASISTRATUS (c.275) were the first persons to measure the pulse rate, separate arteries from veins, and discover that the brain is the center of the nervous system. GALEN, in the second century of our time (AD 130-200), summarized these tremendous Hellenistic achievements in medicine, and his works served as the standard textbook for the next 1500 years.

These great scientific achievements were not, however, followed up in subsequent centuries. Three reasons have been offered as an explanation. First, science had reached the limits of human observation. Without microscopes, telescopes, and other instruments, the exploration of nature could not be pushed any further. Second, slavery and the abundance of cheap labor made the invention of machinery unprofitable. There was no industrial revolution or machine age to further stimulate scientific discovery. Third, the growing preoccupation with religion and salvation worked against the rational spirit on which scientific knowledge depends.

What were some of the accomplishments of Archimedes?

What did Hellenistic medicine achieve?

How did Hellenistic art differ from that of the classical period?

Hellenistic Art — In the 4th century B.C., art changed radically from the idealized, unemotional art of the classical or Hellenic period. It became more naturalistic and emotional. There was also a growth of ornateness and size. Hellenistic monarchs, as well as wealthy individuals, could commission statues, temples, and palaces. They were ostentatious and wanted their buildings and art far more ornate and luxurious than the simple designs of the 5th century.

Everyday subjects were sculpted with realism, showing blemishes, wrinkles, and disfigurations. These included such subjects as an old market woman, a boxer, young children, and a Gaul dying in a pool of blood. The second-century bronze sculpture of *The Boxer*, for example, illustrates the harsh reality of the sport. As one looks into the boxer's battered face, one sees a large protrusion on one cheek as well as a damaged ear. His expression shows the pain he has experienced. Not quite the same as today, but easily identifiable as protective covering, his hands are bound with leather straps and a pad. His body pose is not erect and standing, but rather resting in anticipation of the next round. This statue is far removed from the unblemished beauty and vertical pose of the classical period. The *Winged Victory of Samothrace* and the *Laocoon* are also dynamic expressions of Hellenistic art, studied today for their flowing motion and evocative poses.

Name some examples of Hellenistic Art.

Assessment

The polis was both the glory and the downfall of the Hellenic Civilization. The small city-state generated a degree of loyalty to the community rarely reached in human history. Its smallness made it possible for direct democracy to evolve. But this intense local patriotism made it impossible for the Greeks to form larger political communities. The attempt by Athens to create an Empire failed with the Peloponnesian War. Sparta was ill-suited to take the leadership of the Greek world, given its peculiar garrison state. After 404 B.C., the system of independent poleis degenerated into perpetual warfare and internally most city-states divided into class warfare between rich oligarchs and mob-ruled democracies. The Macedonian King Philip II succeeded in subjecting the Greek city-states to his hegemony. Even though Plato and Aristotle lived during the declining years of the poleis, they never addressed the fundamental problem of how to create a polity larger than that of a single city-state.

Alexander the Great used Macedonian and Greek soldiers to conquer the Persian empire and to spread a hybrid Greek-Macedonian culture to the entire eastern Mediterranean. This cosmopolitan culture of Greek, Persian, Babylonian, Hebrew, and Egyptian elements is generally called the Hellenistic Civilization. Three main Hellenistic Kingdoms developed after the death of Alexander (323 B.C.). Each was in turn conquered by the Roman State. The last, Egypt, fell in 30 B.C. Thus the Hellenistic period of history extended from 323 B.C. to 30 B.C. The Romans adopted most of this Hellenistic culture and merged it with their own traditions to produce what is usually called the Greco-Roman Civilization. We will discuss the rise of Rome and the formation of its empire in the next section.

Look at the *Old Market Woman* pictured at the end of this section. Why is this statue representative of Hellenistic art?

Figure 2.3. The Old Market Woman. Pentelic Marble Statue, Second Century B.C. This marble statue illustrates the naturalism and realism and the Hellenistic Age as opposed to the idealistic, unblemished, expressionless statues of the Hellenic Period. Look at the twist of her torso, the draping of her garment, and the lines around the mouth that give her character and personality. She is not an idealized beauty. *Courtesy of The Metropolitan Museum of Art, Rogers Fund, 1909. (09.39)*

6

The Roman Republic

ITALY is a large peninsula which juts south into the Mediterranean Sea from the Alps. It has the shape of a boot; and at its toe, there is a large island called Sicily. Italy's prehistoric period extends back to the Paleolithic Age. Primitive agricultural settlements were in existence by 5000 B.C. and Bronze Age cultures developed by 2000 B.C. Iron was introduced about 1000 B.C.

During the eighth century, GREEK COLONIES were established in SOUTHERN ITALY AND SICILY. To the North between the ARNO AND TIBER Rivers, the ETRUSCANS developed their civilization. The Etruscan culture was formed during the eighth, flourished and grew during the sixth, began to be seriously challenged during the fifth, became subordinate to the Romans during the third, and lost its remaining cultural distinctiveness during the first century before Christ.

It is still not clear whether the Etruscans represent an indigenous development or outside colonists. The Greek historian Herodotus suggested that the Etruscans came from Lydia. What is clear is that the Etruscan language was neither Indo-European nor Semitic. It appears unrelated to any other known language. The Etruscans did, however, adopt the Greek alphabet for their writing system, which they, in turn, transmitted to the Romans. None of their literature, other than some short inscriptions in their language, have survived. The language has not yet been

Where were the Greek and Etruscan settlements located in Italy?

When did Etruscan culture flourish?

From where did the Etruscans get their alphabet?

Did the Etruscans have a significant influence on the Romans?

deciphered. Most likely the Etruscan culture was a mixture of indigenous Italian elements and outside, probably Eastern, elements including Greek. The Etruscans had a significant impact on Rome, which they ruled for about 100 years. Important Etruscan city-states included Caere, Tarquina, and Veii.

The Founding of Rome: 753 to 613 B.C.

Where is Rome located?

Rome is located near the center of Italy on the Tiber River in the Latin plain. People have been living near Rome continuously since about 1000 B.C., but villages do not constitute a city. The Romans themselves placed the founding of their city at 753 B.C. when their first king, the legendary Romulus, laid out the borders of their city and built its first fortifications. This traditional date for the founding of Rome has generally been accepted by historians with various reservations. The Rome of 753 B.C. was at best a very small city-state of little power or significance and would remain so for many more centuries.

When was Rome founded?

The Romans of later centuries invented many LEGENDS about the origin of their city. The great poet VIRGIL, 70 - 19 B.C., wrote an epic called the *Aeneid* in which the foundation of Rome is linked to the fall of Troy. Aeneas escaped from Troy after its destruction by the Greeks and had many adventures including a serious love affair with the queen of Carthage, whom he jilted and who thereupon committed suicide. Aeneas, who finally settled in Italy, ended up marrying the daughter of Latinus, king of the region near the Tiber. Aeneas founded the town of Livinium,, parent town of both Alba Longa and Rome.

It is doubtful that any Trojans ever migrated to Latium, but the legend was useful to Rome in claiming historical parity to the Greeks. Although the Romans ended up conquering the entire land area surrounding the Mediterranean Sea, they always had an inferiority complex with regard to the Greeks, from whose culture they borrowed massively.

The immediate founding of Rome is linked to the legend of ROMULUS AND REMUS. They were the twin sons of the god Mars and Rhea Silvia, the daughter of the ousted king of Alba Longa. Rhea Silvia had been forced to become a vestal virgin by the usurper. Vestal virgins were required, on pain of death, to remain chaste, but who can refuse a god? After birth, Romulus and Remus were set adrift on the river Tiber. But through the miraculous interventions of Mars, they survived and were nursed by a she-wolf until found by a shepherd. The twins later restored the ousted king to his throne and founded the city of Rome. In a dispute over the boundaries of Rome, Romulus killed his brother Remus and became the sole king.

This legend dates back at least to the 400s B.C. and may have been intended to explain Rome's military power. Having the war god Mars as the father of the founder of your city, as well as having the god as its protector, goes a long way toward explaining Rome's growth and success.

The last legend to be mentioned is that of the RAPE OF THE SABINE WOMEN. After Romulus had built the city walls and established Rome, there was a shortage of women for the eligible bachelors. Romulus organized a war party and invaded the neighboring territory of the Sabines. All the young Sabine women were abducted and raped by the Romans. After each man had taken his

Summarize the legend of Romulus and Remus.

What purpose do legends, such as the miraculous birth and survival of Romulus and Remus, serve?

What lessons might the tale of the rape of the Sabine women teach?

What was the language of Rome?

What did the Romans owe to the Etruscans?

woman, he married her. When the Sabine men came to revenge this outrage, the now-married Sabine women intervened and prevented a war. A peace was signed between the Romans and the Sabines.

This legend confirms what many historians believe based on other evidence, namely that Rome may have started as a mixed settlement. Latins, Sabines, and maybe other groups joined to become Romans. Rome may have started as a settlement for outlaws who were ousted from their own tribe and community. This may have given the Romans a cohesion and loyalty which preserved them through many centuries of war. Whatever the mixed origins of Rome, what is clear is that the language of Rome was always LATIN, the language of the people of the Latin plain. Latin is an Indo-European language related to Greek.

Etruscan Rome: 613 to 509 B.C.

The last three of the traditional seven kings of Rome were Etruscans. The Tarquin dynasty ruled from 613 through 509 B.C.. When the son of the last king seduced and raped the Roman matron LUCRETIA, she denounced her defiler publicly and then committed suicide, even though she was blameless and her husband would have forgiven her. The Romans, outraged, ousted the Etruscans and sent their kings packing. The Roman SENATE declared the REPUBLIC.

The Etruscans significantly and permanently influenced Roman culture. The Romans became literate during this time and the Latin alphabet is based on the Etruscan. Roman religious practices dealing with divination and augury came from Etruria. Under

Figure 2.4. Sarcophagus. Etruscan. Terra Cotta. III-II Centuries B.C. This funerary urn is representative of Etruscan art. This rich culture flourished north of Rome, in what is now Tuscany. Rome was under the rule of Estruscan kings until 509 B.C. and incorporated many Etruscan cultural elements into their society. From the Etruscans, the Romans picked up ideas concerning funeral practices, divination, engineering skills, chariot racing, and gruesome gladiatorial combats. *Courtesy of The Metropolitan Museum of Art. Purchased by subscription, 1896. (96.9.223 ab)*

What is a republic?

the Etruscan kings, Rome became a real city with the ancient Roman Forum (business or market area) as its center. Many of their engineering skills may also have been borrowed from the Etruscans.

The Roman Republic: 509 - 27 B.C.

Who were the Patricians? oligarchy.

PATER = father

Any political system which is not ruled by a monarch or an hereditary aristocracy is a REPUBLIC. In a republic, the rulers must be chosen by some form of election. Depending on the size of the electorate, such a republic may become a democracy. The Roman Republic did not become a democracy in the sense that Athens had been democratic. The Republic was always dominated by the Roman SENATE, whose unelected members were chosen because they had previously held political office.

Distinguish between consuls and councils.

The Roman Republic began with the overthrow of the Etruscan kings by the Patricians. The PATRICIANS were the large property owners, the aristocratic element within Rome. At the beginning of the Republican period, the Patricians dominated all aspects of politics in Rome. Only Patricians could become CONSULS, who were the chief leaders of Rome. The consuls, of which there were always only two, held the IMPERIUM, that is the power to govern, lead armies into war, and pronounce the death sentence. The IMPERIUM might be described as the prerogative power which generally belongs to the king or other chief executive. Consuls were the chief executives of the Republic and were elected for a single term of one year by the popular assembly called the COMITIA CENTURIATA. After their year was up, consuls joined the ranks of the Senate.

Technically, the Roman Senate was merely an advisory body. It gave advice to the consuls, other municipal magistrates, and the popular assemblies. But the prestige of the Senate was such that its advice was usually taken, particularly in matters of foreign policy and war. The 300 Senators came from the wealthiest, most powerful families and clans of Rome and, since ex-consuls joined their ranks, it always had a large reservoir of experienced men of affairs.

The popular assemblies were similar to those in Greece. The most important was the COMITIA CENTURIATA, composed of hundred-man units, or centuries, from the Roman army. Since, as in Greece, citizenship and military service went together, the Roman people were represented. But voting was based on the military equipment of the unit. Cavalry units had greater voting power than infantry. This voting arrangement allowed the wealthy, who could afford a horse and armor, to dominate the centurian assembly and to elect their candidates as consuls and other magistrates. This centurian assembly voted on matters of war and peace, public policy, and legislation. The COMITIA TRIBUTA, assembly of the tribes, was dominated by the plebeians and became powerful at a later time during the Republic.

Other elected magistrates besides the consuls included the praetors, quaestors, aediles, and censors. The PRAETORS were the judges, who also exercised the imperium. The QUAESTORS were responsible for the finances of Rome. The AEDILES supervised the public works of Rome, that is the water supply system, the aqueducts, the road system, and the public buildings. The CENSORS maintained the census rolls of Roman citizenship; in addition, they maintained public morality by censoring those who did not

Why was the Senate so important?

How did the Comitia Centuriata and the Comitia Tributa differ? 100 men units.

Plebian.

Describe some of the elective offices of the Roman Republic.

What events mark the beginning and the end of the Early Republic?

conform. All these positions were originally restricted to Patrician families.

The Republic lasted for almost five hundred years, a long time frame that can be divided into the Early Republic, Imperial Republic, and Late Republic. In the end the Republic gave way to an Emperor, who in effect, though not in title, became a new king. Under the Emperors, Rome survived for almost another five hundred years.

The Early Republic: 509 to 264 B.C.

What was Rome's foreign policy during this period?

The Early Republic can be dated, from the ouster of the Etruscan kings in 509 B.C., to the beginning of the First Punic War against Carthage in 264 B.C. During this period, two broad developments took place.

Rome slowly changed from a small, weak city-state on the Latin plain and became the dominant power on the Italian peninsula. During this time, Rome was almost continually at war with its neighbors. The Romans lost battles, but they did not lose wars. Steadily, the Romans conquered their neighbors through fighting and skillful diplomacy.

What was the focus of domestic concern?

Another development is called **THE STRUGGLE OF THE ORDERS**. It was the political struggle between the **PATRICIANS** and the **PLEBEIANS**. The **PLEBEIANS** were the small farmers who, despite being Roman citizens, were excluded by the Patricians from participation in the political affairs of Rome. Initially, even intermarriage was prohibited between Patricians and Plebeians. There were no racial differences between these two political classes, only wealth and social status. The larger landowners enjoyed their domination over their less wealthy fellow citizens. This class struggle was very similar to the one described during the Archaic Period in Greece. As in Greece, the Plebeians gradually wrested concessions from the Patricians until, by 264 B.C., they had achieved legal equality with the Patricians.

The Plebeians won their victories slowly over a two hundred-year period. The Plebeians were always the majority. In the perpetual wars of Rome, the Plebeians were needed as the foot soldiers in the Roman legions. We might make the analogy that the Patricians were the officers, while the Plebeians were the enlisted men. The Roman Patricians could not win their wars without the loyalty of their common people. That gave the Plebeians an unbeatable hand in their power struggles. The threat of mass mutiny forced the Patricians to make concessions.

The first came in 494 B.C. when the TRIBUNES were recognized officially by the Patrician government as protectors of Plebeian interests. The tribunes were elected for a one-year term by the Plebeian Assembly. Originally, there were only two, but over time the number increased to ten. The tribunes could veto legislation that negatively impacted on the Plebeian order, they could intercede in the law courts on behalf of a Plebeian, appeal cases to the Senate, and countermand orders of the consuls. The tribunes were SACROSANCT during their year of office, which meant that anyone who harmed a tribune could legally be put to death immediately.

In 450 B.C., the Plebeians succeeded in having the traditional laws of Rome written on wooden tablets and promulgated as the Law of the Twelve Tables. Codification of the law is always an important first step in the transformation of a traditional, aristocratic society to one more commercial and urban. The Law of the Twelve Tables was the first step in 1000 years of legal developments. The last was the *Corpus Juris Civilis* issued by

What was the role of the tribunes?

How do you think the Plebeians benefited from a <u>written</u> Law of the Twelve Tables?

To what extent was Rome a democracy?

the Emperor JUSTINIAN in the sixth century A.D.

In 445 B.C., the law forbidding inter-marriage between the two orders was repealed. This repeal benefited the wealthier plebeians, who could now marry into the families of the patricians. In 367 B.C., Plebeians became eligible to run for the office of consul. In 287 B.C., the ASSEMBLY OF THE TRIBES replaced the Assembly of the Centuries as the most important law-making body. Laws enacted by the Assembly of Tribes became binding on all Roman citizens. Since each person had an equal vote in the Assembly of Tribes, theoretically Rome had become a democracy. What was true in theory, however, was never true in fact. The Senate and the magistrates continued to dominate the Republic throughout its history.

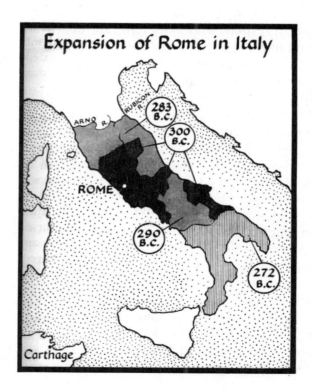

In this evolution of Roman government and power, it must be noted that as late as 390 B.C., Rome was conquered by the Gauls, a Celtic people originally from across the Alps. Because the Gauls destroyed Rome's fortifications, the city had to be rebuilt after they left. Despite this great setback, the Romans managed to regain their power within the Latin region and go on to expand it. By 264, the Greeks in Southern Italy had become subject to Roman rule, as had the Etruscans to the North of Rome. The Italian peninsula was in Roman hands. For eight hundred years, no other enemies penetrated Rome's walls.

What had Rome achieved by 264 B.C.?

The Imperial Republic: 264 to 133 B.C.

It is only with the successful conquest of the Italian peninsula that Rome became a Great Power. It was drawn into the politics of the Eastern and Western Mediterranean, first the West and then the East.

What were the origins of Carthage?

Phoenicians

Punic Wars CARTHAGE was located in Northern Africa near the site of the modern city of Tunis in Tunisia. Carthage was originally founded by PHOENICIANS from the city of TYRE, during the eighth century before Christ. When the Phoenician cities were conquered by the Chaldeans and later the Persians, Carthage became an independent city-state and created its own empire. While at one time allied to Rome, by 264 B.C. these two cities had become rivals for the domination of the Western Mediterranean.

Three wars were waged between Rome and Carthage. The Romans called these wars the Punic wars, after the Latin name for the Phoenician ancestors of the Carthaginians. The FIRST PUNIC WAR, from 264 to 241 B.C., was waged over control of SICILY. Sicily had been colonized by the Greeks, but

Who were the principal rivals in the Punic Wars?

What caused the First Punic War?

as always Greek poleis tended to be factionalized and to engage in war with each other. Rival factions in the city of Messina were supported by Rome and Carthage, respectively. The city of Syracuse became involved, and a general war between Carthage and Rome ensued. The "big boys" brushed aside the clients in whose name they initially intervened. Small states are always ill-advised to ask for help from powerful allies. The cat tends to swallow the canary. Rome initially lacked a fleet. Even after it built one, lack of experience in seamanship led the Romans to lose more ships during storms than in battle.

By 241 B.C., Rome was only slightly less exhausted than Carthage. It is estimated that twenty percent of Rome's citizen soldiers perished during this conflict. But when an unprepared Carthaginian fleet was destroyed by the Romans near the Aegates Islands in 241 B.C., the Carthaginians asked for peace terms. They were required to surrender their possessions on Sicily and to pay a huge indemnity. Sicily became Rome's first overseas province. The Roman Republic was becoming an IMPERIAL REPUBLIC. It has often been said that the expansion of Rome within Italy had been the result of defensive wars. The wars against Carthage were imperialistic wars. Rome was now deliberately seeking to conquer new provinces for the wealth they contained. In 238 B.C., Rome continued its march of conquest by seizing control of Sardinia and Corsica.

What did Rome gain after the end of the war?

The First Punic War had ended in a Roman victory, but from Carthage's point of view this was really a draw, a stalemate, a breathing space for the next round of fighting. Carthage had been blocked on Sicily, but the Carthaginians were an industrious people who now redoubled their efforts to establish colonies and trading posts in Spain. The more the Carthaginians succeeded in Spain, the more the Romans envied them. It was only a matter of time for war to be renewed.

The SECOND PUNIC WAR was fought from 218 to 201 B.C. The Romans declared it, but the Carthaginians struck the first blows. Hannibal, the great Carthaginian general during this war, led an army from Spain, through southern France, over the Alps, into Italy. This army included war elephants. In battle after battle, Hannibal defeated the Romans. The Battle of Cannae in 216 B.C. is still studied today in war colleges for its tactical brilliance. Four Roman legions were destroyed in Hannibal's trap. But while Hannibal ravaged the Italian countryside and won his battles, he was unable to win the war. Rome's allies, with few exceptions, remained loyal. And the Roman will to carry on at all costs, never wavered. Rather than fighting Hannibal, the Romans decided to delay and harass his forces. After ten years of war and living off the land without reinforcements, his army was worn out. The Romans also decided to bring the war to Carthaginian territories. The Roman General Scipio Africanus defeated the Carthaginians in Spain in 206 B.C., crossed over into Africa in 204 B.C., and began to threaten Carthage. Hannibal was recalled from Italy by his government. The Romans had achieved indirectly what they could not win directly. At the Battle of Zama in 202 B.C., Hannibal was defeated by Scipio Africanus. A peace was negotiated in 201 B.C. whereby Carthage gave up its possessions in Spain, paid another huge indemnity, had its fleet reduced to ten ships, and agreed never to go to war without Roman permission. Carthage survived as a city-state, but it ceased to be a major power. Rome had become the dominant power in the Western Mediterranean.

The THIRD PUNIC WAR took place half a century later after Rome had become

What brought about the Second Punic War?

To what extent was Hannibal a success?

What were the consequences of this war?

What brought Rome into the Third Punic War?

the most powerful state throughout the Mediterranean. It was an uneven conflict, a David and Goliath struggle, where Goliath wins. It was a war of pure vindictiveness and imperialistic aggression. The Romans did not like to be reminded that Carthage had once been their equal and almost bested them. When the Carthaginians defended themselves against unprovoked attacks from the King of Numidia, who was Rome's ally, the Roman Senate declared that the Carthaginians had violated the peace treaty that ended the Second Punic War. They refused to permit Carthage to defend itself against these marauders. Rome declared war. A Roman Senator named CATO THE ELDER (c. 234 - 149 B.C.) had for years ended all his public speeches with the words: "Carthago delenda est." Delete or eradicate Carthage! For three long years, from 149 to 146 B.C., the Carthaginians withstood a Roman siege, but in the end their walls were breached, their remaining soldiers butchered, their women and children sold into slavery, and their agricultural lands were strewn with salt to prevent anyone from living there. Carthage had been destroyed. A century later, a new Carthage of Romans arose on the site of the old Phoenician city.

How did Rome treat the conquered Carthaginians?

Conquest of the Hellenistic East

In 200 B.C., after their costly triumph in the Second Punic War, the Romans were drawn almost immediately into the politics of the Eastern Mediterranean. The Hellenistic East had divided into three major kingdoms and several minor states. Rome fought four wars with the Antigonids of Macedonia.

The FIRST MACEDONIAN WAR was from 215 to 205 B.C., during the Second Punic War, when King Philip V of Macedonia, 221 - 179 B.C., allied himself with the Carthaginians after the Roman defeat at

Cannae. The Romans allied themselves with the Aetolian League of Greek city-states and were able to bottle up the Macedonians. A peace treaty, signed in 205 B.C., confirmed the stalemate.

The SECOND MACEDONIAN WAR broke out in 200 B.C. and lasted till 197 B.C. The Achaean and the Aetolian Leagues of Greek States fought on the side of Rome against the Macedonians, who were defeated. The Romans, who deluded themselves into believing that they were the defenders of Greek liberty, declared these two Leagues of States to be completely independent. What the Romans expected was gratefulness and obedience to Rome. When the Greeks made alliances in opposition to Roman interests, a new war arose.

The Aetolian League had allied itself with Antiochus III, 223 - 187 B.C., the Seleucid king of Syria. In the SYRIAN WAR, 192 - 189 B.C., the Romans first defeated the Aetolian League (191 B.C.) and then the main forces of Antiochus (189 B.C.). Antiochus was forced to pay a huge indemnity and had to transfer his Anatolian lands to Rome's ally Pergamum. Rome itself took no territory.

The THIRD MACEDONIAN WAR was from 171 to 167 B.C. Under a new king, the Macedonians sought once again to expand. When the Greek city-states asked for help, Rome was happy to comply. After their victory, the Romans divided the Macedonian kingdom into four separate states and confiscated the Macedonian treasury for themselves.

When that settlement proved unstable, the FOURTH MACEDONIAN WAR broke out from 149 to 148 B.C. This time, finally, the Romans made Macedonia into a Roman province. An uprising by the Achaean League was also put down. CORINTH, the leader of the uprising, was razed to the ground in 146 B.C., the same year that Carthage was finally

Summarize the events of the Macedonian Wars.

What part did the Greek city-states play in these wars?

What was the extent of Roman control of the Mediterranean Sea area by 133 B.C.?

taken. Greece was made a part of the Roman province of Macedonia.

The Romans had become the dominant power in the Mediterranean. Except for Egypt, the Romans had established either direct control over the entire Mediterranean through Roman provinces, or indirect control through allied and associated rulers. The Republic had built an extensive empire. The loot from that empire made it possible for the Roman republican government, in 167 B.C., to eliminate the payment of direct taxes for all Roman citizens. But this huge new empire created problems for Rome that ultimately destroyed the republic and ushered in the era of the principate.

The Late Republic: 133 to 27 B.C.

What were the consequences of Roman success for the small farmers of the Republic?

History is full of ironies, unintended side effects of great achievements. The sturdy, patriotic farmers of Republican Rome, the plebeians, the very social class which had made expansion possible, was gradually destroyed by its very success. The further Roman legions marched, the longer the legionnaires stayed away from their small farms. While their wives were able to maintain a small garden, the farm lands generally deteriorated during these absences. Some soldiers were killed and their widows had to sell their land. The spoils of war were not evenly distributed: officers, praetors, and consuls took the largest share. The patricians used their wealth to buy up, when possible, more farmland. Even those soldiers who returned often found farm work less exciting than residence in Rome as a client of the rich. Slaves were brought back to Italy and forced to do agricultural labor on the developing large estates of the rich. Small homestead farmers were losing out to the plantation system, or LATIFUNDIA, worked by slaves. The social class of small farmers was being destroyed by the very successes which that class had made possible. But without an adequate supply of citizen-soldiers, the very survival of the Republic and Rome were threatened.

From 133 to 27 B.C., the Republic was in crisis facing serious internal and external challenges. It solved the crisis by transforming the republic into a military dictatorship run by a single person called the *princeps*, or first citizen, who later became the Emperor.

Internally, Rome changed from a simple agrarian society to a complex military empire. A new social structure developed. Most patrician and the wealthiest of plebeian families formed a new Senatorial nobility. Below them, the equestrian order (originally cavalrymen) supplied the armies and collected taxes. A sizable citizen proletariat developed in Rome. The small farmer class declined. Slaves increased in number in Italy. In the conquered provinces, society divided into the indigenous nobility, the curiales, and the growing mass of the poor, including slaves. Wealthy provincials were gradually given the legal status of Roman citizens, which carried with it important legal advantages. But the larger the number of Roman citizens, the less significant citizenship was from a political point of view. Republican Rome became less and less democratic, and ultimately ceased to be a republic.

During the late Republic, the Senatorial ruling class came to be divided into two broad factions: the optimates and the populares. The OPTIMATES were the conservatives who sought to preserve their patrician privileges. The POPULARES were the popular leaders who appealed to the masses in order to advance their own agendas. It is

What were the latifundia?

Describe the changing Roman social structure.

Distinguish the Optimates from the Populares.

Why did the Romans experience administrative difficulties?

What were the problems with the Roman tax system?

doubtful that either faction was much concerned with the welfare of all.

Externally, the very size of the empire created problems of administration. The governmental institutions designed for a small city-state were now responsible for an empire that had begun to stretch around the entire Mediterranean Sea. Annual elections for consuls and other municipal officials in Rome continued to be held; only those citizens who could attend the popular assemblies at the time of the elections could vote. A whole new system of how to administer far-away armies and far-away provinces had to be invented. The Roman government needed to become more professional and bureaucratic.

In particular, the Romans had an inadequate system of collecting taxes. Instead of an Internal Revenue Service with public employees serving as tax collectors, the Romans had a privatized tax system. Their system is called TAX FARMING. A private individual would bid for the right to collect taxes in a given province. He would guarantee to the Roman government a certain, fixed amount of money if he won the contract. The person who guaranteed the largest amount would get the contract. It was then up to the tax farmer to squeeze the maximum amount of money from that province. If he collected less than what he had guaranteed, he was still liable for the full amount. If he collected more, the excess was his profit. Obviously tax collectors always collected more than what they had bid. Since there was no maximum limit, tax farming tended to become confiscatory. Confiscatory taxes are taxes that are so high that the person who is forced to pay them must sell his property to pay. Desperate men faced with ruinous taxation will often rise up against their oppressors. Rome's tax system almost guaranteed perpetual revolts in the provinces which had been conquered. The Roman legions upheld the system of tax farming. Obviously Roman commanders were bribed by the tax farmers to aid them in brutalizing those who might resist or hide some of their wealth. Since the Senatorial class, and indirectly all Roman citizens, profited from this system, it was very difficult to reform.

It has often been said that power corrupts. The wealthier Rome became, the greedier grew its ruling classes. Even the Romans at the time were aware that the old values that had made Rome great were in decline. Roman virtues of honor, loyalty, self-sacrifice, duty, piety, and patriotism gave way to licentious living, self-gratification, greed, brutality, and cruelty. It is not even clear whether moralists like Cicero (106 - 43 B.C.), the famous orator and Republican statesman, were sincere in their criticisms or grandstanding. While indulging yourself, it is always easy to preach virtue to the poor.

The crisis of the Republic lasted over one hundred years. It went through several stages which are discussed below.

The Reforms of the Gracchi Brothers

TIBERIUS GRACCHUS was elected as a tribune of the people in 133 B.C. He ran on a reform program intended to restore the small farmer to his position of prominence. Invoking an obscure law which limited the size of farms, he urged that excess land be given to small farmers as new homestead land. The Senatorial classes opposed these reforms. When Tiberius sought to run for re-election as tribune, the Senate declared his election illegal. In the rioting that followed, Tiberius was murdered by followers of his political rivals in the Senate.

Ten years later, in 123 B.C., Tiberius' younger brother, GAIUS GRACCHUS ran and was elected to the tribuneship. He advo-

To what extent were the Romans an exception to the adage that power corrupts?

What was the focus of Tiberius Gracchus's reforms?

were killed

Why didn't he succeed?

What reforms did Gaius Gracchus propose?

cated policies very similar to those of his brother: more land reform for the poor, free grain distribution in Rome, public works projects to put workers on the public payroll, and the extension of citizenship rights to Rome's Italian allies. This last item was actually unpopular among the Romans because they feared that it would dilute their privileges as citizens. When Gaius failed to win his race for a third term as tribune, he gathered an armed following to prevent the repeal of his legislation. In the ensuing conflict, Gaius was murdered.

What did the reform attempts of the Gracchi brothers illustrate?

Both reformers were killed by their enemies. Both had been guilty of violating the traditions of the Roman Republic and their efforts at reform were in part motivated by self-interest. The Gracchi brothers came from an old Roman family. They wished to have a large client following and sought personal power. Nonetheless, their deaths made it clear that peaceful reform was impossible. The plebeian family farm was being swept aside by economic and political forces.

> **The Military Reforms of Marius**

MARIUS, who was born about 157 B.C. and died in 86 B.C., came from the equestrian order and rose through his successful military commands to the highest position in Rome. He was elected an unprecedented seven times to the position of consul: in 107 B.C., from 104 to 100 B.C., and a last time in 86 B.C. Marius transformed the Roman conscript armies of citizen soldiers into a professional army of mercenaries loyal to their general.

What was the focus of Marius's reforms?

The declining number of small farmers created a crisis for the army. Marius solved this problem by waiving the traditional property requirements for service in the military. He admitted the landless poor into the army. Because these soldiers depended for their equipment and livelihood on the army, their loyalties were no longer to the abstract ideal of the republic, but to the concrete benefits which their general could grant them. Armies whose loyalty was to their general would do anything the general commanded, including marching on the Roman Senate and government.

Marius' new armies won major victories for the Romans. Marius defeated JUGURTHA, KING OF NUMIDIA. He ousted the invading Germanic tribes of the Teutoni and Cimbri from Italy. He also fought against MITHRIDATES VI OF PONTUS. Marius was repeatedly drawn into politics when the Senate refused to pay his veterans what was owed them. Though a popular leader and reformer, Marius laid the basis for military dictatorship. He set the precedent that the army could be used to threaten the government.

What were the consequences of the reforms initiated by Marius?

Who was Sulla?

Sulla Throughout much of Marius' life, he was assisted by his second in command, Sulla, who gradually turned on his mentor and became his rival. Sulla, who was born about 138 B.C. to a minor patrician family and died in 78 B.C., had actually captured Jugurtha in 105 B.C., as a quaestor under Marius.

In 90 B.C., Rome's Italian allies rose up to protest the unfair distribution of the spoils of war. While required to fight in Rome's armies, they received no benefits. This uprising is called the SOCIAL WAR. Sulla was given military command during the war from 90 to 89 B.C. and succeeded in defeating this most serious challenge to Rome. As part of the settlement, Rome extended the rights of Roman citizenship to most of its Italian allies.

In 88 B.C., Sulla was elected consul. His troubles with Marius began shortly there-

What was the Social War?

Did Sulla conquer Marius or Marius conquer Sulla? Explain.

Contrast the reforms of Sulla with those of the Gracchi brothers.

after. Sulla was given command against Mithridates VI, only to be replaced by Marius. Sulla then raised an army, marched on Rome, and drove Marius into exile. When Sulla returned to Anatolia to resume the fight against Mithridates, Marius, in turn, raised an army and captured Rome. Marius was elected consul for a last time in 86 B.C., but died shortly after assuming that position.

After defeating and making a peace treaty with Mithridates, Sulla returned to Rome to confront his enemies. Sulla defeated them and took Rome in 82 B.C. Sulla then got even with his enemies by setting up a PROSCRIPTION LIST and having those on the list executed. The Senate legalized these massacres and murders by retroactively granting Sulla the title of DICTATOR. Sulla then proceeded to rewrite Roman constitutional law in such a way that all political power was returned to the old patrician families.

In a way, Sulla's reforms were the mirror image of those of the Gracchi brothers. The Gracchi brothers had wanted to make Rome truly democratic by restoring and increasing the power of the plebeians, the people. Sulla was a conservative, an optimas. He wanted to return all power to the Senate, to make Rome as it had been before the plebeians, the people, gained equality and power. The problem with Rome, according to Sulla, were all these newfangled ideas of participation. The populares were stirring up the people and attacking the best sort of men, the natural-born Senatorial elite. If only the virtuous Senate was restored to full power, the uprisings and political problems of Rome would disappear. For the Gracchi brothers, it had been the corrupt and venal Senators who misgoverned Rome; because of their greed, the Senators were the causes of Rome's problems. Both Sulla and the Gracchi brothers sought to restore some ideal past which in fact had never existed.

After Sulla's bloodbath, proscription, and reorganization of the government, he served as regular consul in 80 B.C. and retired after that term, believing that his reforms had restored the glory of the Republic. He died shortly thereafter, and the Senate returned to its incompetent, corrupt rule of the Republic.

It should be noted that the Gracchi brothers and Sulla, in their very different ways, were republicans. They believed that their reforms would preserve the republic. They were wrong. The problems which confronted the republican form of government could not be solved without breaking the old constitution.

The road to the future had been charted by Marius with his new professional army loyal to their general. After Sulla's death, new ambitious generals tried their hand at dominating Rome and its Empire.

Were Sulla's attempts at reform any more successful than those of the Gracchi brothers? Explain.

The First Triumvirate and Julius Caesar

Sulla's proscription had murdered most, but not all, of the leaders of the populares. Rome's tax farming again and again drove desperate peoples to rebel. War requires competent generals and until those can be found, defeat on the battlefield is likely. A new generation of leaders emerged after Sulla's death.

The most important of these leaders were Pompey, Crassus, and Julius Caesar. Between 60 to 53 B.C., these three men formed what is called the FIRST TRIUMVIRATE. They cooperated with each other against the dominant Senate oligarchy.

Pompey the Great was born in 106 B.C. He was a great general who first fought during the Social War (90 - 89 B.C.). He was active in Roman politics thereafter. His coop-

Who were the members of the First Triumvirate?

What were the fates of Pompey and Crassus?

eration with Julius Caesar ended in 53 B.C., leading to civil war with Caesar from 49 to 48 B.C. After losing to Caesar, he fled to Egypt and was assassinated there in 48 B.C.

Crassus was born about 115 B.C. He was held to be the richest man in Rome and helped finance the others during the First Triumvirate. He had held military command in 72 B.C. and put down the slave revolt on Sicily led by SPARTACUS. In 70 B.C. and again in 55 B.C., Crassus and Pompey were the two consuls for those years. In 55 B.C., Crassus maneuvered to gain the command over a military expedition against the Parthian Empire. Crassus was trapped by the Parthians and his army was destroyed. The standards (flags) of several Roman legions were captured. This was the greatest disgrace which could befall a Roman general. Fortunately for him, Crassus died during this disastrous military campaign.

What did the command in Gaul do for Caesar?

JULIUS CAESAR was born in 100 B.C. to an ancient, but not previously important, patrician family. Caesar was the brains of the First Triumvirate. He married his daughter Julia to Pompey. It is after Julia died that the three-man alliance broke down. Caesar's share of the spoils that could be squeezed from the Triumvirate was the governorship of Roman Gaul and its large army. He used this army to conquer the remainder of Gaul from 58 to 51 B.C. Caesar's tremendous victories in Gaul stimulated the envy of Pompey and the fear of the Senate. The Senatorial oligarchy saw Pompey as the lesser of two evils and succeeded in co-opting Pompey in helping them destroy Caesar. Caesar's official positions and command were coming to an end. He faced the prospect of returning to Rome as a private citizen, surely to encounter trumped up charges of corruption and near-certain death. In 49 B.C., Caesar crossed the RUBICON River, which separated the prov-

Why were some Senators concerned about Caesar's success?

ince of Gaul from Italy. Taking his army across this boundary violated Roman law and was, in effect, the start of Civil War. Crossing the Rubicon has come to be a phrase signifying that one has taken a decisive step which cannot be reversed. One has burnt one's bridges. Caesar crossed the Rubicon either to become master of Rome or to die trying.

The veterans of Caesar's army quickly conquered Italy, took Spain, and pursued Pompey to Greece. After suffering a defeat, Caesar decisively turned tables on Pompey's army at Pharsalus in August 48 B.C. despite being outnumbered. Pompey fled to Egypt, where he was murdered. Caesar followed to Egypt and became involved in the dynastic politics of the Ptolemies. He sided with CLEOPATRA against her brother Ptolemy XIII. He made Cleopatra queen of Egypt and married her in an Egyptian ceremony, even though he was still married to his Roman wife. The relationship did produce a son, Caesarion, who was later murdered by Caesar's adopted heir, Augustus.

The defeat of Pompey was not the end of the internal wars. Caesar had to fight further battles against the allies and sons of Pompey, but by 45 B.C. the last of these opponents had been overcome. During national emergencies, the Romans had, even in the early days of the Republic, granted dictatorial powers to a single man to solve the crisis. During the late Republic, the grant of dictatorial power became more common. Sulla had been dictator in 82 B.C. Caesar was declared dictator by the Senate for the year 49 B.C., after he had crossed the Rubicon and become master of Italy. He was again named dictator in 48, for ten years beginning in 46, and for life in 44 B.C. Caesar also held the consulship in 48 and from 46 to 44 B.C.

What did Caesar's crossing the Rubicon signify? Today, what does "crossing the Rubicon" mean?

What did Caesar do after he achieved victory?

Were there limits to the ambition of Julius Caesar?

By 44 B.C., having become master of the Roman world, it was quite clear that Caesar was not about to surrender his powers or to retire. What were Caesar's future plans? That was the question that agitated Romans in March 44 B.C. It was known that Caesar was planning an attack on the Parthian Empire. Like Alexander, to whom he compared himself, Caesar knew no limits and wanted to conquer the world. It was feared that Caesar wanted to make himself into an absolute monarch on the Hellenistic model. There were even rumors that he might move his capital to Alexandria.

Fear of Caesar's absolute power led to conspiracies against the dictator. On March 15, 44 B.C., the Ides of March, Caesar was scheduled to give a speech to the Senate outlining his future plans. On the steps up the capitol, he was murdered by two Senators. CASSIUS and BRUTUS stabbed Caesar in the back and killed "the greatest Roman of them all." Was this the foul deed of cowards or the heroic act of patriots trying to save the Republic? Historians and great literary figures have wrestled with this question. If someone had successfully assassinated Adolf Hitler, would we not consider that person a hero today? Was Julius Caesar a Hitler who was stopped?

Were Cassius and Brutus heroes?

With hindsight we can say that Cassius and Brutus did not save the republic. They merely plunged it into another round of civil war, until a new Caesar fought his way to the top, that is until AUGUSTUS Caesar became the first Roman Emperor.

| The Second Triumvirate and Augustus |

Great generals, who seize power and become dictators, do not act alone. They have loyal soldiers who have fought under their command. There are seconds in command who have implemented the strategic vision of their commander-in-chief. Julius Caesar's most important lieutenant was MARK ANTONY. Born about 83 B.C., he fought with Caesar against Pompey at the decisive Battle of Pharsalus in 49 B.C. and was consul with Caesar in 44 B.C., when the assassination took place. Together with LEPIDUS and OCTAVIAN (Julius Caesar's grand-nephew), he formed the Second Triumvirate in 43 B.C. to avenge the murder. Mark Antony was responsible for unleashing a proscription against the Republican cause, during which CICERO and many others were executed. In 42 B.C., he was primarily responsible for the military victory over Cassius and Brutus at the Battle of PHILIPPI.

The triumvirs had won their factional struggle against the Senatorial optimates. They divided the Roman possessions amongst themselves. All three would share in ruling Italy. Lepidus would administer the provinces in Africa, Octavian would bring order to Gaul and Spain, and Mark Antony decided to rule in the ever-rebellious East.

Egypt, which was being drawn into the Roman orbit, was still nominally independent. Its queen, Cleopatra VII, had been in Rome when Caesar was assassinated. She returned to Egypt with her infant son, whom she crowned co-ruler as Ptolemy XV. Cleopatra continued her politics of sexual and marital alliances by wooing Mark Antony. The not-unrealistic dream was to forge an Egyptian-Roman alliance which might rule the world. She formed an alliance with Mark Antony in 41 B.C., became his lover, and married him in 37 B.C., in accord with Egyptian law.

Three-man rule is inherently unstable in that each seeks more power over the others. Just as the First Triumvirate broke down into a conflict between Julius Caesar and Pompey, so the Second Triumvirate became a struggle between Octavian and Mark Antony. Lepidus

How did the Second Triumvirate secure its power?

Who were the members of the Second Triumvirate?

Does Cleopatra deserve praise or condemnation?

What happened to Lepidus?

Why was there friction between Mark Antony and Octavian?

Why is the Battle of Actium important?

was removed as a serious contender for power when Octavian forced him to retire in 36 B.C. Lepidus lived on till 13 B.C. and died peacefully in his bed.

The inherent rivalries between powerful men were aggravated in the case of Octavian and Mark Antony in that Mark Antony was married to Octavia, the sister of Octavian. The relationship with Cleopatra made matters worse. It must be noted that marriages among the Roman elite were political alliances. Octavia had been previously married, as had Mark Antony. After Mark Antony's death, Octavia raised the children from all these marriages. Three of Mark Antony's grandchildren became Roman Emperors: Caligula, Claudius, and Nero.

We must now focus on OCTAVIAN. Born in 63 B.C. as a grandnephew of Julius Caesar, he was eighteen-years old when Caesar was assassinated in 44 B.C. Julius Caesar had adopted Octavian as his son in his political will, which was made public after the assassination. Caesar's own son was illegitimate in Roman eyes and he was too young to defend his heritage. Octavian skillfully used the venerated name of Julius Caesar and his designation as the heir to climb to power. After Philippi, it became clear that only one man would rule Rome: either Octavian or Mark Antony.

The showdown was carefully prepared by Octavian. He skillfully strengthened his hold on the Western half of the Roman possessions, depicted Mark Antony as an oriental despot, and propagandistically turned a sordid power struggle into a crusade between Rome and the orientals. At the naval Battle of ACTIUM in September 31 B.C., Octavian decisively defeated the combined forces of Mark Antony and Cleopatra. The two fled to Egypt where Octavian pursued them. Octavian conquered Egypt and Mark Antony committed suicide. Cleopatra tried her sexual charms once more, but when they failed, she, too, committed suicide by having an asp, or cobra snake, bite her. Octavian was master of the Roman world.

What was the fate of Antony and Cleopatra?

Figure 2.5. Cubiculum (bedroom) from Villa at Boscoreale (near Pompeii). Roman, 40-30 B.C. The world of ancient Rome was revealed by excavations at Pompeii and Herculaneum, two cities covered by ash when Mt. Vesuvius erupted in 79 A.D. This bedroom, as a result, is extremely well preserved. Note the intricate design of the mosaic floor tile and the wall paintings that give an illusion of looking outside into a garden. *Courtesy of The Metropolitan Museum of Art, Rogers Fund, 1903. (03.4.13)*

NOTES

[1] Charles M. Bakewell, ed. <u>Source Book in Ancient Philosophy</u>, rev. ed. (New York: Charles Scribner's Sons, 1939), pp. 1-3.

[2] Bakewell, pp. 36-42.

[3] Bakewell, p. 33.

[4] Bakewell, p. 30.

[5] Bakewell, pp. 28-35.

[6] Bakewell, pp. 57-66.

[7] Bakewell, p. 67.

[8] Bakewell, p. 67.

[9] Bakewell, pp. 67-85.

[10] A. H. Armstrong, <u>An Introduction to Ancient Philosophy</u> (Boston: Beacon Press, 1947), pp. 35-36.

[11] Armstrong, p. 71.

[12] "Epicurus to Menaecus" in <u>The Lives and Opinions of Eminent Philosophers, Book X, The Life of Epicurus</u> by Diogenes Laertius (c.230 A.D.), trans. by C. D. Yonge (Internet, <http://www.cluon.com/~ea/Lives.html>, 30 January 1997).

PLATO

The Republic

Plato (c. 428-348 B.C.), who came from a prominent Athenian family, was a student of Socrates. When Socrates was executed in 399 B.C., Plato left the politically unfriendly climate of Athens to travel abroad. He returned to Athens in 387 and founded a school of philosophical instruction called the Academy. The passages that follow, taken from his greatest work, *The Republic* (c. 370 B.C.), reflect his hostility to democracy and suggest that the ideal state is one ruled by philosopher-kings.

The first selection is often called the Allegory of the Cave. An allegory is a literary construct whose characters and events can be interpreted at some deeper level to reveal important concepts or principles. Ordinary persons are like people chained in a cave so that they see shadows cast on the wall of the cave by objects illuminated by the light of a fire behind them and mistake these shadows for real things. The philosopher is someone who has come out of the cave into the world above lit by sunlight. Through the process of education, he or she comes to understand not only particular objects, but the more permanent world of ideas which the objects reflect. The philosophers are the truly enlightened ones who should rule the city and who alone can provide a just society.

The second selection, which actually comes first in Plato's *Republic*, is the Myth of the Metals. In order to get the rest of society to accept the rule of the philosopher-kings by a myth is proposed which future generations might believe to be true. People are to be told that a god created all citizens out of the same earth. But some he mixed with gold and they are to be the rulers or guardians, and some he mixed with silver and these are auxiliaries. Those mixed of brass or iron are the common people, the farmers and the craftsmen. A man of brass or iron must not come to rule over the state, or it is predicted that the city will be destroyed.

In both selections Plato presents his ideas through a literary device called a dialogue, a discussion between two or more people. Socrates is the first speaker and Glaucon the second in the discussions.

Plato's ideas have had great influence on philosophers and statesmen down through the centuries. Some—noting his antipathy to democracy and his willingness to deceive—have accused him of totalitarian leanings, others—noting his respect for education and the life of the intellect, his interest in a just and good society, and his gifted writing style—have been unstinting admirers of his work. Hopefully, you will want to read more than these few pages before passing judgment on his contributions to Western culture.

[The Allegory of the Cave]

The people in the cave can be thought of as ordinary citizens. The chains that prevent them from looking around are similar to the cares, the wants, and the material concerns of everyday life which keep people busy and discourage them from the rigorous thought which is needed for the intellectual life.

AND[*] now, I said, let me show in a figure how far our nature is enlightened or unenlightened: Behold! human beings living in a underground den, which has a mouth open towards the light and reaching all along the den; here they have been from their childhood, and have their legs and necks chained so that they cannot move, and can only see before them, being prevented by the chains from turning round their heads. Above and behind them a fire is blazing at a distance, and between the fire and the prisoners there is a raised way; and you will see, if you look, a low wall built along the way, like the screen which marionette-players have in front of them, over which they show the puppets.

I see.

And do you see, I said, men passing along the wall carrying all sorts of vessels, and statues and figures of animals made of wood and stone and various materials, which appear over the wall? Some of them are talking, others silent.

You have shown me a strange image, and they are strange prisoners.

The people chained in the cave see only the shadows of things, not the real objects which are hidden from them.

Like ourselves, I replied; and they see only their own shadows, or the shadows of one another, which the fire throws on the opposite wall of the cave?

[*]Plato, The Republic, trans. by Benjamin Jowett, M.A. (the Internet Wiretap Online Edition prepared by <dell@wiretap.spies.com>, <http://ockham.philos.phil.tu-bs.de:80/Texte/plato-republic-0.html>, 2 March 1997, the paper edition published in New York: P. F. Collier & Son, 1901).

True, he said; how could they see anything but the shadows if they were never allowed to move their heads?

And of the objects which are being carried in like manner they would only see the shadows?

Yes, he said.

And if they were able to converse with one another, would they not suppose that they were naming what was actually before them?

Very true.

The shadows are thought to be real things which can speak and which receive names from the cave dwellers.

And suppose further that the prison had an echo which came from the other side, would they not be sure to fancy when one of the passers-by spoke that the voice which they heard came from the passing shadow?

No question, he replied.

To them, I said, the truth would be literally nothing but the shadows of the images.

That is certain.

And now look again, and see what will naturally follow if the prisoners are released and disabused of their error. At first, when any of them is liberated and compelled suddenly to stand up and turn his neck round and walk and look towards the light, he will suffer sharp pains; the glare will distress him, and he will be unable to see the realities of which in his former state he had seen the shadows; and then conceive some one saying to him, that what he saw before was an illusion, but

If anyone is freed of his or her chains and forced to look directly at the fire, it will be a frightening experience. The new position will bring unaccustomed strain, the glare will cause anxiety.

Since his eyes are unaccustomed to seeing objects in this light, they will appear unclear to him, even though they have greater reality than the shadows he formerly took to be real.

that now, when he is approaching nearer to being and his eye is turned towards more real existence, he has a clearer vision—what will be his reply? And you may further imagine that his instructor is pointing to the objects as they pass and requiring him to name them—will he not be perplexed? Will he not fancy that the shadows which he formerly saw are truer than the objects which are now shown to him?

Far truer.

And if he is compelled to look straight at the light, will he not have a pain in his eyes which will make him turn away to take refuge in the objects of vision which he can see, and which he will conceive to be in reality clearer than the things which are now being shown to him?

True, he said.

And suppose once more, that he is reluctantly dragged up a steep and rugged ascent, and held fast until he's forced into the presence of the sun himself, is he not likely to be pained and irritated? When he approaches the light his eyes will be dazzled, and he will not be able to see anything at all of what are now called realities.

Not all in a moment, he said.

The problem of clear vision becomes even more acute when he is dragged from the cave into the upper world and exposed to the dazzling rays of the sun. At first, he will see shadows best, then reflections of objects in the water, later the objects themselves.

He will require to grow accustomed to the sight of the upper world. And first he will see the shadows best, next the reflections of men and other objects in the water, and then the objects themselves; then he will gaze upon the light of the moon and the stars and the spangled heaven; and he will see the sky and the stars by night better than the sun or the light of the sun by day?

Certainly.

Last of he will be able to see the sun, and not mere reflections of him in the water, but he will see him in his own proper place, and not in another; and he will contemplate him as he is.

Certainly.

He will then proceed to argue that this is he who gives the season and the years, and is the guardian of all that is in the visible world, and in a certain way the cause of all things which he and his fellows have been accustomed to behold?

Clearly, he said, he would first see the sun and then reason about him.

And when he remembered his old habitation, and the wisdom of the den and his fellow-prisoners, do you not suppose that he would felicitate [congratulate] himself on the change, and pity them?

Certainly, he would.

And if they were in the habit of conferring honors among themselves on those who were quickest to observe the passing shadows and to remark which of them went before, and which followed after, and which were together; and who were therefore best able to draw conclusions as to the future, do you think that he would care for such honors and glories, or envy the possessors of them? Would he not say with Homer,

"Better to be the poor servant of a poor master,"

and to endure anything, rather than think as they do and live after their manner?

At last he will see the sun as it is. Then he will say that the sun is the guardian of the visible world.

When he recalls the den and his fellow-prisoners, he will pity them. He will not be envious of those among them honored for their wisdom in recognizing shadows or predicting the future of life in the cave.

If he, who had been in the sunlight, were suddenly brought back into the cave, his eyes would have a very difficult time adapting to the darkness. The prisoners in the den, observing his troubles, would be convinced that it was dangerous to leave the cave. In fact, if somebody were to attempt to lead another one of them out to the upper world, they would put him to death if they caught him. [This appears to be a reference to the fate of the real-life Socrates who led youths to the light of philosophy and was condemned to death for corrupting the youth.]

Plato, in the role of Socrates, then explains the allegory of the cave. The prison is the world of sight.

Yes, he said, I think that he would rather suffer anything than entertain these false notions and live in this miserable manner.

Imagine once more, I said, such an one coming suddenly out of the sun to be replaced in his old situation; would he not be certain to have his eyes full of darkness?

To be sure, he said.

And if there were a contest, and he had to compete in measuring the shadows with the prisoners who had never moved out of the den, while his sight was still weak, and before his eyes had become steady (and the time which would be needed to acquire this new habit of sight might be very considerable) would he not be ridiculous? Men would say of him that up he went and down he came without his eyes; and that it was better not even to think of ascending; and if any one tried to loose another and lead him up to the light, let them only catch the offender, and they would put him to death.

No question, he said.

This entire allegory, I said, you may now append, dear Glaucon, to the previous argument; the prison-house is the world of sight, the light of the fire is the sun, and you will not misapprehend me if you interpret the journey upwards to be the ascent of the soul into the intellectual world according to my poor belief, which, at your desire, I have expressed—whether rightly or wrongly God knows. But, whether true or false, my opinion is that in the world of knowledge the idea of good appears last of all, and is seen only with an effort; and, when seen, is also inferred to be the universal author of all things beautiful and right, parent of light and of the lord of light in this visible world, and the immediate source of reason and truth in the intellectual; and that this is the power upon which he who would act rationally either in public or private life must have his eye fixed.

I agree, he said, as far as I am able to understand you.

Moreover, I said, you must not wonder that those who attain to this beatific vision are unwilling to descend to human affairs; for their souls are ever hastening into the upper world where they desire to dwell; which desire of theirs is very natural, if our allegory may be trusted.

Yes, very natural.

And is there anything surprising in one who passes from divine contemplations to the evil state of man, misbehaving himself in a ridiculous manner; if, while his eyes are blinking and before he has become accustomed to the surrounding darkness, he is compelled to fight in courts of law, or in other places, about the images or the shadows of images of justice, and is endeavoring to meet the conceptions of those who have never yet seen absolute justice?

Anything but surprising, he replied.

Anyone who has common-sense will remember that the bewilderments of the eyes are of two kinds, and arise from two causes, either from coming out of the light or from going into the light, which is true of the mind's eye, quite as much as of the bodily eye; and he who remembers this when he sees any one whose vision is per-

The journey first towards the fire, and then into the outer world to see the sun itself is a simile for a soul turning from the prison of material things to enter into the intellectual world. The sun it a metaphor for the idea of the good, which is seen with great effort, but is the source of reason and truth in the intellectual world. For Plato ideas or forms were the ultimate reality, rather than sensible objects which were but pale reflections of ideas. The highest of these ideas was the idea of the good.

Once the philosopher has attained the idea of the good and the other ideas of the intellectual world, it is difficult for him to turn back to the everyday world and accept its mistaken concept of justice.

The philosopher who comes out of the dazzling sunlight into the dark cave should not be laughed at if his vision is weak in the unaccustomed darkness. It is he who has remained in the cave and mistakes the shadow of justice for real justice who is more worthy of laughter.

The "certain professors of education " are apparently the sophists, who were intellectual enemies of Socrates.

Unlike the Sophists, Socrates held that a teacher does not put knowledge into the soul of a pupil. The knowledge is already there [from a prior existence]. The whole soul must turn its attention from the world of becoming (material things) to the world of being (immaterial ideas or forms) to know the good.

plexed and weak, will not be too ready to laugh; he will first ask whether that soul of man has come out of the brighter life, and is unable to see because unaccustomed to the dark, or having turned from darkness to the day is dazzled by excess of light. And he will count the one happy in his condition and state of being, and he will pity the other; or, if he have a mind to laugh at the soul which comes from below into the light, there will be more reason in this than in the laugh which greets him who returns from above out of the light into the den.

That, he said, is a very just distinction.

But then, if I am right, certain professors of education must be wrong when they say that they can put a knowledge into the soul which was not there before, like sight into blind eyes.

They undoubtedly say this, he replied.

Whereas, our argument shows that the power and capacity of learning exists in the soul already; and that just as the eye was unable to turn from darkness to light without the whole body, so too the instrument of knowledge can only by the movement of the whole soul be turned from the world of becoming into that of being, and learn by degrees to endure the sight of being, and of the brightest and best of being, or, in other words, of the good.

Very true.

And must there not be some art which will effect conversion in the easiest and quickest manner; not implanting the faculty of sight, for that exists already, but has been turned in the wrong direction, and is looking away from the truth?

Yes, he said, such an art may be presumed.

And whereas the other so-called virtues of the soul seem to be akin to bodily qualities, for even when they are not originally innate they can be implanted later by habit and exercise, the virtue of wisdom more than anything else contains a divine element which always remains, and by this conversion is rendered useful and profitable; or, on the other hand, hurtful and useless. Did you never observe the narrow intelligence flashing from the keen eye of a clever rogue—how eager he is, how clearly his paltry soul sees the way to his end; he is the reverse of blind, but his keen eyesight is forced into the service of evil, and he is mischievous in proportion to his cleverness.

Very true, he said.

But what if there had been a circumcision of such natures in the days of their youth; and they had been severed from those sensual pleasures, such as eating and drinking, which, like leaden weights, were attached to them at their birth, and which drag them down and turn the vision of their souls upon the things that are below—if, I say, they had been released from these impediments and turned in the opposite direction, the very same faculty in them would have seen the truth as keenly as they see what their eyes are turned to now.

Very likely.

A clever rascal may use his intelligence in the service of evil. But if this person had been cut off from sensual pleasures in youth, his or her soul could have turned in the opposite direction and seen the higher truths.

Neither the uneducated, nor those who never finish their education, make capable rulers.

Those with the best minds must be forced to continue their education until they have arrived at a knowledge of the good. Then they must be compelled to descend into the den to dwell among those who are imprisoned by material things. For only those who are philosophers, who have a knowledge of the good, ought to be the administrators of the state.

Yes, I said; and there is another thing which is likely. or rather a necessary inference from what has preceded, that neither the uneducated and uninformed of the truth, nor yet those who never make an end of their education, will be able ministers of State; not the former, because they have no single aim of duty which is the rule of all their actions, private as well as public; nor the latter, because they will not act at all except upon compulsion, fancying that they are already dwelling apart in the islands of the blessed.

Very true, he replied.

Then, I said, the business of us who are the founders of the State will be to compel the best minds to attain that knowledge which we have already shown to be the greatest of all-they must continue to ascend until they arrive at the good; but when they have ascended and seen enough we must not allow them to do as they do now.

What do you mean?

I mean that they remain in the upper world: but this must not be allowed; they must be made to descend again among the prisoners in the den, and partake of their labors and honors, whether they are worth having or not.

But is not this unjust? he said; ought we to give them a worse life, when they might have a better?

You have again forgotten, my friend, I said, the intention of the legislator, who did not aim at making any one class in the State happy above the rest; the happiness was to be in the whole State, and he held the citizens together by persuasion and necessity, making them benefactors of the State, and therefore benefactors of one another; to this end he created them, not to please themselves, but to be his instruments in binding up the State.

True, he said, I had forgotten.

Observe, Glaucon, that there will be no injustice in compelling our philosophers to have a care and providence of others; we shall explain to them that in other States, men of their class are not obliged to share in the toils of politics: and this is reasonable, for they grow up at their own sweet will, and the government would rather not have them. Being self-taught, they cannot be expected to show any gratitude for a culture which they have never received. But we have brought you into the world to be rulers of the hive, kings of yourselves and of the other citizens, and have educated you far better and more perfectly than they have been educated, and you are better able to share in the double duty. Wherefore each of you, when his turn comes, must go down to the general underground abode, and get the habit of seeing in the dark. When you have acquired the habit, you will see ten thousand times better than the inhabitants of the den, and you will know what the several images are, and what they represent, because you have seen the beautiful and just and good in their truth. And thus our State which is also yours will be a reality, and not a dream only, and will be administered in a spirit unlike that of other States, in which men fight with one another about shadows only and are distracted in the struggle for power, which in their eyes is a great good. Whereas the truth is that the State in which the rulers are most reluctant to govern is always the

Socrates argues that compelling philosophers to rule is not an injustice. These philosophers have received their training to benefit the whole state, not merely so that they could please themselves by pursuing knowledge. They must rule because, unlike the masses in the cave, they "have seen the beautiful and just and good in their truth."

The philosophers, with this knowledge, can make the ideal state a reality. They are unlike typical rulers who mistake shadows for reality and think power is a good worth struggling for.

The best state is run by rulers who are reluctant to govern and the worst by rulers hungry for power.

Those who go into public affairs thinking their own interest is the chief good cannot govern well. Their greed will lead to all types of fights. But the philosopher would prefer to concentrate more on exploring the world of ideas than governing the ignorant masses. He governs out of a sense of stern duty and accepts the burdens of office as a just demand of those who have provided his education. Only philosophers, lovers of wisdom, look "down upon the life of political ambition."

best and most quietly governed, and the State in which they are most eager, the worst.

Quite true, he replied.

And will our pupils, when they hear this, refuse to take their turn at the toils of State, when they are allowed to spend the greater part of their time with one another in the heavenly light?

Impossible, he answered; for they are just men, and the commands which we impose upon them are just; there can be no doubt that every one of them will take office as a stern necessity, and not after the fashion of our present rulers of State.

Yes, my friend, I said; and there lies the point. You must contrive for your future rulers another and a better life than that of a ruler, and then you may have a well-ordered State; for only in the State which offers this, will they rule who are truly rich, not in silver and gold, but in virtue and wisdom, which are the true blessings of life. Whereas if they go to the administration of public affairs, poor and hungering after their own private advantage, thinking that hence they are to snatch the chief good, order there can never be; for they will be fighting about office, and the civil and domestic broils which thus arise will be the ruin of the rulers themselves and of the whole State.

Most true, he replied.

And the only life which looks down upon the life of political ambition is that of true philosophy. Do you know of any other?

Indeed, I do not, he said.

And those who govern ought not to be lovers of the task? For, if they are, there will be rival lovers, and they will fight.

No question.

Who then are those whom we shall compel to be guardians? Surely they will be the men who are wisest about affairs of State, and by whom the State is best administered, and who at the same time have other honors and another and a better life than that of politics?

They are the men, and I will choose them, he replied.

****

[The Myth of the Metals]

How then may we devise one of those needful falsehoods of which we lately spoke—just one royal lie which may deceive the rulers, if that be possible, and at any rate the rest of the city?

What sort of lie? he said.

Nothing new, I replied; only an old Phoenician tale of what has often occurred before now in other places, (as the poets say, and have made the world believe), though not in our time, and I do not know whether such an event could ever happen again, or could now even be made probable, if it did.

How your words seem to hesitate on your lips!

Those who govern because they love to dominate others are bound to get into disputes with rival lovers of power. Only the philosophers, who can envision a better life than politics, are fit to provide the best government.

Plato is concerned that people may reject the rule of the intellectuals who have been specially educated to govern. So, in the persona of Socrates, he proposes to tell one big lie to deceive the rest of the city, and perhaps even the rulers themselves. The function of the lie is to win acceptance of his rulers by all classes.

One purpose for this lie or myth is to create social bonds within society. All the citizens of the state were created in the womb of the same mother earth. All citizens are to be regarded as brothers and they are to serve and defend their country as their mother.

Another purpose of the myth is to establish a class structure justifying the power of the rulers. People are to be told that while they are all brothers, God created them differently. Some he mixed with gold and they are to be the highest rulers or guardians. Those mixed with silver are to be auxiliaries or helpers. Those mixed with brass and iron are meant to be farmers and craftsmen.

You will not wonder, I replied, at my hesitation when you have heard.

Speak, he said, and fear not.

Well then, I will speak, although I really know not how to look you in the face, or in what words to utter the audacious fiction, which I propose to communicate gradually, first to the rulers, then to the soldiers, and lastly to the people. They are to be told that their youth was a dream, and the education and training which they received from us, an appearance only; in reality during all that time they were being formed and fed in the womb of the earth, where they themselves and their arms and appurtenances were manufactured; when they were completed, the earth, their mother, sent them up; and so, their country being their mother and also their nurse, they are bound to advise for her good, and to defend her against attacks, and her citizens they are to regard as children of the earth and their own brothers.

You had good reason, he said, to be ashamed of the lie which you were going to tell.

True, I replied, but there is more coming; I have only told you half. Citizens, we shall say to them in our tale, you are brothers, yet God has framed you differently. Some of you have the power of command, and in the composition of these he has mingled gold, wherefore also they have the greatest honor; others he has made of silver, to be auxiliaries; others again who are to be husbandmen and craftsmen he has composed of brass and iron; and the species will generally be preserved in the children. But as all are of the same original stock, a golden parent will sometimes have a silver son, or a silver parent a golden son. And God proclaims as a first principle to the rulers, and above all else, that there is nothing which they should so anxiously guard, or of which they are to be such good guardians, as of the purity of the race. They should observe what elements mingle in their offspring; for if the son of a golden or silver parent has an admixture of brass and iron, then nature orders a transposition of ranks, and the eye of the ruler must not be pitiful towards the child because he has to descend in the scale and become a husbandman or artisan, just as there may be sons of artisans who having an admixture of gold or silver in them are raised to honor, and become guardians or auxiliaries. For an oracle says that when a man of brass or iron guards the State, it will be destroyed. Such is the tale; is there any possibility of making our citizens believe in it?

Not in the present generation, he replied; there is no way of accomplishing this; but their sons may be made to believe in the tale, and their sons' sons, and posterity after them.

I see the difficulty, I replied; yet the fostering of such a belief will make them care more for the city and for one another.

The myth demands that parents from the guardian class show no mercy to a less capable son. Instead, the child must to be given the status of a farmer or laborer. Similarly offspring of the commoners are to receive higher ranks if they have higher intelligence. A man of brass or iron, that is a man of lesser capacity, must not be allowed to rule lest a prophecy predicting the destruction of the state comes true.

To future generations, this tale will appear believable, and serve to sanctify the rule of the intellectuals.

THE ALLEGORY OF THE CAVE

1. Why do you think Plato uses the dialogue between Socrates and Glaucon as a teaching device?

2. What are the differences between the people in the cave and those outside? How does each group view the world?

3. Why does Plato describe two separate and distinct worlds?

4. Explain how and why the prisoners in the cave view the shadows as real things. What happens when the prisoner is turned into the daylight? How does Plato view reality?

5. Why must the prisoner return to his fellow prisoners in the cave? What purpose does he now have?

6. Using Plato's allegory, how are we like the prisoners in the cave today?

7. What and where is the other world beyond our sense experience? Do you believe this world exists?

THE MYTH OF THE METALS

1. Describe the classes of citizens in Plato's ideal state. What is the difference in function between the guardians and the craftsmen? What privileges does each class have? What limitations?

2. What is the grand lie that Socrates proposes? Why does he propose this big lie?

3. What is Plato's position on those who should govern the state? Explain carefully.

4. What specific criticisms would you offer to Plato about his ideal state?

Self-Test

Can you identify each of the following? Tell who, what, when, where, why, and/or how for each term.

1. Mt. Olympus
2. Aeschylus
3. Sophocles
4. Euripides
5. Greater Dionysia
6. *Lysistrata*
7. Herodotus
8. Thucydides
9. Parthenon
10. Thales
11. Pythagoras of Samos
12. Heraclitus
13. Democritus
14. Sophists
15. Socrates
16. Plato
17. *The Republic*
18. Aristotle
19. Hellenistic Civilization
20. Euclid
21. Aristarchus of Samos
22. Eratosthenes
23. Archimedes of Syracuse
24. Cynics
25. Epicureans
26. Logos
27. Etruscans
28. Virgil or Vergil
29. *Aeneid*
30. Patricians
31. Plebeians
32. Struggle of the Orders
33. Consul
34. *Imperium*
35. Law of the Twelve Tables
36. Punic Wars
37. Cannae
38. Scipio Africanus
39. Latifundia
40. The Gracchi Brothers: Tiberius and Gaius
41. Marius
42. Sulla
43. First Triumvirate
44. Second Triumvirate
45. Pompey the Great
46. Julius Caesar
47. Spartacus
48. Battle of Actium
49. Marc Antony
50. Cleopatra
51. Octavian
52. Caesar Augustus

Part II: Multiple Choice Questions

Circle the best response from the choices available.

1. The Greeks conceived their chief gods as
    a. all-powerful forces of nature.
    b. divine spirits capable only of evil.
    c. pure spirits far removed from human affairs.
    d. magnified human beings leading very human lives.

2. The Greek drama originated in
    a. public celebrations of military victories.
    b. attempts by politic leaders to propagandize their reform programs.
    c. religious festivals.
    d. attempts to popularize democratic ideas.

3. Viewed collectively, the Greek dramatists succeeded in
    a. making man seem ridiculously weak.
    b. exploring nearly all facets of human nature with great profundity.
    c. ridiculing religious ideas.
    d. undermining the Greek love of the city-states.

4. The question that <u>first</u> occupied the Greek philosophical mind was a search for the
    a. ideal political system.
    b. nature of man.
    c. nature of the gods.
    d. fundamental force behind and giving unity to the universe.

5. A trait common to most classical Greek sculptors was their
    a. violent emotionalism.
    b. idealization of the human figure.
    c. disregard for the human figure.
    d. effective use of geometric design.

6. The Pythagoreans differed from the Ionians in that they
    a. lived on the Greek mainland.
    b. relied completely on a mythical explanation of the universe.
    c. sought to explain the universe mathematically.
    d. chose fire as the primary substance of the universe.

7. Socrates believed that truth could be discovered by
    a. controlled observations of the senses.
    b. logical thinking and critical discussion.
    c. translating facts into mathematical forms.
    d. analyzing the writing of leading Greek poets and philosophers.

8. Plato believed all of the following <u>except</u>
    a. the common people cannot be expected to think intelligently about important questions of state.
    b. democracy could degenerate into anarchy.
    c. true knowledge is found in the world of Forms.
    d. it is dangerous to trust the care of the state to philosophers.

9. The great historian of the Persian Wars was
    a. Herodotus.
    b. Thucydides.
    c. Polybius.
    d. Parmenides.

10. The Peloponnesian War was caused by
    a. Spartan militarism.
    b. Athenian aggressiveness and exploitation of her empire.
    c. Persian intrigue.
    d. Macedonian power.

11. The Hellenistic world created by Alexander
    a. was a mixture of Greek and Eastern elements.
    b. carried Greek ideals to victory in the Siberia.
    c. had no permanence at all since Alexander died at age 32.
    d. saw the Greeks swallowed up by the higher culture of the East.

12. After Alexander's death, his empire
    a. was inherited intact by his son.
    b. was recovered by the Persians.
    c. fragmented into a series of independent city-states extending from Greece to India.
    d. was disputed over by his generals and ultimately divided into several kingdoms.

13. Generally, Hellenistic monarchs
    a. were subservient to an Assembly of all citizens.
    b. allowed the cities in their realm complete control over domestic and foreign affairs.

    c. discouraged commerce and trade among cities.
    d. encouraged the oriental practice of worshipping the king as a god or representative of the gods.

14. The philosophy of the Hellenistic Age which taught that the individual should withdraw from public life to cultivate the pleasures of the mind with a few close friends in pleasant surroundings was
    a. Epicureanism.
    b. Stoicism.
    c. Cynicism.
    d. Skepticism.

15. The theoretical basis of the Stoic belief in the oneness of humanity is found in the idea that
    a. the absence of any gods in the universe means that no person is better than any other person.
    b. all humans are equal in that they share in the Divine Reason that rules the cosmos.
    c. since nobody can possess knowledge that is absolutely true, one person cannot be better than another.
    d. the God of the Hebrews is the God of all humanity.

16. Cynics were
    a. Hellenistic gods.
    b. philosophers who taught that inner peace was achieved by living according to the traditions of one's society.
    c. supreme individualistss who rebelled against established values and conventions.
    d. people who attempted to restore the values of the polis.

17. The traditional founding date for Rome is 751 B.C., but a more realistic beginning of Roman history is
    a. the Etruscan rule of Rome during the 7th and 6th centuries B.C.
    b. the expulsion of the Etruscan kings and the founding of the Roman Republic in 509 B.C.
    c. the end of the Struggle of the Orders in 287 B. C.
    d. the end of the 2nd Punic War in 201 B. C.

18. Under the government system of the Roman Republic the chief magistrate(s) of the state was (were)
    a. two elected consuls.   b. the Senate.
    c. the tribunes.   d. the king.

19. The principal organ of patrician power was
    a. Tribal Assembly.   b. Senate.
    c. tribunate.   d. Plebeian Assembly.

20. Which of the following did not contribute to the growth of plebeian political strength during the fifth century B. C.?
    a. the establishment of a tribal assembly.
    b. the codification of the Twelve Tables of Roman law.
    c. the right to elect tribunes.
    d. plebeian control of the Senate.

21. The Roman Republic's conquest of a large empire
    a. generated huge spoils of war.
    b. caused tremendous social changes within Rome and Italy.
    c. contributed to the ultimate collapse of the republican form of government.
    d. all of the above.

22. The Gracchi brothers sought to
    a. gain personal power and make themselves rulers of Rome.
    b. increase the power of the Roman Senate.
    c. redistribute land to the poorer farmers.
    d. none of the above.

23. The leader of the Senatorial faction (*optimates*) who ruthlessly killed many of the followers of Marius and the *populares* was
    a. Sulla.
    b. Pompey.
    c. Brutus.
    d. Marc Anthony.

24. The collapse of the Roman Republic may be explained by all of the following except
    a. a deterioration in the quality of senatorial leadership.
    b. a decline in devotion to the city.
    c. foreign invasion of Italy in the first century A.D.
    d. civil war.

25. Augustus succeeded where Julius Caesar failed because
    a. he destroyed the remaining critics of monarchy in the Senate.
    b. he established a legitimate monarchy.
    c. maintained the appearance of a Republic while in reality centralizing most power in his own hands.
    d. successfully restored the Republic by reforming the corrupt Senate.

Part III: Review and Thought Questions

1. How do Plato and Aristotle differ in their philosophic thought? Give at least two differences.

2. Differentiate between the Apollonian and Dionysian elements in the Greek religion.

3. What and where is the other world beyond our sense experience, according to Plato?

4. How do Herodotus and Thucydides differ in their historical approach?

5. Explain how we are indebted to the Greeks for the beginnings of drama. What examples of plays do you recall from your reading?

6. Explain Aristotle's contributions to philosophic thought in your own words?

7. How did Hellenic and Hellenistic art differ? Explain fully. Give examples of each.

8. Describe and explain the political structure of the Roman Republic. Did it have a constitution? Include specific offices, legislative bodies, such as the Senate and the assemblies, and their functions.

9. Explain how the Punic Wars made Rome into the dominant power in the Western Mediterranean.

10. How did class tensions grow as small plebeian farmers were dispossessed from their land?

11. What did the Etruscan culture contribute to the Roman civilization?

12. Relate the legend of Romulus and Remus.

13. What reforms did the Gracchi wish to achieve?

14. How did Marius change the status of the military?

15. How and why did the First and Second Triumvirates destroy the Republic?

16. What were the gains of the plebeians as a result of the Struggle of the Orders?

17. How did Caesar gain dictatorial power? What were three of his reforms? Why was he assassinated?

18. List and describe the divisions of Alexander's empire after this death.

19. How did Alexander the Great contribute to the cosmopolitanism of the Hellenistic Age?

20. How did each one of the following philosophies believe an individual could achieve happiness: Stoicism, Cynicism, Epicureanism, Skepticism? Which advice would you follow if given a choice?

21. Compare and contrast the 5th century B.C. Hellenic Greek philosophy of Plato with that of the Stoics.

22. What were the contributions of Hellenistic science to Western Civilization? Why were they so progressive and forward-looking for the time period?

Part IV: Full-Length Essays

1. Discuss the contributions of the 5th century B.C. Hellenic Greeks to Western civilization in the areas of history, drama, philosophy, and democracy. Give examples in each area.

2. Explain the beliefs of three Pre-Socratic philosophers. How do these beliefs differ from Socrates, Plato, and Aristotle?

3. Describe and explain the political structure of the Roman Republic. How did it differ from the direct democracy practiced by the 5th century B.C. Greeks?

4. Describe the power struggles of the First and Second Triumvirate. How did they bring about a downfall of the Republic? Explain fully.

5. Describe the gods and goddesses and their domains of concern that were immortalized by the Greeks. How did the early Greeks' beliefs in mythology influence their culture?

6. Explain how the effects of the Punic Wars transformed Rome and Roman society. Include the addition of colonies, the changed social class structure, and the redistribution of agricultural wealth.

7. Describe the philosophies of the Cynics, the Stoics, and the Epicureans.

8. Discuss the achievements of Hellenistic math and science. Include Euclid, Eratosthenes, Aristarchus, Archimedes, Herophilus in your discussion of the achievements.

Chapter III

THE ROMAN EMPIRE

AND

ITS SUCCESSORS

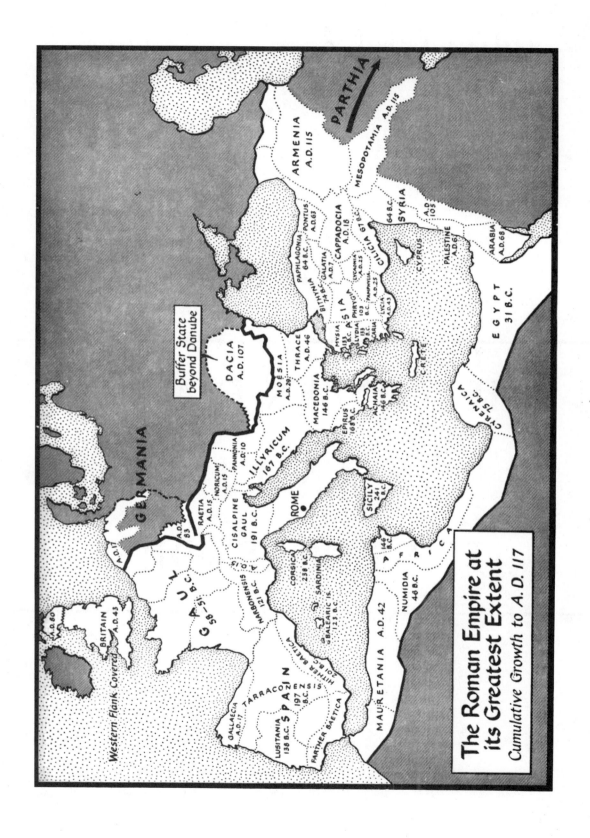

The Roman Empire at its Greatest Extent
Cumulative Growth to A.D. 117

7

The Roman Empire and Roman Culture

The Principate: 27 B.C. to 180 A.D.

Conquering an empire is not the same as ruling it. Alexander the Great and Julius Caesar have taught that lesson to those who are willing to learn. Octavian realized that he had to transform his MILITARY POWER into LEGITIMATE AUTHORITY. Julius Caesar had been killed because many Romans feared that he wanted to make himself king. For almost five hundred years, every Roman schoolchild had learned about the evils of the Etruscan kings and that kingship was an unjust form of government. Any move by Octavian to make himself king might have produced another stab in the back by a fanatic who saw himself as a patriotic defender of Republican virtues.

The Roman Senate, on the other hand, had also learned a lesson. Cassius and Brutus had been defeated. The death of Caesar had not restored the republic; instead, it had led to another round of civil wars. Many old patrician families were no more. Mark Antony's proscription had killed many of them. Killing Octavian would lead, no doubt, to yet another dictator.

The Senate and Octavian were both willing to compromise. They needed to find a form of government that would preserve the illusion of a republic while accommodating to the necessity of strong one-man rule. They needed a king without the title. The title that Octavian did accept was that of *princeps* or

What challenge faced Octavian after he defeated Antony and Cleopatra?

Why might the Roman Senate be willing to tolerate a one-person rule?

What was the Principate?

first citizen. From this word has come the name for the government: the PRINCIPATE.

The principate was a DYARCHY, essentially a compromise between rule by one and rule by the few, the Emperor and the Senate. The Emperor would rule for life, but with the assistance of the Senatorial class. The many, the Roman people, the ordinary male citizens who had participated in the popular assemblies, lost whatever political power they may have had previously.

Why wasn't it hereditary?

But the principate was not a monarchy. The hereditary principle of succession was never quite established. This was due, to a considerable degree, to the fact that emperors usually did not have an heir to succeed them. But it was also due to a residual sense of republicanism. The emperors always ruled in the name of the Senate and the Roman People (S.P.Q.R.). Legal fictions are important even when they seem to be contradicted by the facts.

The principate, established in 27 B.C. and lasting until 180 A.D., marked the most prosperous period in Roman history. This period was also the time of the PAX RO-MANA, the Roman Peace. The Mediterranean Sea had become a Roman lake and was governed by Roman law. We will discuss this period in terms of the emperors who ruled during this time.

How long did the Principate last?

Augustus: 27 B.C. to 14 A.D.

What was the *Pax Romana*?

In 27 B.C., Octavian was ready to establish his new system. He had carefully reorganized the Senate on a basis of wealth and with his own supporters. With great show, he surrendered all his powers to the Senate and the Roman people. The Senate responded with an equal act of ceremony, asking Octavian to resume the burden of government. They made him consul for life, praetor for life, quaestor for life, and tribune for life. Octavian was the first citizen of Rome, the PRINCEPS. The Senate also declared him IMPERATOR, that is victorious general, and they called him the exalted one, *augustus*. After 27 B.C., Octavian, no longer called by that name, is called AUGUSTUS, the first Roman Emperor.

What offices did Augustus hold?

| Arrangement with the Senate | But the Senate also got something out of the deal. They remained as the chief advisory body to the Emperor. They were also allowed to continue to rule the old provinces which had been conquered before 133 B.C., that is Sicily, Africa, and Spain. The Senate appointed the praetors and proconsuls who governed those provinces and, most important, the Senate disposed of the tax revenues from Senatorial provinces. Augustus controlled the newer, and always troublesome, provinces in the East, which had really been reconquered during the civil wars of the First and Second Triumvirates. Above all, Egypt was incorporated into the Roman Empire.

What powers did the Senate get?

| Arrangement with the Army | Augustus recognized that he had risen to power on the swords of his soldiers. The army had to be reorganized to prevent future commanders from seizing power. Augustus created a professional army, under strict discipline, with long-term (20 years) enlistments, and a land grant to veterans after mustering out. Civilian and military authority was divided in the provinces so that one could be used to check the other. Strict rules prohibited military commanders from moving their soldiers from one province to another without permission.

Augustus also created a special 20,000-man legion, called the PRAETORIAN

How did August seek to control the army?

What was the function of the Praetorian Guard?

GUARD, over which he exercised direct military command. The Praetorian Guard protected the emperor. They could be used to intimidate the Senate should that body challenge the will of the princeps. They could also put down an uprising by the Roman mob, formerly known as the Roman people. Finally, the Guard would serve as the centerpiece of the Emperor's army should insurrection break out in the provinces.

What Augustus did not consider, and what did not become a problem while he lived, was that the Praetorian Guard might itself become a political force. The commander of the Praetorian Guard might challenge the emperor for leadership.

Was the establishment of the Guard an unmixed blessing? Explain.

Religious Adjustment Government is always linked to religion, even when the effort is made to separate the state from the church. Until our modern age and the formation of the United States of America, governments always imposed an official religion. The Romans believed in many gods. Polytheistic societies find it easy to incorporate additional gods into their mythologies. But when many independent city-states, tribal societies, and kingdoms are conquered by a new Babylon, the imperial city's gods must be accorded some primacy. Religion, like the military, law, and trade, can serve as a unifying force.

Why do you think Augustus was concerned about religion?

The Romans, even during the period of the Republic, had adjusted *their* religion to that of the Greeks and the Hellenistic world into which they expanded. With Augustus, the next step was taken. Julius Caesar and Augustus had temples built in their name. The Emperors were worshipped as gods. The possibility that a mortal could become immortal was rooted in Greek thought, where Hercules and other men were thought to have joined the gods at Mount Olympus for their heroic deeds on earth. Alexander had claimed immortality, and the pharaohs of Egypt had been king-gods.

What were the benefits of emperor worship?

Emperor worship began under Augustus and gradually became an official cult. It was, like saying the Pledge of Allegiance or saluting the flag, a sign of loyalty to Rome. The people in Egypt and the eastern provinces were more familiar with the deification of their rulers, and were presumed to be less loyal to Rome than Italians. But even in the West, emperor worship grew steadily.

The peace which followed the establishment of the principate under Augustus, after all these decades of war, would seem to prove the divine nature of the man. It is reassuring to have a god as your ruler, at least as long as he maintains peace. Rulers like to be worshipped, and the ruler benefits when his subjects believe him to be a god. His commands will be obeyed more readily. Opponents might hesitate to kill a god and commit sacrilege against all the gods. Moreover, as an immortal, he might be invincible and revenge himself.

Why did Augustus undertake public works programs and provide grain and games for the masses?

The Augustan Age Augustus encouraged this emperor worship and the glorification of Rome. Seeking to make Rome the greatest city of the empire, he built new temples, baths, stadia, and roads. Rome became a city of more than a million people. Public works provide employment. The riches of the empire were used to bring free grain to the poor. Gladiatorial games entertained the masses.

There is often a prudish side to dictators. Augustus sought to restore public morality. He legislated against prostitution, male and female, and he passed new marriage laws requiring that adults marry and have children.

Why did Augustus treat the poets Virgil and Ovid so differently?

Augustus encouraged the artists of his day to glorify Roman history. VIRGIL'S *Aeneid* fit perfectly into that picture. The poet OVID, on the other hand, was exiled because his poetry and writings on love did not conform to the emperor's morality.

Augustus was married twice. His second wife, LIVIA DRUSILLA, had two sons from a previous marriage but bore Augustus no children. He had a daughter, Julia, from his first marriage. JULIA was his hope for a suitable son-in-law and grandsons as heirs. Julia had several marriages arranged for her, but her husbands kept dying. Her third husband was Tiberius, the son of Livia Drusilla from her first marriage. He, ultimately, succeeded Augustus, because Julia's sons by her second marriage died before Augustus. Julia cheated on her husband, conspired to murder her father, and died in exile. The morality which Augustus preached was not practiced in his own household.

Was Augustus a success? Explain.

Augustus, who died at the age of 76 in 14 A.D. outlived those whom he had hoped would succeed him. He had no sons; his grandsons had died; his daughter had turned on him and was in exile. But the empire which he had helped to construct would last for centuries. Not a bad achievement for a mortal.

Tiberius: 14 A.D. to 37 A.D.

Tiberius was born in 42 B.C. and became emperor in 14 A.D. at the age of 55. He was Augustus's last choice and seemed to have resented that fact. Tiberius was a competent general and had the loyalty of the soldiers when he became emperor. As emperor, he became more and more suspicious and executed his real and imagined enemies. Tiberius had a palace built on the island of

CAPRI, and he ruled from there from 26 A.D. to his death in 37 A.D., at the age of 78.

Identify and distinguish Tiberius, Caligula, and Claudius.

> Gaius Julius Caesar Germanicus, a.k.a. Caligula: 37 A.D. to 41 A.D.

AUTOCRATIC. ERRATIC -

Caligula was the grandson of Tiberius's brother. He was born in 12 A.D. and became emperor at age 25. Two of his older brothers and his mother had been accused of treason and were murdered by Tiberius. He nonetheless ingratiated himself with Tiberius and lived with him on Capri from 32 A.D. onward. As emperor, he became increasingly autocratic and erratic. His hatred of the Senate led him to have his horse elected as consul. After military failures, he was assassinated by the Praetorian Guard in 41 A.D., at the age of 29.

> Claudius: 41 A.D. to 54 A.D.

Rampaging through the palace, the soldiers found the hunchbacked and supposedly retarded uncle of Caligula. They proclaimed him emperor. Claudius was born in 10 B.C. and became emperor at the age of 50. He was a younger brother of Caligula's father. Contrary to the opinion of his family, Claudius was not retarded. In fact, he may have been one of the last Romans to be able to speak the Etruscan language.

Which of these was the most able ruler?

He was an effective emperor under whom the conquest of Britain, first attempted by Julius Caesar, was completed. He also added provinces in North Africa, Mauritania, and the Balkans, Thrace. Claudius used his freedmen as administrators, which made him unpopular with the Senate. The Roman writer SUETONIUS wrote a scandalous biography on *The Lives of the Caesars*, which served as the basis of Robert Graves's novel *I,*

What seem to be the failings of Nero?

Claudius. That novel became a PBS series and aired on public television.

Claudius married his fourth wife, his niece Agrippina II, at the age of 57. Excluding his own son, Germanicus, he adopted Nero, her son from a previous marriage as his heir. Agrippina, the sister of Caligula, may have poisoned her husband to assure Nero's succession. Nero reciprocated the favor and murdered his mother.

Nero: 54 A.D. to 68 A.D.

Nero was born in 37 A.D. and became emperor at the age of 17. He was under the control of his mother until he had her murdered in 59 A.D. After 62 A.D., Nero ruled unrestrainedly and had his enemies accused of treason and executed. In 64 A.D., the Great Fire of Rome destroyed much of the city. Many accused Nero of having set the fire as an urban renewal project so that he could build a new palace. Nero sought to shift the blame by accusing a newly formed religious sect in Rome, the CHRISTIANS. This was the FIRST GREAT PERSECUTION of the Christians.

Why did he persecute the Christians?

Whether Nero was clinically insane can be debated, but it is clear that the absolute power which he enjoyed as emperor unbalanced him. Nero fancied himself as an artist and free spirit. He publicly sang, played music, and raced chariots. In 67 A.D., he went on a tour of Greece and entered various competitions. He won all of them, of course.

By 68 A.D., these antics provoked insurrection in several provinces. Even the Praetorian Guard turned against him. Nero committed suicide at the age of 31, lamenting at his own death what a great artist the world would be losing.

Nero was the last of the emperors who in some way were related to the Julian and Claudian clans that had produced Julius Caesar and Caesar Augustus. They were known for that reason as the JULIO-CLAUDIAN EMPERORS.

After Nero's death, three military commanders vied for the purple, that is the color of the emperor's robes. Three emperors died between 68 and 69 A.D. until the fourth contender, Vespasian, took control. Vespasian was the founder of the FLAVIAN DYNASTY OF EMPERORS. The Flavians include Vespasian and his two sons, Titus and Domitian. They had no relation whatsoever to Nero and his ancestors.

Vespasian: 69 A.D. to 79 A.D.

Vespasian was born in 9 A.D. and seized the emperorship in 69 A.D., at the age of 60. He was a capable ruler who restored the finances of the empire both by economies and higher taxes. He began the construction of the Colosseum. Rights of Roman citizenship were extended. He made his son Titus head of the Praetorian Guard and heir. When Vespasian died in 79 A.D., at the age of 70, his son succeeded smoothly.

Titus: 79 A.D. to 81 A.D.

Titus, a military man, was born 39 A.D. and became emperor at the age of 40. During his brief rule, the volcano on Mount Vesuvius erupted and buried the provincial cities of POMPEII and HERCULANEUM in 79 A.D. In 80 A.D., a plague and fire brought great destruction to Rome. Titus actively aided the victims of these disasters. When Titus died unexpectedly in 81 A.D., his

Distinguish between the Julio-Claudians and the Flavians.

What did Vespasian and Titus accomplish?

Was Domitian an able ruler? Explain.

younger brother succeeded unopposed even though he had held no major previous offices under his brother and father.

Domitian: 81 A.D. to 96 A.D.

Domitian was born 51 A.D. and became emperor unexpectedly at the age of 30. Domitian persecuted both Christians and Senators. Subsequent historians, who have largely come from those two groups, have denounced Domitian as an autocratic emperor. He weakened the power of the Senate, forced those who came in his presence to prostrate themselves, and had himself addressed in oriental fashion as "lord and god." Domitian did manage to maintain order within the empire, but his autocratic policies generated the very opposition which he feared. He was murdered in 96 A.D., probably by agents of his wife.

Who were the Good Emperors?

There were no candidates in the wings to compete for the emperorship. By default, the Senate had an opportunity to determine the future. They debated about the restoration of the republic, but finally decided to elect one of their own, an elderly Senator by the name of NERVA as emperor. With Nerva begins the period of THE GOOD EMPERORS. What is good about these emperors is that they adopted a competent official as their heir while still alive. This method of adoption solved the succession problem from 96 to 180 A.D.

Nerva: 96 A.D. to 98 A.D.

Nerva was chosen by the Roman Senate, just when one had reason to believe that its power was gone. Nerva did not live long enough to do much of anything, except for one important thing. He adopted the general TRAJAN as his heir. This set a pattern and made Nerva the first of the Good Emperors.

Trajan: 98 A.D. to 117 A.D.

Trajan was born in Roman Spain in 53 A.D. and became emperor at the age of 45. Under Trajan, Rome reached the height of its imperial expansion. He pushed the borders beyond the Rhine-Danube frontiers and conquered Dacia (modern-day Romania) on the northeastern side of the Danube. Trajan also went to war against the Parthian Empire, that perennial enemy of the Romans to the East. Although he captured the Parthian capital and reached the Persian Gulf at the mouth of the Tigris-Euphrates Rivers, he could not overcome all resistance. By the end of his life the Parthians had reconquered most of their territory. Trajan, who was a good administrator, engaged in a massive building program and subsidized the poor in Rome. He died at the age of 64.

Hadrian: 117 A.D. to 138 A.D.

Hadrian, who was Trajan's cousin and adopted successor, was born in 76 A.D. and became emperor at the age of 41. He did not continue the expansionary policies of Trajan. Dacia was retained, but the effort to conquer the Parthian empire was given up. Instead Hadrian developed a defensive strategy against the many tribes who lived on the borders of the Roman Empire. He had heavy fortifications built on the frontier where there were no natural barriers such as a river. These fortifications were similar to the Great Wall of China, which was built at about the same time in history. The most famous of

What did Nerva accomplish?

Distinguish between the policies of Trajan and Hadrian.

What was Hadrian's Wall?

these fortifications is HADRIAN'S WALL, which marked the border between Roman Britain and Scotland. Parts of that wall are still standing.

Hadrian was extremely well educated and a connoisseur of classical philosophy and art. Strongly opposed to the monotheistic religion of Judaism, he outlawed circumcision and had a temple to Jupiter Capitolinus built on the site of the Temple in Jerusalem. This provoked a serious uprising, which he ruthlessly quelled. Toward the end of his life, he adopted Antoninus Pius as his heir. He died at age 62.

Who was Antonius Pius?

Antoninus Pius: 138 A.D. to 161 A.D.

Antoninus Pius, who was born in 86 A.D. and became emperor at the age of 52.; he continued the defensive policies of his predecessor. These policies brought prosperity to the Empire. He was popular with the Senate, which continued to play an important role in government. He adopted his wife's nephew, Marcus Aurelius, as his heir. He died at the age of 75.

How was Marcus Aurelius different from the other emperors we have discussed?

Marcus Aurelius: 161 A.D. to 180 A.D.

Marcus Aurelius, who was born in 121 A.D. and became emperor at the age of 40, was a Stoic philosopher. While on military campaigns against the Marcomanni and other Danubian tribes Marcus Aurelius kept a private diary called the *Meditations* in which he confesses that he would rather be in a secluded study philosophizing than on the battlefield. He will do his duty, however, as a good Stoic and Roman must. Doing one's duty, no matter what one's station in life, was a prime belief of the Stoics.

Marcus Aurelius was less successful on the battlefield. He spent a great deal of Rome's treasure on a war against the Germans, which had not been won by the time of his death. He made one other fatal mistake. He adopted his son, as is natural, to be his heir, although he knew that the son was unsuited for the position. As a Stoic philosopher, he should have valued his duty to Rome above his duty to his family.

What was the most serious mistake of Marcus Aurelius?

> ### Lucius Aelius Aurelius Commodus: 180 - 192. A.D.

Commodus was born in 161 A.D., was co-ruler with his father from 177 A.D., and became sole emperor in 180 A.D., at the age of 19. Abandoning the war against the Germanic tribes on the Danube, he engaged in lavish orgies for his friends and squandered the already depleted resources of the empire. Those he thought critical of his ways, he had executed. Commodus was not a good emperor. It is under his emperorship that the principate collapses and we have the start of what historians call The Third Century Decline. Like Caligula before him, Commodus fancied himself a gladiator. He thought that he was the embodiment of Hercules. Whether that belief suffices to have him classified as mad is left to the reader. His "friends" had him strangled to death during one of his wrestling matches. He was 31 years of age.

What were the failings of his son, Commodus?

Summation The principate was a hybrid form of government. It was the union of a single, almost all-powerful emperor ruling in conjunction with the upper classes of Rome, the patricians and the equestrians, centered on the traditional Roman Senate. There was always a tension between the emperor and the Senate. Wise

Describe the succession problem in the principate.

emperors cooperated and manipulated; foolish ones attacked and executed the men who helped govern the Empire. Over time, the power of the Emperor seems to have grown over that of the Senate.

The principate never resolved the succession problem. The emperorship was never strictly governed by the hereditary principle. If Emperors had sons, they would often, but not always, try to make them their successors. It is strange how many emperors were childless or without sons. It has been suggested that the gold dishes and cups used at the emperor's table had high concentrations of lead. Lead poisoning can produce both sterility and insanity. Without sons, the emperors would often seek their heirs within the extended families of their clans. Despite the fact that the Romans were a patriarchal society, Roman women of the upper classes played powerful roles within their clans. The Julio-Claudian Emperors were all related.

The principate used adoption as a method for regulating the succession. These adoptions could be of competent but unrelated officials. The Good Emperors fall mainly in this category. Only once did the Senate elect an Emperor.

Why did the principate fail?

The ultimate principle of succession and the source of the emperor's power was the military. Julius Caesar and Augustus had fought their way to the top. Vespasian had seized power. Even Trajan and Hadrian owed their emperorship not only to adoption, but also to the support they enjoyed within the military. The principate was a disguised military dictatorship, an iron fist within the velvet glove.

The principate ended when the emperors were no longer able to deal effectively with the problems of this huge empire. For example, having an incompetent like Commodus at the head of the empire accelerated problems that even Marcus Aurelius had barely managed to contain. The Pax Romana and the principate lasted 200 years and constituted the high point of Rome and of Roman Civilization. Let us take a look at the cultural legacy of Greco-Roman Civilization at its height before it begins its long centuries of decline and transformation.

Discuss the Roman road system.

The Cultural Legacy of the Romans

The Romans were a practical people. They were good soldiers, administrators, lawyers, and engineers.

Engineering and Architecture *ARch.*

Do you think the Romans cared enough about sanitation? Explain.

Over five centuries, they built one of the greatest road systems of antiquity, whose total length would have encircled the earth ten times at the equator. The phrase "all roads lead to Rome" derives from the fact that Roman roads began at the FORUM ROMANUM; each mile was marked with a six-foot circular pillar measuring the distance from Rome. These roads were usually straight, using tunnels and viaducts to cut through hills and bridge valleys. Some of these roads, such as the APPIAN WAY, are in use today.

The Romans built elaborate water systems to supply their cities with water for fountains, public baths, and to flush the streets of Rome which also served as sewers. Aqueducts ported water from more than 100 miles away to supply the water needs of ancient Rome.

What material did the ancient Roman builders have that was unknown to earlier builders?

The Romans invented CONCRETE, made of lime and sand. They built four-story apartment buildings to house the million

Who was Vitruvius?

While the Greeks are noted for their columns, for what are the Romans noted?

inhabitants of their city. Their public buildings like the COLOSSEUM, the PANTHEON, and the BATHS OF CARACALLA were immense structures.

Engineering skills link naturally to the development of architecture. VITRUVIUS (c.70-25 B.C.) wrote a ten-volume book on architecture, which remains important to our own age. It inspired much of the Renaissance revival of classical building styles. The Romans continued to build temples using various types of columns to support the building. They also built BASILICAS, large rectangular buildings surrounded on all sides by a colonnaded gallery. They developed the TRIUMPHAL ARCH commemorating the great victories of their generals. The Romans used the round arch, vault, and dome effectively so that very large buildings could be constructed.

Law

What was the *jus gentium*?

Roman law developed for a thousand years from the Law of the Twelve Tables (450 B.C.) through the *Corpus Juris Civilis* (527 A.D.). In ancient times, law was not territorial but communal. Two Athenians in Rome would be tried according to Athenian law. Any Roman in conflict with a foreigner would obviously be treated according to Roman law. But what if an Athenian came in conflict with someone from Alexandria? What law should apply? A special judge, the *praetor peregrinis*, handled these cases and came to develop a special kind of law, the *jus gentium*. The *jus gentium* (law of the tribes or peoples) was a common law which derived from legal principles common to different legal systems. In all legal traditions, murder is prohibited, so is theft. There are common commercial practices. The Romans came to identify this *jus gentium* with the *jus natu-rale*. NATURAL LAW is the idea that there are universal moral principles inherent in human nature and in the divine order of the cosmos.

Here are a few of the principles of Roman law which are valid today. No one suffers a penalty for what he thinks. No one may be forcibly removed from his own house. The burden of proof is on the party affirming, not on the party denying. In inflicting penalties, the age and inexperience of the guilty party must be taken into account.

Roman administrators and soldiers began with a single city-state and slowly conquered an empire that covered all the lands surrounding the Mediterranean Sea. No people since, not even in our own age, have ever duplicated this feat. The Romans did this without modern machines or guns and cannons. The Roman legion with short swords and armor overcame the Hellenistic phalanx. Their discipline and organizational skills, as well as their determination and ruthlessness, cannot be overemphasized.

Religion

Even their religion was practical. In its earliest forms, the religion appears to have been animistic. The world was full of spirits, or *noumena*. These spirits were indifferent to humans, amoral, and could be either good or bad. With proper ritual, these noumena could be appeased. It was like a contract: do this for me and I'll do that for you. Some of the most important noumena were VESTA, the spirit which guarded the hearth fire; LARES, which guarded the house and its boundaries; PENATES, the spirit of the larder. The head of the household, the PATERFAMILIAS, performed the various rituals to keep these

Distinguish the *jus naturale* from the *jus gentium*.

What are some of the principles of Roman law with us even today?

What were the Vesta. the Lares. and the Penates?

Who were the vestal virgins and the pontifex maximus?

spirits friendly. These household gods were also the gods of Rome. The VESTAL VIRGINS, for example, tended the eternal flame of Rome.

The Etruscans had brought more complex ritual to the Romans. Divination and augury became important. Several colleges of priests and priestesses formed, headed by the PONTIFEX MAXIMUS (chief priest). Under the influence of the Greeks, these spirits took human form and were anthropomorphized. The twelve Olympian gods of Greece took on Roman names.

How similar was the Roman religion to that of the Greeks?

THE GREEK GODS AND THEIR ROMAN NAMES

GREEK NAME	ROMAN NAME
ZEUS	JUPITER
HERA	JUNO
ARES	MARS
POSEIDON	NEPTUNE
ATHENA	MINERVA
APOLLO	APOLLO
ARTEMIS	DIANA
DIONYSUS	BACCHUS
APHRODITE	VENUS
DEMETER	CERES
HEPHAESTUS	VULCAN
HERMES	MERCURY

The Capitoline Hill, one of the seven hills on which Rome was built, was the religious center of the city. The Capitoline Temple, the oldest of many temples there, was divided into three sections, one each for the worship of Jupiter, Juno, and Minerva. Mars, another important Roman deity, was not only the god of war, but also of the state and of agriculture. The Romans may have adopted Greek names, but their gods were profoundly different from those of the Greeks. There was none of the charm and ribaldry of the Greek immortals.

Literature

Roman literature was influenced by Greek examples. Homer's *Odyssey* influenced the poet VIRGIL (70 - 19 B.C.), who wrote the *Aeneid*, a national epic linking the founding of Rome with the Trojan War. The poem pleased Augustus, who was seeking to revive Roman patriotism. Virgil also wrote the *Georgics*, a poem about farming. A contemporary of Virgil was the poet HORACE (65 - 8 B.C.), whose *Odes*, influenced by Sappho, celebrate the beauty of Italy and the trials of romance. His *Satires* mocked everyday social mistakes. Another famous poet of the Augustan age was OVID (43 B.C. - c.17 A.D.), whose greatest works are *Metamorphoses* and the *Art of Love*. This last work purports to instruct men on how to seduce women. The *Art of Love* incensed Augustus, who banished Ovid from Rome.

The prose writer who had the greatest influence on the style of later generations was CICERO (106 - 43 B.C.). He was an ardent defender of republican institutions, famous for the elaborateness of his speeches against the conspirator Cataline, and notable for the Stoic ethics of his writings on *Friendship* and *Old Age*. At the insistence of Mark Antony, a political enemy, he was executed during the Second Triumvirate.

During the reign of Augustus, LIVY (59 B. C. - 17 A.D.) wrote a *History of Rome* *Historian* from 753 to 9 B.C. Unfortunately, much of

Discuss the poetry of Virgil.

Who was Horace?

Would you rather read Cicero or Ovid? Why?

Compare the work of the historians Livy and Tacitus.

also Roman medieval.

Discuss some Roman playwrights.

What did Marcus Aurelius write?

this work has been lost. From the portions that are extant, it is obvious that he is more concerned with depicting, in dramatic terms, Rome's destiny than in giving a factual analysis of events. This book, with its emphasis on moral character, was widely admired by later generations. The historian TACITUS (c.56 - c.115) was also concerned with moral issues. His *Germania*, from which we get much of our knowledge about the early *were not romans* German tribes, contrasts the virtues of the unpolished barbarians with the vices of the decadent Romans.

While Roman drama had several good comedians, including PLAUTUS (c.254 - 184 B.C.) and TERENCE (c.185 - 159 B.C.), the most noted writer of tragedies was SENECA (c.4 B.C. - 65 A.D.), whose work influenced medieval and Renaissance authors. Seneca, noted for his devotion to Stoicism, served as a tutor of Nero. He later committed suicide with stoic fortitude when accused of conspiracy against that emperor. Another adherent of Stoicism was the emperor MARCUS AURELIUS (161 - 180 A.D.), whose *Meditations* offered spiritual comfort to many.

The Romans were not creative. In the arts, literature, and philosophy, they imitated Greek models and rarely succeeded in equaling the original. The influence of Greek did, however, enrich the Latin language and that enrichment has come down to us. Latin has been the doorway through which we have come to understand the ancient world. Their language is another of their great legacies to us. Latin, the language of the Roman Catholic Church until the 1960s, was the language of all the educated during the Middle Ages and remained influential until well into the modern age. The Italian, French, Spanish, Portuguese, and Romanian languages derive directly from Latin. English is a Germanic language, but it has borrowed many Latin words.

Third Century Collapse of the Roman Empire: 180 A.D. to 284 A.D.

Who was Septimius Severus?

The Third Century Collapse of the Roman Empire may be divided into three segments: the decline, the collapse, and the effort to rebuild.

The decline began with Commodus, 180 to 192. His murder was followed by a brief civil war out of which SEPTIMIUS SEVERUS (193-211) emerged victorious. He was the first of what are called the BARRACKS EMPERORS.

He was succeeded by his oldest son CARACALLA, who ruled from 211 to 217. Caracalla engaged in a massive building program. The BATHS OF CARACALLA in Rome are one surviving example. To pay for his huge expenditures, he lowered the silver content of the Roman *denarius* to 60%. This debasement of the currency and increases in taxation had disastrous economic effects. He extended Roman citizenship to all free-born persons, probably for economic reasons, since only citizens paid inheritance taxes.

Caracalla also committed his share of atrocities by murdering his younger brother, and co-ruler, GETA. He fought a successful war against Germanic tribes on the upper Rhine River. His war against the Parthians was also successful, until he was murdered by one of his officers named MACRINUS.

Macrinus was emperor for two years (217 to 218), until he was killed in a revolt led by Septimius Severus's Syrian wife. She placed her thirteen-year old grandnephew, ELAGABALUS (218 to 222), on the throne.

Discuss the deeds of Caracalla.

The Pretorian guard put the person in charge (emperor).

Why do you think Marcinus was killed?

Who were the Severan Emperors?

What was the most notable feature of the period from 235-284?

What caused the anarchy within the Empire?

Elagabalus was dominated by his mother, who had him adopt a cousin as his heir, just in case. Elagabalus was murdered by his troops, and the cousin became emperor.

SEVERUS ALEXANDER (222 to 235) was the last of the emperors who had some remote connection to Septimius Severus and who are collectively called the SEVERAN EMPERORS (193 to 235). Severus Alexander appears to have had the makings of a good general and was able to stabilize the frontier with Persia. In 234, he was forced to deal with an invasion of the ALEMANNI on the Rhine, whom he sought to buy off rather than fight. His troops murdered him in 235. With his death, the last semblance of maintaining old traditions and keeping some civilian control over the military ended.

From 235 to 284, COMPLETE ANARCHY descended on the Empire. There were 22 emperors during these 49 years, of whom almost all were murdered or died in battle. The central administration of the empire all but collapsed. It looked like the end of the Roman world.

What were the causes of this anarchy? Two primary reasons are usually given. First, the Empire was too large geographically and when the pressures on the frontiers became too great, the existing military forces could not prevail. The Germanic tribes were pushing at Rome from the North, at the Rhine and Danube frontiers. The Parthian and then the Persian Empires attacked from the East. It was just too much.

The second reason is that the Roman economy began to collapse. The increase of taxes, debased currency, extractions of goods or produce, and an ever-increasing bureaucracy undermined the vitality of the empire. Enlarging the army to meet the challenges posed by invaders merely increased the pressures on the economy. The more the government regulated economic activities and the more centralized power became, the less room there was for initiative and enterprise.

It is clear that a profound crisis hit the Roman Empire during the third century. This crisis produced a total transformation in government, society, and religion. What the Third Century Anarchy did not achieve was the end of the Roman world. There was enough strength left to make yet one more beginning. The Emperors DIOCLETIAN and CONSTANTINE created a new political system that we call the AUTOCRACY. This Autocracy will be discussed later. But first, we will take a look at the rise of Christianity, which will triumph during the Autocracy and provide the basis for a new social order.

How severe was the Third Century Crisis?

Figure 3.1. Head of Constantine I (c. 325 A.D.). Roman Sculpture. Marble. The Emperor Constantine (306-337 A.D.) issued the Edict of Milan in 313 A.D., giving religious toleration to Christians in the Roman Empire. He was attracted to Christianity, reputedly, after seeing a cross in the sky before his great victory at the Milvian Bridge Battle. Look at the otherworldly expression on his face and in the pupils of his eyes. *Courtesy of The Metropolitan Museum of Art, Bequest of Mrs. F. F. Thompson, 1926. (26.229)*

8

The Rise of Christianity and the End of the Empire

The Rise of Christianity

Jesus Christ was not a Christian. He was born into the Jewish religion, he was circumcised, he learned the Torah, and he sacrificed at the Temple in Jerusalem. Christianity, as a religion, began only after the death of Jesus. It began with the Resurrection, which to his followers was proof that He was the Messiah, that what he had implied was true, He was the Son of God. Easter is the most important Christian holiday and the first Easter marks the beginning of Christianity.

Why is the Resurrection so important to Christians?

The Four Gospels

We know about the person of Jesus of Nazareth through the New Testament, the Christian Bible. The four GOSPELS tell the story of Jesus's life, teachings, and crucifixion. They were written more than one generation after the events described. It is generally held that MARK is the earliest Gospel and was written about 68 to 70 A.D., probably in Rome. If correct, it is the only Gospel written prior to the destruction of the Temple in Jerusalem by the Romans in 70 A.D. MATTHEW and LUKE are held to have been

Who were the four Gospel writers?

When did they write their Gospels?

Distinguish the Synoptic Gospels from the Gospel of St. John.

written about 85 A.D., and JOHN between 95 and 100 A.D. Each of the Gospels differs in details, but the first three are more similar and are called the SYNOPTIC Gospels. There appears to have been a source book of the sayings of Jesus, which is used by Matthew and Luke. Unfortunately, this source book, called *Q* for the German word Quelle, has been lost. The Gospel of John, written later and apparently based on different sources, differs from the Synoptic Gospels. John used longer narratives and appears to have been concerned to rebut the beliefs of rivals, such as the Gnostics, about the nature of Jesus.

Give some details of Jesus's life.

Jesus of Nazareth

According to the Gospel stories, JESUS was born in BETHLEHEM during the rules of Emperor AUGUSTUS and King HEROD THE GREAT of Judea. King Herod died in 4 B.C., so Jesus must have been born previously. Many centuries later, Christians decided to date the Christian calendar from the time of the birth of Christ. About 525 A.D., a monk by the name of DIONYSIUS EXIGUUS placed the date of birth at least four years too late.

We know little about Jesus's early life, but the Gospels tell us that in the fifteenth year of the rule of the emperor TIBERIUS (14 to 37 A.D.), Jesus was baptized by JOHN THE BAPTIST, who acknowledged him as the MESSIAH, the expected king and deliverer of the Jews. While Christ's public ministry began at that point, it is not clear how many years Jesus preached. One of the Gospels has Jesus in Jerusalem for the Passover three times, the other three only once. There is considerable evidence, according to the historian Joseph Ward Swain, that Jesus was crucified on April 7, 30 A.D.[1]

Conditions in Judea at the Time of Jesus.

Why did devout Jews dislike the Herods?

Jesus lived in Judea at a time of extreme turbulence. In 63 B.C., POMPEY, the rival of JULIUS CAESAR, had entered Jerusalem as part of his campaign to pacify the East. He ended Maccabeean rule, aided in the establishment of HEROD's family as rulers for the Romans, and began the process of turning Judea into a Roman province. HEROD THE GREAT, assuming the legacies of his grandfather and father, became king of Judea in 37 B.C. and ruled from Jerusalem with Roman support. Pious Jews found these puppet rulers of Rome almost more hateful than the Romans even though they were of their own religion.

As we have said before, Judaism was the only monotheistic religion in the world at that time. The polytheistic worship of the Romans offended pious Jews at almost every point of contact. The Jews had rebelled against and liberated themselves from the SELEUCID rulers of Syria. The faction known as the ZEALOTS wanted to do the same against the Romans.

Distinguish among the Zealots, the Sadducees, and the Pharisees.

The SADDUCEES were the aristocratic faction who controlled the Temple worship. They were willing to cooperate with the Romans since they realized that armed opposition would result in the destruction of the Temple. The Sadducees accepted only the Five Books of Moses, the PENTATEUCH, as the law, did not accept the oral tradition, and rejected such ideas as the immortality of the soul and resurrection.

The PHARISEES, who came largely from the middle classes, believed in a strict adherence to the Torah, but were willing to supplement it with the oral tradition. They

Discuss the beliefs of the Essenes.

followed Jewish rituals to the letter and sought to practice in their daily lives the same rules of purity usually practiced only within the Temple. They believed in the immortality of the soul and resurrection. By concentrating on their religion, they hoped to minimize contact with the Romans.

The ESSENES took this idea of separation one step further by actually withdrawing from the larger society and living in separate monastic communities. An Essene community at QUMRAN has been excavated and the DEAD SEA SCROLLS, which were found beginning in 1947 in caves nearby, are assumed to have been written by this community. The Dead Sea Scrolls were written from about 150 B.C. onwards until the destruction of the community by the Romans in 68 A.D. The Essenes believed in a Teacher of Righteousness and were waiting for the messiah. It has been suggested that John the Baptist may have belonged to an Essene community at some time. There appear to be many parallels between the Essenes and early Christianity.

What were the Dead Sea Scrolls?

Who were the Samaritans?

In addition to these four factions within Judaism, the SAMARITANS and the HELLENIZED JEWS living outside Judea must also be mentioned. The Samaritans were Jews who had remained in JUDAH when the leadership had been carried off to BABYLON after the destruction of the FIRST TEMPLE (586 B.C.). When the exiles returned and built the SECOND TEMPLE, the Samaritans had opposed them. Pious Jews discriminated against the Samaritans.

Contrast the Jews of the Diaspora with the Jews within Judea.

Not all the exiles returned and a large DIASPORA COMMUNITY existed outside Judea. After Alexander the Great, these Diaspora Jews adopted Greek as their language. The Jews in the Diaspora became HELLENIZED and were in many ways more liberal than those who remained in Judea.

The Historical Jesus

The historical Jesus is difficult to assess. Saying that he was not here to break the Law but to fulfill it, he confined himself to preaching to Jews and he did not seek out Romans. Jesus offended the PHARISEES by working on the Sabbath (healing the sick), by consorting with outcasts (tax collectors and Samaritans), and by allowing himself to be touched by the unclean (women). He deliberately attacked the SADDUCEES by criticizing their stewardship of the Temple and driving the money lenders out.

It is not clear whether he thought of himself as the MESSIAH and, if he did, just what that meant to him. He clearly saw himself as more than a PROPHET, and did not prevent others from calling him the Messiah. Jesus called himself the SON OF MAN, another term that is unclear.

It is clear that many Jews in Judea during the Roman occupation were looking for a MESSIAH. What they were looking for was another DAVID who would drive out the Romans just as the original had defeated the PHILISTINES. Jesus' preaching attracted large crowds, and crowds are always feared by foreign rulers anticipating insurrections. Jesus disappointed the ZEALOTS, saying his kingdom was not of this world. But the Romans crucified him with the ironic caption "KING OF THE JEWS."

It must be noted that Julius Caesar and Augustus had temples built for them. EMPEROR WORSHIP was becoming part of the CIVIC RELIGION of the Roman Empire, but the idea that Caesar was a god was SACRILEGE to the Jews. The idea that any living man could claim to be a god or the son of a god, let alone the son of the One God, was

Who did Jesus offend?

Why were so many Jews looking for a Messiah?

renegates, anarchist jews

What did the Romans intend when they placed a sign on his cross reading "King of the Jews"?

What was the Sanhedrin?

Who was Pontius Pilate?

Who actually crucified Jesus?

How did his followers react to his death and the news of his Resurrection?

unthinkable. If Jesus made such claims, or did not publicly deny them, he was indeed guilty of violating the First Commandment under Jewish law as the highest Jewish court, the SANHEDRIN, understood it.

The fact that Jesus was not stoned to death in accord with Jewish law, but was turned over to the Romans, illustrates that the Jewish people were no longer a self-governing state. They had become a Roman province ruled by PONTIUS PILATE, the sixth Roman governor from 26 to 36 A.D. However much some of the Jews may have wanted his death, it was the Roman authorities who crucified him. The Gospels downplay the Roman guilt, in part perhaps because they were written after the break with Judaism had been made and were aimed largely at a gentile (non-Jewish) audience.

There is also that other aspect to the crucifixion. Until the last moment on the cross when he died, even his disciples expected a MIRACLE, with the Messiah smiting his enemies and inaugurating His Kingdom. They went away dejectedly when no miracle took place.

The issue is not, however, who killed Jesus. There is an inevitability to the crucifixion like in a Greek tragedy. If Christ had not been killed, if he had been pardoned and sent into exile somewhere, if he had gathered a great army and defeated Tiberius, what then?

It is only the RESURRECTION which proves the Divine nature of Christ. For those who believe that the Resurrection is a historical event, there can be no doubt about the true nature of Christ. It galvanized the APOSTLES who spread THE GOOD NEWS. Not many met the risen Christ, and many who were told the story second-hand did not believe. FAITH is the essential requirement for being a Christian.

The Acts of the Apostles

more historical than the gospels

The Acts of the Apostles follows the four Gospels in the New Testament. It tells the story of the development of the early Christian Church from about 30 A.D. to 63 A.D. Christianity began as a SECT within Judaism. All of Jesus's disciples and all of the apostles were Jewish, and most of the early converts were Jews. Christianity benefited from the fact that there was a large Jewish community outside of Judea. These Hellenized Jews became a prime target for the early missionaries.

The Hellenized form of Judaism was extremely attractive to many Greeks, particularly those familiar with Greek philosophy. Almost immediately the early Christian missionaries began to make converts from among the GENTILES. This posed the question whether gentile converts to Christianity should be required to follow all the Jewish customs, in particular CIRCUMCISION.

Saint Paul

SAUL OF TARSUS, born before 10 A.D. and educated as a Pharisee, persecuted the early Christians. He had a conversion experience about 36 A.D. while on the road to Damascus, in which the living Jesus spoke to him. Saul converted to Christianity, and as St. Paul he became, next to Christ, the most important person in the shaping of that religion. St. Paul founded many new Christian churches in the Greek-speaking eastern half of the Roman Empire. Some of the earliest Christian writings were penned by him. He wrote thirteen of the EPISTLES of the New Testament. He was the first great THEOLOGIAN of the Church, making the CHRISTOS,

What were the Acts of the Apostles?

What do the Acts tell us about the early Christians?

Give the background of Paul, the Apostle to the Gentiles.

How did Paul leave his imprint on the development of Christianity?

the Anointed One, the center of the new religion.

St. Paul was the chief advocate of the position that gentile converts did not have to become Jews. This position was ultimately accepted by the early Church. This decision transformed Christianity from a sect within Judaism into a SEPARATE RELIGION.

About 58 A.D., St. Paul was in Jerusalem. He was arrested, and after two years imprisonment invoked his right as a ROMAN CITIZEN to be tried in the Imperial city. About 63 A.D., St. Paul is under house arrest in Rome, still preaching and writing letters. At that point, the Acts of the Apostles ends abruptly. Other sources indicate that he was acquitted of the charges, went on a missionary trip to Spain, was rearrested in Rome, and was martyred during the Christian persecution under the Emperor NERO, about 67 A.D. ST. PETER, the favorite disciple of Jesus, is believed to have been killed in Rome at about the same time. St. Peter is held to have been the FIRST BISHOP OF ROME.

When did Peter and Paul die?

By the time of St. Paul's death, many Christian churches had been established in the major cities of the Roman Empire. Gentile conversion to Christianity was now possible with only minimal obligations toward Judaism. Jewish converts, however, were expected to keep their Jewish traditions.

> Destruction of the Second
> Temple in Jerusalem: 70 A.D.

What task did Nero give to Vespasian?

In 66 A.D., rebellion broke out in Judea. The general VESPASIAN was ordered by the Emperor NERO to quell it. Systematically, Vespasian set about reconquering Judea with the utmost brutality. In 68 A.D., Nero committed suicide and a struggle for power ensued. Vespasian was proclaimed emperor by his troops in 69 A.D. after several other candidates had failed. Once he had secured his position, he left his son TITUS to complete the conquest of Jerusalem. The Temple was taken in 70 A.D. after bitter fighting. Temple worship and the central authority which the High Priest had exercised over all Jews came to an end.

Jerusalem, which had also been the center of the early Christians, was a burnt city. The destruction of the Second Temple produced a major crisis for Judaism. Judea, though conquered, still seethed and guerrilla warfare continued in the hills. MASADA held out till 73 A.D. A final, futile Jewish uprising against the Romans took place from 132 to 135 A.D. under BAR KOCHBA. Emperor HADRIAN took drastic measures to bring it to an end.

In the aftermath of these events, Judaism turned inward. Under the leadership of the rabbis, Judaism became the religion which it is today. Christianity, on the other hand, became ever more universal and embraced the gentile world of the Romans and Greeks.

Under what circumstances was the Second Temple destroyed?

How did this affect Judaism?

Formation of the Early Christian Church

The earliest Christians seem to have met in private homes. They expected the SECOND COMING to be imminent. There was no need to worry about tomorrow because the KINGDOM OF GOD was at hand and the Lord would provide. Property may have been held in common in these earliest of Churches. The faithful prayed, shared the common meal, and aided one another.

The organizational structure of the early Church, if any, is unclear. Obviously, the TWELVE APOSTLES had immense standing in the early Church. Anyone who had been with Jesus, including his family, and

Do you think the early Christians were closer to one another than today's Christians?

Describe the organizational structure as it evolved in the early Christian Church.

who could tell some story about the Master would have found an eager audience. There were also 72 wandering MINISTERS sent out by Jesus (Luke 10:1), EVANGELISTS like Philip (Acts 8:5), and CHARISMATIC PROPHETS (Acts 11:27). When the Church began, it was centered on Jerusalem, but it spread rapidly throughout the Mediterranean.

Acts 6:1-6 reports on the selection of seven OVERSEERS, who would take care of the distribution of food to the widows and orphans while the apostles continued to preach. In 1Timothy 3:1-13, St. Paul describes the characteristics required of OVERSEERS and DEACONS. 1Peter 5:1-4 calls upon the ELDERS of the Church to be shepherds to their flock, serving as overseers but not lording it over their congregations.

Overseers gradually became BISHOPS. Elders became PRESBYTERS and later PRIESTS. CLERGY came to be distinguished from LAITY. Deacons served an intermediary function between the two. Slowly bishops began to exercise greater control. They claimed their authority derived not from their congregations, but through the laying on of hands by other bishops who were successors to the Apostles (APOSTOLIC SUCCESSION). A definite body of official, or ORTHODOX, doctrine and practice developed. Those who deviated from orthodoxy came to be called HERETICS.

What is Apostolic Succession?

What are heretics?

One of the earliest HERESIES appears to have been the GNOSTIC heresy. Gnostics challenged not only orthodox beliefs, claiming to have a secret knowledge taught by Christ, but they also challenged the growing hierarchical structure of the Church.

Give an example of an early heresy.

By the third century, the Christian Church had become well organized, with a definite doctrine, and a sizable membership. Despite persecutions, it could not be eradicated.

The Autocracy: 284 to 395

With the failure of the Principate and the anarchy of the Third Century, a new basis for the Roman Empire had to be found if it was to survive at all. Part of that restructuring required a new religious basis. The mystique of the divine Emperor could not be upheld with every general murdering his rival and proclaiming himself ruler. The old mythologies on which the polytheistic religions of the Greeks and Romans had depended were losing their credibility. Greek philosophy had undermined traditional religion among the educated. The turmoil of the Third Century was driving the masses to seek new answers.

A variety of MYSTERY RELIGIONS were coming out of Egypt, Syria, and Greece. The Eleusian mysteries, the cults of Dionysus, Orpheus, Isis, Serapis, and Mithra all made their way to Rome. In all these cults, there is a mystical union with the god and a promise of immortality. Some have suggested that Christianity could also be considered a mystery religion.

The Emperor Decius (249 to 251) sought to destroy these mystery religions. He launched the first empire-wide persecutions of the Christians. His effort failed because his tenure in office was too short. The Emperor Aurelian (270 to 274) considered seriously making the Cult of Mithra the official religion of the Roman Empire. Mithraism is derived from Persian Zoroastrianism and postulated a dualistic struggle between the forces of good and evil. Mithra, the Invincible Sun, led the forces of Good. Mithraism was particularly popular within the military. The Emperor Constantine (306 to 337) took the fateful step of first legalizing Christianity in 313 and then actively favoring it. During the course of the

Why were Roman emperors more willing to consider new religions?

What were the mystery religions?

Why do you suppose the Emperor Decius persecuted the Christians?

Who first legalized Christianity?

Who was Diocletian?

Autocracy, Christianity became the official religion of the Roman Empire. That decision produced a total transformation of values. As paganism died, so did the classical world of Greco-Roman civilization. A new Christian world of the Middle Ages began to take shape.

Diocletian: 284 to 305

How was the tetrachy supposed to work?

Rome has decision to make defend the western part attack by Germans or constrict the Empire

DIOCLETIAN is considered the founder of the AUTOCRACY. Diocletian was a general who restored order not only through force of arms, but also through a far-reaching reorganization of the Empire, dividing it into an Eastern and a Western half. He ruled the Eastern half as AUGUSTUS and appointed a colleague as CO-AUGUSTUS in the West. Each half was further split into two so that there were four PREFECTURES. Each Augustus had a subordinate who was given the title of CAESAR. Note that "augustus" and "caesar" had become titles rather than names of a person. These four generals formed what has been called the TETRACHY.

Diocletian hoped that this system had solved the succession problem. The plan was that whenever an augustus died, his caesar would move up to augustus and appoint a new caesar. When the senior augustus died, his co-augustus would assume the leadership.

As long as Diocletian was in control, this system worked and there was no doubt as to who was in charge. With four generals fighting under Diocletian's direction to restore order, the Empire revived.

Distinguish between prefectures and dioceses.

Diocletian further divided the four prefectures into smaller DIOCESES, which replaced the earlier provinces. He increased the military from about 300,000 during the principate to 500,000 soldiers, while seeking to counteract the economic burden which this entailed by increasing economic regulations. Every person was frozen into the occupation of his father. Farmers were forced to stay on the land. In many ways these rules formed the basis of serfdom, which developed during the Middle Ages. The magistrates of the cities, the so-called CURIALES, were also frozen in their positions. They became little more than extractors of taxes. Cities lost most of their administrative independence and civic pride. This regimentation of society, that is the AUTOCRATIC SYSTEM created by Diocletian, restored some stability but at the very high price of individual freedom.

It should be noted that Diocletian had picked the Eastern half of the empire to rule personally. This, too, was a permanent readjustment. The center of power of the Empire shifted from the West back to the East, as if civilization was contracting to its origins. The East was more populous, more prosperous, and easier to defend. Rome ceased to be the capital of the Roman Empire.

In 305, Diocletian appeared to have had a mental breakdown. He gave up his position, forced his co-augustus to step down, and retired to a magnificent palace which he had built near modern-day Split in Croatia. There he lived out the rest of his days until his death in 313, refusing to play a role in the civil wars which his resignation had caused.

The tetrachy broke down as soon as Diocletian retired. A free-for-all ensued among the remaining generals, until CONSTANTINE, the son of one of Diocletian's caesars, emerged supreme in 324.

> ### Constantine: 306 to 337

Constantine began his struggle for power in 306, when his father, who was by then the augustus of the West, died. During

Describe the economic reforms instituted by Diocletian.

Do you think they were a good idea? Explain.

Why do you think Diocletian's reformed system has been call the Autocracy?

Evaluate the effectiveness of the system.

What was the Edict of Milan?

Why did Constantine want the Council of Nicaea?

What was decided at the Council of Nicaea?

Why do you think Diocletian and Constantine preferred to rule from the East?

his climb to power, Constantine sought the support of Christians and their God. In 312, he won an important battle against his rival with the sign of the cross on his banner. Constantine became the champion of Christianity and gradually moved toward making Christianity the official religion of the Empire. He issued the EDICT OF MILAN in 313, which granted official status to the Christian churches for the first time.

In 325, Constantine presided over the first general meeting of all the major Christian churches to insure unity with the religion that he wished to use as a source of strength for his restructured Empire. This COUNCIL OF NICAEA was convened to resolve a division within the Christian churches regarding the relationship between God the Father and God the Son, that is the nature of the TRINITY. The ARIANS held that since logically a father is prior in time to his son, so God the Father must have existed prior to God the Son. The orthodox position held that both are one, and have existed together forever. There is no priority or superiority between them.

The Council of Nicaea declared Arianism to be a heresy, and developed a creed on the official meaning of the Trinity. Acceptance of the NICENE CREED on the Trinity has ever since been the standard for defining a non-heretical or orthodox Christian. The Nicene Creed declared that God the Father, God the Son, and God the Holy Spirit are co-equal and co-eternal.

Constantine followed Diocletian's pattern of ruling from the East. He founded a new capital city at the site of the Greek city of Byzantium. He named this new capital after himself, CONSTANTINOPLE. Strategically located at the entrance to the Black Sea, Constantinople straddles the narrows that separate the continents of Europe and Asia. The center of the city is located on the Asiatic side. Constantinople flourished as the capital city of the Roman Empire, the Eastern Roman Empire, and the Byzantine Empire until 1453, when it was conquered by the Ottoman Turks. Constantine had chosen a superb location for his new Capital City, his Second Rome.

Constantine was also able to repulse an attack by the Goths, reorganize the army into stationary frontier guards backed up by more mobile forces, revalue the currency to prevent further inflation, and strengthen the central bureaucracy. Constantine began the building of the HAGIA SOPHIA (Holy Wisdom) Church, one of mankind's greatest architectural achievements. Repeatedly rebuilt, the Church became the symbol of the new Christian Empire. Constantine died in 337 at the age of about 57.

Was Constantinople a good choice for an eastern capital? Explain.

Constantius II: 337 to 361

Constantius II, the third son of Constantine, ruled together with his brothers, until, by 350, he emerged as sole ruler. The three brothers had continued to favor Christianity, however in its Arian form. In 360, Constantius II was challenged by his cousin, Julian the Apostate. Constantius II died while preparing to wage war against Julian.

What was the attitude toward Christianity of the emperors who followed Constantine?

Julian the Apostate: 360 to 363

Julian is called the Apostate because, while baptized as a Christian, he reverted back to paganism. The last Roman Emperor who was a pagan, he rescinded the privileges which his predecessors had granted to Christian churches. Julian sought to reform paganism and restore its vitality. While gaining the approval of a few romantic admirers of classical literature, the effort generally failed.

Discuss the return of the barracks emperors.

Whether his policies would ultimately have led to a major wave of Christian persecution remains speculation because he died in 363 while campaigning against the Persians. He was the last member of the family of Constantine.

The Return of Barracks Emperors

With the death of Julian, the army once again picked the emperors. First, they chose JOVIAN (363 to 364), who made peace with the Persians and surrendered the territory won from them by Diocletian. He died the following year. Then, the army chose Valentinian and his younger brother Valens. VALENTINIAN I (364 to 375) ruled in the West and VALENS (364 to 378) ruled in the East.

In 376, the Germanic tribe of the Visigoths crossed the Danube in force. Individual tribesmen, adding up to tens of thousands, had settled in the Empire before, but never had a whole tribal army succeeded in crossing the frontier. In 378, this army defeated Valens and his legions at the Battle of ADRIANOPLE. The emperor was killed.

What made the migration of the Visigoths especially threatening?

In the West, GRATIAN (375 to 383) succeeded his father Valentinian I, and also his uncle, Valens, in the East for a year. In 379, Gratian appointed the general THEODOSIUS to assume command in the East and to halt the advancing Goths. In 383, Gratian died and was succeeded by his younger brother VALENTINIAN II (383 to 392) as Emperor in the West. When Valentinian II died, Theodosius became sole ruler.

Theodosius I The Great: 379 to 395

Theodosius, the last Roman Emperor to rule a united Roman Empire, started as ruler of the East after the debacle of Adrianople. He made peace with the Goths by granting them land and allowing them to serve *en masse* in the army. With his people split in half between Arianism and orthodoxy, Theodosius convened the second Ecumenical Council, the first Council of Constantinople, to deal again with the issue of Arianism. He found a formula that persuaded most of the Arians to accept orthodoxy. In 380, Theodosius ordered all pagans to become Christians, and in 392, he forbade all sacrifices in honor of the old gods.

Despite the obvious services which Theodosius had rendered toward the victory of orthodox Christianity, he ran afoul of ST. AMBROSE (c.340-397), bishop of Milan. After Theodosius had ordered a massacre of a large number of persons in Thessalonica because they had rioted, Ambrose excommunicated the Emperor and forced him to do penance before readmitting him into the Christian community. This was the first time that the Church asserted its primacy over the state.

From 392 to 395, Theodosius was the sole ruler of the Empire. Upon his death, he left two young children as his heirs. The older boy Arcadius became the Eastern Roman Emperor and the younger son Honorius became Western Roman Emperor. What had begun as a sharing of power became in fact a division of the empire. Never again would both parts of the empire be under the jurisdiction of one person.

The Western Roman Empire and the Germanic Invasions: 395 to 476

Germanic tribes had been living on the borders of the Roman empire for centuries

Examine the accomplishments of Theodosius the Great.

What problems did he have with Ambrose, Bishop of Milan?

How were these problems resolved?

Describe the contacts between Germans and Romans before 376 A.D.

dating back to the beginning of the Principate. As the Romans expanded further east into the European plain after their conquest of Gaul, they encountered the Germans. The Emperor Augustus had expanded the frontier to the Rhine and Danube. In 9 B.C., three Roman legions were destroyed by German forces in the Teutoburg Forest. After that defeat, Augustus gave up the effort to bring the Germanic tribes into the Roman Empire. Four centuries later, many Germanic peoples had been Romanized. Their warriors had been accepted into the Roman legions. Indeed, most Roman forces were made up of provincials and border folk.

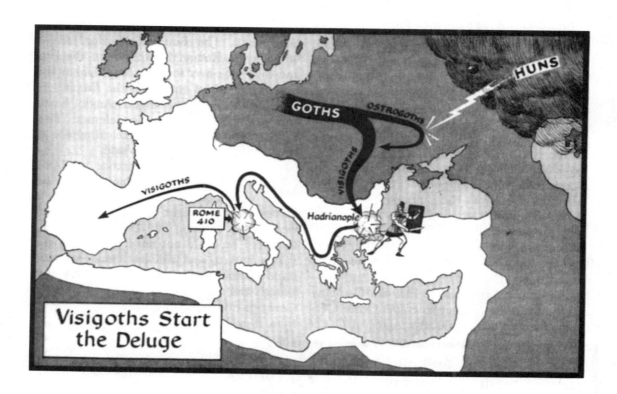

Visigoths Start the Deluge

When the VISIGOTHS crossed the Danube in 376 and defeated Valens at Adrianople in 378, the final chapter in the relationship between Romans and Germans had begun. It opened the period of the Germanic invasions and the collapse of the Roman Empire in the West.

Historians are divided on the question whether these were invasions or migrations of peoples. The term VOELKERWANDERUNG is used by many to describe these events. The Germanic peoples were themselves being attacked by the HUNS, a Mongolian people who were nomadic raiders. The greatest leader of the Huns was ATTILA. Between 434 and his death in 453, Attila collected tribute and raided large parts of the Empire. The Germanic tribes actually cooperated with the Romans against the Huns. It was this general upheaval and resettling of peoples, the destruction of cities, the decline of commerce, depopulation in many areas, and a lowering of cultural levels generally, which brought Roman administration to an end.

We shall not treat in detail the various tribes and their leaders. But a few highlights need to be presented. The Visigoths, Ostrogoths, Lombards, Vandals, Franks, Angles, Saxons, and Jutes all settled in different parts of the Western Roman Empire. Between 395 and 476, the Emperors, who supposedly ruled in the West, were weak and ineffective. The last of them, a twelve-year old boy ironically named ROMULUS AUGUSTULUS, was unceremoniously booted out of office by the Germanic chief ODOACER in 476. Let us take a look at these different tribes.

The Visigothic Kingdom of Spain

The Visigoths were the western branch of the great Germanic tribe of the GOTHS. It

What was the effect of the German invasions or migrations upon the Roman Empire?

What role did the Huns play?

Who were Romulus Augustulus and Odoacer?

Recount the journeys of the Visigoths.

How does St. Augustine defend the reputation of the God of the Christians in the *City of God?*

What was the ultimate fate of the Visigothic Kingdom in Spain?

was they who first invaded the Roman Empire in strength. After their victory at Adrianople, they signed a peace treaty and became allies under Theodosius. After 395, they moved West under their leader ALARIC. In 410, Alaric and his Visigoths sacked Rome, the first time that Rome had fallen to a conqueror in almost 800 years. The taking of Rome sent shock waves throughout the empire, but was not enough to rally the Romans. Many pagans blamed the Christians for the fall. While the pagan gods had protected Rome, the Christian God did not. ST. AUGUSTINE, bishop of Hippo in North Africa, was stimulated to write his greatest work, *The City of God*. In it, he argued that Christians need not worry about the fall of Rome. All earthly cities are temporary and will all fall. Only the heavenly City of God is eternal. Christians should focus on the Heavenly City, that shining city on a hill, which is forever. This was hardly a call to arms for the defense of the Empire.

After Rome, the Visigoths moved to Aquitaine in southwestern France and later expanded into Spain. After the Franks pushed them out of Aquitaine, the Visigoths established an important Germanic Kingdom in Spain. The Visigothic Kingdom lasted to 711, when it was conquered by the Muslims.

The Ostrogothic Kingdom of Italy

The Ostrogoths or Eastern Goths had fallen under the domination of the Huns. After the death of Attila and the rapid collapse of the Huns' dominions thereafter, the Ostrogoths rallied and produced their greatest leader, THEODORIC THE GREAT.

Theodoric, born about 455, succeeded his father Theodemir as king of the Goths in 471. He settled his followers in modern-day Bulgaria. In 488, the Eastern Roman Emperor

Zeno encouraged Theodoric to move West to drive out Odoacer. Theodoric was successful, murdered Odoacer at a banquet, and established an Ostrogothic Kingdom in Italy, which he ruled from 493 until his death in 526.

Theodoric had been raised as a child in Constantinople and was appreciative of the fact that the Romans had much to teach to semi-barbarians like his own people. Theodoric hoped to merge the military vigor of the Goths with the administrative talents of the Romans to forge a new society. He utilized Romans in his administration. His efforts to reconcile conquerors with the conquered proved difficult because there was a religious gulf. The Goths were Arian Christians, whereas the Italians were orthodox, that is Roman Catholics.

Theodosius was succeeded by his daughter and her husband. The daughter, Amalasuntha, was an ally of the Eastern Roman Emperor Justinian. When her husband, Theodahad, murdered her in 535, the Emperor Justinian launched an invasion of Italy.

Who was Theodoric the Great and what were his achievements?

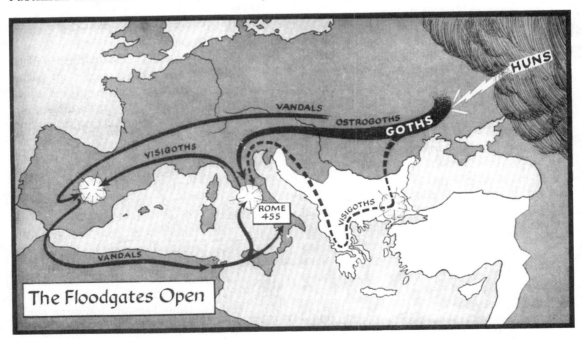

The Floodgates Open

Describe the exploits of the Vandals.

The Vandal Kingdom of North Africa

The Vandals were a relatively small Germanic tribe. It is estimated that their warriors numbered no more than 20,000. They were pushed by the advancing Huns to cross the Rhine and invade Roman Gaul in December 406. By 409, they had reached Spain. They produced a great leader, GAISERIC, who became king in 428.

Gaiseric took the tribe from Spain across the Strait of Gibraltar to North Africa in 429. By 439, he had conquered Carthage, the most important Roman city. Gaiseric dominated North Africa, built a significant fleet, and in 455 used it to plunder Rome. The looting done at that time gave the tribe its Roman name, Vandals. In the English language, to vandalize remains as a verb meaning to trash or destroy something without reason. An effort by the Eastern Roman Emperor Leo I to destroy the Vandals in 468 failed. Gaiseric finally died in 477.

It is illustrative of the weakness of the Roman Empire that such a small tribe could migrate at will throughout Roman lands from the Rhine to Tunisia. In the days of Augustus such a tribe would have been eradicated.

Gaiseric's heirs ruled until 534, when the Vandal Kingdom was destroyed by Belisarius in the service of the Emperor Justinian. Roman rule over North Africa was ended by the Muslims of the Umayyad period, who conquered Tunisia in 670 and reached the Strait of Gibraltar by 750.

What do these raids tell us about the state of the Roman Empire?

The Angles, Saxons, and Jutes

The Romans abandoned Britain in 410 when they withdrew their legions because they were needed on the continent. The Angles,

Saxons, and Jutes invaded the island during the second half of the fifth century. Gradually driving the romanized Celtic population towards Wales and Cornwall, they established small kingdoms in Mercia, Northumbria, and Wessex from the seventh through eleventh centuries. They were Christianized at the end of the sixth century when St. Augustine of Canterbury became the first archbishop. The history of England will be discussed in detail in the following chapters.

Why did the Angles, the Saxons, and the Jutes find the invasion of Britain to be so easy?

The Frankish Kingdom

Of all the Germanic peoples, the Franks did the least migrating. They simply moved across to the other side of the Rhine river near the city of MAINZ and expanded from there. Some of the clans were allies of the Romans during the fourth century. The Merovingian leader CLOVIS (481 to 511) conquered most of Roman Gaul. About 496, Clovis converted to Catholic Christianity, which gained him the support of the bishops in Gaul. Clovis and the Franks are discussed in more detail in the next section.

Who Christianized England?

The Papacy, Monasticism, and the Formation of Western Civilization

We have discussed the growth of Christianity during its first three centuries and its establishment as the official religion of the Roman Empire during the fourth. This triumph was linked to the establishment of an effective Church organization, which adopted the diocesan pattern of the Autocracy. Each diocese was headed by a bishop, who exer-

Where did the Merovingian King Clovis focus his efforts?

Who were the patriarchs?

What did St. Jerome do for the Western church?

Some argue that the Catholic Church was the true inheritor of the Roman Empire in the West. Do you agree or disagree? Why?

cised not only spiritual but also increasingly secular authority. The bishops in the major cities of the Empire exercised some spiritual authority over the bishops in provincial cities. By the sixth century, the bishops in five major cities were recognized as having the superior status of patriarchs. The five patriarchates were Rome, Constantinople, Alexandria, Antioch, and Jerusalem.

Christianity had spread from Jerusalem to Antioch and Alexandria, then to Rome, and last to Constantinople after it became the capital of the Empire under Constantine. Four of these major cities were located in the East. Only Rome was in the West.

The early Christian Church conducted its services in Greek, even in Rome. It is not clear when the Latin Rite of the Mass developed. It is clear that the Bible was first translated into Latin by St. Jerome about 380. Called the *Vulgate*, it became the official Bible for the Church in the West.

With the collapse of the Roman Empire in the West, the bishops assumed many functions previously performed by the government. Of all the bishops' seats in the West, that of Rome has the greatest historical and religious significance. When the Emperors moved their Western capital from Rome to Milan in 305, the bishops of Rome filled the vacuum of power. The Germanic invasions and the end of the Empire further increased the significance of the Bishop of Rome. These bishops had assumed the title pontiff or pope. The pontifex maximus had once been the head of the Roman state religion.

Even during the period of the Autocracy, Christianity was dividing, along with the Empire, into an Eastern Orthodox Christianity and a Western Catholic Christianity. The East spoke Greek and the West used Latin in the Mass. While the earliest Church Councils had been called by the Emperor and had been presided over by him, both the Patriarch of Constantinople and the Pope of Rome were asserting spiritual supremacy.

The Papacy

We need not trace the rise of the papacy historically. It suffices to say that from at least 500 to 1500, the Roman popes were the spiritual leaders of Latin Christendom. For Roman Catholics, the pope remains the head of their Church. Orthodox Christians and Protestant Christians do not accept the claim that the pope is the head of the Christian Church.

The pope's claim is based on the DOCTRINE OF PETRINE SUCCESSION. Jesus said to his favorite disciple Peter that "upon this rock I will build my Church."[2] This is one of the few word plays in the New Testament. Peter is a name, but "petra" means "rock" in Latin. Peter is held to have been the founder of the Christian community in Rome and its first bishop. All subsequent bishops of Rome, according to the DOCTRINE OF APOSTOLIC SUCCESSION, have been invested by the previous bishop. Thus there is held to be a direct line of bishops from Jesus to Peter to the current incumbent, Pope John Paul II. The pope is the VICAR OF CHRIST. When speaking on matters of faith and doctrine, the pope is infallible according to Catholic Church doctrine.

There have been many great popes. POPE LEO I, pope from 440 to 461, is credited with having persuaded Attila the Hun in 452 to turn away from Rome without destroying it. He was less successful with Gaiseric the Vandal, who sacked Rome in 455. Leo asserted forcefully the primary position of the papacy.

What is the papacy?

Explain the basis of papal claims to ecclesiastical supremacy.

Was Leo I a strong pope? Explain.

How did Pope Gregory I increase the prestige of the papacy?

POPE GREGORY I, pope from 590 to 604, was the first pope to gain this office after having been a monk. He came from a rich patrician family and was relatively cultured for his day. The Gregorian Chant of church music is named after him. He dispatched monks to England to try to convert the Anglo-Saxons. St. Augustine of Canterbury was one of the men whom he had chosen. Asserting the right of the Pope to intervene in secular matters, Gregory appointed governors of Italian cities. He was a good administrator, reorganized the estates of the Church, and actively aided the poor. He was the first to call himself the "servant of the servants of God."

At a time when most institutions were crumbling, only the Catholic Church survived. It saved the heritage of the classical world through the wreckage of the Barbarian Invasions. Strong popes helped to convert the pagan tribes to Christianity.

What motivated people to become monks?

Monasticism

Monasticism has its roots in the East, particularly in Egypt and Syria. Christian hermits isolated themselves from the world to fast and pray. Some sought to mortify the flesh in imitation of the pain Christ suffered on the cross. There is a strand of thought within Christianity that holds that only the spirit is holy and that the flesh is corrupt. The joys of this life, including sexual pleasure, are to be renounced in favor of meditation and prayer. It may be difficult in our age to understand the ASCETIC, who believes that disciplined self-denial, poverty, celibacy, solitude, silence, fasting, long vigils without sleep, and prayer are pleasing to God.

Who is the founder of Christian monasticism?

ST. ANTHONY is considered to be the father of Christian monasticism. He lived about 251 to 355 in Egypt and became a hermit. Others congregated around him, but lived in isolation from each other.

The founder of Western monasticism is considered to be ST. BENEDICT OF NURSIA, who lived from 480 to 543 and established the monastery of MONTE CASSINO. St. Benedict established a communal rule that included prayer, work, and sleep. He did not believe in the physical mortification of the flesh. The fact that productive work was included in the BENEDICTINE RULE was of tremendous significance, especially since this approved work included the copying of manuscripts. Special SCRIPTORIA were created where the monks copied not only religious text, but also much of classical literature. Without the Benedictine monasteries, it is probable that literacy would have disappeared in the West during the Dark Ages.

The monks were also instrumental in most of the missionary work designed to convert various heathen tribes. With the encouragement of the popes, the Benedictines converted the Anglo-Saxons and other Germanic tribes.

The Formation of Western Civilization

The Germanic invasions during the fifth century destroyed Roman civilization in the West. But the civilization which they destroyed had already undergone a Christian transformation. The Goths, Vandals, and Franks did not encounter the old Romans of the Republic or the Principate. Moreover, the Christian element in the form of the Roman Catholic Church not only survived, but civilized the Germanic tribes.

After the invasions ended, a new Western Civilization began to form, based on the mixture of populations: Germanic, Ro-

Who founded Christian monasticism in the West?

Why was the Benedictine Rule so important?

Erasmus and other Renaissance thinkers belittled the monks, depicting them as ignorant and lazy. Was this historically correct?

To what extent do you think the Catholic Church was a conduit for the transmission of Greco-Roman values?

man, and Celtic. Germanic customs were modified by older traditions. Both the Judeo-Christian and the Greco-Roman traditions came to impact on this new Western Civilization, which will be explained in the following chapters.

Conclusion We have followed the rise of the primitive tribes of the Latins and Sabines to the height of their power during the days of the Roman Republic and the Principate, between 200 B.C. to 200 A.D. We saw the decline during the Third Century and the transformation into a new Christian Commonwealth during the Autocracy. And then in the fifth century, primitive tribes, much like the Latins, swept into Italy and sacked Rome repeatedly. Only the Catholic Church survived in the West to civilize and Christianize the barbarians. Many of us are the heirs of those barbarians and all of us have benefited from the survival of much of the Greco-Roman heritage.

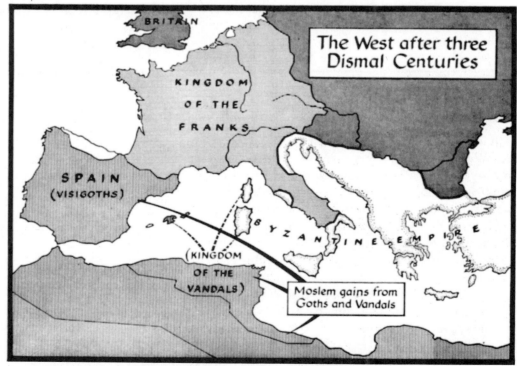

The West after three Dismal Centuries

9

The Byzantines, the Arabs, and the Franks

Just as the collapse of the Soviet Union in the late twentieth century gave rise to a number of successor nations, so also the collapse of the Roman Empire was followed by the rise of successor states. In the east, a Roman emperor continued to rule from Constantinople after the deposition of the western emperor, Romulus Augustulus, in 476 AD. Many historians speak of an Eastern Roman Empire, which came to be known as the Byzantine Empire when the predominant language of the court changed from Latin to Greek. Also in the East, we find the rise to prominence of the Arabs who were transformed and energized by a new religious faith, Islam. In the West, a number of barbarian kingdoms were formed which together comprise Medieval Europe. In the transition period, the most conspicuous kingdom was that of the Franks, which will be described here.

What states succeeded the collapse of the Western Roman Empire?

What distinguishes the Eastern Roman Empire from the Byzantine Empire?

The Byzantines

The word Byzantine is derived from Byzantium, the original name for the imperial capital of Constantinople. One of the greatest emperors to rule from Constantinople was Justinian I, the Great, who ruled from 527 to 565. This Latin-speaking Emperor, who was very conscious of the Roman heritage, sought

Contrast the reigns of Justinian and Heraclius.

With the benefit of hindsight, would you say these emperors were successes in the foreign policy arena?

to regain control of the western portions of the Roman Empire that had been lost and to maintain the eastern extremities against the Persians. He enjoyed considerable, if temporary, success with the help of his able generals, BELISARIUS (c.505-565) and NARSES (478-c.573). At the time of Justinian's death, the Eastern Roman Empire included Italy, North Africa, part of Spain, Palestine, Syria, and Asia Minor. The costs of his wars severely taxed the resources of his empire. Riots against his tax policies actually threatened his rule in 532, but the Empress Theodora helped him find the fortitude to prevail over the rioters. Theodora, who had been an actress and a prostitute, became one of his key advisors. When she died in 548, Justinian's rule lost much of its cutting edge. After his death in 565, many of his western conquests were lost. Plague and taxes left his empire exhausted.

HERACLIUS, who reigned from 610 to 641, renewed imperial vitality. Since the official language of the court had become Greek, Heraclius was truly a Byzantine emperor. He regained the provinces of Syria, Palestine, and Egypt from the Persians. Heraclius initiated the THEMES, originally army divisions that controlled lands from which peasant soldiers could be recruited. Under Heraclius's successors the themes became the backbone of civil as well as military administration.

The successes of Heraclius in Syria, Palestine, and Egypt were indeed short-lived. In 634, Muslim Arabs began an invasion of these areas. By 650 not only were these lands taken, but Persia itself fell to the Arabs. Sea power ultimately saved the Byzantine Empire from Arab conquest. While Constantinople was besieged by Arab forces for the first time in 674, the most serious siege in 717 was lifted by the forces of Emperor Leo III (717-

741). Each time, Byzantine naval superiority was a decisive factor in turning back the Arabs. The Byzantine navy used GREEK FIRE, a mixture of flammable materials such as sulfur, pitch, and quicklime. This fire, shot from ship board tubes, quickly consumed the wooden ships of the enemy.

Against the TURKS, nomadic people originally from Asia, the Byzantines were much less successful. The Seljuk Turks delivered a major blow to the Byzantines at MANZIKERT in Asia Minor in 1071. A greatly reduced Byzantium turned to Western Europe for help. The result was the Crusades, which did more to assert revived western power than to save the Byzantine Empire. In fact in 1204, during the Fourth Crusade, the Crusaders actually stormed Constantinople and established the short-lived Latin Empire of Constantinople (1204-1261). Although Greek rulers regained control of the Byzantine Empire, they were not able to completely overcome the negative effects of the Fourth Crusade. Most importantly, the Italian city states, led by Venice, established dominance in the Mediterranean Sea. Byzantine inferiority at sea was a fatal weakness. The Ottoman Turks were able to capture Constantinople in 1453 and finally extinguish the Byzantine Empire.

Byzantine Christianity

The Christian religion, a predominant factor in Byzantine civilization, developed in a different path than in the West. One reason for this was the role of the emperor. As far back as the first Christian ruler of the Roman Empire, Constantine, the emperor had played an active role in church affairs. He called the Council of Nicaea (325) to deal with the

Why was sea power important to the Byzantine Empire?

What was Greek fire?

To what extent did the Crusades help the Byzantine Empire?

What is Caesaropapism?

Who were the Iconoclasts?

What was the *filioque* controversy?

Arian controversy. The emperors in the East helped to determine the teachings of the state church and to depose patriarchs in Constantinople and elsewhere who did not meet their approval. The popes, who had turned to the Frankish kings in the mid-700s for protection, and the other clergy in the West were outside the reach of the emperor. In the East, the emperors often acted as both the political and the religious head of state. This practice of serving as both emperor and pope is called CAESAROPAPISM.

Disputes about religious dogma served to justify the existence of different political factions within Byzantium and hastened the separation of eastern and western churches. ICONOCLASM was one such dispute. The Iconoclasts insisted on breaking the images of Christ and the saints so that they might not be worshipped as false idols. Several emperors, starting with Leo III in 726, favored the Iconoclasts. The emperors were opposed by the monks and the popes. Finally in 843, the dispute was settled and the veneration of icons was permitted in both east and west.

The *FILIOQUE* (and the Son) controversy was another dispute that played a key part in splitting eastern and western churches. The creed, or statement of faith, adopted at Nicaea, speaks of the Holy Spirit proceeding "from the Father." In the West, the phrase "and the Son" was added. The difference was used by Photius (858-67, 877-86), the patriarch of Constantinople, to call a church council in 867 which condemned a supposedly heretical pope. Despite an eventual reconciliation of the churches, friction between eastern and western churches remained. The *filioque* dispute was resurrected in 1054 in a quarrel between the Patriarch Michael Cerularius (1043-58) and the reforming Pope Leo IX (1048-1054). Excommunications were issued by both sides. The result was a permanent schism between eastern (Orthodox) and western Christianity that has lasted to this day. When the churches were temporarily reunited in 1204 by Crusaders who captured and sacked Constantinople, anti-western sentiment among Orthodox adherents only hardened.

Many of the Slavic peoples, including the Russians, were converted to the Orthodox form of Christianity. Saints CYRIL (c.826-869) and METHODIUS (c.815-884), often called the Apostles to the Slavs, were Greek missionaries and brothers who translated the Bible into Slavonic, using a written alphabet they invented. Slavs who received Christianity from Constantinople have been generally less friendly to the West and to the values of Western Civilization. For example, in the Balkans, the Serbs, who are Orthodox Christians, are bitter enemies of their fellow South Slavs, the Croatians, who are Catholics.

How did the western and eastern Christian churches split apart?

The Byzantine Legacy

Constantinople left its mark on the cultures of both east and west. Justinian I not only reconquered Italy, but also caused the collection of Roman laws in the form of the *Corpus Juris Civilis* ("Body of Civil Law"), the first part of which was published in 529. This work contains (1) a Code of Law, bringing together in accessible form the accumulated law cleansed of contradictions, (2) a Digest of the writings of legal scholars, (3) the Institutes, which is a textbook for beginning students, and (4) the Novels or new laws enacted during Justinian's reign. This code not only became the basis of the Byzantine Empire's legal system, but also much of Western Europe's as well.

It was also during Justinian's reign that the Church of the Hagia Sophia (Holy

What was the *Corpus Juris Civilis*?

Does Western Civilization owe much to the Byzantine Empire? Explain.

Wisdom) was rebuilt. The church has a huge central dome 100 feet in diameter that rests on four large arches. The effect was to allow its many windows to transmit seemingly heavenly light to the interior of the much admired and imitated building. When the Turks took over in 1453, they preserved the great church as a mosque. Byzantine icons or images, usually painted on wooden panels and frequently portraying Christ, the Virgin Mary, or one of the saints, have also been influential, especially in Russia.

Western Civilization is deeply indebted to Byzantium for other things besides architecture and art. The Byzantines were not only interested in Christianity, but also in the pre-Christian Greek classics. Their love of this literature helped preserve the texts of Plato and Thucydides for our profit. The West is also indebted to the Greeks for their resistance to Islam. The fact that Constantinople did not fall until 1453, gave Western Europe time to gather resources to resist the force of Islam. The anti-Islamic crusades began at the invitation of a Byzantine emperor in 1095. In the first half of the sixteenth century, we find the Holy Roman Emperor Charles V preoccupied by the threat the Turks posed. Had Constantinople fallen along with Persia in the seventh century, this book might be exploring a very different, more Islamic, western civilization. Who is to say for sure?

Who are the Arabs?

The Arabs

independent tribal groups. in the south.

The Arabs, who began as a Semitic people like the Jews, speak Arabic as their native language. Today the Arab world includes much of North Africa and the Middle

East. Most Arabs are Muslims, adherents of Islam, which began in Arabia, a large peninsula between Africa and Asia. Arabia is separated from Jordan and Syria to the north by deserts and it borders on the Indian Ocean in the south.

Who was Muhammad?

The Life of Muhammad

The great prophet of Islam is Muhammad who was born about 570 AD in Mecca, a city in western Arabia. Muhammad's father died before his son was born and Muhammad's mother died when he was six years old. He was raised in the care of relatives. Mecca was located along a caravan route used for transporting goods from Asia to Syria and other parts of the Middle East. Muhammad became involved in this trade and became the business agent of a wealthy widow, Khadijah, whom he married when he was about twenty-five and she was forty. Muhammad appears to have spent much time fasting and praying. In 610 he received a revelation from the angel Gabriel that he was to be the Messenger of God — to recite the words of God for his people. These recitations were later collected into the holy book of Islam, the KORAN (or "Qur'an").

What were some of his ideas?

QURAN

While pagan polytheism was the predominant religious belief of Arabia, there were Christians and Jews there with whom Muhammad had come into contact. Muhammad preached a message that there was but one God, ALLAH, and Muhammad was his prophet. He warned of a judgment day and urged the Meccans to renounce false idols and to accept the bounty and compassion of the one God. The dominant Quraysh tribe rejected his message. They feared that Mecca would lose its place as a pilgrimage center where numerous gods could be worshipped in an

Did he find ready acceptance in Mecca? Explain.

What was the Hegira?

Was Muhammad's relocation to Mecca a success?

Was Muhammad anti-Meccan? Explain

ancient building known as the Kaaba. Muhammad became subject to a boycott. He was nevertheless safe as long as his uncle, Abu Talib, who was the head of the Hashim clan of the Quraysh tribe, offered him protection. But in 619 both his uncle and his wife, Khadijah, died. The new clan leader refused to grant Muhammad protection, which meant that he could be killed without fear of retaliation. In 622, Muhammad and about 70 of his followers decided to flee Mecca and go to MEDINA (originally called Yathreb), which is located about 250 miles to the north. The move is known as the HEGIRA (emigration) and is celebrated as the year one in the Muslim lunar calendar.

Muhammad had been invited to Medina to act as a peace arbitrator among the feuding tribes. Medina was a city with three Jewish clans as well as a large Arab population. Muhammad made himself the leader of the Arabs of the city and eventually eliminated the Jews (some by execution) who resisted his efforts at conversion. He began attacks on the caravans of Mecca, and this led to large-scale war. In 627, he successfully resisted a siege of Medina by a force of ten thousand Meccans. In 629, he reached a truce with the Meccan leaders and, in 630, he marched into Mecca with little bloodshed. He granted a general amnesty and made Mecca the center of worship of his new religion. When Muhammad died in 632, Islam was the religion of the greater part of the Arabian peninsula.

The Teachings of Islam

someone's vow to the word of Allah.

Islam means "surrender" and a Muslim is one who has surrendered or committed himself or herself completely to the one God ("Allah" in Arabic). There are no priests in the Islamic faith who provide the sacraments as a means to heaven, as in Christianity. The teachings of Islam are found above all in the Koran, but also in certain rules or practices ("sunna") and sayings ("hadith"). The Five Pillars summarize the duties of the individual Muslim who is required (1) to profess that there is no god but Allah and that Muhammad is the Messenger of God; (2) to pray five times daily facing Mecca and to partake in other ritual prayers; (3) to give donations to poor Muslims; (4) to fast from sunrise to sunset during Ramadan which is a month in the lunar calendar; and (5), health and wealth permitting, to make a pilgrimage ("hajj") to Mecca at least once in a lifetime.

Islam also accepts angels, lesser spirits called jinns, a day of judgment, and heaven and hell. The family is the basic nucleus of Muslim society. Women are under male protection. The Koran prescribes the veiling of adult women and permits a husband to have up to four wives, providing he treats each of them equally.

Christians and Jews are considered to be people of the Book, believers in the one, true God. They have a tolerated, if subordinate place, in Muslim societies. Such figures as Jesus and Moses are seen as prophets, but Muhammad is the final prophet, sent by Allah, whose message is for all peoples.

The Expansion of Islam

After Muhammad's death in 632, Abu Bakr (632-634) was chosen as CALIPH or successor to the Prophet. He had been an early supporter and his daughter, Aisha, had been married to Muhammad. Abu Bakr put down revolts in Arabia and led campaigns into Syria and Palestine. The next three suc-

Explain the basic teachings of Islam.

How would you compare Islam to Christianity or Judaism?

Describe the expansion of Islam.

cessors, who were also early converts and related to the Prophet by marriage, were also all assassinated. The last of these caliphs, Ali, Muhammad's first cousin and son-in-law, (656-661) died in 661. Under these rulers Egypt, Palestine, Syria, Mesopotamia, and Persia became part of the Muslim Empire. This phenomenal success is explained by several factors. The Arab tradition of raiding was now focused outside Arabia since fighting was forbidden within the House of Islam; the Byzantine and Persian Empires were both exhausted from fighting each other and less able to stop the Arab advance; and finally, in places like Egypt and Syria, heretical Christians found the followers of Islam to be more tolerant than Byzantine emperors.

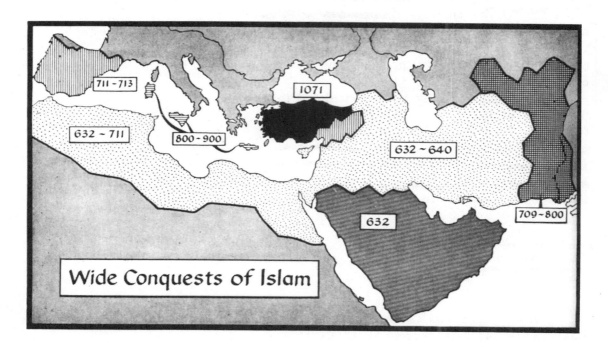

Wide Conquests of Islam

Divisions Within Islam

Distinguish between the Sunnites and the Shiites.

Ali had married Fatima, the daughter of Muhammad. When he was assassinated in 661, his place as caliph was taken by Muawiyah, a member of an old Meccan family which had originally been opposed to Islam. Muawiyah (661-680) founded a dynasty of caliphs known as the Umayyads, who ruled over the whole Islamic Empire to 750. They made Damascus, in Syria, their capital. The accession of Muawiyah led to a split or schism in Islam that continues to this day. Those who accepted the Umayyads were known as the Sunnites. They followed the Koran and the Sunna (practices) that complemented the holy book. The Shiites or partisans, on the other hand, insisted that only Ali and his descendants were legitimate caliphs. Today, approximately 90% of Muslims are Sunnites. The Shiites though are especially prominent in some areas, such as Iran, southern Iraq, and Lebanon.

In 750, a new dynasty, the Abbasids, overthrew the Umayyads, most of whom were massacred. (Umayyad rulers continued in Spain until 1031.) The Abbasids moved the capital of the empire from Damascus to Baghdad, a new city in present-day Iraq. The new regime opened up positions of power to non-Arabs. Persian influence was especially strong. The Abbasids used Seljuk Turks as soldiers in the caliph's bodyguard. Eventually (around 945) the Seljuks became the dominant force in the Baghdad caliphate. The political unity of Islam was not only broken by Umayyad Spain, but other areas, nominally a part of the Abbasid Empire, obtained practical independence. These included southern Iraq, Syria, Egypt, and Arabia. In 1258, the Mongols ended Abbasid rule in Baghdad.

Who were the Umayyads, the Abbasids, and the Seljuks?

Figure 3.2. Leaf from manuscript of Dioscorides. Mesopotamian. XIII Century. In the first century A.D., a Roman army surgeon, Pedanius Dioscorides, compiled a treatise on herbal medicine, *De Materia Medica.* Included in this manuscript was a recipe for cough medicine; the preparation of this remedy is shown here. Classical medicine was preserved and transmitted to Islamic countries. In turn, Europe learned from Islamic physicians such as Ibn Sina or Avicenna (980-1037), whose *Canon of Medicine* was translated from the Arabic in the twelfth century and remained a standard work in European medical schools until the seventeenth century. *Courtesy of The Metropolitan Museum of Art, Rogers Fund, 1913. (13.152.6)*

Arab Culture

What are some of the achievements of Arab culture?

The language of the Koran was Arabic and believers were not supposed to translate it into other languages. The Umayyads especially pushed the adoption of Arabic as the common language of the empire. The result was both religion and language were sources of Muslim unity.

While poetry had inspired the Arabs long before Muhammad, the Umayyad period is noted for the development of new forms of love lyrics and hunting poems. The ascent of the Abbasids brought in Persian influences. In the West, the best known work of Arab literature is *The Thousand and One Nights,* or the *Arabian Nights*, in which the bride Scheherazade keeps telling a woman-hating king stories to forestall the time of her execution.

beautiful architect work.
mathematics.

The Arabs adopted Indian numerals, including the zero, to serve their own needs and passed these on to the west. Such Arabic words as alcohol, algebra, cipher, and zenith have entered the vocabularies of Western languages. The Arabs eagerly adapted governance structures from the Persians and the Greeks. The philosophy of Aristotle and Plato deeply influenced the Islamic world. Medieval Europe rediscovered the work of Aristotle through the commentaries of the Spanish Muslim, Averroes (Ibn Rushd, 1126-98). Medicine, too, was another area in the Middle Ages where the Arabs were more advanced than Europeans. The *Canon of Medicine,* by the philosopher Avicenna (Ibn Sina, 980-1037), was translated from the Arabic in the twelfth century and remained a standard work in European medical schools until the seventeenth century.

Does the West owe anything to the Arabs? Explain.

Why did the popes seek the protection of the Franks?

The Franks

After Justinian's death (565), his gains in the West began to evaporate. The Arabs took over most of Spain. The Lombards, a Germanic tribe, conquered large sections of Italy. At first the popes depended on the Byzantine emperors for protection from the Lombards, but the Iconoclastic Controversy put increasing strains on the relationship between the pope in Rome and the emperor in Constantinople. Also, Byzantine might was weakening in the West. Instead, the popes found protection from a new source, the Franks, who had both military might and a friendlier disposition towards Catholic Christianity.

Clovis

Was Clovis a hero or a villain? Explain.

The Franks, who gave their name to France, were a Germanic tribe. One branch of the Franks, the Salians, had settled in northern Gaul. They were united by Clovis (481-511), who proceeded to conquer most of Gaul. Clovis was helped in his task of conquest by the support of the Gallo-Roman settlers as well as the Franks. Clovis had converted to the Catholic form of Christianity, which made him more acceptable to the old Roman population than other Germanic leaders, who had adopted the Arian form of Christianity. Clovis used his alleged distaste for Arians to justify his expansionist policy. He also systematically killed off relatives who might threaten his position on the throne.

When Clovis died, his kingdom was divided among his four sons as was traditional among the Franks who did not yet have the notion that the first born should inherit everything (PRIMOGENITURE). Clovis was the founder of a dynasty known as the MEROVINGIANS (after a previous chief, Merovech, the grandfather of Clovis). His sons bitterly fought one another, until only one, Chlotar (511-561) survived. He was temporarily able to reunite the Frankish realm, but the kingdom was once again divided among the sons of Chlotar when he died in 561. The Merovingian dynasty was to continue until 751. But there was great turmoil and weakness. Royal brother fought brother to increase his share of the patrimony, the Frankish kingdom. Many of the kings were disinterested and left the way open for the nobles and chief ministers to increase their own power.

Who were the Merovingians? What weakened their dynasty?

The Carolingians

The most important official in the Frankish kingdom, after the king, was the MAYOR OF THE PALACE. He administered the royal estates and often led the army. Just as there could be more than one king, there could also be more than one mayor of the palace. In 687, Pepin II of Heristal (680-714) defeated a rival mayor to become the only mayor of the palace for the Frankish kingdom. His son, CHARLES MARTEL (the hammer) also became mayor of the palace (714-741). He added greatly to the prestige of the family by defeating in 732 a Muslim raiding party from Spain which was attempting to reach the wealthy monastery of St. Martin of Tours in France. He also conquered Burgundy and encouraged the Christianizing of Germany. It was the son and successor of Charles, PEPIN III, THE SHORT, who was to start a new

What did Charles Martel accomplish?

Why did Pepin the Short and Pope Zacharias need each other?

What was the Donation of Pepin?

What was the Donation of Constantine?

dynasty of Frankish kings. This dynasty is known as the CAROLINGIANS in honor of Charles (*Carolus* in Latin) Martel.

Pepin the Short, who began his career as mayor of the palace in 741, had ambitions to be king. When he sent envoys to Pope Zacharias (741-752), Pepin received support for his ambitions from the pope. The envoys asked the pope whether it was good for one person to have the title of king while another actually ruled. The pope not only denounced this arrangement, but also issued a papal pronouncement deposing the last of the Merovingian kings, Children III (743-51). With papal legitimization, it was safe for Pepin to assume the throne as King of the Franks. He was crowned by St. Boniface (c.673-754) in 751 and later Pope Stephen II (752-757) reanointed Pepin as king.

Pepin, in turn, embraced a particularly pro-papal policy. He attacked and defeated the Lombards when they threatened the pope's control of Rome (754 and 756). By the DONATION OF PEPIN in 756, he gave the pope lands in central Italy. This Donation was to serve as the basis for the PAPAL STATES, an independent country which would be ruled by the popes until 1870. The rights of the popes were further enhanced by a forgery, the Donation of Constantine. This document was drawn up in the papal chancery, apparently in the second half of the eight century. The document, purported to be written by the Roman Emperor Constantine in 313, gave to the pope the imperial dignity and control of Italy and the western regions of the empire. It was not proven to be a forgery until 1440! A consequence of these events was that the popes had vastly increased their temporal authority and gained the continuing protection of the Frankish kings, ending papal reliance on the ineffectual and frequently hostile Byzantine emperors.

Charlemagne

Pepin the Short was an able ruler who established the Carolingian dynasty, crushed internal revolts, and extended royal control over Aquitaine. Yet, his accomplishments are overshadowed by those of his son, CHARLEMAGNE (Charles the Great), who ruled from 768 to 814. Charles doubled the territory under royal control by conquering the Saxons, the Lombards, the Avars, the duchy of Bavaria, Brittany, some territory south of the Pyrenees (the Spanish March), and making many Slavs on the eastern frontier into tributary peoples.

The pope, as we saw, was dependent upon the Frankish king for protection. This was even truer of Pope Leo III (795-816), who had fled a revolt in Rome and was restored to power by Charles. The king then went to Rome to bring about a permanent settlement. Charlemagne attended mass in Rome on Christmas day 800 A.D. While there, the pope, apparently without warning, placed a crown on Charles's head and proclaimed him Emperor of the Romans. In doing so, the pope was setting a dangerous precedent by arrogating to himself the power to make an emperor. Charlemagne later entered protracted negotiations with the Byzantine emperor from whom he eventually received recognition of his title. When Charlemagne's son, Louis, was crowned emperor in the presence of Charles, it was in the Frankish capital of Aachen, outside of the reach of the pope. The imperial title itself was clearly valued by Charlemagne and captured the imagination of westerners. While the imperial title fell into disuse among the Carolingians by 925, German rulers revived the use of the title in 962 and a Holy Roman Emperor continued to

Compare the achievements of Pepin the Short and Charles the Great.

Do you think Charlemagne really liked the title of Emperor? Explain.

Why was Charlemagne considered to be an effective ruler?

reign in the West until 1806, when the office ended — a victim of Napoleon's aggression.

Charlemagne was an effective ruler who strengthened administrative control and encouraged cultural development. The powers of local government were most often in the hands of counts chosen from prominent families. To make sure the counts were obeying his orders and giving justice to their people, Charlemagne instituted the practice of sending *missi dominici*, royal inspectors. These envoys were teams of two or three, and included both a clergyman and a lay lord. They traveled in particular areas to meet local officials and made reports back to the emperor.

Education was advanced by importing the monk ALCUIN OF YORK (c.735-804) from England. Alcuin established a palace school at Aachen where he gathered a group of scholars from different areas of Europe. The result was an educational system that at least served the needs of the few clergy and laity used in administering Frankish government. Later Alcuin was made abbot of St. Martin of Tours. At the scriptorium of that abbey was developed a reformed handwriting known as Carolinigian minuscule. That script provides the basis for the lowercase letters we use today.

Who was Alcuin of York?

What was Carolinigian minuscule?

There was also a revival of interest in painting and architecture. The monasteries produced illuminated portraits and geometric designs in the gospel manuscripts copied there. Charlemagne eventually established his capital at Aachen (Aix-la-Chapelle). A palace complex was built influenced by Byzantine and Roman designs. The most famous of these buildings was the palace chapel modeled after the church of San Vitale in Ravenna built by Justinian. The two-story, octagonal building, with marble columns and a central dome, was the most impressive new building in the

Europe of its day. Later scholars were sufficiently impressed with all of these cultural achievements to speak of a CAROLINGIAN RENAISSANCE. Certainly Carolingian scholarship and art outlasted the political structure established by Charlemagne.

Is the term "Carolingian Renaissance" justified? Explain.

The Breakup of the Carolingian Empire

When Charlemagne died, his empire was inherited by his son, Louis the Pious (813-840). Charles's earlier plans had called for dividing the empire, but Louis was the only surviving son at the time of his father's death in 814. Louis was unlucky enough to have three sons survive him. Compared to his father, he had a less forceful personality and tended to be overly scrupulous. The clergy and his wives (by successive marriages) often controlled him. His unruly sons took advantage of him and the empire was plunged into a series of civil wars during his reign. After his death in 840, the sons of Louis fought on until they agreed to a more permanent division of the Carolingian empire in the 843 TREATY OF VERDUN. That treaty divided the empire into three kingdoms. The west Frankish lands went to Charles the Bald (843-877); the east Frankish lands came under the rule of Louis the German (843-876); and Lothair I (843-855), who also held the title of emperor, ruled over a Middle Kingdom consisting of a swath of land from what today would be the Netherlands, by the North Sea, through the middle of the Italian peninsula below Rome. The western kingdom of Charles the Bald spoke a Romance language and formed the basis of modern France, while the eastern kingdom of Louis was German-speaking and formed a nucleus from which modern Germany developed. The two kingdoms would fight over the lands of the Middle

What were the provisions of the Treaty of Verdun? Why was it significant?

What followed the breakup of the Carolingian empire?

Kingdom, such as Alsace-Lorraine (derived from Lothair), for the next thousand plus years.

The Carolingian empire split up for several reasons. Its people had significant differences of language and custom. It required a strong personality, such as Charlemagne's, to hold it together. The feuds of his successors and the Frankish custom of dividing the inheritance among all surviving males obviously encouraged disunity. Finally, the lands of the empire had to face a new series of invaders. Magyars (Hungarians) came from the east to invade Germany, France, and Italy. Muslim invaders attacked Italy and southern France. Scandinavian Vikings or Norsemen struck many parts of Europe, establishing settlements in Ireland and England, in Normandy in France, in southern Italy, and at Kiev in the Ukraine. Out of this chaos grew new institutions described in the next section.

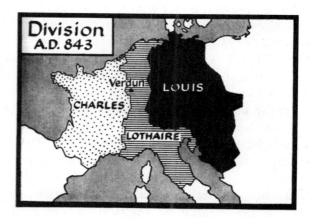

ROMAN EMPERORS[3]

Augustus	27 BC-14 AD	Alexander Severus	222-235
Tiberius	14-37	Various Emperors	235-249
Gaius (Caligula)	37-41	Decius	249-251
Claudius	41-54	Various Emperors	251-284
Nero	54-68	Diocletian	284-305
Galba	68-69	Maximian	286-305
Otho	69	and	306-308
Vitellius	69	Constantius I	305-306
Vespasian	69-79	Galerius	293-311
Titus	79-81	Constantine I	306-337
Domitian	81-96	Constantius II	337-361
Nerva	96-98	Constantine II	337-340
Trajan	98-117	Magnentius	350-353
Hadrian	117-138	Julian	361-363
Antoninus Pius	138-161	Jovian	363-364
Marcus Aurelius	161-180	Valentinian I	364-375
L. Verus	161-169	Valens	364-378
Commodus	180-192	Gratian	367-383
Pertinax	192-193	Valentinian II	375-392
Didius Julianus	193	Theodosius I	379-395
Septimius Severus	193-211		
Caracalla	211-217	Western Roman Emperors:	
Geta	211-212	Honorius	395-423
Macrinus	217-218	Various Emperors	423-475
Elagabulus	218-222	Romulus Augustulus	475-476

NOTES

[1] Joseph Ward Swain, The Ancient World, Vol. 2 The World Empires: Alexander and the Romans After 334 B.C. (New York: Harper & Brothers, 1950), p. 477.

[2] Matthew 16: 16 - 19.

[3] This select list is adapted from "Emperors of Rome," The 1997 Grolier Multimedia Encyclopedia (CD-ROM, Danbury, Ct.: Grolier Interactive, 1997) and from "The Imperial Index: The Rulers of Rome," De Imperatoribus Romanis (Internet, <http://www.salve.edu/~dimaiom/impindex.html>, 10 March 1997).

Figure 3.3. Mosaic: The Miraculous Draught of Fishes. Byzantine. Early 6th Century A.D. Developed in ancient Greece, mosaic is the art of placing small pieces of cut stone or pigmented glass in a plaster bed to effect designs. This early mosaic, illustrating a New Testament story, is found in S. Apollinare Nuovo, a church in Ravenna, Italy. Justinian I (527-565) was the Eastern emperor who carried the Byzantine style of art to the West. *Courtesy of The Metropolitan Museum of Art, Johnston Fund, 1924. (24.144.7)*

AUGUSTINE

Confessions

One of the Fathers of the early Christian church was St. Augustine. He was born in what is now Algeria in North Africa in 354. His mother, Monica, was a deeply committed Christian, but his father was a pagan. He received an excellent classical education, became a teacher of rhetoric, and eventually moved to Milan, which at the time was the capital of the Roman Empire. Augustine had a long-term mistress by whom he had a son, Adeodatus (gift of God). For nine years he was a Manichaean. This religion made a dualistic division of the world into realms of light or spirit ruled by God and of darkness ruled by Satan. The body, being material, was considered evil. He also came under the influence of Neoplatonist philosophy before embracing Christianity. Augustine was not baptized as a Christian until 387.

The passages which follow are from his *Confessions* in which he recounts his conversion struggle. He is at pains to attack the doctrine of the Manichees, at the same time admitting how the desires of the flesh held him back from embracing Christianity. Augustine felt called to take up what he considered the highest form of Christianity, which like Manichaeism, involved total chastity or continence, the complete abstinence from sexual relations. He found the will to do this in the exhortation of the Apostle Paul to "put on the Lord Jesus Christ, and make no provision for the flesh to fulfill the lusts thereof." Modern readers may find it difficult to comprehend Augustine's struggle for continence, but if they think how some alcoholics or drug users' struggling for sobriety find strength in a Higher Power, the meaning of this passage becomes clearer.

After his conversion, Augustine returned to Africa, became the Bishop of Hippo, and wrote many works of Christian theology, including *The City of God* which is discussed elsewhere in this book. He died in 430 as the Vandals were besieging Hippo.

BOOK TWO, CHAPTER I[1]

1. I wish now to review in memory my past wickedness and the carnal corruptions of my soul—not because I still love them, but that I may love thee, O my God. For love of thy love I do this, recalling in the bitterness of self-examination my wicked ways, that thou mayest grow sweet to me, thou sweetness without deception! Thou sweetness happy and assured! Thus thou mayest gather me up out of those fragments in

[1] From Augustine, *Confessions*, trans. by Albert C. Outler (1955, Internet, <http://www.fortnet.org:80/~ftp/pub/religion/Early_Church/fathers/augustine/confessions/confessions.html>, 27 February 1997).

which I was torn to pieces, while I turned away from thee, O Unity, and lost myself among "the many."[1] For as I became a youth, I longed to be satisfied with worldly things, and I dared to grow wild in a succession of various and shadowy loves. My form wasted away, and I became corrupt in thy eyes, yet I was still pleasing to my own eyes—and eager to please the eyes of men.

CHAPTER II

2. But what was it that delighted me save to love and to be loved? Still I did not keep the moderate way of the love of mind to mind—the bright path of friendship. Instead, the mists of passion steamed up out of the puddly concupiscence of the flesh, and the hot imagination of puberty, and they so obscured and overcast my heart that I was unable to distinguish pure affection from unholy desire. Both boiled confusedly within me, and dragged my unstable youth down over the cliffs of unchaste desires and plunged me into a gulf of infamy. Thy anger had come upon me, and I knew it not. I had been deafened by the clanking of the chains of my mortality, the punishment for my soul's pride, and I wandered farther from thee, and thou didst permit me to do so. I was tossed to and fro, and wasted, and poured out, and I boiled over in my fornications—and yet thou didst hold thy peace, O my tardy Joy! Thou didst still hold thy peace, and I wandered still farther from thee into more and yet more barren fields of sorrow, in proud dejection and restless lassitude.

3. If only there had been someone to regulate my disorder and turn to my profit the fleeting beauties of the things around me, and to fix a bound to their sweetness, so that the tides of my youth might have spent themselves upon the shore of marriage! Then they might have been tranquilized and satisfied with having children, as thy law prescribes, O Lord—O thou who dost form the offspring of our death and art able also with a tender hand to blunt the thorns which were excluded from thy paradise![2] For thy omnipotence is not far from us even when we are far from thee. Now, on the other hand, I might have given more vigilant heed to the voice from the clouds: "Nevertheless, such shall have trouble in the flesh, but I spare you,"[3] and, "It is good for a man not to touch a woman,"[4] and, "He that is unmarried cares for the things that belong to the Lord, how he may please the Lord; but he that is married cares for the things that are of the world, how he may please his wife."[5] I should have listened more attentively to these words, and, thus having been "made a eunuch for the Kingdom of Heaven's sake,"[6] I would have with greater happiness expected thy embraces.

---

[1] Yet another Plotinian phrase; cf. *Enneads*, I, 6, 9:1-2. [This and subsequent footnotes are by the translator, Albert C. Outler.]

[2] Cf. Gen. 3:18 and *De bono conjugali*, 8-9, 39-35 (*N-PNF*, III, 396-413).

[3] 1 Cor. 7:28.

[4] 1 Cor. 7:1.

[5] 1 Cor. 7:32, 33.

[6] Cf. Matt. 19:12.

4. But, fool that I was, I foamed in my wickedness as the sea and, forsaking thee, followed the rushing of my own tide, and burst out of all thy bounds. But I did not escape thy scourges. For what mortal can do so? Thou wast always by me, mercifully angry and flavoring all my unlawful pleasures with bitter discontent, in order that I might seek pleasures free from discontent. But where could I find such pleasure save in thee, O Lord—save in thee, who dost teach us by sorrow, who woundest us to heal us, and dost kill us that we may not die apart from thee. Where was I, and how far was I exiled from the delights of thy house, in that sixteenth year of the age of my flesh, when the madness of lust held full sway in me—that madness which grants indulgence to human shamelessness, even though it is forbidden by thy laws—and I gave myself entirely to it?

BOOK EIGHT, CHAPTER I

1. O my God, let me remember with gratitude and confess to thee thy mercies toward me. Let my bones be bathed in thy love, and let them say: "Lord, who is like unto thee?[1] Thou hast broken my bonds in sunder, I will offer unto thee the sacrifice of thanksgiving."[2] And how thou didst break them I will declare, and all who worship thee shall say, when they hear these things: "Blessed be the Lord in heaven and earth, great and wonderful is his name."[3]

Thy words had stuck fast in my breast, and I was hedged round about by thee on every side. Of thy eternal life I was now certain, although I had seen it "through a glass darkly."[4] And I had been relieved of all doubt that there is an incorruptible substance and that it is the source of every other substance. Nor did I any longer crave greater certainty about thee, but rather greater steadfastness in thee.

But as for my temporal life, everything was uncertain, and my heart had to be purged of the old leaven. "The Way"—the Saviour himself—pleased me well, but as yet I was reluctant to pass through the strait gate.

And thou didst put it into my mind, and it seemed good in my own sight, to go to Simplicianus, who appeared to me a faithful servant of thine, and thy grace shone forth in him. I had also been told that from his youth up he had lived in entire devotion to thee. He was already an old man, and because of his great age, which he had passed in such a zealous discipleship in thy way, he appeared to me likely to have gained much wisdom—and, indeed, he had. From all his experience, I desired him to tell me—setting before him all my agitations—which would be the most fitting way for one who felt as I did to walk in thy way.

2. For I saw the Church full; and one man was going this way and another that. Still, I could not

[1] Ps. 35:10.
[2] Cf. Ps. 116:16, 17.

[3] Cf. Ps. 8:1.
[4] 1 Cor. 13:12.

be satisfied with the life I was living in the world. Now, indeed, my passions had ceased to excite me as of old with hopes of honor and wealth, and it was a grievous burden to go on in such servitude. For, compared with thy sweetness and the beauty of thy house—which I loved—those things delighted me no longer. But I was still tightly bound by the love of women; nor did the apostle forbid me to marry, although he exhorted me to something better, wishing earnestly that all men were as he himself was.

But I was weak and chose the easier way, and for this single reason my whole life was one of inner turbulence and listless indecision, because from so many influences I was compelled—even though unwilling—to agree to a married life which bound me hand and foot. I had heard from the mouth of Truth that "there are eunuchs who have made themselves eunuchs for the Kingdom of Heaven's sake"[1] but, said he, "He that is able to receive it, let him receive it." Of a certainty, all men are vain who do not have the knowledge of God, or have not been able, from the good things that are seen, to find him who is good. But I was no longer fettered in that vanity. I had surmounted it, and from the united testimony of thy whole creation had found thee, our Creator, and thy Word—God with thee, and together with thee and the Holy Spirit, one God—by whom thou hast created all things. There is still another sort of wicked men, who "when they knew God, they glorified him

[1]Matt. 19:12.

not as God, neither were thankful."[2] Into this also I had fallen, but thy right hand held me up and bore me away, and thou didst place me where I might recover. For thou hast said to men, "Behold the fear of the Lord, this is wisdom,"[3] and, "Be not wise in your own eyes,"[4] because "they that profess themselves to be wise become fools."[5] But I had now found the goodly pearl; and I ought to have sold all that I had and bought it—yet I hesitated.

CHAPTER VI

14. On a certain day, then, when Nebridius was away—for some reason I cannot remember—there came to visit Alypius and me at our house one Ponticianus, a fellow countryman of ours from Africa, who held high office in the emperor's court. What he wanted with us I do not know; but we sat down to talk together, and it chanced that he noticed a book on a game table before us. He took it up, opened it, and, contrary to his expectation, found it to be the apostle Paul, for he imagined that it was one of my wearisome rhetoric textbooks. At this, he looked up at me with a smile and expressed his delight and wonder that he had so unexpectedly found this book and only this one, lying before my eyes; for he was indeed a Christian and a faithful one at that, and often he prostrated himself before thee, our God, in the church in constant daily prayer.

[2]Rom. 1:21.
[3]Job 28:28.
[4]Prov. 3:7.
[5]Rom. 1:22.

When I had told him that I had given much attention to these writings, a conversation followed in which he spoke of Anthony, the Egyptian monk, whose name was in high repute among thy servants, although up to that time not familiar to me. When he learned this, he lingered on the topic, giving us an account of this eminent man, and marveling at our ignorance. We in turn were amazed to hear of thy wonderful works so fully manifested in recent times—almost in our own—occurring in the true faith and the Catholic Church. We all wondered—we, that these things were so great, and he, that we had never heard of them.

15. From this, his conversation turned to the multitudes in the monasteries and their manners so fragrant to thee, and to the teeming solitudes of the wilderness, of which we knew nothing at all. There was even a monastery at Milan, outside the city's walls, full of good brothers under the fostering care of Ambrose—and we were ignorant of it. He went on with his story, and we listened intently and in silence. He then told us how, on a certain afternoon, at Trier,[1] when the emperor was occupied watching the gladiatorial games, he and three comrades went out for a walk in the gardens close to the city walls. There, as they chanced to walk two by two, one strolled away with him, while the other two went on by themselves. As they rambled, these first two came upon a certain cottage where

lived some of thy servants, some of the "poor in spirit" ("of such is the Kingdom of Heaven"), where they found the book in which was written the life of Anthony! One of them began to read it, to marvel and to be inflamed by it. While reading, he meditated on embracing just such a life, giving up his worldly employment to seek thee alone. These two belonged to the group of officials called "secret service agents."[2] Then, suddenly being overwhelmed with a holy love and a sober shame and as if in anger with himself, he fixed his eyes on his friend, exclaiming: "Tell me, I beg you, what goal are we seeking in all these toils of ours? What is it that we desire? What is our motive in public service? Can our hopes in the court rise higher than to be 'friends of the emperor'[3]? But how frail, how beset with peril, is that pride! Through what dangers must we climb to a greater danger? And when shall we succeed? But if I chose to become a friend of God, see, I can become one now." Thus he spoke, and in the pangs of the travail of the new life he turned his eyes again onto the page and continued reading; he was inwardly changed, as thou didst see, and the world dropped away from his mind, as soon became plain to others. For as he read with a heart

---

[1]Trèves, an important imperial town on the Moselle; the emperor referred to here was probably Gratian. Cf. E.A. Freeman, "Augusta Trevororum," in the *British Quarterly Review* (1875), 62, pp. 1-45.

[2]*Agentes in rebus*, government agents whose duties ranged from postal inspection and tax collection to espionage and secret police work. They were ubiquitous and generally dreaded by the populace; cf. J.S. Reid, "Reorganization of the Empire," in *Cambridge Medieval History*, Vol. I, pp. 36-38.

[3]The inner circle of imperial advisers; usually rather informally appointed and usually with precarious tenure.

like a stormy sea, more than once he groaned. Finally he saw the better course, and resolved on it. Then, having become thy servant, he said to his friend: "Now I have broken loose from those hopes we had, and I am determined to serve God; and I enter into that service from this hour in this place. If you are reluctant to imitate me, do not oppose me." The other replied that he would continue bound in his friendship, to share in so great a service for so great a prize. So both became thine, and began to "build a tower", counting the cost—namely, of forsaking all that they had and following thee.[1] Shortly after, Ponticianus and his companion, who had walked with him in the other part of the garden, came in search of them to the same place, and having found them reminded them to return, as the day was declining. But the first two, making known to Ponticianus their resolution and purpose, and how a resolve had sprung up and become confirmed in them, entreated them not to take it ill if they refused to join themselves with them. But Ponticianus and his friend, although not changed from their former course, did nevertheless (as he told us) bewail themselves and congratulated their friends on their godliness, recommending themselves to their prayers. And with hearts inclining again toward earthly things, they returned to the palace. But the other two, setting their affections on heavenly things, remained in the cottage. Both of them had affianced brides who, when they heard of

---

[1]Cf. Luke 14:28-33.

this, likewise dedicated their virginity to thee.

CHAPTER VII

16. Such was the story Ponticianus told. But while he was speaking, thou, O Lord, turned me toward myself, taking me from behind my back, where I had put myself while unwilling to exercise self-scrutiny. And now thou didst set me face to face with myself, that I might see how ugly I was, and how crooked and sordid, bespotted and ulcerous. And I looked and I loathed myself; but whither to fly from myself I could not discover. And if I sought to turn my gaze away from myself, he would continue his narrative, and thou wouldst oppose me to myself and thrust me before my own eyes that I might discover my iniquity and hate it. I had known it, but acted as though I knew it not—I winked at it and forgot it.

17. But now, the more ardently I loved those whose wholesome affections I heard reported—that they had given themselves up wholly to thee to be cured—the more did I abhor myself when compared with them. For many of my years—perhaps twelve—had passed away since my nineteenth, when, upon the reading of Cicero's Hortensius, I was roused to a desire for wisdom. And here I was, still postponing the abandonment of this world's happiness to devote myself to the search. For not just the finding alone, but also the bare search for it, ought to have been preferred above the treasures and kingdoms of this world; better than all bodily pleasures, though they were to be had for the taking.

But, wretched youth that I was—supremely wretched even in the very outset of my youth—I had entreated chastity of thee and had prayed, "Grant me chastity and continence, but not yet." For I was afraid lest thou shouldst hear me too soon, and too soon cure me of my disease of lust which I desired to have satisfied rather than extinguished. And I had wandered through perverse ways of godless superstition—not really sure of it, either, but preferring it to the other, which I did not seek in piety, but opposed in malice.

18. And I had thought that I delayed from day to day in rejecting those worldly hopes and following thee alone because there did not appear anything certain by which I could direct my course. And now the day had arrived in which I was laid bare to myself and my conscience was to chide me: "Where are you, O my tongue? You said indeed that you were not willing to cast off the baggage of vanity for uncertain truth. But behold now it is certain, and still that burden oppresses you. At the same time those who have not worn themselves out with searching for it as you have, nor spent ten years and more in thinking about it, have had their shoulders unburdened and have received wings to fly away." Thus was I inwardly confused, and mightily confounded with a horrible shame, while Ponticianus went ahead speaking such things. And when he had finished his story and the business he came for, he went his way. And then what did I not say to myself, within myself? With what scourges of rebuke did I not lash my soul to make it follow me,

as I was struggling to go after thee? Yet it drew back. It refused. It would not make an effort. All its arguments were exhausted and confuted. Yet it resisted in sullen disquiet, fearing the cutting off of that habit by which it was being wasted to death, as if that were death itself.

CHAPTER VIII

19. Then, as this vehement quarrel, which I waged with my soul in the chamber of my heart, was raging inside my inner dwelling, agitated both in mind and countenance, I seized upon Alypius and exclaimed: "What is the matter with us? What is this? What did you hear? The uninstructed start up and take heaven, and we—with all our learning but so little heart—see where we wallow in flesh and blood! Because others have gone before us, are we ashamed to follow, and not rather ashamed at our not following?" I scarcely knew what I said, and in my excitement I flung away from him, while he gazed at me in silent astonishment. For I did not sound like myself: my face, eyes, color, tone expressed my meaning more clearly than my words.

There was a little garden belonging to our lodging, of which we had the use—as of the whole house—for the master, our landlord, did not live there. The tempest in my breast hurried me out into this garden, where no one might interrupt the fiery struggle in which I was engaged with myself, until it came to the outcome that thou knewest though I did not. But I was mad for health, and dying for life; knowing what evil thing I was, but not knowing what good thing I was so shortly to become.

I fled into the garden, with Alypius following step by step; for I had no secret in which he did not share, and how could he leave me in such distress? We sat down, as far from the house as possible. I was greatly disturbed in spirit, angry at myself with a turbulent indignation because I had not entered thy will and covenant, O my God, while all my bones cried out to me to enter, extolling it to the skies. The way therein is not by ships or chariots or feet—indeed it was not as far as I had come from the house to the place where we were seated. For to go along that road and indeed to reach the goal is nothing else but the will to go. But it must be a strong and single will, not staggering and swaying about this way and that—a changeable, twisting, fluctuating will, wrestling with itself while one part falls as another rises.

20. Finally, in the very fever of my indecision, I made many motions with my body; like men do when they will to act but cannot, either because they do not have the limbs or because their limbs are bound or weakened by disease, or incapacitated in some other way. Thus if I tore my hair, struck my forehead, or, entwining my fingers, clasped my knee, these I did because I willed it. But I might have willed it and still not have done it, if the nerves had not obeyed my will. Many things then I did, in which the will and power to do were not the same. Yet I did not do that one thing which seemed to me infinitely more desirable, which before long I should have power to will because shortly when I willed, I would will with a single will. For in this, the power of willing is the power of doing; and as yet I could not do it. Thus my body more readily obeyed the slightest wish of the soul in moving its limbs at the order of my mind than my soul obeyed itself to accomplish in the will alone its great resolve.

CHAPTER IX

21. How can there be such a strange anomaly? And why is it? Let thy mercy shine on me, that I may inquire and find an answer, amid the dark labyrinth of human punishment and in the darkest contritions of the sons of Adam. Whence such an anomaly? And why should it be? The mind commands the body, and the body obeys. The mind commands itself and is resisted. The mind commands the hand to be moved and there is such readiness that the command is scarcely distinguished from the obedience in act. Yet the mind is mind, and the hand is body. The mind commands the mind to will, and yet though it be itself it does not obey itself. Whence this strange anomaly and why should it be? I repeat: The will commands itself to will, and could not give the command unless it wills; yet what is commanded is not done. But actually the will does not will entirely; therefore it does not command entirely. For as far as it wills, it commands. And as far as it does not will, the thing commanded is not done. For the will commands

that there be an act of will—not another, but itself. But it does not command entirely. Therefore, what is commanded does not happen; for if the will were whole and entire, it would not even command it to be, because it would already be. It is, therefore, no strange anomaly partly to will and partly to be unwilling. This is actually an infirmity of mind, which cannot wholly rise, while pressed down by habit, even though it is supported by the truth. And so there are two wills, because one of them is not whole, and what is present in this one is lacking in the other.

CHAPTER X

22. Let them perish from thy presence, O God, as vain talkers, and deceivers of the soul perish, who, when they observe that there are two wills in the act of deliberation, go on to affirm that there are two kinds of minds in us: one good, the other evil. They are indeed themselves evil when they hold these evil opinions—and they shall become good only when they come to hold the truth and consent to the truth that thy apostle may say to them: "You were formerly in darkness, but now are you in the light in the Lord."[1] But they desired to be light, not "in the Lord," but in themselves. They conceived the nature of the soul to be the same as what God is, and thus have become a thicker darkness than they were; for in their dread arrogance they have gone farther away from thee, from thee "the true Light, that lights every man that comes into the world."

Mark what you say and blush for shame; draw near to him and be enlightened, and your faces shall not be ashamed.[2]

While I was deliberating whether I would serve the Lord my God now, as I had long purposed to do, it was I who willed and it was also I who was unwilling. In either case, it was I. I neither willed with my whole will nor was I wholly unwilling. And so I was at war with myself and torn apart by myself. And this strife was against my will; yet it did not show the presence of another mind, but the punishment of my own. Thus it was no more I who did it, but the sin that dwelt in me—the punishment of a sin freely committed by Adam, and I was a son of Adam.

23. For if there are as many opposing natures as there are opposing wills, there will not be two but many more. If any man is trying to decide whether he should go to their conventicle [religious gathering] or to the theater, the Manicheans at once cry out, "See, here are two natures—one good, drawing this way, another bad, drawing back that way; for how else can you explain this indecision between conflicting wills?" But I reply that both impulses are bad—that which draws to them and that which draws back to the theater. But they do not believe that the will which draws to them can be anything but good. Suppose, then, that one of us should try to decide, and through the conflict of his two wills should waver whether he should go to the theater or to our Church. Would not those also waver about the

---

[1]Eph. 5:8.

[2]Cf. Ps. 34:5.

answer here? For either they must confess, which they are unwilling to do, that the will that leads to our church is as good as that which carries their own adherents and those captivated by their mysteries; or else they must imagine that there are two evil natures and two evil minds in one man, both at war with each other, and then it will not be true what they say, that there is one good and another bad. Else they must be converted to the truth, and no longer deny that when anyone deliberates there is one soul fluctuating between conflicting wills.

24. Let them no longer maintain that when they perceive two wills to be contending with each other in the same man the contest is between two opposing minds, of two opposing substances, from two opposing principles, the one good and the other bad. Thus, O true God, thou dost reprove and confute and convict them. For both wills may be bad: as when a man tries to decide whether he should kill a man by poison or by the sword; whether he should take possession of this field or that one belonging to someone else, when he cannot get both; whether he should squander his money to buy pleasure or hold onto his money through the motive of covetousness; whether he should go to the circus or to the theater, if both are open on the same day; or, whether he should take a third course, open at the same time, and rob another man's house; or, a fourth option, whether he should commit adultery, if he has the opportunity—all these things concurring in the same space of time and all being equally longed for, although impossible to do at one time. For the mind is pulled four ways by four antagonistic wills—or even more, in view of the vast range of human desires—but even the Manicheans do not affirm that there are these many different substances. The same principle applies as in the action of good wills. For I ask them, "Is it a good thing to have delight in reading the apostle, or is it a good thing to delight in a sober psalm, or is it a good thing to discourse on the gospel?" To each of these, they will answer, "It is good." But what, then, if all delight us equally and all at the same time? Do not different wills distract the mind when a man is trying to decide what he should choose? Yet they are all good, and are at variance with each other until one is chosen. When this is done the whole united will may go forward on a single track instead of remaining as it was before, divided in many ways. So also, when eternity attracts us from above, and the pleasure of earthly delight pulls us down from below, the soul does not will either the one or the other with all its force, but still it is the same soul that does not will this or that with a united will, and is therefore pulled apart with grievous perplexities, because for truth's sake it prefers this, but for custom's sake it does not lay that aside.

CHAPTER XI

25. Thus I was sick and tormented, reproaching myself more bitterly than ever, rolling and writhing in my chain till it should be utterly broken. By now I

was held but slightly, but still was held. And thou, O Lord, didst press upon me in my inmost heart with a severe mercy, redoubling the lashes of fear and shame; lest I should again give way and that same slender remaining tie not be broken off, but recover strength and enchain me yet more securely.

I kept saying to myself, "See, let it be done now; let it be done now." And as I said this I all but came to a firm decision. I all but did it—yet I did not quite. Still I did not fall back to my old condition, but stood aside for a moment and drew breath. And I tried again, and lacked only a very little of reaching the resolve—and then somewhat less, and then all but touched and grasped it. Yet I still did not quite reach or touch or grasp the goal, because I hesitated to die to death and to live to life. And the worse way, to which I was habituated, was stronger in me than the better, which I had not tried. And up to the very moment in which I was to become another man, the nearer the moment approached, the greater horror did it strike in me. But it did not strike me back, nor turn me aside, but held me in suspense.

26. It was, in fact, my old mistresses, trifles of trifles and vanities of vanities, who still enthralled me. They tugged at my fleshly garments and softly whispered: "Are you going to part with us? And from that moment will we never be with you any more? And from that moment will not this and that be forbidden you forever?" What were they suggesting to me in those words "this or that"? What is it they suggested, O my God? Let thy mercy guard the soul of thy servant from the vileness and the shame they did suggest! And now I scarcely heard them, for they were not openly showing themselves and opposing me face to face; but muttering, as it were, behind my back; and furtively plucking at me as I was leaving, trying to make me look back at them. Still they delayed me, so that I hesitated to break loose and shake myself free of them and leap over to the place to which I was being called—for unruly habit kept saying to me, "Do you think you can live without them?"

27. But now it said this very faintly; for in the direction I had set my face, and yet toward which I still trembled to go, the chaste dignity of continence appeared to me—cheerful but not wanton, modestly alluring me to come and doubt nothing, extending her holy hands, full of a multitude of good examples—to receive and embrace me. There were there so many young men and maidens, a multitude of youth and every age, grave widows and ancient virgins; and continence herself in their midst: not barren, but a fruitful mother of children—her joys—by thee, O Lord, her husband. And she smiled on me with a challenging smile as if to say: "Can you not do what these young men and maidens can? Or can any of them do it of themselves, and not rather in the Lord their God? The Lord their God gave me to them. Why do you stand in your own strength, and so stand not? Cast yourself on him; fear not. He will not flinch and you will not fall. Cast yourself on him without fear, for he will receive and heal you." And I blushed violently, for I still heard

the muttering of those "trifles" and hung suspended. Again she seemed to speak: "Stop your ears against those unclean members of yours, that they may be mortified. They tell you of delights, but not according to the law of the Lord thy God." This struggle raging in my heart was nothing but the contest of self against self. And Alypius kept close beside me, and awaited in silence the outcome of my extraordinary agitation.

CHAPTER XII

28. Now when deep reflection had drawn up out of the secret depths of my soul all my misery and had heaped it up before the sight of my heart, there arose a mighty storm, accompanied by a mighty rain of tears. That I might give way fully to my tears and lamentations, I stole away from Alypius, for it seemed to me that solitude was more appropriate for the business of weeping. I went far enough away that I could feel that even his presence was no restraint upon me. This was the way I felt at the time, and he realized it. I suppose I had said something before I started up and he noticed that the sound of my voice was choked with weeping. And so he stayed alone, where we had been sitting together, greatly astonished. I flung myself down under a fig tree—how I know not—and gave free course to my tears. The streams of my eyes gushed out an acceptable sacrifice to thee. And, not indeed in these words, but to this effect, I cried to thee: "And thou, O Lord, how long? How long, O Lord? Wilt

thou be angry forever? Oh, remember not against us our former iniquities."[1] For I felt that I was still enthralled by them. I sent up these sorrowful cries: "How long, how long? Tomorrow and tomorrow? Why not now? Why not this very hour make an end to my uncleanness?"

29. I was saying these things and weeping in the most bitter contrition of my heart, when suddenly I heard the voice of a boy or a girl I know not which—coming from the neighboring house, chanting over and over again, "Pick it up, read it; pick it up, read it."[2] Immediately I ceased weeping and began most earnestly to think whether it was usual for children in some kind of game to sing such a song, but I could not remember ever having heard the like. So, damming the torrent of my tears, I got to my feet, for I could not but think that this was a divine command to open the Bible and read the first passage I should light upon. For I had heard[3] how Anthony, accidentally coming into church while the gospel was being read, received the admonition as if what was read had been addressed to him: "Go and sell what you have and give it to the poor, and you shall have treasure in heaven; and come and follow me."[4] By such an oracle he was forthwith converted to thee.

So I quickly returned to the bench where Alypius was sitting, for there I had put down the apos-

---

[1]Cf. Ps. 6:3; 79:8.

[2]This is the famous *Tolle, lege; tolle, lege.*

[3]Doubtless from Ponticianus, in their earlier conversation.

[4]Matt. 19:21.

tle's book when I had left there. I snatched it up, opened it, and in silence read the paragraph on which my eyes first fell: "Not in rioting and drunkenness, not in chambering and wantonness, not in strife and envying, but put on the Lord Jesus Christ, and make no provision for the flesh to fulfill the lusts thereof."[1] I wanted to read no further, nor did I need to. For instantly, as the sentence ended, there was infused in my heart something like the light of full certainty and all the gloom of doubt vanished away.[2]

30. Closing the book, then, and putting my finger or something else for a mark I began—now with a tranquil countenance—to tell it all to Alypius. And he in turn disclosed to me what had been going on in himself, of which I knew nothing. He asked to see what I had read. I showed him, and he looked on even further than I had read. I had not known what followed. But indeed it was this, "Him that is weak in the faith, receive."[3] This he applied to himself, and told me so. By these words of warning he was strength

ened, and by exercising his good resolution and purpose—all very much in keeping with his character, in which, in these respects, he was always far different from and better than I—he joined me in full commitment without any restless hesitation.

Then we went in to my mother, and told her what happened, to her great joy. We explained to her how it had occurred—and she leaped for joy triumphant; and she blessed thee, who art "able to do exceedingly abundantly above all that we ask or think."[4] For she saw that thou hadst granted her far more than she had ever asked for in all her pitiful and doleful lamentations. For thou didst so convert me to thee that I sought neither a wife nor any other of this world's hopes, but set my feet on that rule of faith which so many years before thou hadst showed her in her dream about me. And so thou didst turn her grief into gladness more plentiful than she had ventured to desire, and dearer and purer than the desire she used to cherish of having grandchildren of my flesh.

---

[1]Rom. 13:13.
[2]Note the parallels here to the conversion of Anthony and the *agentes in rebus*.
[3]Rom. 14:1.

---

[4]Eph. 3:20.

Questions for Critical Thinking and Discussion

1. To what is St. Augustine confessing?

2. What is his dilemna?

3. What insight(s) do you receive into St. Augustine's character and motives?

4. What mental and spiritual satisfaction did St. Augustine receive from writing his Autobiography? How did the writing help him reflect on his past life?

5. St. Augustine finds in Romans 13:13 a response to his struggle. What does this New Testament verse tell him?

6. Can you describe Augustine's journey from paganism to Christianity?

7. What qualities does the pre-Christian character of Augustine have that make you sympathetic to the torments of his soul?

8. How might a study of the *Confessions* help people with modern-day problems such as alcohol or drug abuse?

Self-Test

Part I: Identification

Can you identify each of the following? Tell who, what, when, where, why, and/or how for each term.

1. Principate
2. *Pax Romana*
3. Praetorian Guard
4. Mt. Vesuvius eruption
5. Julio-Claudian Emperors
6. Flavian Dynasty
7. "Good Emperors"
8. *Jus gentium*
9. *Jus naturale*
10. Paterfamilias
11. Noumena
12. Vestal Virgins
13. *Pontifex Maximus*
14. Cicero
15. Autocracy
16. Diocletian
17. Constantine
18. Dead Sea Scrolls
19. St. Paul
20. Mithraism
21. Tetrachy
22. Council of Nicaea
23. St. Augustine
24. *The City of God*
25. Vulgate
26. Petrine Succession
27. St. Benedict of Nursia
28. Byzantium
29. Justinian
30. Theodora
31. Hagia Sophia
32. *Corpus Juris Civilis*
33. "Greek fire"
34. Caesaropapism
35. Iconoclasts
36. *Filioque* controversy
37. Muhammad or Mohammed
38. Hejira or Hegira
39. Koran or Qur'an
40. Five Pillars of Faith
41. Sunnites
42. Shiites
43. *The Canon of Medicine*
44. Clovis
45. Merovingian dynasty
46. Charlemagne
47. Mayor of the palace
48. Donation of Pepin
49. Alcuin of York
50. Carolingian minuscule
51. Carolingian Renaissance
52. Donation of Constantine
53. *Missi dominici*
54. Treaty of Verdun

Part II: Multiple Choice Questions

Circle the best response from the choices given.

1. *The Aeneid* is a(n)
    a. satire on Roman life.
    b. accurate history of the Roman Republic.
    c. short lyric poem glorifying Rome.
    d. long epic poem glorifying Rome.

2. Rome's greatest achievements are generally believed to have been in the areas of
    a. literature and philosophy.
    b. science and mathematics.
    c. law and government.
    d. religion and morality.

3. The brief reign of the Emperor Nerva is memorable because he
    a. built the Colosseum in the city of Rome.
    b. started the adoptive system of selecting emperors.
    c. defeated the Jews in the second Hebrew revolt.
    d. extended the borders of the Roman Empire to the Persian Gulf.

4. During the period 180 A.D. to 284 A.D. all of the following are true <u>except</u>
    a. The Roman empire almost collapsed.
    b. Germanic tribes and Parthian soldiers invaded the empire.
    c. Christianity became the official religion of Rome.
    d. The city of Rome ceased to be the center of the Roman empire.

5. The key to the understanding of Christianity as an organized religion was
    a. the birth of Christ.
    b. Jesus' baptism by John the Baptist.
    c. the Resurrection.
    d. the writing of the gospels.

6. Jesus Christ
    a. consciously and deliberately set out to convert the entire world to the new religion of Christianity which he founded.
    b. taught that the old Mosaic law had been replaced through Him.
    c. clearly stated that he was the Messiah as the Jews understood that term.
    d. none of the above.

7. St. Paul is given credit for
   a. stressing personal salvation through Christ.
   b. developing a larger Church organization.
   c. spreading Christianity beyond the Jews to the larger population of pagans.
   d. all of the above.

8. One of the two central ritual acts in early Christianity was the
   a. confession of sin.
   b. giving of alms.
   c. sacrament of penance.
   d. Lord's Supper.

9. "And I say also unto thee, that thou art Peter, and upon this rock I will build my church; and the gates of hell shall not prevail against it. And I will give unto thee the keys of the kingdom of heaven ..." The words of this quotation are important to which of the following:
   a. the doctrine of the Resurrection.
   b. the claims of the bishops of Rome to supremacy in the Church.
   c. the belief of the Jews that they were a Chosen People.
   d. the development of Christianity as a universal faith.

10. Diocletian's system of administration
   a. removed the army from the emperor's control.
   b. divided the Empire into four prefectures.
   c. centralized all authority in Rome.
   d. separated religion and government.

11. The Arian heresy held that
   a. Christ is not equal to God the Father.
   b. Father and Son both derive from the Holy Ghost.
   c. Father, Son, and Holy Ghost are one and the same.
   d. none of the above.

12. The Council of Nicaea is significant because it
   a. provided for the separation of the Eastern (Greek) Church from the Western (Roman) Church.
   b. established the bishop of Rome as pope in the West.
   c. stated the orthodox doctrine of the Church on the Trinity.
   d. proclaimed baptism to be the central act of Christian ritual.

13. After the division of the Empire in 395 A.D., the
    a. two emperors made war against each other.
    b. western half fell to barbarian rulers.
    c. prosperity of the West increased.
    d. East fell under the sway of the West.

14. In the West, the successor state to the Roman empire eventually turned out to be
    a. the Byzantine Empire.
    b. the kingdom of Granada.
    c. the Visigothic kingdom.
    d. the kingdom of the Franks.

15. The last Eastern Roman Emperor to attempt the reconquest of the West was
    a. Theodosius.
    b. Justinian.
    c. Diocletian.
    d. Constantine.

16. Justinian's *Corpus Juris Civilis*
    a. was a law code applied exclusively in the Western Roman Empire.
    b. codified and preserved much of Roman law.
    c. was the largest church building in Christendom.
    d. never went into effect.

17. The political structure of the Byzantine state
    a. was dominated by the Russian nobility.
    b. resembled that of the Frankish kingdom.
    c. emphasized local self-government.
    d. placed absolute power in the hands of the emperors.

18. The Byzantine state was characterized by a strong linkage between the head of the government and the head of the Christian Church. This is known as
    a. separation of church and state.
    b. caesaropapism.
    c. spiritual supremacy of the church.
    d. spiritual supremacy of the god.

19. Which of the following was not a religious practice of Islam?
    a. fasting during the daylight hours of the month of Ramadan.
    b. praying five times a day.
    c. ceremonial wine drinking.
    d. making a pilgrimage to Mecca at least once during a Moslem's lifetime.

20. The flight from Mecca to Medina was a turning point in Muhammad's career because it
  a. ended the lunar calendar.
  b. removed him from politics.
  c. demonstrated the impossibility of centering the new religion in Arabia.
  d. marked the beginning of a militant phase of this new movement.

21. The caliphs immediately following Muhammad
  a. retained the allegiance of all Muslims.
  b. were all related to the Prophet.
  c. united the Christians to conquer their neighbors.
  d. refused to protect new converts.

22. The expansion of Islam in the West was stopped at the battle of Tours in 732 A.D. by
  a. Charlemagne.
  b. Clovis.
  c. Charles Martel.
  d. Alcuin.

23. The Frankish kingdom under the Merovingians
  a. was dominated by the Arian heresy.
  b. was constantly at war against the Church.
  c. worked with the Church against pagans and Arian Christians.
  d. set a high standard of public morality for all of Christian Europe.

24. The popes welcomed a political alignment with the Frankish kings
  a. in order to convert them from Arian Christianity to orthodoxy.
  b. because they hoped to do away with images in the churches.
  c. to increase their dependence on the Byzantine emperors.
  d. to gain protection from Lombard invaders.

25. Charlemagne controlled local government officials by
  a. turning local government over to the Church.
  b. sending out royal inspection agents.
  c. relying on the loyalty of his counts.
  d. adopting the Roman system of administration.

Part III: Review and Thought Questions

1. Explain the role of religion in the in the Roman state. Include gods and noumena in your response.

2. How do the mystery religions influence Christianity?

3. What went wrong with the Roman Empire in the third century? Give specific examples.

4. How did the "Good Emperors" solve the problem of succession?

5. Explain the government structure and the reforms introduced by Diocletian. Were they successful in achieving stability?

6. What role did politics play in the Iconoclastic Controversy?

7. What is the historical importance of the crowning of Charlemagne as Holy Roman Emperor?

8. Describe the Treaty of Verdun. Why is it called the most important treaty of the Middle Ages?

9. Discuss Augustus' arrangements with the Senate and the Praetorian Guard. Why was his reign called the Golden Age? Explain fully.

10. What was the Donation of Pepin? Why is it important to the history of the Church?

11. What are the differences between the Sunnites and the Shiite Muslims?

12. Describe the basic teachings of Islam.

13. What were the principal Jewish sects before the advent of Christianity? Did they play any role in the development of Christianity?

14. What led to a permanent schism between Eastern (Orthodox) and Western Christianity?

15. Why couldn't the Carolingian Empire hold together? What happened?

16. How did the Germanic and Asiatic tribes contribute to the weakness of the Roman Empire?

17. Describe the organization and functions of the early Christian church.

18. How, when, and why did the Byzantines save Christianity from invading Muslims?

19. How did the writings of Saint Augustine contribute to Christianity?

20. Can you explain the Arian heresy and the role of the Council of Nicaea in its disposition?

Part IV: Full-Length Essays

1. Describe Augustus' arrangements with the Senate, the Army, the poets, and Roman people. How did these arrangements glorify the state?

2. Explain the cultural legacy of Rome in the areas of law, government, engineering, architecture and literature to Western civilization. Give specific examples.

3. Compare and contrast the teachings of Islam with the teachings of Christianity.

4. Imagine you are a Christian living in the time of Constantine. What changes have you seen since he became Augustus?

5. Describe the political organization and educational practices that occurred during the reign of Charlemagne.

6. What was the legacy of the Arabs and the Byzantines to Western civilization?

Figure 4.1. Plaque from a medieval book cover displays the symbolds of the four evangelists carved in ivory. The man with a halo and wings represents St. Matthew, the line—St. Mark, the calf—St. Luke, and the eagle—St. John. The center symbol of the Lamb of God (*Agnus Dei*) in the cross represents Jesus. *Courtesy of The Metropolitan Museum of Art, Gift of J. Pierpont Morgan, 1917. (17.190.38)*

Chapter IV

THE MIDDLE AGES

Figure 4.2. Tabernacle. Ivories. French. Early XIV Century. The smiling Madonna along with Biblical scenes carved on the four panels is representatve of medieval church art. Do you recognize the pointed arch design that illustrates the Gothic style of architecture? *Courtesy of The Metropolitan Museum of Art, Gift of George Blumenthal, 1941. (41.100.122)*

Middle age → they write about religion + Local stories also.
they did hand craft.

10

The Development of Medieval Society

The Origins of Feudalism

Because of constant turmoil, rape, pillage, famine, disease, and the lack of a strong central government, the weak sought protection from the strong after the breakup of the Carolingian Empire. During the Middle Ages, three basic classes emerged in society: those who worked (peasants bound to the land), those who prayed (clergy), and those who fought (warriors). The nobles (lords) were the warriors, and they were granted land (fiefs) by a higher noble in return for military service. The lords built fortified castles and manors in strategic locations, such as on a mountain promontory or a river confluence, where as warriors they could fend off attacks and take the peasants (serfs) into their fortress in times of distress.

In these turbulent times, few monetary transactions occurred and land was the primary basis of wealth. A monarch or other lord (duke, count, baron, earl) would grant territory to another lord, who was a member of the same social class (a vassal), in exchange for his services as a warrior. This contractual relationship was called feudalism. The land grant would provide the vassal (the grantee) with the wherewithal (the produce from the land and rents from tenants) to equip his knights with horses, armor, and weapons. Great lords (the grantors) now had armed vassals at their disposal who had sworn per-

Describe the class structure of medieval society.

What was feudalism?

What were the obligations of the vassal?

sonal allegiance and fealty (faithfulness) in return for their land grants.

The formal ceremony whereby the vassal pledged his fealty and loyalty to his overlord was called HOMAGE; at the same ceremony the vassal was "invested" with a clod of earth or a sheaf of grain, representing his fief. An oath of loyalty bound the two nobles together until death or mutual dissolution. The vassal promised to be the lord's man, and had the following obligations. He had to fight for his lord, usually 40 days a year, ransom him if he were to be captured, sit at his court in order to hear criminal and civil cases, provide hospitality and entertainment for a specified number of days each year, and give generous gifts upon the knighting of the lord's eldest son or the marriage of his oldest daughter. Customarily, in a system called primogeniture, the vassal's eldest son inherited the land, the title, and the privileges and obligations of his rank.

How were vassals trained?

Male offspring were schooled for entrance into the aristocratic warrior class. Beginning at seven or eight years of age, a noble might send his son to a close relative—a brother, a cousin, an uncle—to serve as a page in the household and to train in the arts of warfare and chivalry, the code of conduct becoming the warrior. After appropriate skill training in horsemanship, jousting, archery, arms and armor, there would be a solemn knighting ceremony. After a twenty-four hour vigil of prayer and fasting, the knight pledged to aid the "Just and the Right," to defend the weak and the helpless, and to fight in the service of God. (He did not have to slay a dragon.) Even 12-year old knights in training learned to balance themselves on a horse wearing 30 to 35 pounds of armor.

Females were not eligible to inherit because they could not be warriors. If there were no male heirs, the daughter had to patiently wait until her parent or guardian found her a knightly husband, who could then be invested with the fief.

Did women enjoy equal rights under feudalism?

The Church also fit into the feudal system. Church land was held as a collective entity by a monastic order or perhaps a wealthy lord would die without heirs, donating his fief to the Church. Archbishops, bishops, abbots would subdivide, then parcel out these fiefs to professional knights to fight on their behalf. Sometimes "a man of the cloth" would swear fealty to a king, prince, duke, count and find himself embroiled in an armed conflict. *The Song of Roland,* a heroic epic written about 1100 in a French dialect, recounts how an archbishop fights the Muslim infidel, then dies a hero warrior's death on the battlefield. Customarily, the clergy were not warriors or professional soldiers, except in unusual circumstances.

How did the Church fit into feudalism?

Subinfeudation

Subinfeudation was the subletting of a portion of a fief to another noble. The noble tenant became the vassal to the original holder of the fief, who was now a lord as well as a vassal to whoever had granted him the fief. Even the lower vassals in this fragile pyramid often could parcel out fiefs. Sometimes a vassal held fiefs from two or more overlords, and they later became enemies. Perhaps you can see how a lord could be caught in a conflict of interest. Usually in the vassal's oath of homage he would specify exactly to whom he owed primary allegiance (liege homage). In other words, he designated by name the lord for whom he would fight first in the event of an armed conflict. As tenuous as this system was, it worked for approximately 500 years in a Europe lacking strong central government.

What was subinfeudation?

What was manorialism?

Manorialism *basic system of middle ages. monasticism was part of it*

Castle central administrator places.

Alongside the many varied local customs of feudalism, which was a political system, there was an economic and social system called manorialism. As part of the fief, the manor (estate) was the principal unit of agricultural production. Those who worked on the manor were peasants or serfs (not "surfs") bound to the land. The fields, which the serfs worked in common, were divided into strips for particular families and strips reserved for the lord as part of the lord's demesne (that part of the manor dedicated to the lord's use, perhaps a quarter to a third of the whole estate). The peasants worked the demesne land for the lord.

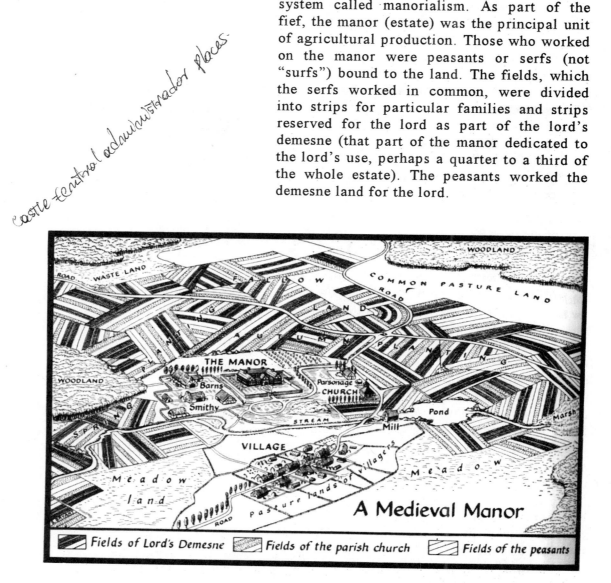

A Medieval Manor

Fields of Lord's Demesne | Fields of the parish church | Fields of the peasants

A large manor might have a village of several hundred peasant families and contain over a thousand acres of forest, swamp, streams, and arable land. A smaller fief might have a dozen families and contain less than 400 acres. Travel was precarious, roads were primitive, and robbers were numerous (Remember Robin Hood and his Merry Men!). Most serfs were born, lived, and died on the same manor, very provincial and limited in their outlook. Later, if a runaway serf escaped to a town without being caught for a year and a day, he could gain his freedom and become a freeman. As the Middle Ages progressed, a serf could buy his freedom, then become a tenant farmer, and pay rent to the lord of the manor. The lords preferred monetary payment rather than payments in kind because produce would spoil easily and money was a more convenient medium for the purchase of luxury goods.

In terms of creature comforts and variety of food, the serfs' lives were quite miserable by our standards. Adults, children, and, in the winter, farm animals infested with bugs and fleas lived in a one-room thatched hut, which often had a dirt floor and a hole in the roof for a chimney. In this crowded environment, accidents, disease, and malnutrition often took their toll, reducing life expectancy to thirty or forty years. The overworked peasants had meat only a few times a year, usually at Christmas, Easter, and Pentecost; their everyday fare was the perpetual cabbage soup, grain bread, and maybe cheese and ale for dinner. Not aware of the germ theory of disease, medieval serfs rarely washed their utensils or their hands. The hunting of game was reserved for the lord and his vassals. Serfs turned over one-tenth (the tithe) of their produce to the church. Each serf worked perhaps three days a week for the lord and one day for the church, leaving him two days

How did serfs differ from vassals?

Describe the life-style of the typical serf.

What obligations did the serf owe his lord?

for himself and his family. The peasant had to pay his lord for the use of his wine press, bake oven, gristmill, and even a stud fee. In addition, he was expected to perform a labor corvee of repairing the roads and bridges on his lord's estate. Does this type of lifestyle strike you as less than luxurious?

Agricultural Revolution

What were some of the new methods used in the agricultural revolution?

Around the eleventh century, an agricultural revolution dramatically increased the food supply. New lands were cultivated as serfs drained swamps and marshes, cleared dense forests, and discovered new technology. For example, the invention of the iron horseshoe enabled the horses' hoofs to sustain traction for plowing over uneven, rocky fields. A new shoulder harness collared both horses and oxen in tandem so they worked as a team. A heavy plow, drawn on wheels, which could overturn heavy, wet soil was another plus. Now fields did not have to be plowed twice, both vertically and horizontally, as they had in the past. With the invention of the windmill and improvements in the waterwheel, greater quantities of grain could be ground. Perhaps the most striking advance was the creation of the **THREE-FIELD SYSTEM** in which farmers planted one field in the fall for spring harvesting, another field in the spring for fall harvesting, leaving one field fallow to rejuvenate throughout the year. Legume crops (peas, beans, clover) that added nitrogen to the soil would also be rotated in the various fields. With all these advances, agricultural production increased by at least a third. As a result of food surpluses, population increased and commercial activity burgeoned.

The Rise of Towns

Surplus agricultural products were bartered at fairs in the spring and fall throughout Europe, especially in the Champagne region of France. Exchanges of grain or wine for furs, spices, salt, silk and woolen cloth, metalwork, pottery, tapestries, and other luxury goods revived long-distance trade and commercial activity. For instance, the Italian cities of Venice, Genoa, and Pisa established commercial arrangements with Constantinople and the Orient for the outfitting of the Crusaders and the trade in luxury goods desired by the nobility. New cities arose in northern Europe, such as Hamburg in Germany and Edinburgh in Scotland. The population of cities of Medieval Europe rarely exceeded 50 thousand, which was approximately the population of fifteenth-century London. There were some exceptions. Paris had perhaps 200 thousand inhabitants in the fourteenth century. Today, London has a population of over 6 million, while more than 2 million people live in Paris proper.

Trade occurred outside a castle or inside a walled community where some measure of security might be enforced. Some examples still remain in Europe today, such as the walled city of Carcassone in southern France, where a version of Robin Hood was filmed. Towns permitted artisans and merchants to trade, set up shops, and establish their own political and social systems. These middle-class burghers, later called bourgeoisie, were neither serfs nor lords. They would become the dominant commercial force in the Later Middle Ages.

Name some towns that came into being in the Middle Ages.

How large were medieval towns?
10,000 people.
15,000
mostly sk~~ill~~ people.

Who were the burghers or bourgeoisie? (sociological)
middle class.

Pretzels were invented by monks. also spices, herbs and Perignon wine.

The Guild System

Explain the guild system.

Technical education

Controlled by these burghers, the guild system became a potent stimulus in the distinctive manufacture of quality hand-crafted goods. Today most of our products are mass-produced in quantities of scale; it would be unthinkable to take three years to hand loom a rug or tapestry. But weaving was a highly skilled craft for a long time.

The guild system that developed in towns in that era was the forerunner of the skilled labor union system still in use today (with apprenticeship training and state licensing of plumbers, electricians, stonemasons, hairdressers, etc.). The artisan system took a child of approximately seven to apprentice for a trade under a guild master. In exchange for food, lodging, and training, the apprentice would perform menial and gradually more skilled tasks. After seven years, the apprentice could make a masterpiece for the guild wardens to evaluate. If the quality and workmanship of the masterpiece proved exemplary, the apprentice would then be promoted to journeyman. As a journeyman, he could work for wages under another master in the same trade. If he acquired sufficient funds and a good reputation, he then could become a full-fledged guild master himself and perhaps move to another town to open his own shop. The terms and conditions for each craft or merchant guild varied; for example, a goldsmith and a cooper (barrel maker) would not have the same requirements. The guild set the "fair" price for a product, the terms and conditions of employment, hours of work, the standards of production, and specified the training requirements for apprentices. However, the guild was more than an employment agency; it was also a social and fraternal organization where the sick and injured were

How did the guild system differ from most business situations today?

given succor, the dead buried with dignity, weddings and births celebrated, and parades held on religious holidays in honor of the guild's patron saint. For example, St. Joseph was the patron saint of the carpenters' guild. Fines and ostracism were imposed on those members who disregarded the rules, but those who followed "the party line" prospered.

How was the university connected to the guild system?

Medieval Culture

The University System

Medieval universities followed many of the same principles as the merchant or artisan guilds; however, these were guilds or corporations of students or masters (professors). The word *universitas* means corporation in Latin; the masters or students united for their protection and self-interest, thereby constituting the first universities or educational guilds. These universities produced or "manufactured" educated men with certificates of competency (degrees) in prescribed programs.

How and why did they originate? Kings, princes, and popes were not the only ones looking for a trained elite. Merchants in towns and law courts also required literate individuals knowledgeable in the arts, government, or judicial procedures. During the Early Middle Ages, monastic schools educated the would-be clergy, the priests and monks of the Church. Limited in their number and in their curriculum, these monastic schools were never meant to serve society as

How did universities originate?

next layer of the middle age society. they need to keep records

How did the organization of the University of Bologna differ from that of the University of Paris?

Compare the college student of the Middle Ages to today's student.

a whole. In the High Middle Ages cathedral schools located near the seats of bishops in large towns began to exceed the monastic schools in their numbers and importance. The number of students attending cathedral schools increased so much that the bishop would turn the direct control of the school over to a church officer, called the chancellor, who was obliged to instruct the rich or poor without a fee. As time went on, these cathedral schools attracted students from a wide geographic area, gradually evolving into universities. These "cathedrals of learning" played a pivotal role in the intellectual life of the Middle Ages.

As a growing number of students traveled to cities like Paris, Bologna, and Salerno in search of the best teachers, they unofficially established themselves in rented halls or rooms, hired the professors, and set the terms and conditions of their apprenticeship. These included the length and content of the lectures, the length of the academic term, the fines the masters would have to pay for absence, for not covering the text in the required time, or for drawing less than five students to their lectures. At the University of Bologna, formally established by Emperor Frederick Barbarossa in 1158, the corporation of students controlled the university. At the University of Paris, established by Robert de Sorbon in 1257, the masters set the regulations.

Not unlike university students of today, medieval students (all male) attended lectures, took notes, studied for examinations, learned the art of oral disputation, questioning and thinking on one's feet. However, there were notable differences. Classes were taught in Latin, the universal language of the Church and scholarship, not in the everyday tongue (the vernacular). Every student who entered the university was expected to be well versed

The 1st ones
monks recorded (written notes) music.

in classical Latin grammar and literature. (How many students do you know who can read Virgil?) For lectures professors read authoritative texts, such as the Bible or the work of Aristotle, and made comments on these texts.

The curriculum consisted of studying the seven liberal arts, the *trivium* (grammar, rhetoric, and logic) and *quadrivium* (arithmetic, geometry, music, and astronomy). Upon completion of the liberal arts curriculum after three or four years, if the student passed rigorous, comprehensive examinations, he would be awarded a baccalaureate degree, which is similar to our Bachelor of Arts. A significant difference between then and now is that students were examined orally and in public after a program of study rather than after a specific course. Students also had individual tutors and studied under a master. Today we have a great variety of programs from animal behavior to underwater archaeology, but we have the Middle Ages to thank for our degree system.

After three or four more years of study, further examinations, and the writing of a Master's thesis (still used), the student would be granted a Master's Degree. Graduation in the arts, the Master of Arts degree, was the common entrance into the professional studies. Now the student could decide to specialize in law, medicine, or theology. Most doctors of theology studied for fifteen years, obtaining their doctorate after age thirty-five. More popular as a source of job placement and advancement, however, was a doctorate in law, which took seven years. Because kings, merchants, and law courts required trained individuals to interpret and adjudicate, legal studies were the route to upward mobility, much the same as they are now.

What were the *trivium* and the *quadrivium*?

*geocentric idea of the Universe.
science to improve time.*

Do you see similarities in degree programs? Explain.

Name some medieval universities and indicate their areas of specialization.

Most universities specialized in specific areas of study. For example, the University of Bologna devoted itself to the study of the law; Paris specialized in the study of theology and logical thinking; and Salerno became a center for the teaching of medicine. Interestingly, the medical student at Salerno did not dissect cadavers, as this activity went against the teachings of the Church; they only studied their medical textbooks (Hippocrates, Galen, Averroes, and others) and took lecture notes.

At times many of the students were rambunctious (perhaps too much studying, gambling, or drinking). There were riots and altercations between the townspeople and the students, who frequently were clergy and wore clerical robes. Many students felt abused by excessive price gouging for food and lodging charged by the townspeople. The townspeople thought the students were rowdy, snooty, and above the law. For example, the University of Cambridge evolved out of a "town" and "gown" riot when, in 1209, students left Oxford University over the turmoil. Rather than being informal locations in rented rooms, "colleges" eventually emerged with residence halls endowed by wealthy patrons. For example, Robert de Sorbon endowed the Sorbonne, the College of Liberal Arts at the University of Paris.

How did the phrase "town and gown" originate?

From the handful of universities brought into existence in the twelfth century, there were at least eighty known universities at the end of the fifteenth century, including schools at Heidelberg, Prague, Vienna, and Salamanca. It is ironic that many students who wear a cap and gown at their graduation are unaware of the tradition that medieval students wore clerical gowns all the time, not only at graduation, and that their degree of Bachelor, Masters, or Doctorate conferred by the chancellor of the university, which may be written in Latin, dates back to the twelfth century.

Scholasticism

Scholasticism is a term used to describe both the teaching methods and the theological and philosophical doctrines taught in the schools of Medieval Europe. Scholastics would examine the writings of famous authorities, make comments on them, and attempt to resolve conflicts through the use of logical reasoning. An intellectual problem that especially preoccupied the Scholastics was the relationship between faith and reason.

ST. ANSLEM (1033-1109), sometimes considered to be the father of Scholasticism, demonstrated the use of reason to bolster rather than question Christian faith. He used reason to prove the existence of God. His ontological (ontology is the study of being) proof holds that a being who exists in reality is greater than one who merely exists in the mind. Since we think of God as a being greater than any other, God must really exist.

PETER ABELARD (1079-1142) also encouraged the use of reason. His book *Sic et Non* (Yes and No) contains over 150 theological propositions and shows that different authorities can be used to support or oppose each thesis. The only way to resolve these conflicts is through reason. Abelard was a popular and contentious teacher who fell in love with a pupil of his, Heloise. He seduced her and when she had a child, he secretly married her, even though he was supposed to be a celibate cleric. When her uncle Fulbert found out, he had Abelard castrated. She went off to a convent and he became a monk. Their

What is Scholasticism?

believe Faith + reason are together.

Explain St. Anslem's ontological proof for the existence of God.

How did Abelard contribute to Scholastic thought?

Describe the major works of St. Thomas Aquinas.

analize god,
Jesus,

What is the relationship between faith and reason according to Aquinas?

age of faith.

love story has caught the imagination of students ever since. Today the lovers are reunited in a cemetery in Paris.

While Abelard's theological work is not widely known today, that of ST. THOMAS AQUINAS (1224-1274) is. Aquinas, a Dominican monk, wrote the *Summa Theologica* (Summary of Theology), a celebrated compendium on God, morality, and just about every theological question of his day. The rigorous scholastic methodology applied in this work is quite challenging for the beginning student, who is better advised to look at the *Summa Contra Gentiles* (Summary Against the Gentiles) which uses reason to defend Christianity against Islam. Aquinas wrote numerous other works, including commentaries on the works of Aristotle (the Philosopher for Aquinas), whose major writings had been reintroduced to the West at that time.

When Aquinas considers the relationship between faith and reason, he believes both are sources of truth since both are given to humans by God. He was convinced, for example, that we can know the existence of God by faith and can prove God's existence by reason. He believed, however, that the mysteries of the Christian faith, such as the Trinity, could neither be proven nor disproven by reason. But what if there appeared to be a conflict between reason and faith? Aquinas was persuaded that any conflicts were due to faulty human reasoning rather than errors in faith, which came directly to man by divine revelation. For Aquinas the concepts of faith are more certain than ideas reached by mere human deliberation. Contrast Aquinas's world view with that of many contemporary scholars who consider the beliefs of faith to be much less certain than scientifically-validated facts.

Art and Architecture

Why do you think so many great cathedrals were built in the Middle Ages?

In this **AGE OF FAITH**, the Church was the central, unifying force in people's lives. All eyes are focused on glorifying God and achieving eternal life. Nowhere is this focus better revealed than in the achievements of Christian art as exemplified in the churches, monasteries, and the cathedrals of this period.

Romanesque Architecture

The first architectural style to appear was Romanesque, in the manner of the Romans. Around the ninth and tenth centuries, the Magyar and Viking invaders had looted and burned hundreds of wooden churches and monasteries throughout Europe. Starting in the eleventh century, in combination with the Cluniac reform movement, abbeys and monasteries were reconstructed of stone, a more permanent building material, in the Romanesque style. The ancient Roman form of the basilica, rectangular in shape, was changed to add a transept, crossing the central part (nave) of the church at right angles. This extension created the shape of a cross or cruciform floor plan, symbolizing Christ crucified. An apse (a semicircular opening that extended the church) was present at the head of the cross. The altar, positioned at the intersection of the cross, traditionally faced east, the main entrance west. Arched barrel vault ceilings, now constructed of stone, required massive walls to support their weight. In some cases the walls were 10 to 12

When did the Romanesque style begin?

small windows
fortification structures.
use stones.

What are the origins of the term?

What are the characteristics of the Romanesque style?

feet thick with narrow slit-like apertures for windows. These small, rectangular openings allowed little light to enter, creating an air of mystery, gloom, and impregnability. Other features of Romanesque architecture include rounded arches, twin towers, and large interior piers supporting the weight of the roof.

Brightly colored mosaics (pieces of colored tile or glass) and frescoes (freshly painted wet plaster) brightened the dark interior. Stiff, elongated, expressionless sculptures of saints, apostles, and the holy family, stationed inside and outside, were meant to awe and to inspire the churchgoer. It seems that the stonemasons of that era were unfamiliar with either classical Greek or the more naturalistic Roman figures; however, the elongated figures heightened dramatic effect. More interesting to students are the bizarre demons, fanciful monsters, mythological creatures that fill the tops of columns. These creatures were artists' visions of what hell might hold. Some of the more dramatic examples of Romanesque architecture are found at England's Southwell monastery, France's Church of the Madeleine at Vezelay, dedicated to Saint Mary Magdalen, and Spain's Santiago de Compostela, which contains the body of St. James as a relic. The major cathedrals housed relics, such as the body, the bones, the teeth, the hair of a saint, who could intercede for the petitioner. Vast numbers of worshippers went on pilgrimages to cathedrals to pray for miraculous cures, the souls of their dead relatives, spiritual renewal, or to receive indulgences (remission of the punishment due for their sins).

What are some examples of Romanesque style churches?

Gothic Architecture

Starting in twelfth-century France, there developed a new style of architecture know as the Gothic. Some of the more well-known examples of Gothic cathedrals include France's Chartres, Reims, and Notre Dame; England's Salisbury and Canterbury; and Germany's Strasbourg. Much time, energy, pride, deep religious faith, and financial resources were devoted to their construction. Some cathedrals took 50 to 350 years to complete; for example, Reims in France took 79 years to finish.

The word *cathedral* comes from cathedra or seat of a bishop's see or diocese. A cathedral is a much larger version of a church, housing a large school, choir, and pilgrimage site. The town had to be large enough to finance and support its construction. Not only did the townspeople give donations, but also the guild members, wealthy merchants, bankers, and nobles gloried in being part of the process. Towns would vie with one another to have the most magnificent cathedral, for it was also a symbol of urban pride.

Distinctive characteristics of the Gothic style of cathedrals, which evolved in the twelfth and thirteenth centuries, include pointed arches (the shape of hands folded in prayer), lofty spires, stained glass windows, ribbed vaults in the ceiling, and flying buttresses. These buttresses are outside arched stone piers, which support the much thinner walls of the Gothic style. The open ceilings reveal unbelievable spaciousness; in some cases the ribbed vaults soar to celestial heights, such as the one at Beauvais built to 167 feet before it collapsed.

The sculptures on the Gothic style were more human and naturalistic. For example, the smiling angel of the Annunciation at Reims Cathedral does not appear foreboding, but rather appealingly cheerful. Also the plants, vines, flowers, and leaves that were now sculpted displayed a love of nature that

When did Gothic architecture develop?

What are some examples of Gothic cathedrals?

wood
beautiful design of TAPESTRY
walls (Cloister museum).
above George Washington Bridge.

What are some of the characteristics of the Gothic style of architecture?

most important
stained glass windows.

Contrast the Gothic and Romanesque styles of sculpture.

Why was stained glass used?

was not present in the Romanesque style. Some of the cathedrals, such as Notre Dame in Paris, had gargoyles used as downspouts. These are fanciful, grotesque creatures that ward off evil spirits, according to medieval beliefs. The interior was illuminated by the exquisitely designed stained glass windows. An extremely large stained glass window, called the rose window from the blending of colors at Chartres Cathedral, appeared over the west portal entrance to these houses of worship. Their brilliant hues of reds, blues, golds, greens figuratively inspired the love of God. The illiterate could stare at the representations of the Bible stories, trying to understand as well as reconstruct them. Some of the vivid colors with their artistic placement in the lead frames made the reflected light burst into a million diamond sparklers. This is why these cathedrals are called MONUMENTS IN STONE, truly symbolizing the medieval devotion to the glory and splendor of God.

Literature

Latin was the universal language of the Church, scholars, and the very few literate lay individuals of the Middle Ages. Some of the finest examples of Latin are found in the hymns, chants, and devotional works of the Church. The Gregorian chants of the monks are not only still sung, but have also found their way into top-selling European recordings. Exuberant, lusty poems written by anonymous university students were part of the counterculture of the time. Cleverly constructed and witty, these Goliardic (in honor of a fictitious St. Golias) verses praised the pleasures of this world as opposed to the glories of the next.

Written in the vernacular (everyday tongue of the French, Spanish, German, Italian) were the epic poems. The earliest Anglo-Saxon heroic poem *Beowulf* was written in Old English by a Northumbrian monk in the late eighth or ninth century. Extolling loyalty, heroism, and bravery, *Beowulf* recounts the legend of a Swede who journeys to Denmark to slay a dragon/monster. One of the most famous epics written in an early French dialect is *The Song of Roland*, a tale of another stalwart hero. Other epic poems of warfare, chivalry, and loyalty to one's overlord include the *Nibelungenlied* (German) and the *Poem of El Cid* (Spanish).

Long poems sung by minstrels and troubadours at nobles' courts were called *chansons de geste* ("songs of great deeds"). Extremely popular, these poems recounted magical events, with wizards and fairies possessing supernatural powers, and were overlaid with romantic themes. With the forces of good pitted against the forces of evil, these songs of heroic deeds provided dramatic intrigue long before the soap operas of today engaged the eager viewer. In the Reading from the Time section, you will discover the lay of Marie de France, which is representative of these romantic poems. Chretien de Troyes was another author who launched the romances of King Arthur, Queen Guinevere, Sir Lancelot, Sir Galahad, Merlin, and others in their legendary court of Camelot. During this Age of Chivalry, noblewomen were placed figuratively on a pedestal to be worshipped from afar and were thought to be worthy of unrequited love and daring deeds. In reality, they were very much subordinate to their fathers and husbands and carried substantial household responsibilities. However, in these long poems, romantic love was an

What was the subject matter of Goliardic verse?

Name some epic poems of the Middle Ages.

long epics, has to have romance.

Were there medieval equivalents to today's romance novels? Explain.

Why is Dante Alighieri the best known poet of the Middle Ages?

Who are some of the characters found in Chaucer's *Canterbury Tales*? Do they ring true to life?

ennobling, fiercely exciting force that tore people apart as well as glued them together with dramatic intensity.

Medieval dramas were originally enacted in churches. Morality plays such as *Everyman* with personified virtues and vices, offered insight into the human condition and tried to inspire people to live saintly lives. Passion plays dramatized the last days of Christ, including his crucifixion. Miracle plays revolved around the lives of the saints, such as St. Catherine of Siena. There were pageants on religious holidays, such as Christmas, Easter, and Whitsunday.

The poet laureate of the High Middle Ages who created a treasure of vernacular literature is an Italian, Dante Alighieri (1265-1321). The *Divine Comedy*, his allegory of the soul's journey through hell, purgatory, and paradise, left a lasting impression on Western Civilization. With his vivid images of sinners consigned to one of the nine concentric circles of Hell according to their earthly misdeeds, Dante immortalized visions of the afterlife for all time. In his 100-canto long poem, Dante synthesized the medieval quest for the divine as the purpose of life.

Geoffrey Chaucer (c.1340-1400), in his *Canterbury Tales,* wrote of pilgrims on a journey to the shrine of Thomas à Becket at Canterbury, England. He developed memorable descriptions of people representative of their times and of the human condition. The scholarly Clerk of Oxenford cares more for books than fine clothing, while the Wife of Bath claims that what women really want is to be dominant over their husbands. These tales still amuse and delight readers, just as they did the readers in Chaucer's day.

11

Popes, Emperors, and Crusaders

The Medieval Church

Expressions of Popular Piety

In the Western Europe of the Middle Ages the Christian church, what today is called the Roman Catholic Church, played a central role in the lives of the people. Most medieval humans were not concerned with whether God existed, which was a given, but rather how they could be sure of reaching heaven.

Sacraments By the twelfth century, the church had established seven sacraments. The sacraments were visible signs of the inward reception of God's grace, which was necessary for salvation. Baptism ushered the new-born into the Christian life, freeing one from the taint of original sin. Confirmation prepared the adolescent to take on adult responsibilities. Extreme unction prepared the Christian for death. The sacrament of penance absolved him of grave sin, which would otherwise land him in hell. A form of union with Christ was possible through the reception of the Eucharist, which was thought to contain the actual body and blood of Jesus under the appearance of bread and wine (after a priest had said the words of consecration during the ceremony known as the Mass). If a man became a priest, he received the sacrament of holy orders, while

What are the sacraments?

Name some of the sacraments and describe their function.

Why did the sacraments increase clerical power?

heterosexual couples celebrated their ties with the sacrament of marriage. Most of these sacraments (baptism and marriage were the exceptions) had to be administered by a priest. Thus the clergy controlled the flow of grace needed for eternal bliss.

Saints Popular worship had many outlets besides the sacraments. We have already mentioned the great cathedrals of the Middle Ages. There was also the veneration of the saints, persons who had led especially holy lives and were believed to be capable of interceding with God on behalf of ordinary sinners. Mary, the mother of Jesus, was especially honored since it was believed that she had particular weight with God. In fact, she was recognized as the Queen of Heaven and believed to be a compassionate mother for every Christian.

Who was the most important saint?

What are relics?

Relics Along with the honoring of the saints came the veneration of relics, which were objects closely associated with the departed saint. A limb or some other body part was a prime relic. But clothes of the departed saint, splinters of the cross on which Christ died, even remnants of the five loaves Jesus used to feed the multitude were venerated during the medieval period without great concern for their authenticity. There were many reports of miracles produced by touching relics. A relic's value was measured by the reports of miracles it performed, not by established historical pedigree. Relics were prized possessions of churches.

Pilgrimages People made pilgrimages to churches and shrines, especially if they contained important relics associated with holy persons. The practice of going on a pilgrimage might be compared to going on a tour to some popular attraction today. The setting for Chaucer's *Canterbury Tales* was a pilgrimage to the Cathedral in Canterbury, England, where the martyred St. Thomas à Becket was buried. It was believed that many cures were worked at the invocation of the saint. The refusal of the Seljuk Turks to permit Western European pilgrims to visit the Holy Land was one of the justifications used to launch the crusades. The church encouraged the practice of visiting holy shrines by granting to the pilgrims indulgences or the remission of penance due for sins.

What were some of the benefits that encouraged pilgrimages? Were pilgrims always welcomed?

Religious Orders and Reform

The founding of the Benedictine monks by Benedict of Nursia was mentioned earlier. The endeavors of these monks and similar religious orders or groups, whether in manual labor on farms or in copying texts, contributed to strengthening both the church and society in general. It was not long before their services were used by kings, dukes and counts, as well as bishops and popes. The abbots found themselves responsible for providing knights for feudal armies and wise counsel to the politicians of their day. As the scope of their activities broadened and as generous contributions poured in from wealthy benefactors anxious about the next life, it was easy to grow complacent and indulgent of the flesh. Fortunately for the church, there were periodic movements for reform and renewal, which provided new groups of men and women dedicated to God and church.

Describe some of the activities of the monks.

paper reform

Why was there a need for periodic reform?

Cluniacs One such group developed around the monastery of Cluny in Burgundy, France. Founded in 910 by William I, Duke of Aquitaine, Cluny was free of the

Who were the Cluniacs?

jurisdiction of local bishops and dukes and subject only to papal authority. Its regime represented a modification of Benedict's rule. More stress was put on copying of manuscripts and elaborate liturgical services than on field labor and private prayer. Corrupt living within the monastery was not tolerated. The influence of the Cluniacs quickly spread to other monastic establishments throughout Europe. Many of these monasteries were daughter houses of the original in Cluny and were ruled by priors appointed by the abbot in Cluny, whose authority they accepted. Cluny's influence spread beyond the monastic circle to the church in general.

The Cluniac campaign stressed several areas of reform. Simony, or the selling of sacred objects and offices, was to be stopped. All priests were to adhere to the requirement of celibacy by giving up concubines or wives. Just as Cluny was free from the jurisdiction of the local duke, all church officials were to be freed from the control of political authorities. The practice of kings and others appointing church officials was to be ended. In the eleventh century many of the reforms sought by the Cluniac movement were instituted by reforming popes. In 1059, Pope **NICHOLAS II** (1059-1061) decreed that the **COLLEGE OF CARDINALS**, which had served as assistants to the pope, were to elect new popes. The idea was to free the papacy from the control of political officials. When Hildebrand, who was a monk from a Cluniac monastery, became Pope **GREGORY VII** (1073-1085) the papacy itself came to be an outpost of the movement. Success brought wealth and deep involvement in the political system. By the middle of the twelfth century, the Cluniac order was itself in need of reform.

What were some of their proposed reforms?

What was the College of Cardinals?

dominate the church to the present day

want to recapture the shrine of Jesus Christ

| Cistercians | Fortunately for the church, other religious orders with

fresh zeal came forward. One of these was the CISTERCIANS, an order founded in 1098 at Citeaux, in a remote area not far from Dijon, France. By the middle of the next century, there were over 300 monasteries with 11,000 monks and nuns. They led austere lives following the rule of Benedict with greater rigor than Benedict himself probably contemplated. Great emphasis was put on manual labor. Cistercian farming activities in remote areas helped to bring more land under cultivation and contributed to the development of western European commerce. The best known Cistercian of the Middle Ages was SAINT BERNARD OF CLAIRVAUX (1090-1153) who became a counselor to popes and kings. He led the attack on the rationalist teachings of Peter Abelard.

Franciscans The thirteenth century saw a new development: the rise of religious orders whose members did not stay in secluded cloisters, but went out into the towns and the countryside to preach to ordinary folks. Members of these orders were often called FRIARS (brothers) or MENDICANTS since they would beg to earn their bread rather than concentrate on farming as the Cistercians. The Franciscans were one of these mendicant orders. Their founder, ST. FRANCIS OF ASSISI (c.1182-1226) in Italy, embraced a life of idealized poverty and service to the poor. Initially this order owned nothing in common or individually, but some modifications of this strict poverty were eventually made. The Franciscans were encouraged by the church as an attractive alternative to groups such as the Waldenses, who also embraced poverty but were more critical of abuses within the church and were condemned as heretics. By 1220, Francis had thousands of followers and Franciscan mis-

Who was the most famous Cistercian?

How did the friars differ from more traditional monks?

Why do you think Francis of Assisi attracted so many people?

How did the Dominicans differ from the Franciscans?

sions were established in many places in Europe and even in the Holy Land.

Dominicans A contemporary of Francis was St. Dominic (c.1171-1221), born in Spanish Castile. Dominic became interested in converting the Albigenses of southern France, who were heretical dualists, believing all material things were evil. After working among the Albigenses or Cathari, Dominic was inspired to found a new order, popularly known as the DOMINICANS, who would seek to convert the world to the Catholic version of Christianity. In order to create effective preachers, Dominic placed more emphasis on education than Francis did. He followed the example of Francis in requiring his followers to take vows of poverty and live on donations. By the time of Dominic's death in 1221, there were some 500 friars and 60 priories throughout western Europe. The Dominicans became famous educators. Albert the Great and Thomas Aquinas, leading medieval intellectuals, were members of the order. As leaders in the campaign against heretics, they also came to staff the offices of the INQUISITION, the church tribunal charged with suppressing heresy.

Name some famous Dominicans.

The Holy Roman Empire

What part of the Carolingian empire became Germany? For how long did the Carolingians rule?

The grandsons of Charlemagne divided his empire into three parts in the Treaty of Verdun of 843. This division proved to be permanent. The eastern part became Germany, the western part France, and the middle never coalesced into a single state but was often the battle ground between France and Germany.

The Carolingian line of rulers died out in the East Frankish kingdom in 911. Thereupon the dukes of the tribes making up this

Eastern Carolingian realm, the future Germany, elected one of their own as king. Conrad the Franconian was chosen. Throughout his rule his chief rival was the duke of Saxony. Perhaps to get even, Conrad helped to select his rival, Henry I, the Fowler, Duke of Saxony, to be the next king of Germany. Henry I ruled from 918 to 935 and was the first of a line of Saxon kings that governed till 1024.

Otto the Great

Otto I the Great (936 - 973) was the most important of the Saxon kings in that he decisively defeated the Magyars in 955 at the Battle of Lechfeld. Otto extended his influence into northern Italy and came to Rome in 962 where he was crowned Emperor by Pope John XII (955 - 964). He was granted the title which Charlemagne and the Carolingian rulers had held but which had fallen into disuse after 925. Later, the name Holy Roman Empire was applied to the realms ruled by the German emperors. Many date the Holy Roman Empire from this coronation in 962. Critics have pointed out that this kingdom certainly was not holy, was not Roman (it was essentially a German kingdom), and was not an empire (it was a collection of tribal duchies barely held together by the emperor).

The Saxon kings governed with the aid of the bishops. Since clergymen must be celibate, they could not bequest their bishops' sees to their sons. Whenever one bishop died, the king could appoint another loyal follower to replace him. This system depended on the king appointing the bishops and other high prelates in his kingdom. During the early Middle Ages, the Church had become thoroughly intertwined with the feudal system. Bishops controlled sizable territories which

Name some of the German kings.

Why was Otto I so important?

Was the Holy Roman Empire well named?

What was the relationship between the Holy Roman Emperors and the Catholic Church?

What were the consequences of the Investiture Struggle?

How great a help were their Italian possessions to the Holy Roman Emperors?

they received from the king or other lord as a fief. They were expected to provide military service. Even the pope was often appointed by these Holy Roman Emperors. Obviously, the bishops of this time were greatly lacking in spirituality.

The Catholic Church was in danger of losing its spiritual mission. But excesses within the Church have often produced reform movements. The Cluniac Reform movement sought to disentangle the Church from feudalism and secular control. Under the Franconian or Salian line of rulers (1024 - 1125), a great power struggle erupted between the Popes and the Holy Roman Emperors. This power struggle is called the INVESTITURE STRUGGLE, which centered on the question whether the Emperor or the Pope would appoint bishops in Germany. The climax of this struggle took place between the Holy Roman Emperor Henry IV (1056 - 1106) and Pope Gregory VII (1073 - 1085). The Papacy won this struggle and worked to undermine the power of the German Emperors.

The dukes and other powerful lords had chafed under powerful rulers. They used the Investiture Struggle to further their own powers. Having lost Church support and without loyal bishops appointed by themselves, the German kings were unable to control effectively their diverse lands. The fact that Otto the Great had acquired most of Northern and Central Italy further complicated the job of these rulers. When they were in Italy, their German vassals rebelled; and when they were in Germany, the reverse was true.

The Hohenstaufen Dynasty

The Hohenstaufen family from Swabia, governed the Empire from 1138 to 1254. It produced two strong rulers, Frederick I Barbarossa (1152 - 1190) and Frederick II (1220 - 1250), who sought to restore the imperial power. Frederick Barbarossa lost the decisive Battle of Legnano in 1176 against an alliance of North Italian cities called the LOMBARD LEAGUE, which had Papal support. That defeat and the following Peace of Constance (1183) forced the Emperor to give up meaningful control over the Lombard cities of northern Italy. This marked the beginning of the independent city-states of Italy which would play a decisive role during the Renaissance.

Name two powerful Hohenstaufen rulers.

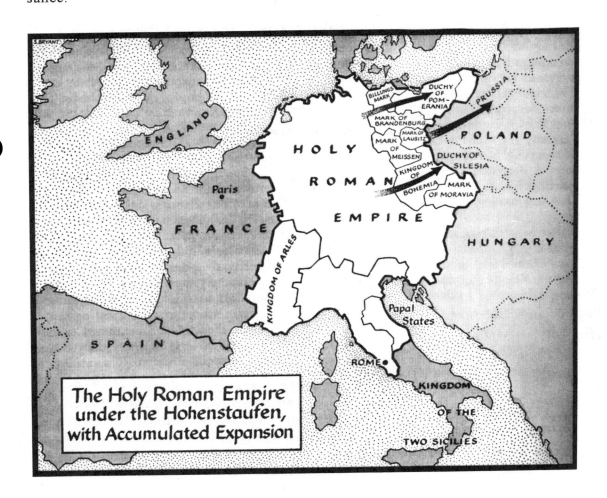

The Holy Roman Empire under the Hohenstaufen, with Accumulated Expansion

What followed the death of Frederick II?

Frederick II had inherited the Norman kingdom of Sicily through his mother. He was more concerned about his Italian possessions than his German title. He came close to politically uniting all of Italy and breaking the independent power of the Papacy. He died unexpectedly of illness in 1250 when victory was within his grasp. The popes never forgot this near defeat. They called the remaining Hohenstaufen heirs "a brood of vipers" and successfully prevented them from gaining the imperial title. In particular, the popes fought against having the Imperial title based on hereditary rights. They advocated an electoral system, as had been customary in Germanic tribal practice. The period from 1250 to 1273 is called the GREAT INTERREGNUM when there were no recognized Holy Roman Emperors.

What was the Golden Bull?

The Golden Bull

The German monarchy had always contained an elective element but after 1273, it becomes purely elective. Emperors could not pass their title to their sons. Each emperor was elected by a small group of powerful princes. In 1356, the GOLDEN BULL of Emperor Charles IV delegated this electoral power to seven Imperial Electors. The feudal lords of Germany made sure that they did not elect the most powerful candidate. The popes, the free cities, and the feudal lords had triumphed over the emperors. While the Holy Roman Empire survived until 1806 when the self-made Emperor Napoleon I of France finally abolished it, the Empire became a weak confederation of ultimately more than 300 independent little states. Neither Italy nor Germany was unified until the 1860s and 70s. Just as France and England emerged as powerful monarchical states in the thirteenth

What distinguished France and England from Italy and Germany after the thirteenth century?

century, the Holy Roman Empire went into decline.

We discuss the investiture struggle in greater detail below. Our focus shifts from the perspective of the Empire to the perspective of the Popes and the Church.

The Pope versus the Holy Roman Emperor

The use of the title Roman Emperor had fallen into disuse among the Carolingian descendants of Charlemagne after 925. But the title was revived by the Saxon king of Germany, Otto I (936-973) in 962. Otto received the crown from Pope John XII (955-964) as a reward for rescuing the pope from an Italian enemy. Otto established tight control over the clergy within his domain, which included much of Germany, Burgundy, and northern Italy. He also dominated the papacy itself, since he later deposed John and saw to the appointment of a pope more to his liking.

Gregory VII We have mentioned above that Pope Gregory VII, who became pope in 1073, was a product of the Cluniac reform movement. In 1059, even before becoming pope, he had supported the election of the popes by the College of Cardinals as a means of getting rid of the influence of both Holy Roman Emperors and the Italian nobility. As a former Cluniac monk and papal secretary, Gregory VII believed he should reform and purify all of Christian society. In addition, he also wished to continue the program of his predecessor Leo X by eliminating the abuses of simony (the buying and selling of church offices), clerical marriage, or concubinage. Believing his mission in life was to be a reformer, he issued papal pronouncements that no one should question his power. God alone would judge his actions; as a re-

Was Emperor Otto I subservient to the pope who had crowned him emperor? Explain.

What were the ambitions of Gregory VII?

What weapons were available to an ambitious pope?

sult, he alone had the power to depose emperors and to select bishops. This announcement had far-reaching implications.

Yes, the pope did indeed have authority to EXCOMMUNICATE Christian followers. By denying them membership in the church and the right to partake of the sacraments, which were needed for salvation, the pope doomed the excommunicated to an eternity in Hell. He also had a more formidable authority, called INTERDICT. This most terrible punishment was the forbidding of any Christian within a prescribed geographic region the right to enter a church to receive the sacraments. Consequently, entire populations could be prohibited from entering a church so that Christians believed themselves to be in danger of dying in mortal sin. They would then burn in hell forever.

What was lay investiture?

Holy Roman Emperor Henry IV (1056-1106)

was Pope Gregory VII's nemesis. The emperor had the power to select higher church prelates (archbishops, bishops, and abbots) loyal to him, and invest them with the symbols of their office (the ring and the staff) as well as their fiefs (land). The practice of non-clerics or lay people investing clerics with the symbols of their office became known as LAY INVESTITURE. Holy Roman Emperors found lay investiture to be very much to their liking since they depended on clerical vassals as administrators. Generally, the cleric who received his appointment from the emperor was more dependable than the lay vassal whose position was largely a matter of inheritance.

Why was it so important to the Holy Roman Empire?

Canossa In 1076, one of the most dramatic conflicts in medieval history arose because both pope and emperor had a candidate for the open Bishopric of Milan, a major town in the Holy Roman Empire. As a result of this dispute, first Emperor Henry IV deposed Gregory VII as pope, then Gregory deposed Henry as Holy Roman Emperor, excommunicating him and placing an interdict on the Holy Roman Empire. Although most of the bishops supported Henry, his nobles were edgy, restless, and considered the Emperor's deposition an opportunity to rebel. As Gregory journeyed to meet with the German nobles, Henry "cut him off at the pass" by going to Canossa, a palace of the pope in the Italian Alps, in January 1077. Dressed as a penitent in sackcloth (burlap) and ashes, Henry stood barefoot in the snow for three days. As a priest, Gregory was forced to forgive Henry. But jockeying for supremacy continued with Henry going back on his word of giving obedience to the Pope. After being excommunicated a second time, Henry had his troops occupy Rome in 1084. They held Gregory captive at the fortress of St. Angelo outside Rome where he died in exile.

After 50 years of strife, this struggle for church-state supremacy ended with a compromise, the CONCORDAT OF WORMS (1122). This agreement on lay investiture was reached by another pope, Calixtus II (1119-24), and Henry's son, Henry V (1106-25). The emperor would invest the prelate with his fief, and the church would grant him his spiritual symbols. Bishops and abbots would be elected by appropriate church officials, but the emperor could be present at elections and settle disputes. The church had gotten rid of lay investiture, but the emperor retained very real influence in the selection process.

Innocent III

With his theory of papal preeminence, the most resplendent, capable, and successful

Explain the dispute between Emperor Henry IV and Pope Gregory VII.

What is the symbolism of Canossa?

What was the Concordat of Worms?

Who do you think won—the pope or the emperor?

How comprehensive were the assertions of authority made by Pope Innocent III?

medieval pope was Innocent III (1198-1216). Elected unanimously by the College of Cardinals, his pontificate illustrates the culmination of power politics, diplomacy, and an exalted vision of the papacy's place in Christendom. Describing himself as the Sun in his bull (pronouncement) entitled *The Sun and the Moon* (1198), he writes as follows:

> ...As God, the creator of the Universe, set two great lights in the firmament of heaven, the greater light to rule the day, and the lesser light to rule the night, so He set two great dignities in the firmament of the universal church...the greater to rule the day, that is, souls, and the lesser to rule the night, that is, bodies. These dignities are the papal authority and the royal power. And just as the moon gets her light from the sun, and is inferior to the sun in quality, quantity, position, effect, so the royal power gets the splendor of its dignity from the papal authority...[1]

What is meant by Papal Monarchy?

The claims of papal authority over the monarchs of the world made in this quote is sometimes called PAPAL MONARCHY. Other popes, including Gregory VII had made similar assertions, but it was Innocent III who came closest to realizing these claims in fact. Believing in the righteousness of his cause, Innocent interfered in the affairs of several European monarchs. For example, by placing an interdict on France, he forced the king, Philip Augustus, to take back his Danish wife after the French prelates had annulled the king's marriage. Of course, the fact that the king's second wife had died in the meantime certainly made Philip Augustus more willing to acquiesce. But Innocent also made the king of Castile relinquish his wife because she was too close a relative.

King John of England Innocent III also tangled with King John of England (1199-1216) over who should be the Archbishop of Canterbury, the highest ranking prelate in the country. When John refused to accept Stephen Langton, Innocent's candidate, the pope excommunicated John and placed all of England under interdict in 1208. Though this meant that the ordinary English man or woman was deprived of the sacraments, John was not particularly intimidated. Indeed, the king took the occasion to seize the revenues of the church. It was a different matter, however, when Innocent encouraged Philip II of France to make preparations for the invasion of England in order to depose John. Philip was most anxious to oblige the pope and destroy an old enemy. John's own vassals were not too reliable, given their distaste for the king. So, in 1213, John did a sharp about face and not only accepted the pope's candidate for archbishop, but also gave his country, England, to the pope. He then received it back as a fief, making the king the pope's vassal. John profited by securing the pope's support, but papal prestige was enhanced by having the king of England as a vassal.

Innocent Chooses a Holy Roman Emperor Like Gregory VII, Innocent was also involved with the affairs of the Holy Roman Empire. It was a very complex situation. When Innocent took the throne, he found the Papal States threatened by the power of the Holy Roman Empire which had traditional claims to northern Italy. More recently, through a royal marriage, the Empire had also become associated with the Kingdom of Sicily, which included much of

How did Pope Innocent use marriage laws as instruments of papal power?

How did the king of England become a vassal of the pope?

Why did Pope Innocent III fear Imperial control of Sicily?

What actions did Innocent III take to prevent the union of Sicily with the Holy Roman Empire?

the southern Italian mainland. Under the Hohenstaufen Emperor Henry VI, who was the son of the celebrated Holy Roman Emperor Frederick I or Frederick Barbarossa (1155-1190), territory claimed by the pope had come into the possession of the emperor. Innocent feared that the Papal States, which lay in between The Holy Roman Empire and the Kingdom of Sicily, would continue to be squeezed by ambitious emperors as long as they ruled both empire and kingdom.

The pope, who ascended the papal throne in 1198—the year following the death of Henry VI, launched an aggressive counter-offensive. Innocent made himself the guardian of the young son of Henry VI, Frederick (later Frederick II), who was only three when his father died. Frederick was the recognized ruler of Sicily.

In the Holy Roman Empire itself, the position of king of Germany was contested. Philip of Swabia, a Hohenstaufen and brother of the former Henry VI, was challenged by Otto of Brunswick, a member of the rival Welf family. The pope initially supported Otto in order to separate Sicily from Germany. He crowned Otto Holy Roman Emperor after the unexpected death of Philip in 1208. Otto proved faithless and immediately attacked Sicily. Innocent's response was to support Frederick, his ward, for the position of Holy Roman Emperor. He first made Frederick agree to give up Sicily so that Germany and Sicily would remain under separate rulers. Innocent's gambit succeeded when Otto was defeated by the pope's ally, Philip II of France, at Bouvines in 1214. At the Lateran Council of 1215, Innocent III had the pleasure of declaring Otto deposed and confirming Frederick as emperor-elect of the Holy Roman Empire. It is ironic that after Innocent's death, in 1216, Frederick II reestablished his rights to Sicily, which was actually the possession that interested him most. Nevertheless, Pope Innocent had succeeded, through the fortunate victory of his ally at Bouvines, in determining who should be Holy Roman Emperor. Certainly, this represented the reversal of the earlier situation in which the Holy Roman Emperor had deposed Pope Gregory VII.

It would be possible to give further evidence of Pope Innocent III's effectiveness here by discussing the crusade he launched against the Albigensian heretics of southern France or his domination of the Byzantine Church as a result of the Fourth Crusade, which will be discussed later. But the examples of his dealings with the kings of France and England, and with the Holy Roman Emperors, should leave no doubt why historians consider the medieval papacy to have reached the height of its political power under Innocent.

It is interesting to note that the conflict between Welf and Hohenstaufen families became translated in Italy into a conflict between two factions, the Guelphs (Welfs) and the Ghibellines (a term derived from the Hohenstaufen castle of Waiblingen). The term Guelphs became associated with the supporters of the papacy, while Ghibellines came to designate those favoring the empire. The words continued in use into the fifteenth century, long after they had lost any connection with the original German families.

Boniface VIII

Innocent III died in 1216. By the end of the century, under Boniface VIII (1294-1303), the papacy's fortunes were in steep decline. The French and English monarchs, preparing for war against one another, sought to tax their clergy to raise funds. Boniface

Summarize the evidence demonstrating the political power of Innocent III.

Who were the Guelphs and the Ghibellines

What were the sources of friction between Pope Boniface VIII and King Philip IV?

What did Boniface VIII claim in *Unam Sanctam*?

What happened to Boniface?

challenged both these rulers by issuing in 1296 a bull or official letter, *Clericis Laicos*, which forbade the clergy to pay taxes to royal authorities without the explicit permission of the pope. The French king, PHILIP IV or Philip the Fair (1285-1314), took up the challenge. He cut off the flow of funds from France to the papal court and began a war of words against the pope. Boniface was obliged to back down. He tried to be conciliatory, even canonizing Philip's grandfather, King Louis IX. But in 1301, Philip's lawyers drew up phony charges against a French bishop whom Philip wished to try in a royal court. Boniface came to the defense of the bishop and Philip turned on Boniface calling him a heretic. The fracas led Boniface to issue, in 1302, the bull *Unam Sanctam*, one of the most extreme assertions of papal monarchical authority ever written. This bull declared that earthly power is subordinated to spiritual power. A spiritual power can only be judged by a higher spiritual power. If the highest spiritual power, the pope, errs, God alone can be the judge, not any earthly ruler. Philip's response was to send a loyal henchman, William de Nogaret, to kidnap the pope so that he could be brought to France for trial in a royal court. On September 7, 1303, Boniface was seized at his residences in Anagni. Though rescued by townspeople, the eighty-year old man was badly shaken up and died from the shock of the experience about three weeks later.

| Avignon Papacy | One would have expected the subsequent moral outrage to have carried the day for Boniface's cause. But this was not so. The next pope, Benedict XI (1303-1304), removed the excommunication against King Philip and sought instead to blame Nogaret, who had attempted the actual kidnapping. The next

pope, Clement V (1305-1314), a Frenchman, was even more ready to accommodate the French king. He quickly appointed nine French cardinals and altered those parts of *Clericis Laicos* and *Unam Sanctam* to which Philip objected. More significantly, he refused to go to Rome. Instead he relocated papal headquarters to Avignon, a city then within the Holy Roman Empire, but just across the Rhone River from France. The papacy would remain at Avignon from 1309 to 1377, leaving the impression (not necessarily true) that it was under the thumb of the French king.

What was the Avignon Papacy?

The Popes in Perspective

Clearly the outcome of the struggle between Philip IV and Boniface VIII was a victory for the French king and a decline in the prestige of the papacy. Pope Boniface VIII had claimed that all lay leaders had to be subservient to him, the highest spiritual power. Unlike his predecessor, Innocent III, he did not come even close to making good his claims. The question arises: how should we judge the demands of a Boniface or an Innocent. Surely the demands seem excessive to those of us who have been raised to accept the separation of church and state and to regard religion as a private matter. Some will grant that we cannot judge historical figures by the reigning assumptions of our own day. Others will see the struggle of popes against emperors and kings as merely examples of the struggle for power and dominance that continues, perhaps eternally, between the preeminent persons in any social system. Still others will see the struggle of the popes to limit and even subordinate the power of political rulers as establishing historical precedents that find full fruition in contemporary constitutional systems. These set limits on the

Do you think the popes were right in pressing their claims to superiority over political authorities? Explain.

How did the Crusades start?

What motivated the Crusades?

power of the government over the governed. How do you judge the popes described here?

The Crusades

The power of the medieval church is seen not only in the attempts of the popes to dominate the political leaders of their time, but also in the phenomena of the Crusades, which sent whole armies off to the Middle East to rescue the Holy Land. The time is November 27, 1095; the place is Clermont, France. The Byzantine Emperor Alexius I Comnenus (1081-1118) had asked the pope for aid against the advance of the Seljuk Turks. Pope Urban II (c. 1088-1099), at the Council of Clermont, delivers an impassioned speech to a crowd of nobles and commoners, urging them to take up the cross (*Crux* in Latin, hence Crusade) and wrest the Holy Land from the Muslims. The crowd goes wild, shouting in unison, "It is the will of God." With this phrase as a slogan, thousands will fight for 177 years to recapture the shrines in Jerusalem, embark on other worthy (or nefarious) endeavors, slaughtering and pillaging in the name of religion, politics, and greed.

When we talk about this period, we have to focus on the religious climate of the times. All classes of medieval people were concerned about their souls passing into heaven, about receiving absolution for their sins and achieving eternal salvation. So when the reigning pope promised remission for sins for the recapture of the Holy Land, the response was overwhelming. If the Crusaders were successful, the Pope would again be acknowledged as the leader of all Christendom.

Because there was an excess of young warriors and no real conflict to focus their energies, the Pope wished to channel their aggressiveness into a Crusade. This excess was caused by the inheritance laws of the time. Under PRIMOGENITURE, only the eldest son inherited land, estates, and the title. The younger sons were left to seek land, glory, plunder, and adventure in other outlets. By diverting these energetic knights into a Crusade, the Pope would rid Europe of excess militaristic zeal. The armed warriors would now fight Muslims instead of each other.

How did primogeniture encourage the crusading spirit?

Peasants' Crusade: 1096

Long before the knights could organize after Pope Urban II's sermon, a firebrand preacher, Peter the Hermit (c.1050-1115), excited and inspired a group of French peasants to take off for Jerusalem. Two French contingents and three German peasant groups abandoned their rural lives to march across Europe. The tragedy was that the Germans vented their anti-Semitic hatred as they went along, massacring Jews in the Rhineland despite the efforts of bishops to save them. When the sick and exhausted survivors of the Peasants' Crusade arrived in Constantinople, Emperor Alexius prudently shipped them off to be slaughtered in Asia Minor by the Seljuk Turks.

What was the Peasants' Crusade?

First Crusade: 1096-1099

The soldiers of the First Crusade were largely French under the leadership of Godfrey of Bouillon, his brother, Baldwin of Flanders, Raymond of Toulouse, and others. In July 15, 1099, Jerusalem fell into the hands of the Crusader knights. First-hand accounts relate horrible atrocities and blood up to the knees of the Crusaders' horses in

When did the Crusaders capture Jerusalem?

the Temple of Solomon. Christians massacred both Muslims and Jews in a savage orgy of blood lust. The following testimony is an account from an actual participant in the First Crusade:

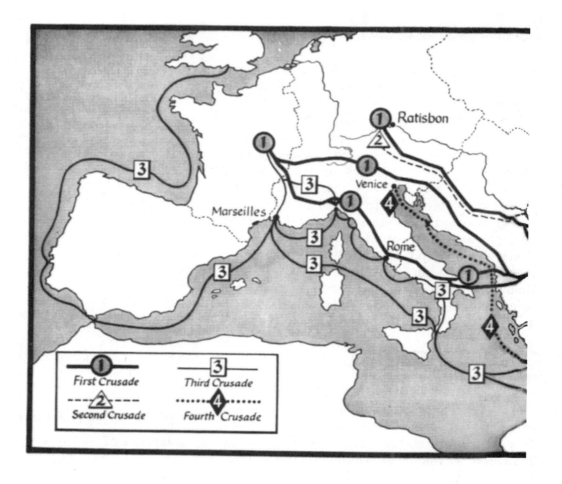

...But now that our men had possession of the walls and towers, wonderful sights were to be seen. Some of our men (and this was more merciful) cut off the heads of their enemies; others

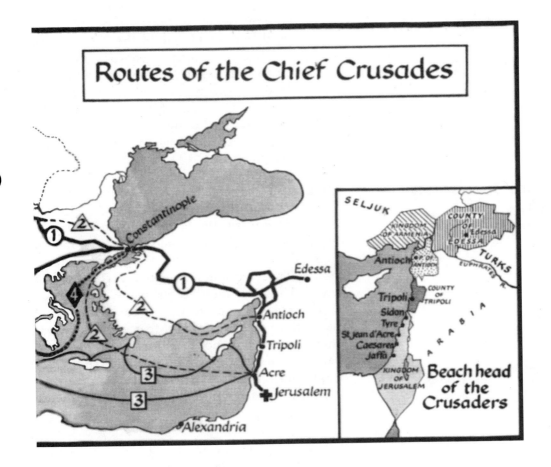

Routes of the Chief Crusades

Beach head of the Crusaders

What judgments do you make about the capture of Jerusalem?

shot them with arrows, so that they fell from the towers; others tortured them longer by casting them into the flames. Piles of heads, hands, and feet were to be seen in the streets of the city. It was necessary to pick one's way over the bodies of men and horses. But these were small matters compared to what happened at the Temple of Solomon, a place where religious ceremonies are ordinarily chanted. What happened there? If I tell the truth, it will exceed your powers of belief. So let it suffice to say this much, at least, that in the Temple and porch of Solomon, men rode in blood up to their knees and bridle reins. Indeed, it was a just and splendid judgment of God that this place should be filled with the blood of unbelievers, since it had suffered so long from their blasphemies.[2]

Was the First Crusade a success? Explain.

After the Muslim defeat, the Crusaders held four principalities in the Holy Land: the County of Edessa, the Principality of Antioch, the County of Tripoli, and the capstone of their conquests—the Latin Kingdom of Jerusalem. These kingdoms lasted for about 45 years. The Crusader States were beachheads of Christendom, stretching 500 miles along the eastern shore of the Mediterranean Sea. There were six more major Crusades and many more minor expeditions to the Holy Land, but the spirit and success, judged by Western standards, of the First Crusade were never duplicated.

Second Crusade: 1147-1149

Because the Crusaders were supplied by the sea and were small pockets of warriors in Muslim territory, their stronghold at Edessa was easily captured by Islamic armies. Abbot Bernard of Clairvaux, one of the most saintly monks of the time, convinced two monarchs, Emperor Conrad of Germany and Louis VII of France to pursue the Second Crusade from 1147 to 1149. Since the two monarchs were at odds with each other and the Muslims had superior military strength, their efforts achieved nothing. This Crusade failed miserably.

Assess the success of the Second and Third Crusades.

Third Crusade: 1189-1192

When in 1187 Jerusalem fell to Saladin, an exceptionally competent Muslim commander, three of the most powerful rulers in Europe called for the Third Crusade (1189-1192). These monarchs were: The Holy Roman Emperor Frederick Barbarossa, King Philip Augustus of France, and King Richard I (Richard the Lionhearted) of England. Due to lack of coordination, their combined forces could not retake Jerusalem. However, they did manage to capture a port, Acre, on the Mediterranean. Richard the Lionhearted negotiated a pact with Saladin, allowing Christian pilgrims access to their holy shrines once more.

Fourth Crusade: 1202-1204

How did the Fourth Crusade get started?

Pope Innocent III, the vigorous pope at the apex of the movement of papal power, summoned this paradoxical Crusade. When the Crusaders could not pay for the sea passage they had booked to the Holy Land from the commercial trading city-state of Venice, the doge (leader) of Venice suggested an alternative mode of payment: the capture of a Christian city, Zara, on the coast of the Adriatic Sea. This city was a commercial

What made the Fourth Crusade so unusual?

rival of Venice, and the doge saw in the Crusaders an opportunity to subdue his enemies. Incensed over the capture of Zara, Pope Innocent excommunicated all who took part (though he later rescinded the excommunication of the warriors).

Now the unimaginable happens. A pretender to the Byzantine throne, Alexis IV, promises the Latin Christian warriors an enormous sum of money if they would help restore the throne to him and his father, who would then become co-rulers of the Byzantine Empire. As you may have guessed, the Crusaders do as they are asked; however, when it comes time to pay, the now Emperor Alexis reneges on his agreement. The Crusaders sack, loot, and pillage Constantinople in retaliation, establishing Latin Christian control over this Byzantine capital. Christians are slaughtering fellow Christians at both Zara, Constantinople, and in other victories over the Byzantines. The Crusaders never reached the Holy Land. They took control of Constantinople and established a sixty-year Latin Empire of Constantinople. The Roman Catholic crusaders were pleased with their acquisition of Constantinople because they felt the Easterners were heretics who had left the fold.

What was the Children's Crusade?

Children's Crusade

The purity and innocence of children was tested in the Children's Crusade of 1212. A band of French youngsters heeded the call of Stephen of Cloyes, a shepherd boy. He and a German lad, Nicholas from Cologne, had visions of Christ calling them to liberate the Holy Land. Poor and believing French and German youngsters reached Marseilles, and possibly Pisa, to embark for the Holy Land. Some drowned in storms; others were sold to

Islamic slave traders in North Africa or to brothels in Italy. There may have been fifty thousand souls altogether. Very few of these unfortunate children ever returned home.

Effects of the Crusades

As we have seen, thousands of Jews, Muslims, Christians, men, women, and children, were slaughtered for the goal of recapturing the Holy Land. Although Palestine was held for short periods, holding it on a long-term basis was not an attainable objective for the West. It remained in Muslim hands until 1918, when it was captured by General Allenby in World War I.

Some historians feel that by outfitting the Crusaders, the Italian commercial cities of Genoa, Pisa, and Venice became wealthy. Other historians argue these cities would have traded with the eastern world anyway, without the benefit of supplying the Crusaders. These cities prospered, became commercial rivals among themselves, and by 1350 paved the way for the Age of Exploration and the Italian Renaissance.

One long-term legacy of the Crusades was the enmity aroused between Christians and Moslems. Many of our problems in the Middle East have come from this continued animosity. However, while the young Crusading warriors were away, there was more peace in Europe. The absence of these knights led to the growth of nationalism and an increase in the powers of the kings of England and of France. In other words, the powers of the nobles declined; and with this decline, the institution of feudalism lost some of its prestige. Geography, travel, and tales of the East stimulated interest in exploring faraway lands. The enthusiasm for crusading gradually lost its appeal among the nobles and common

What were some of the effects of the Crusades?

Are you inclined to condemn or praise the Crusades?

Under what circumstances might a Western crusade into the Middle East be launched today?

folk as they became more and more preoccupied with affairs in their nation-states. By the conclusion of the thirteenth century, the Crusading movement had lost most of its appeal.

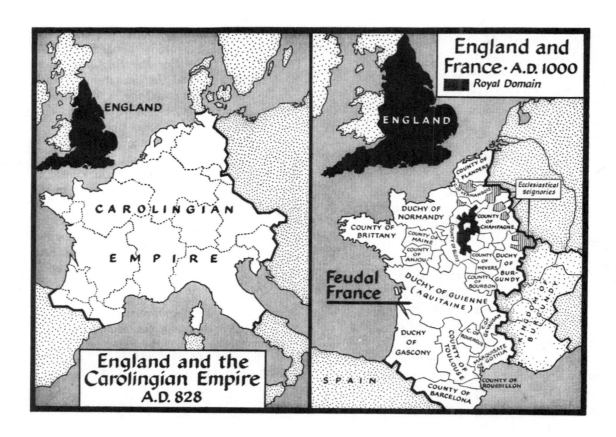

England and the Carolingian Empire A.D. 828

England and France · A.D. 1000
Royal Domain

Feudal France

12

France, England, and the Later Middle Ages

The Capetian Dynasty in France

Hugh Capet and the Early Capetians

The Treaty of Verdun in 843 had divided the Empire of Charlemagne among his grandsons. The western portion, which was to become France, was given to Charles the Bald. Carolingian family members succeeded to the throne after Charles, but their strength was weakened by the feudal system, which placed greater power in the hand of the vassals of the king—the counts and dukes, than in the king himself. The king came to be elected by the great feudal lords.

On a few occasions, rivals of the Carolingians were elected. Hugh Capet (987-996), who was not a Carolingian, was elected to the French throne in 987. He was smart enough to associate his son, Robert, with the throne by the end of the year. Association meant establishing a kind of joint reign by crowning one's successor while continuing to rule. When Hugh died in 996, Robert, his son and chosen successor, became the sole king. The Capetians used the process of associating their sons with the royal office and were fortunate to have a continuing line of male heirs at a time when women were normally

Why did the feudal system tend to weaken the French monarchy?

Who was Hugh Capet?

How did the Capetians succeed in establishing a new dynasty?

Why is Louis the Fat remembered?

What factors hurt the marriage of Eleanor of Aquitaine?

denied the right to rule. The result was that the French throne became a hereditary monarchy and the Capetian family ruled France until the last of the direct line of the Capetians died out in 1328.

The early Capetians had very limited resources. Their royal holdings or demesne, from which they drew most of their revenues, consisted of a number of scattered regions. The most important cities within their territories were Paris and Orleans. Hugh Capet could not freely travel through his domain without encountering robber vassals willing to plunder the land. It was Louis VI the Fat (1108-1137), the great great grandson of Hugh, who finally succeeded in gaining control over his own lands by pacifying the robber lords. Louis the Fat, who was obese, brutal, and ambitious, was fortunate enough to have an able advisor in the person of Abbot Suger (c.1081-1151) of Saint-Denis. Suger not only advised Louis the Fat, but he also wrote a flattering biography of the monarch that was to create a favorable image for later historians.

Louis VII and Eleanor of Aquitaine

The son and successor to Louis the Fat was Louis VII, who reigned from 1137 to 1180. The young king was able to draw upon the advice of Suger until the Abbot's death in 1151. The father had arranged the marriage of his son to Eleanor of Aquitaine, who was the heiress to the large duchy of Aquitaine in the south of France. Wed in 1137 when Eleanor was only fifteen and he was sixteen, the marriage did not go well. Eleanor bore Louis two daughters, but no male heirs. Perhaps more important, the king suspected her of having an affair with a handsome Muslim she met while on a crusade with Louis. The marriage was annulled in 1152. Eleanor then found herself surrounded with suitors anxious for her possessions. She chose to marry Henry Plantagenet, Count of Anjou, whose holdings in France included Anjou, Maine, and Normandy. In 1154, he also became king of England.

The result was a political disaster for Capetian interests. Henry and Eleanor together, as vassals of Louis VII, held the entire west coast of France! They had more territory under their direct control than Louis had in the royal domain, known as the Île de France. Moreover, Henry was king of England in his own right, not as the vassal of Louis, and owed no feudal obligations to Louis for his English possessions. The Angevin (the adjectival form of Anjou) threat to France was very real and would preoccupy Louis's son, Philip II.

Why was the marriage of Henry of Anjou to Eleanor of Aquitaine such a threat to the French crown?

Expansion of the French Monarchy in the Thirteenth Century

In the thirteenth century France had three great kings: Philip II, Louis IX, and Philip IV.

Who was Richard the Lion-Hearted?

Philip Augustus

Philip II (1180-1223) Augustus, the son of Louis VII, crushed Angevin power in France. Philip fought Richard, king of England, from 1194-1199. Richard, nicknamed the Lion-Hearted, was a very skilled fighter, able to inspire his vassal warriors. Things did not go very well for Philip until Richard was killed by an arrow in a minor skirmish in

What were some of the character defects of King John of England?

What circumstances helped Philip II of France in his quest for the Angevin territories in France?

Why was the Battle of Bouvines so significant?

1199. John, the youngest son of Henry II, succeeded his brother Richard as king of England. Subject to great mood swings of furious energy and great indolence, John kept faith with no one and was distrusted by all. He was a suitable target for the ambitions of Philip Augustus.

The opportunity came for Philip when John married, in 1200, Isabel of Angoulême who was betrothed to one of John's vassals. When the vassal could get no satisfaction from John, he appealed to John's lord, who was Philip Augustus. Philip summoned John to Paris to answer charges. When John failed to answer the summons to the king's court, Philip had an excuse for taking John's fiefs in France by force, thereby greatly enriching the house of Capet. In 1204, Normandy was made part of Philip's royal domain. After a truce in 1206, John had little of what had been the Angevin possessions in France, except Gascony in the south.

John did not give up hope of regaining his lost territories in France. He made an alliance with Otto IV, the Guelf emperor of the Holy Roman Empire, against Philip and his ally, Frederick of Hohenstaufen. The plan was for Otto to move against Philip from the east and John to move against Philip from the west in the summer of 1214. While John was held at bay by Philip's son, a battle was fought between Philip and Otto in the east at Bouvines on July 27, 1214. The result was a decisive victory for Philip II. Otto lost his position as Holy Roman Emperor. John went back to England, where he had to deal with a rebellion of his barons. John died in 1216. Too tied up with affairs in England for the rest of his reign, John was not an effective threat to Philip. The Angevin power in France had been broken.

Saint Louis

Louis IX (1226-1270) was the son of Louis VIII and the grandson of Philip II. His mother was Blanche of Castile, the granddaughter of the Angevin Henry II and Eleanor of Aquitaine. The queen mother, an able woman, was responsible for the royal government when the twelve-year old Louis IX came to the throne and later (1248-1252), when Louis was off on a crusade. The only king of France to be a canonized saint of the Catholic Church, he did much to earn that honor. This pious king washed the feet of lepers, gave alms to the poor, built hospitals, and led two crusades, actually dying from illness while on a crusade. He negotiated peace settlements with England and Spain's monarchs, when he might, instead, have chosen to go to war. He was so respected internationally that he was asked to arbitrate a dispute between the English king, Henry III, and his barons.

We must understand, however, that Louis's virtues were in keeping with his time. Intolerant of non-Christians, both Muslims and Jews, he also attacked the Christian Albigensians, whom he considered heretics, in the south of France. Royal power in France was enhanced. The king has been described sitting under an oak tree hearing the cases of all who appealed to him for justice, whether rich or poor. This quest for justice served to check the power of subordinate feudal nobles. The king also sent *enquêteurs*, or inspectors, around to the various regions to make sure that the royal officials did not abuse their authority. Neither his nobles nor royal officials found the saintly king to be an easy mark.

Did Louis IX of France deserve to be canonized a saint? Explain.

How did Louis IX increase royal power?

Philip the Fair

To what extent was Philip IV a success?

The grandson of Louis IX was Philip IV, the Fair, who ruled from 1285 to 1314. Philip's nickname, "the Fair," referred to his good looks rather than to any reputation for just dealings with others. Philip IV's struggles with Pope Boniface VIII are described elsewhere. He succeeded in having the papacy transfer its headquarters to Avignon in close proximity to the border of France and in having Boniface's edicts against him nullified.

Philip IV was much less successful in trying to get the English out of Gascony in southern France and in battling the Flemings in the north, whose woolen interests linked them to the English. These wars left the king scrambling for new tax revenues. His search for funds and struggles with the pope, led him to call assemblies which included representatives of the clergy, nobles, and apparently for the first time in 1302, the townspeople. Each of these groups constituted an "estate." The three groups or estates assembled together later became the Estates-General, which resembled a legislature. However, it remained an advisory body and did not acquire the full legislative powers of the Parliament in England or of the Congress in the United States.

What was the Estates General?

The Anglo-Normans in England

The affairs of the French and English monarchies were very intertwined in medieval times. To better appreciate the linkage, it is necessary to look at England in 1066. Harold

II, the last Anglo-Saxon king of England, was crowned on January 16, 1066. While not of royal blood, he had the support of the previous king, Edward the Confessor (1042-1066), and had been elected by the English nobility.

William the Conqueror

Harold's claim to the English throne was disputed by several rivals, the most important of which was William, the duke of Normandy in France. Originally Viking invaders, the Normans had by 1066 adopted the French language, and William held Normandy as a vassal of the French king. William the Bastard (as he was called by virtue of his illegitimate birth) was a second cousin of Edward the Confessor, who had himself been raised in Normandy. William had also been promised the crown in 1051 by the weak Edward, and had allegedly wrung a promise of support at one time from Harold under duress. What made William's claim strong in 1066 was possession of one of the best trained feudal armies in Europe and a papal banner supporting William's claim to England. (The Pope saw an opportunity to get a more submissive Archbishop of Canterbury.)

The Battle of Hastings

King Harold of England was aware of William's intentions to invade and had gathered an army in the south of England to resist the expected Norman invasion across the English Channel. In the meantime, England was invaded from the north by the king of Norway, another claimant to the throne who was allied with Harold's own brother, Tostig. On September 25, 1066, Harold defeated this northern force at the Battle of Stamford

Compare the claims of Harold the Saxon and William of Normandy to the English throne.

Why was the Battle of Stamford Bridge so significant?

Why did the Normans win the Battle of Hastings?

Bridge. But he then had to march hurriedly south to confront William's Norman forces, who had invaded England on September 28th. After a march of 250 miles, Harold's Saxon forces met the Normans at the Battle of Hastings on October 14, 1066. It has been estimated that William had 1500 cavalry and another 300-400 infantrymen whose principal weapon was the bow and arrow. We do not know the size of Harold's army, but some appear to have been ill-trained peasants. While the Saxons had horsemen, they dismounted when fighting. Using newer tactics, the Norman horsemen stayed in the saddle as they fought. They were able to slaughter the Saxons who were on foot and whom William had skillfully drawn out of formation. Harold died after receiving an arrow through the eye and the victory went to William's forces. The Battle of Hastings was depicted in the Bayeux Tapestry traditionally attributed to William's wife Matilda. This battle was the last successful military invasion of England!

What was the Danegeld?

The Norman Conquest Changed England

Why is the Domesday Book important?

William I the Conqueror replaced the Anglo-Saxon nobility with Norman lords. He retained those aspects of Anglo-Saxon government that suited his advantage. For example, he kept the Danegeld, a tax originally imposed by the Anglo-Saxon kings for the purpose of fighting or buying off invading Danes. To get the most revenue from this tax, he commissioned a survey of taxable property in England. This detailed record, which has been of great value to historians, was completed in 1086. It was called the DOMESDAY BOOK because, like the Last Judgment, there would be no appeal from its findings.

The Norman Conquest meant both more efficient and more centralized government for England. An example of centralization is the SALISBURY OATH of 1086 which had landowners of substance take an oath of fealty directly to William—overruling their obligations to their immediate feudal lord and establishing independent bonds directly with the king. William also took care to keep much of the land of England as his personal property. An estimated one-fourth of the land was in the royal demesne at the time of his death in 1087.

What was the Salisbury Oath?

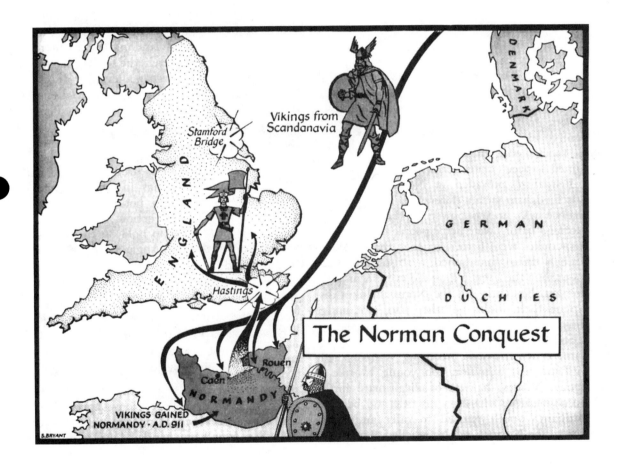

The Norman Conquest

Can you name some of the possessions of Henry II?

Henry II, the First Angevin King of England

Henry of Anjou, one of the most important English kings, ruled England as Henry II from 1154 to 1189. This was the same Henry whose marriage to Eleanor of Aquitaine has already been mentioned. Remember the vastness of the territories he ruled! The Angevin empire in France went from Normandy in the north to Gascony in the south — fiefs held as the vassal of the French king. England was important for the royal title it brought Henry and the resources it gave him in maintaining and expanding the rest of the Angevin empire.

What were the origins of the common law?

Henry took a particular interest in extending the royal system of justice and is credited with furthering the development of what came to be known as the COMMON LAW in England. The common law was the law of the king, which was "common" in the sense that it applied throughout England. Decisions made in the courts of barons or other feudal lords were not common law because they had applicability in only a particular lord's jurisdiction. The common law, as opposed to the Roman law, had its origins in the Germanic and feudal tradition. Law in this tradition was not made by a legislature or by the king's fiat. Rather, law was the remembered customs of the tribal society or group. Henry II had judges ride out regularly from Westminster, his judicial headquarters, to various shires or counties to apply the law in particular cases. These circuit judges were not familiar with who might have committed a crime in a particular area, but they made use of local juries to determine who should stand trial. In the time of Henry II, trial by ordeal was still common in criminal matters. In land disputes, which were civil cases, it became possible to have juries determine who had the right to possess a particular property. The clear division of juries into grand juries to make indictment and petit juries to bring convictions was a later development, as was the heavy reliance on previous court precedents to determine cases. The use of several types of WRITS, or written orders directing that a case be heard in a royal court, became standardized. The historical evidence does not suggest that Henry II expanded the common law primarily because of his thirst for justice. Rather, the expansion of royal justice served to enrich the king and increase his political power. The royal courts collected various fees in connection with these trials and the goods of those convicted in criminal trials were forfeited to the crown. Uncooperative feudal nobles could be and were brought down by adverse property decisions.

Henry II and Thomas à Becket

It was Henry's interest in the expansion of the royal justice that brought him to nominate Thomas à Becket (c.1118-1170) to be Archbishop of Canterbury. Becket had been a favorite of Henry's and rose to the position of the king's chancellor. When the Archbishop of Canterbury died in 1162, Henry persuaded Thomas to become the new Archbishop of Canterbury, hoping to assure himself of a friendly head of the church in England. The church had its own system of church law that competed with royal law.

Becket was one of those persons who puts himself or herself wholeheartedly into whatever they are doing. As the chancellor of

How does common law differ from law made by a legislature (statutory law)?

Why were juries needed?

How did Thomas à Becket get to be Archbishop of Canterbury?

Describe the conflict between Henry II and Becket.

the realm, he had served his king, Henry II, as perfectly as possible. As Archbishop of Canterbury, Becket served his church with the same drive towards perfectionism—fighting any encroachments Henry attempted on church prerogatives.

A special point of conflict between Henry and Becket was what to do with clerics who were accused of such criminal behavior as murder or robbery. Henry was willing for accused clerics to be tried in ecclesiastical courts, but he insisted that, if convicted, they should not only lose clerical status but be handed over to royal authority for punishment. Becket wished that punishment of clerics be the exclusive right of church courts. Since ecclesiastics meted out much less severe punishment than lay judges, and since it was not hard to gain clerical status, there was an incentive to enter clerical orders to avoid full punishment for serious offenses.

Do you think Henry really wanted Becket to be killed in the cathedral? Explain.

The conflict reached the point that Becket fled England in 1164 to escape Henry's reach. A reconciliation of sorts was made in 1170 when Thomas à Becket returned to Canterbury to take up again his duties as archbishop. Upon returning, Becket sought to oust those bishops who had supported the king. Hearing about this, Henry, who was in France, flew into a rage, charging that his followers failed in their loyalty to him and expressing the wish to be rid of the archbishop. Four of Henry's knights crossed the Channel, rode to Canterbury, and murdered Becket in the cathedral. This was not an action Henry really wanted. Becket was now a martyr. To make amends, Henry did penance, permitted the clergy to escape punishment by secular authorities, and even to appeal the decisions of English ecclesiastical courts to the Papal Curia. For Thomas, as for his master Jesus, in death there was victory!

Henry II Opposed by Wife and Sons

Henry had difficulties not only with friends, such as Becket, but with his immediate family as well. Perhaps because of his bedroom activities with other women, his wife Eleanor and he did not get along. In any case, Eleanor encouraged her sons to revolt against their father. In 1173 and 1174, Henry II fought his sons: Henry, Richard, and Geoffrey. Henry crushed the revolts but treated his defeated sons generously. However, he confined Eleanor for the rest of his life, some fifteen years. The sons Henry and Geoffrey died before their father. But Richard quarreled with his father, who wished to leave Aquitaine to his youngest son, John. Even John, whose interest Henry II was protecting, joined his brother against his father! Henry died a broken-hearted man.

Limits on the English Monarchy in the Thirteenth Century

While the French kings of the thirteenth century were enjoying successes and expanding royal prerogatives, the English monarchs of the same period were forced to accept limits on royal power. King John of England had suffered humiliation at the hands of Pope Innocent III in the contest to determine who would be appointed Archbishop of Canterbury. John Lackland had also lost most of his lands in France to the French king, Philip Augustus. After the Battle of Bouvines, all hope of recovering his French territories had to be given up.

Evaluate Henry II as a family man.

Do you think John of England was a loser? Explain.

Magna Carta

What were the origins of the Magna Carta?

When John returned to England from France, his barons demanded that their defeated king remedy their grievances. They resented being subject to heavy and, in their minds, sometimes illegal taxes for unsuccessful wars. They also felt the king had corrupted the law courts to obtain false judgments against baronial families. When John resisted, the barons rose in rebellion against him. In 1215 at Runnymede, about twenty miles southwest of London, which was then in the hand of the rebels, John submitted to the barons, signing the MAGNA CARTA or Great Charter. It was primarily a statement of the rights of the nobles, but it contained clauses of benefit to churchmen and merchants as well.

Explain some of its provisions.

Historians and political figures have debated the meaning of the Magna Carta. Later generations found a broad set of liberties for all English citizens embedded in it. Such interpretations are anachronistic, but the Magna Carta does contain language that sought to limit the powers of the English king and was later interpreted as a statement of general constitutional liberties. For example, one clause reads "No scutage nor aid [forms of taxes] shall be imposed in our kingdom, except by the common council of our kingdom..." and another clause says "No freeman shall be taken or imprisoned...except by the legal judgment of his peers or by the law of the land."[3] It is not difficult to see how later generations could find in these words the principles no taxation without representation and a right to trial by jury.

A committee of twenty-five barons was to be elected and permitted to harass the king by taking his possessions if the king failed to respect the provisions of the charter. This meant that the barons might have to war against their king to enforce their rights!

The Origins of Parliament

Since the time of William the Conqueror, the kings of England had had a *Curia Regis* or King's Court. In this court were the most important nobles, who were summoned as a great council to give advice to the king. Some historians trace the origins of the English parliament from the *Curia Regis*. The word parliament itself derives from the French word *parler*, to speak or talk. When the great barons got together there was quite a bit of talking, just as there is in contemporary legislatures. An important part of the development of parliament can be traced to the thirteenth century.

King John's successor, his son Henry III, who reigned from 1216 to 1272, was disliked by the barons. Henry III used many foreign-born officials and raised taxes. When, at the pope's bidding, he became embroiled in a war to make his second son, Edmund, the king of Sicily, the barons forced Henry III to accept the Provisions of Oxford (1258), which made the king subject to a governing council. The king's reneging on the Provisions led to the Barons' War (1263-1267).

Each side needed support and funds for the war. The leader of the baronial opposition was Simon de Montfort (1208-1265). Simon called a parliament for January 1265 that was not only to include barons, earls, and high churchmen, but also two knights from each shire or county and two citizens from each city and borough. The inclusion of the knights and the town citizens brought together the elements that constitute the English Parliament, though as yet there was no division

How was the Magna Carta supposed to be enforced?

What was the *Curia Regis?*

Describe Henry III's difficulties with the barons.

What was the composition of Simon de Montfort's January 1265 parliament?

into a House of Lords and a House of Commons.

Later, in the year Simon was defeated and killed in a battle with Edward, the eldest son of Henry III. When Henry died, Edward ruled in his own right as Edward I (1272-1307). Edward was a considerably more effective and respected king than his father. Nevertheless, Edward continued to call parliaments frequently, many of them on the model established by Simon de Montfort. In doing this, he assured himself of general support for his policies, and more especially for his taxes.

Why did Edward I continue to call parliaments?

The approval of Parliament came to be required for the imposition of new taxes to be legitimate. This right gave Parliament a measure of power over the king to induce him to grant legislation demanded by and favorable to the king's subjects. Parliament and the Common Law provided some measure of restraint on the royal prerogative. The elements for an effective, yet limited, central government were in place. It would take centuries of further struggles between kings, the great lords, the princes of the church, and the leading citizens of the towns to perfect the national monarchy of England.

The Later Middle Ages

What do historians mean by the Later Middle Ages?

Historians regard the fourteenth and fifteenth centuries (1300-1500) as the Later Middle Ages. It was a time of political and religious upheaval. During this period, much of the medieval social and economic structure came apart. By 1300 most arable land in Europe had been put into cultivation. Given the limits of the agricultural technology then available, it was difficult to increase agricultural productivity. Marginal land, requiring much labor, was already in use. As population grew to somewhere between 80 and 100 million, plots were subdivided and many families found they could not produce enough to feed themselves and pay the landlord. Between 1315 and 1322 heavy rains, cold weather, and unusual frosts had produced insufficient crops for the growing population of Europe. This Little Ice Age caused famine and in some areas over 10% of the population succumbed to either starvation or disease. Perhaps you can see why these fourteenth-century malnourished people would have a high susceptibility to disease.

What factors contributed to food shortages in the first quarter of the fourteenth century?

The Black Death

Suppose an epidemic disease with no available vaccines gripped our nation or planet. Furthermore, in some forms of this deadly disease, people would die in significant numbers, experiencing horrible last moments (high fever, coughing, diarrhea, spitting blood). Scary scenario? But this is exactly what happened in the fourteenth century in European countries when the Black Death or bubonic plague caused pandemonium, fear, and havoc. The bubonic plague still exists in India, China, other Far Eastern countries, and in the southwestern United States.

What are the symptoms of the Black Death?

Remember modern sanitation standards did not exist in 1348-1350. Medieval cities were over-crowded, refuse was dumped into narrow streets, physicians and victims alike had no knowledge of bacteria or viruses—what we now call the germ theory of disease. We have become antiseptic and hygiene conscious only in recent centuries. We now know the bubonic plague is caused by an intestinal bacillus carried in the stomach of fleas living in the hairs of rodents. The bite of the flea would then infect a human, causing large swellings (BUBOES, hence the name bubonic

What caused the Black Death?

How did the plague start?

Describe the societal disruptions caused by the Black Death.

plague) in the lymph glands in the neck, armpit, or groin. Dark blotches appeared on the skin of victims—hence the term Black Death.

The plague arrived from the Far East when a Genoese merchant ship carrying a cargo of grain, infected rats, and dead sailors docked at Messina, Sicily in 1347. The Asian rats exited the ship, rapidly spreading the plague throughout Italy, France, England, northern Germany, and the Scandinavian countries along the trade routes and through the more heavily populated cities. The plague wiped out one-third to one-half of the total population of Europe. Some estimates run as high as 60% in major cities. People living in remote areas were spared for the most part because of the lack of contact with infected rats or humans.

Although some victims could survive the bubonic variety of the plague, most individuals who contracted the pneumonic or septicemic form expired within twenty-four hours. Knowing no cause or no cure, to medieval people, it seemed like the end of the world. God must indeed be punishing them for their sins. Because of the vast number of sudden deaths, corpses were buried in mass graves, often without the benefit of a funeral. The nuns and the priests who ministered to the ill also died in large numbers; as a consequence, there was a shortage of clergy. Urban families, living in proximity to one another, were particularly vulnerable. Houses, monasteries, and fields were left unattended; cattle, sheep, and other animals roamed or died because they were abandoned. The universality of death surrounded everyone in society.

Some survivors turned to hedonism, eating and drinking excessively, while others became intensely religious, praying continuously. One of the most curious groups of religious fanatics were called FLAGEL-

LANTS. They came out of Germany and went about the countryside beating themselves in ritualistic ceremony with whips of knotted leather affixed with little iron spikes. The idea behind their self-inflicted wounds was to do penance so that God would end the plague. Finally the Pope condemned their masochistic behavior, and they were ordered to stop. The Jews were at this time accused of poisoning wells and in many areas of Germany Jews were massacred. Again in history, the Jews were used as scapegoats.

Who got blamed for the Black Death?

Peasant Revolts

The economy of Europe was completely disrupted by the Black Death. Recurrences of the plague occurred in almost every generation throughout the fourteenth and fifteenth centuries. Landowners had to compete for the available serfs, who in turn could demand much higher wages and better working conditions than before the plague. As a result, many landowners gave up farming and leased their lands. Inflation distorted the economy as prices, particularly of goods requiring skilled labor, reached unprecedented levels.

The economic dislocation fostered unrest and there were uprisings in several parts of Europe in the fourteenth century. One of the more famous was the uprising of the JACQUERIE in northern France in 1358, during the Hundred Years' War between England and France. Marauding armies on both sides pillaged peasant dwellings, while taxes were increased to provide ransom for captured French aristocrats, including the king. A contemporary description[4] recounts an instance of peasants invading a lord's castle and raping his wife in front of his eyes; in another case they killed the noble husband before his wife and children and later exe-

What were the Jacquerie?

What did they do?

What caused the Peasant's Revolt of 1381 in England?

Who led the revolt?

How did it end?

Describe the rival claims to the French throne that brought on the Hundred Years' War.

cuted them as well. The revolt lasted for only a few weeks until the military put down the rebels and meted out similarly savage reprisals.

The Black Death also played a role in the Peasant's Revolt of 1381 in England. The scarcity of labor had led to rising wages and some instances of release from serfdom. When the upper-class succeeded in passing laws that attempted to restrict wages to their pre-plague levels, this did not sit well with peasants and urban workers. The incident that actually brought on the revolt was the enactment of a poll tax of a shilling a person regardless of income. Insurrections occurred in both Kent and Essex. The rebel leader, Wat Tyler, met the teenage king, Richard II (1377-1399), in June and persuaded him to abolish serfdom and permit wages to rise. But Tyler was later slain by the mayor of London. The leaderless rebels were hunted down and the economic concessions withdrawn. Aristocratic privilege would be maintained into modern times.

The Hundred Years' War

The rebellions we have been discussing were short-lived, but the Hundred Years' War was a major upheaval that contributed to the decline of the medieval order. Lasting much longer, from 1337 to 1453, this war was not continuous, but a series of intermittent engagements. It originated in rival claims to the French throne. Philip IV of France had three sons and a daughter. Each of the sons ruled France. When the last of the sons died in 1328 without a male heir, the French nobility selected Philip Valois, who became Philip VI (1328-1350). He was the son of Philip IV's brother. However, Edward III (1327-1377), King of England, claimed he had a better right to the throne since his mother was the daughter of Philip IV. French lawyers, who did not want an English king as their ruler, claimed that royal descent could only be through the male line. Other factors helped to foster the war. Edward III was the duke of Gascony in southern France and as duke he was a vassal of the French king, Philip VI. Philip continued the age-old French policy of making life difficult for English kings who tried to maintain their possessions in France. The English and French also had conflicting interests in Flanders, which was a vassal county of France not directly under the control of the French crown. The English, who supplied the Flemish with wool for their important cloth industry, sided with the workers during a period of urban unrest; the French king, seeking to make his claims to Flanders more effective, sided with the wealthy merchants.

The Longbow The first stages of the war saw sweeping English victories. The English, who relied much more than the French on infantry forces, had a superior weapon for the peasant infantryman in the longbow that measured five to six feet in length. Using a longbow, an archer had a rapid-fire weapon that could shoot 10 to 12 arrows a minute. The longbow, capable of piercing armor, had an effective range of around 200 yards. The crossbow, used by French forces, was far inferior. Besides the French nobility loved to charge on horseback in heavy armor. They were slaughtered by the English infantry in several battles: Crecy (August 26, 1346), Poitiers (September 19, 1356), and Agincourt (October 25, 1415). At one point most of northern France recognized the English king as their legitimate ruler. But the French population was always much greater than the English, perhaps 15 million

What other factors helped to bring on this war?

Describe the English longbow and tell why it was so important in the Hundred Years' War.

Name some of the English victories.

Why didn't the English, with their superior tactics, win the war?

Describe the role of Joan of Arc.

What were the consequences of the Hundred Years' War?

to four million. It was easy for the English, with superior tactics, to win battles; it was much more difficult to hold substantial territory on a long-term basis.

Joan of Arc   What the French needed after so many defeats, was someone capable of rallying them and instilling them with hope. Joan of Arc (c.1412-1431), often called the MAID OF ORLEANS, proved to be that person. Voices, which she believed came from heaven, told her she had to liberate France from the English. She persuaded Charles, the DAUPHIN or eldest son of the French king, to let her take command of his troops and lead them in breaking the English siege of Orleans. She also persuaded Charles, who had been disinherited in favor of the English ruler, to be crowned at Reims as the rightful king of France. Later, after falling into the hands of the Burgundians, who were allies of the English, she was turned over to the English. They had her condemned as a heretic and burned at the stake on May 30, 1431. Joan was afterwards exonerated by a different church court and became a national hero of France, actually receiving Catholic sainthood in 1920. By the time of her death, the tide of the war had turned and the French were well on their way to recapturing the territories the English had seized. The war ended in 1453 with the fall of Bordeaux to French forces. The only territory the English retained in France was the port of Calais (until 1558).

The Hundred Years' War had several consequences. The importance of the infantry increased with the use of the longbow, and in the later stages of the war gunpowder and cannons were introduced. The nature of warfare was changing. Heavily armored knights on horseback, the mainstay of feudal armies, were becoming obsolete. Larger armies comprised chiefly of commoners were to become commonplace. National sentiment was increased in both England and France. In France, the king gained the right to additional taxes to maintain a standing army. At the end of the war, France was well on the way to becoming a modern nation-state. Since the English lost, its monarchy did not receive a similar boost. English kings had to keep returning to parliament for the funds to pursue the war.

War of the Roses

Indeed, subsequent to the English defeat suffered in the Hundred Years' War, there broke out in England a civil war known as the War of the Roses. This war, which lasted from 1455 to 1485, involved two main factions: the house of LANCASTER whose emblem was a red rose and the house of YORK whose emblem was a white rose. Henry VI, who began his reign in 1422 as a child of nine months, was from the house of Lancaster. He was a terrible ruler with frequent bouts of insanity. The Yorkists sought first to control Henry and later, in 1461, replaced him. Several battles occurred for control of the kingdom, with first one side successful and then the other. The final battle was won in August 1485 when HENRY TUDOR, related to the house of Lancaster, defeated the Yorkist Richard III (1483-1485) at Bosworth field. (Richard had previously alienated many in England by allegedly arranging the deaths of his two young nephews, who had a better claim on the throne than he.) The result of Henry Tudor's victory was the start of a new royal dynasty, the Tudors. Henry, who took the title Henry VII (1485-1509), was a strong monarch. So were his son, Henry VIII (1509-1547), and his grand-

When did the War of the Roses occur?

Who were the participants?

What was the outcome of this war?

How might the War of the Roses have helped to strengthen the English monarchy?

daughter Elizabeth I (1558-1603). It is quite probable that many in England welcomed a strong national monarchy after the uncertainties brought on by the War of the Roses. The strength of this monarchy, of course, contributed to the waning of the feudal system in England.

The Great Schism

In papal history, what was the Babylonian Captivity?

Not only feudal authority, but papal authority was also challenged in the Later Middle Ages. Earlier, we saw that the French king, Philip IV, came out the better in his struggle with Pope Boniface VIII. In 1309, Pope Clement V established papal headquarters in Avignon on the border of France. While several popes spoke of returning to Rome, none did on a permanent basis until 1377. It was not simply a case of the overwhelming influence exercised by the king of France. Rome itself was the scene of many civil disturbances which would make the life of any pope and his entourage rather difficult. Many popes felt that Avignon was a better location from which to mediate an end to the Hundred Years' War. Nevertheless the European, especially the Italian, perception was that the pope was under the thumb of the French monarch. While at Avignon, the papacy had succeeded in increasing the centralization of church government and, concomitantly, papal revenues. Many of the cardinals were enabled to lead lives of gross luxury. Unhappiness with the situation led critics to speak of this period (1309-1377) as the BABYLONIAN CAPTIVITY of the papacy, suggesting comparison with the exile of the Jews in Babylonia after the fall of Jerusalem in 586 B.C.

Was the papacy truly the captive of the French monarchy?

Finally, in 1377, Pope Gregory XI (1370-1378) returned permanently to Rome.

He appears to have been persuaded by appeals to do the right thing by figures known for their piety, such as St. Catherine of Siena (1347-1380). Gregory died the year after his return. When the College of Cardinals met to elect a successor, they found howling mobs outside demanding an Italian pope and threatening death to the French. Since the majority of cardinals were French at this time, you can imagine their discomfort. In these circumstances they elected in April of 1378 an Italian, Bartolomeo Prignano, the archbishop of Bari, who took the name Urban VI (1378-1389). Urban showed an unexpected zeal for reform and a disposition to harshly scold the cardinals.

When a group of the cardinals later met at Anagni, they declared that the election of Urban VI had been invalid because of the mob pressure. In late September they elected a new pope, a Frenchman, who took the title Clement VII (1378-1394). Urban refused to step down and Clement established his headquarters at Avignon. Each man excommunicated his rival papal claimant. This marks the beginning of what came to be known as the GREAT SCHISM*. A schism is a separation or a division, and from 1378 to 1417 the Western church was separated into factions. At the start there were two factions. One group recognized the pope at Rome, while the other group recognized the pope at Avignon. The result was truly shocking to the pious. It was possible for various nations to play off one side against the other. The popes were in no position to demand all the revenues due the church or to scorn the wishes of political officials in making appointments of bishops and abbots. France, Scotland, Castile, and

---

* There was an earlier Great Schism in 1054, when Eastern and Western churches split apart.

Why did Pope Gregory XI return papal headquarters to Rome?

What were the origins of the Great Schism of the fourteenth century?

How did it weaken the church?

Why did the Great Schism persist?

What was Conciliarism?

Was the Council of Pisa a success? Explain.

southern Italy supported the claimant at Avignon. England, Flanders, the Holy Roman Emperor, many of the German principalities, and most of Italy supported the Roman pontiff.

Conciliarism

A leading question of the day was how to resolve the split since cardinals in each faction kept on electing new popes when the papal claimant they supported passed on. The idea developed that a general council of the church should be called. It was held that since the council represented the whole church, even the pope was subordinate to it. It appeared possible that such a council could depose one or both of the claimants to resolve the issue. This notion, that a general council of the church is superior in authority to the pope, is called CONCILIARISM. It is a theory, not surprisingly, that popes reject to this day. A council, recognized by neither the pope at Avignon nor at Rome, was called at Pisa in 1409. The Council of Pisa declared the popes reigning in both cities deposed, and in their place, they elected another man, Alexander V (1409-1410). When Alexander died within a year, he was replaced by John XXIII (1410-1415). Unfortunately, the other two claimants did not accept the legitimacy of the council. The result was that there were now three people calling themselves pope and the split was worse than ever.

The matter was finally resolved, at the insistence of the Holy Roman Emperor, by convening the Council of Constance which lasted from 1414 to 1418. The pope supported by the Roman faction, Gregory XII (1406-1415), was persuaded (some would say forced) to resign; the other two claimants, John XXIII and Benedict XIII (1394-1417), were deposed. Martin V (1417-1431) was elected with the support of the leading nations of Western Europe. The Schism was over.

The Council of Constance attended to other matters as well. It passed a statement that subordinated papal authority to that of general councils, which were to meet regularly. But Martin and subsequent popes worked successfully to reassert papal supremacy. The council also burned John Huss (c.1372-1415) of Bohemia at the stake for heresy. Some of Huss's ideas, for example the superiority of scripture over the authority of popes or councils, appear to prefigure the Protestant Reformation of the sixteenth century.

The proceedings of the Council of Constance, as indeed the whole of the Great Schism, are quite controversial. Were there three popes or one real pope and one or two false claimants? Did Gregory XII and his Roman predecessors constitute the only true pontiffs? Most Protestant historians opt for three popes. Catholic historians, on the other hand, find only one true pope ruling at any given moment from the time of Urban VI to Gregory XII. Whatever the case, there can be no doubt that the Great Schism and the Conciliar Movement weakened the authority of the popes and undermined the medieval assumption of western Christian unity.

How did the Great Schism finally end?

Do you think there were three popes or only three claimants and one pope?

NOTES

[1] Oliver J. Thatcher and Edgar H. McNeal, eds., <u>A Source Book for Medieval History</u> (New York: Charles Scribner's Sons, 1905), p. 208.

[2] A.C. Krey, <u>The First Crusade: The Accounts of Eye-Witnesses and Participants</u> (Princeton: Princeton University Press, 1921), pp. 261-262.

[3] <u>Magna Carta</u>, in William F. Swindler, <u>Magna Carta: Legend and Legacy</u>, (Indianapolis: Bobbs-Merrill, 1965), p.270, 316-17.

[4] G. C. Macaulay, ed., <u>The Chronicles of Froissart</u>, trans. by Lord Berners (London: Macmillan, 1904), pp. 136-137 in <u>Internet Medieval Source Book</u> (Internet, <http://www.fordham.edu/halsall/source /froissart2.html>, 25 March 1997).

MARIE DE FRANCE

The Lay of Sir Launfal·

Little is known about the life of Marie de France. Scholars agree that she probably lived in England and wrote in the last part of the twelfth century (after 1170). It is quite possible that she was a member of the court of King Henry II of England, who also ruled vast territories in France. The name Marie de France simply meant Mary from France, indicating that she was born in France.

Her lays are written in a French dialect that was common in northern France and at the royal English court of the time. A lay is a short poem intended to be sung. The tale presented here is a romance celebrating one of the knights at King Arthur's Round Table, Launfal, who should be identified with Lancelot. The story uses earlier, Celtic sources and evidences a belief in fairies. In this medieval setting, the fairies are similar in stature to humans, but possess very remarkable magic and beauty. In the end, Launfal goes off to Avalon, the magical island of fairies and heroes.

I WILL tell you the story of another Lay. It relates the adventures of a rich and mighty baron, and the Breton calls it, the Lay of Sir Launfal.

King Arthur—that fearless knight and courteous lord—removed to Wales, and lodged at Caerleon-on-Usk, since the Picts and Scots did much mischief in the land. For it was the wont of the wild people of the north to enter in the realm of Logres, and burn and damage at their will. At the time of Pentecost, the King cried a great feast. Thereat he gave many rich gifts to his counts and barons, and to the Knights of the Round Table. Never were such worship and bounty shown before at any feast, for Arthur bestowed honours and lands on all his servants—save only on one. This lord, who was forgotten and misliked of the King, was named Launfal. He was beloved by many of the Court, because of his beauty and prowess, for he was a worthy knight, open of heart and heavy of hand. These lords, to whom their comrade was dear, felt little joy to see so stout a knight misprized. Sir Launfal was son to a King of high descent, though his heritage was in a distant land. He was of the King's household, but since Arthur

* Marie de France, "The Lay of Sir Launfal," *French Medieval Romances: From the Lays of Marie de France*, translated by Eugene Mason (London: J. M. Dent & Sons; New York: E.P. Dutton & Co., [1911]), pp. 61-76.

gave him naught, and he was of too proud a mind to pray for his due, he had spent all that he had. Right heavy was Sir Launfal, when he considered these things, for he knew himself taken in the toils. Gentles, marvel not overmuch hereat. Ever must the pilgrim go heavily in a strange land, where there is none to counsel and direct him in the path.

Now, on a day, Sir Launfal got him on his horse, that he might take his pleasure for a little. He came forth from the city, alone, attended by neither servant nor squire. He went his way through a green mead, till he stood by a river of clear running water. Sir Launfal would have crossed this stream, without thought of pass or ford, but he might not do so, for reason that his horse was all fearful and trembling. Seeing that he was hindered in this fashion, Launfal unbitted his steed, and let him pasture in that fair meadow, where they had come. Then he folded his cloak to serve him as a pillow, and lay upon the ground. Launfal lay in great misease, because of his heavy thoughts, and the discomfort of his bed. He turned from side to side, and might not sleep. Now as the knight looked towards the river he saw two damsels coming towards him; fairer maidens Launfal had never seen. These two maidens were richly dressed in kirtles [gowns] closely laced and shapen to their persons and wore mantles of a goodly purple hue. Sweet and dainty were the damsels, alike in raiment [clothing] and in face. The elder of these ladies carried in her hands a basin of pure gold, cunningly wrought by some crafty smith—very fair and precious was the cup; and the younger bore a towel of soft white linen. These maidens turned neither to the right hand nor to the left, but went directly to the place where Launfal lay. When Launfal saw that their business was with him, he stood upon his feet, like a discreet and courteous gentleman. After they had greeted the knight, one of the maidens delivered the message with which she was charged.

"Sir Launfal, my demoiselle [damsel], as gracious as she is fair, prays that you will follow us, her messengers, as she has a certain word to speak with you. We will lead you swiftly to her pavilion, for our lady is very near at hand. If you but lift your eyes you may see where her tent is spread."

Right glad was the knight to do the bidding of the maidens. He gave no heed to his horse, but left him at his provand [grazing] in the meadow. All his desire was to go with the damsels, to that pavilion of silk and divers colours, pitched in so fair a place. Certainly neither Semiramis [an Assyrian queen] in the days of her most wanton power, nor Octavian, the Emperor of all the West, had so gracious a covering from sun and rain. Above the tent was set an eagle of gold, so rich and precious, that none might count the cost. The cords and fringes thereof were of silken thread, and the lances which bore aloft the pavilion were of refined gold. No King on earth might have so sweet a shelter, not though he gave in fee the value of his realm. Within this pavilion Launfal came upon the Maiden. Whiter she was than any altar lily, and more sweetly flushed than the new born rose in time of summer heat. She lay upon a bed with napery [sheets] and coverlet of richer worth than could be furnished by a castle's spoil. Very fresh and slender showed the lady in her vesture [slip] of spotless linen. About her person she had drawn a mantle of ermine, edged with purple dye from the vats of Alexandria. By reason of the heat her raiment was unfastened for a little, and her throat and the rondure of her bosom showed whiter and more untouched than hawthorn in May. The knight came before the bed, and stood gazing on so sweet a sight. The Maiden beckoned him to draw near, and when he had seated himself at the foot of her couch, spoke her mind.

"Launfal," she said, "fair friend, it is for you that I have come from my own far land. I bring you my love. If you are prudent and discreet, as you are goodly to the view, there is no emperor nor count, nor king, whose day shall be so filled with riches and with mirth as yours."

When Launfal heard these words he rejoiced greatly, for his heart was litten [lighted] by another's torch. "Fair lady," he answered, " since it pleases you to be so gracious, and to dower so graceless a knight with your love, there is naught that you may bid me do—right or wrong, evil or good—that I will not do to the utmost of my power. I will observe your commandment, and serve in your quarrels. For you I renounce my father and my father's house. This only I pray, that I may dwell with you in your lodging, and that you will never send me from your side."

When the Maiden heard the words of him whom so fondly she desired to love, she was altogether moved and granted him forthwith her heart and her tenderness. To her bounty she added another gift besides. Never might Launfal be desirous of aught, but he would have according to his wish. He might waste and spend at will and pleasure, but in his purse ever there was to spare. No more was Launfal sad. Right merry was the pilgrim, since one had set him on the way, with such a gift, that the more pennies he bestowed, the more silver and gold were in his pouch.

But the Maiden had yet a word to say.

"Friend," she said, " hearken to my counsel. I lay this charge upon you, and pray you urgently, that you tell not to any man the secret of our love. If you show this matter, you will lose your friend, for ever and a day. Never again may you see my face. Never again will you have seisin [possession] of that body, which is now so tender in your eyes." Launfal plighted faith, that right strictly he would observe this commandment. So the Maiden granted him her kiss and her embrace, and very sweetly in that fair lodging passed the day till evensong was come.

Right loath was Launfal to depart from the pavilion at the vesper [evening] hour, and gladly would he have stayed, had he been able, and his lady wished.

"Fair friend," said she, "rise up, for no longer may you tarry. The hour is come that we must part. But one thing I have to say before you go. When you would speak with me I shall hasten to come before your wish. Well I deem that you will only call your friend where she may be found without reproach or shame of men. You may see me at your pleasure; my voice shall speak softly in your ear at will; but I must never be known of your comrades, nor must they ever learn my speech."

Right joyous was Launfal to hear this thing. He sealed the covenant with a kiss, and stood upon his feet. Then there entered the two maidens who had led him to the pavilion, bringing with them rich raiment, fitting for a knight's apparel. When Launfal had clothed himself therewith, there seemed no goodlier varlet [rascal] under heaven, for certainly he was fair and true. After these maidens had refreshed him with clear water, and dried his hands upon the napkin, Launfal went to meat. His friend sat at table with him, and small will had he to refuse her courtesy. Very serviceably the damsels bore the meats, and Launfal and the Maiden ate and drank with mirth and content. But one dish was more to the knight's relish than any other. Sweeter than the dainties within his mouth, was the lady's kiss upon his lips.

When supper was ended, Launfal rose from table, for his horse stood waiting without the pavilion. The destrier [war horse] was newly saddled and bridled, and showed proudly in his rich gay trappings. So Launfal kissed, and bade farewell, and went his way. He rode back towards the city at a slow pace. Often he checked his steed, and looked behind him, for he was filled with amazement, and all bemused concerning this adven-

ture. In his heart he doubted that it was but a dream. He was altogether astonished, and knew not what to do. He feared that pavilion and Maiden alike were from the realm of faery [sphere of magic].

Launfal returned to his lodging, and was greeted by servitors, clad no longer in ragged raiment. He fared richly, lay softly, and spent largely, but never knew how his purse was filled. There was no lord who had need of a lodging in the town, but Launfal brought him to his hall, for refreshment and delight. Launfal bestowed rich gifts. Launfal redeemed the poor captive. Launfal clothed in scarlet the minstrel. Launfal gave honour where honour was due. Stranger and friend alike he comforted at need. So, whether by night or by day, Launfal lived greatly at his ease. His lady, she came at will and pleasure, and, for the rest, all was added unto him.

Now it chanced, the same year, the feast of St. John, a company of knights came, for their solace, to an orchard, beneath that tower where dwelt the Queen. Together with these lords went Gawain and his cousin, Yvain the fair. Then said Gawain, that goodly knight and dear to all,

"Lords, we do wrong to disport ourselves in this pleasaunce without our comrade Launfal. It is not well to slight a prince as brave as he is courteous, and of a lineage prouder than our own."

Then certain of the lords returned to the city, and finding Launfal within his hostel, entreated him to take his pastime with them in that fair meadow. The Queen looked out from a window in her tower, she and three ladies of her fellowship. They saw the lords at their pleasure, and Launfal also, whom well they knew. So the Queen chose of her Court thirty damsels—the sweetest of face and most dainty of fashion— and commanded that they should descend with her to take their delight in the garden. When the knights beheld this gay company of ladies come down the steps of the perron [front entrance], they rejoiced beyond measure. They hastened to lead them by the hand, and said such words in their ear as were seemly and pleasant to be spoken. Amongst these merry and courteous lords hasted not Sir Launfal. He drew apart from the throng, for with him time went heavily, till he might have clasp and greeting of his friend. The ladies of the Queen's fellowship seemed but kitchen wenches to his sight, in comparison with the loveliness of the maiden. When the Queen marked Launfal go aside, she went his way, and seating herself upon the herb, called the knight before her. Then she opened out her heart.

"Launfal, I have honoured you for long as a worthy knight, and have praised and cherished you very dearly. You may receive a queen's whole love, if such be your care. Be content: he to whom my heart is given, has small reason to complain him of the alms."

"Lady," answered the knight, "grant me leave to go, for this grace is not for me. I am the King's man, and dare not break my troth [loyalty]. Not for the highest lady in the world, not even for her love, will I set this reproach upon my lord."

When the Queen heard this, she was full of wrath, and spoke many hot and bitter words.

"Launfal," she cried, "well I know that you think little of woman and her love. There are sins more black that a man may have upon his soul. Traitor you are, and false. Right evil counsel gave they to my lord, who prayed him to suffer you about his person. You remain only for his harm and loss."

Launfal was very dolent [sorry] to hear this thing. He was not slow to take up the Queen's glove, and in his haste spake words that he repented long, and with tears.

"Lady," said he, "I am not of that guild of which you speak. Neither am I a despiser of woman, since I love, and am loved, of one who would bear the prize from all the ladies in the land. Dame, know now and be persuaded, that she, whom I serve, is so rich in state, that the very meanest of her maidens, excels you, Lady Queen, as much in clerkly skill and goodness, as in sweetness of body and face, and in every virtue."

The Queen rose straightway to her feet, and fled to her chamber, weeping. Right wrathful and heavy was she, because of the words that had besmirched her. She lay sick upon her bed, from which, she said, she would never rise, till the King had done her justice, and righted this bitter wrong. Now the King that day had taken his pleasure within the woods. He returned from the chase towards evening, and sought the chamber of the Queen. When the lady saw him, she sprang from her bed, and kneeling at his feet, pleaded for grace and pity. Launfal—she said—had shamed her, since he required her love. When she had put him by, very foully had he reviled her, boasting that his love was already set on a lady, so proud and noble, that her meanest wench went more richly, and smiled more sweetly, than the Queen. Thereat the King waxed marvellously wrathful, and swore a great oath that he would set Launfal within a fire, or hang him from a tree, if he could not deny this thing, before his peers.

Arthur came forth from the Queen's chamber, and called to him three of his lords. These he sent to seek the knight who so evilly had entreated the Queen. Launfal, for his part, had returned to his lodging, in a sad and sorrowful case. He saw very clearly that he had lost his friend, since he had declared their love to men. Launfal sat within his chamber, sick and heavy of thought. Often he called upon his friend, but the lady would not hear his voice. He bewailed his evil lot, with tears; for grief he came nigh to swoon; a hundred times he implored the Maiden that she would deign to speak with her knight. Then, since the lady yet refrained from speech, Launfal cursed his hot and unruly tongue. Very near he came to ending all this with his knife. Naught he found to do but to wring his hands, and call upon the Maiden, begging her to forgive his trespass, and to talk with him again, as friend to friend.

But little peace is there for him who is harassed by a King. There came presently to Launfal's hostel those three barons from the Court. These bade the knight forthwith to go with them to Arthur's presence,

to acquit him of this wrong against the Queen. Launfal went forth, to his own deep sorrow. Had any man slain him on the road, he would have counted him his friend. He stood before the King, downcast and speechless, being dumb by reason of that great grief, of which he showed the picture and image.

Arthur looked upon his captive very evilly.

"Vassal," said he, harshly, "you have done me a bitter wrong. It was a foul deed to seek to shame me in this ugly fashion, and to smirch the honour of the Queen. Is it folly or lightness which leads you to boast of that lady, the least of whose maidens is fairer, and goes more richly, than the Queen?"

Launfal protested that never had he set such shame upon his lord. Word by word he told the tale of how he denied the Queen, within the orchard. But concerning that which he had spoken of the lady, he owned the truth, and his folly. The love of which he bragged was now lost to him, by his own exceeding fault. He cared little for his life, and was content to obey the judgment of the Court. Right wrathful was the King at Launfal's words. He conjured his barons to give him such wise counsel herein, that wrong might be done to none. The lords did the King's bidding, whether good came of the matter or evil. They gathered themselves together, and appointed a certain day that Launfal should abide the judgment of his peers. For his part Launfal must give pledge and surety to his lord, that he would come before this judgment in his own body. If he might not give such surety then he should be held captive till the appointed day. When the lords of the King's household returned to tell him of their counsel, Arthur demanded that Launfal should put such pledge in his hand, as they had said. Launfal was altogether mazed and bewildered at this judgment, for he had neither friend nor kindred in the land. He would have been set in prison, but Gawain came first to offer himself as his surety, and with him, all the knights of his fellowship.

These gave into the King's hand as pledge, the fiefs and lands that they held of his Crown. The King having taken pledges from the sureties, Launfal returned to his lodging, and with him certain knights of his company. They blamed him greatly because of his foolish love, and chastened him grievously by reason of the sorrow he made before men. Every day they came to his chamber, to know of his meat and drink, for much they feared that presently he would become mad.

The lords of the household came together on the day appointed for this judgment. The King was on his chair, with the Queen sitting at his side. The sureties brought Launfal within the hall, and rendered him into the hands of his peers. Right sorrowful were they because of his plight. A great company of his fellowship did all that they were able to acquit him of this charge. When all was set out, the King demanded the judgment of the Court, according to the accusation and the answer. The barons went forth in much trouble and thought to consider this matter. Many amongst them grieved for the peril of a good knight in a strange land; others held that it were well for Launfal to suffer, because of the wish and malice of their lord. Whilst they were thus perplexed, the Duke of Cornwall rose in the council, and said,

"Lords, the King pursues Launfal as a traitor, and would slay him with the sword, by reason that he bragged of the beauty of his maiden, and roused the jealousy of the Queen. By the faith that I owe this company, none complains of Launfal, save only the King. For our part we would know the truth of this business, and do justice between the King and his man. We would also show proper reverence to our own liege [sovereign] lord. Now, if it be according to Arthur's will, let us take oath of Launfal, that he seek this lady, who has put such strife between him and the Queen. If her beauty be such as he has told us, the Queen will have no cause for wrath. She must pardon Launfal for his rudeness, since it will be plain that he did not speak out of a malicious heart. Should Launfal fail his word, and not return with the lady, or should her fairness fall beneath his boast, then let him be cast off from our fellowship, and be sent forth from the service of the King."

This counsel seemed good to the lords of the household. They sent certain of his friends to Launfal, to acquaint him with their judgment, bidding him to pray his damsel to the Court, that he might be acquitted of this blame. The knight made answer that in no wise could he do this thing. So the sureties returned before the judges, saying that Launfal hoped neither for refuge nor for succour [help] from the lady, and Arthur urged them to a speedy ending, because of the prompting of the Queen.

The judges were about to give sentence upon Launfal, when they saw two maidens come riding towards the palace, upon two white ambling palfreys [saddle horses]. Very sweet and dainty were these maidens, and richly clothed in garments of crimson sendal [fine silk], closely girt and fashioned to their bodies. All men, old and young, looked willingly upon them, for fair they were to see. Gawain, and three knights of his company, went straight to Launfal, and showed him these maidens, praying him to say which of them was his friend. But he answered never a word. The maidens dismounted from their palfreys, and coming before the dais where the King was seated, spake him fairly, as they were fair.

"Sire, prepare now a chamber, hung with silken cloths, where it is seemly for my lady to dwell; for she would lodge with you awhile."

This gift the King granted gladly. He called to him two knights of his household, and bade them bestow the maidens in such chambers as were fitting to their degree. The maidens being gone, the King required of his barons to proceed with their judgment, saying that he had sore displeasure at the slowness of the cause.

Sire," replied the barons, "we rose from Council, because of the damsels who entered in the hall. We will at once resume the sitting, and give our judgment without more delay."

The barons again were gathered together, in much thought and trouble, to consider this matter.

There was great strife and dissension amongst them, for they knew not what to do. In the midst of all this noise and tumult, there came two other damsels riding to the hall on two Spanish mules. Very richly arrayed were these damsels in raiment of fine needlework, and their kirtles were covered by fresh fair mantles, embroidered with gold. Great joy had Launfal's comrades when they marked these ladies. They said between themselves that doubtless they came for the succour of the good knight. Gawain, and certain of his company, made haste to Launfal, and said,

"Sir, be not cast down. Two ladies are near at hand, right dainty of dress, and gracious of person. Tell us truly, for the love of God, is one of these your friend? "

But Launfal answered very simply that never before had he seen these damsels with his eyes, nor known and loved them in his heart.

The maidens dismounted from their mules, and stood before Arthur, in the sight of all. Greatly were they praised of many, because of their beauty, and of the colour of their face and hair. Some there were who deemed already that the Queen was overborne.

The elder of the damsels carried herself modestly and well, and sweetly told over the message wherewith she was charged.

"Sire, make ready for us chambers, where we may abide with our lady, for even now she comes to speak with thee."

The King commanded that the ladies should be led to their companions, and bestowed in the same honourable fashion as they. Then he bade the lords of his household to consider their judgment, since he would endure no further respite. The Court already had given too much time to the business, and the Queen was growing wrathful, because of the blame that was hers. Now the judges were about to proclaim their sentence, when, amidst the tumult of the town, there came riding to the palace the flower of all the ladies of the world. She came mounted upon a palfrey, white as snow, which carried her softly, as though she loved her burthen. Beneath the sky was no goodlier steed, nor one more gentle to the hand. The harness of the palfrey was so rich, that no king on earth might hope to buy trappings so precious, unless he sold or set his realm in pledge. The Maiden herself showed such as I will tell you. Passing slim was the lady, sweet of bodice and slender of girdle. Her throat was whiter than snow on branch, and her eyes were like flowers in the pallor of her face. She had a witching mouth, a dainty nose, and an open brow. Her eyebrows were brown, and her golden hair parted in two soft waves upon her head. She was clad in a shift of spotless linen, and above her snowy kirtle was set a mantle of royal purple, clasped upon her breast. She carried a hooded falcon upon her glove, and a greyhound followed closely after. As the Maiden rode at a slow pace through the streets of the city, there was none, neither great nor small, youth nor sergeant, but ran forth from his house, that he might content his heart with so great beauty. Every man that saw

her with his eyes, marvelled at a fairness beyond that of any earthly woman. Little he cared for any mortal maiden, after he had seen this sight. The friends of Sir Launfal hastened to the knight, to tell him of his lady's succour, if so it were according to God's will.

"Sir comrade, truly is not this your friend? This lady is neither black nor golden, mean nor tall. She is only the most lovely thing in all the world."

When Launfal heard this, he sighed, for by their words he knew again his friend. He raised his head, and as the blood rushed to his face, speech flowed from his lips.

"By my faith," cried he, "yes, she is indeed my friend. It is a small matter now whether men slay me, or set me free; for I am made whole of my hurt just by looking on her face."

The Maiden entered in the palace—where none so fair had come before—and stood before the King, in the presence of his household. She loosed the clasp of her mantle, so that men might the more easily perceive the grace of her person. The courteous King advanced to meet her, and all the Court got them on their feet, and pained themselves in her service. When the lords had gazed upon her for a space, and praised the sum of her beauty, the lady spake to Arthur in this fashion, for she was anxious to begone.

"Sire, I have loved one of thy vassals,—the knight who stands in bonds, Sir Launfal. He was always misprized in thy Court, and his every action turned to blame. What he said, that thou knowest; for over hasty was his tongue before the Queen. But he never craved her in love, however loud his boasting. I cannot choose that he should come to hurt or harm by me. In the hope of freeing Launfal from his bonds, I have obeyed thy summons. Let now thy barons look boldly upon my face, and deal justly in this quarrel between the Queen and me."

The King commanded that this should be done, and looking upon her eyes, not one of the judges but was persuaded that her favour exceeded that of the Queen.

Since then Launfal had not spoken in malice against his lady, the lords of the household gave him again his sword. When the trial had come thus to an end the Maiden took her leave of the King, and made her ready to depart. Gladly would Arthur have had her

lodge with him for a little, and many a lord would have rejoiced in her service, but she might not tarry. Now without the hall stood a great stone of dull marble, where it was the wont of lords, departing from the Court, to into the saddle, and Launfal by the stone. The Maiden came forth from the doors of the palace, and mounting on the stone, seated herself on the palfrey, behind her friend. Then they rode across the plain together, and were no more seen.

The Bretons tell that the knight was ravished by his lady to an island, very dim and very fair, known as Avalon. But none has had speech with Launfal and his faery love since then, and for my part I can tell you no more of the matter.

Questions for Critical Thinking and Discussion

1. Why do you think King Arthur excluded Sir Launfal from gifts, honors, and lands?

2. What aspects of this lay would be considered romantic to medieval readers?

3. What role, if any, does lineage and ancestry play in the tale?

4. What characteristics of knighthood and chivalry are described?

5. Explain the lord-vassal relationship between King Arthur and Sir Launfal. When the king called Sir Launfal "vassal," was it meant to be derogatory?

6. What part did the trial play? Why was the judgment so important to the King—to the Queen—to the nobles?

7. What does the author's description of the clothing of the Maiden and her attendants do for the tale? Why is the beauty of the Maiden so important?

8. What do you think is the lesson, if any, taught in the lay?

Self-Test

Part I: Identification

Can you identify each of the following? Tell who, what, when, where, why, and/or how for each term.

1. Vassal
2. Manorialism
3. Guild system
4. *Summa Theologica*
5. Gothic style
6. Dante Alighieri
7. Relics
8. Simony
9. Franciscans
10. Inquisition
11. Interdict
12. Canossa
13. Innocent III
14. *Unam Sanctam*
15. Council of Clermont
16. Hugh Capet
17. William the Conqueror
18. Henry II
19. Magna Carta
20. Flagellants
21. Longbow
22. War of the Roses
23. Babylonian Captivity of the Papacy
24. Fief
25. Three-field system
26. Scholasticism
27. Romanesque style
28. *Beowulf*
29. *Canterbury Tales*
30. Cluniacs
31. Cistercians
32. Dominicans
33. Gregory VII
34 Lay Investiture
35. Concordat of Worms
36. Bouvines
37. Avignon Papacy
38. Sack of Constantinople
39. Eleanor of Aquitaine
40. The Battle of Hastings
41. Thomas a Becket
42. Black Death
43. Hundred Years' War
44. Maid of Orleans
45. Great Schism
47. Council of Constance

Part II: Multiple Choice Questions

Circle the best response from the choices given.

1. The uncertainties of the 9th century Viking, Magyar, and Moslem invasions resulted in the development of
    a. strong central governments.
    b. feudalism.
    c. bureaucratic absolutism.
    d. papal monarchy.

2. The principal force that held the feudal system together as a working organization was the
    a. personal relations of loyalty among the nobles.
    b. disciplinary power of the king.
    c. legacy of Roman law.
    d. mutual self-help among the peasants.

3. Which one of the following was a logical outcome of the acceptance by the Church of land on a feudal basis?
    a. freedom of the Church from the problem of defending the land.
    b. freedom of the Church from taxation.
    c. control of the election of clergymen by the noble who granted the land.
    d. buying and selling of Church land by the clergy.

4. The class structure of medieval society consisted of the following groups except:
    a. clergy.
    b. peasants.
    c. fiefs.
    d. lords.

5. The agricultural system of the early Middle Ages which contributed to economic revival was
    a. feudalism.
    b. serfdom.
    c. investiture.
    d. manorialism.

6. Otto the Great and his four successors
    a. were the only rulers of Europe at the time.
    b. utilized the bishops and abbots to govern their kingdom.
    c. often ruled France.
    d. all of the above.

7. When we say that the German kings of the Middle Ages practiced lay investiture, we mean that they
    a. were chosen by laymen.
    b. were invested with their title by laymen.
    c. received most of their lands from laymen.
    d. filled the chief clerical offices with men of their choice.

8. Since 1059, the Roman popes have
    a. chosen their own successors.
    b. been elected by the bishops.
    c. been elected by the College of Cardinals.
    d. appointed by the Holy Roman Emperors until 1453.

9. After Henry IV begged Gregory VII for forgiveness at Canossa
    a. Henry reestablished his power in Germany.
    b. Henry ousted Gregory as pope and placed his own candidate on the Holy See.
    c. the strong role played by the Holy Roman Emperors never fully recovered.
    d. all of the above.

10. The greatest of the medieval popes in terms of papal supremacy was
    a. Gregory VII.
    b. Urban II.
    c. Innocent III.
    d. Boniface VIII.

11. Within medieval towns, merchants and craftsmen were organized in
    a. universities.   b. corporations.
    c. unions.   d. guilds.

12. The curriculums of medieval universities differed from modern curriculums in that there were no subjects offered in
    a. mathematics.
    b. experimental sciences.
    c. rhetoric.
    d. astronomy.

13. Structurally, a Gothic cathedral can best be described as
    a. a stone skeleton composed of pointed arches and pillars.
    b. a massive building with thick walls and narrow windows.
    c. a building limited in size by the need to support heavy, barrel-vaulted roofs.
    d. a direct heir of the Greek temple.

14. Dante's *Divine Comedy*
    a. combined pre-Christian classics with medieval theology.
    b. was primarily a political diatribe against his enemies.
    c. was a Latin treatise defending vernacular literature.
    d. had little influence until it was rediscovered in the nineteenth century.

15. The most decisive moment in medieval English history was
    a. the Roman conquest of Britain.
    b. the Anglo-Saxon invasions.
    c. the Danish raids on the Anglo-Saxon kingdoms.
    d. the Norman Conquest.

16. Henry I of England sent royal judges traveling throughout his realm thereby creating
    a. canon law.
    b. common law.
    c. Roman law.
    d. municipal law.

17. The Magna Carta was forced on
    a. Henry II in 1188.
    b. John in 1215.
    c. Edward I in 1307.
    d. none of the above.

18. According to the Magna Carta, the king
    a. was elected by the barons.
    b. could arrest anyone he chose to.
    c. could take no action without holding an election.
    d. could not imprison a freeman without a trial.

19. During the rule of Philip Augustus, large French territories in Normandy, Anjou, and Aquitaine were ruled by
     a. the King of England.
     b. the Holy Roman Emperor.
     c. the Roman Pope.
     d. the King of Denmark.

20. The dynasty that ruled France from 986 A.D. to 1328 A.D. was that of
     a. Carolingians.
     b. Capetians.
     c. Burgundians.
     d. Tudors.

21. The Great Schism involved
     a. the election of two popes or three popes at the same time.
     b. a separation of Rome and Avignon over doctrinal questions.
     c. a withdrawal of the French king from papal politics.
     d. a division between the Roman Catholic Church of the West and the Islamic faith of the East.

22. King Edward III of England contested the crown of France after the last of the Capetian male heirs died. Thereby starting the
     a. Hundred Years' War.
     b. Wars of the Roses.
     c. Waldensian heresy.
     d. Third Crusade.

23. Which of the following best characterizes the War of the Roses?
     a. a struggle between the House of York and the House of Lancaster over who would be king.
     b. civil war in England between different noble factions.
     c. a conflict that was not resolved until Henry Tudor became king.
     d. all of the above.

24. Not until Joan of Arc in 1429 at the Battle of Orleans
     a. did the French begin to defeat the English.
     b. did the English win their first victory.
     c. were the two crowns briefly combined.
     d. did the feudal nobility regain the powers they had lost to strong kings, like Philip IV and Edward I.

Part III: Review and Thought Questions

1. Describe some of the new inventions and methods used to increase agricultural production in the eleventh century.

2. How did the First Crusade differ from the Fourth Crusade?

3. What was the conflict between Henry II and Thomas à Becket? How was it resolved?

4. Explain how the two marriages of Eleanor of Aquitaine affected English and French society of the time period.

5. What was the impact of the Norman conquest of England on English society?

6. Why and how did the Papacy lose prestige in the 14th century?

7. Describe the major works of Thomas Aquinas. How did he reconcile faith and reason?

8. How did the guild system differ from today's unions?

9. How and why was the Magna Carta an important step in the political development of England?

10. How does the curriculum and student life differ today from the Middle Ages?

11. Describe the lifestyle of an 11th century peasant.

12. Discuss three differences in the architectural style of the Romanesque and Gothic churches.

13. How could a vassal be caught in a conflict of interest between his lord and another lord? What could he do to protect himself?

14. What was the Investiture Controversy all about? Was there a winner?

15. What was the main reason the Germans did not achieve political unity in the Middle Ages?

16. Explain the conflict between Philip IV and Boniface VIII. What was the outcome?

17. Describe three expressions of popular piety in the Middle Ages. What was the intended outcome of each?

18. What specific areas did the Cluniac reform movement embrace?

19. What were the three weapons the Church could use against heretics?

20. Describe four religious orders and their stated missions.

21. What were three effects of the Black Death? Was it more serious to the people of the fourteenth century than the AIDS epidemic is to today's people?

22. Explain why Innocent III is thought to portray papal power at its apex. Give specific examples.

Part V: Full-Length Essays

1. Describe the literature of the Middle Ages. Include epic poems, Goliardic verses, "songs of great deeds," and vernacular literature of Dante and Chaucer.

2. Explain the political and social structure of feudalism. How did manorialism differ from feudalism?

3. Describe the causes and effects of the Crusades. What Crusade seemed the most ironic to you? Why?

4. Explain how the pontificate of Innocent III illustrates the culmination of power politics. Was he an effective Pope? Why or why not?

5. Discuss the causes, the major events, and the effects of the Hundred Years' War.

6. Explain the functions and the apprenticeship system of the medieval guilds. What purpose did they serve in that time period?

7. Describe and explain some of power struggles between the church and the state, such as the Investiture Controversy, the Avignon Papacy, and/or the Great Schism.

Chapter V

FROM

THE RENAISSANCE

TO

THE WARS OF RELIGION

Figure 5.1. Andrea della Robbia (Florentine, 1435-1525). *Madonna and Child*, c. 1470-1475. Illustrative of Renaissance glazed terra cotta sculpture, this panel of the Madonna and Child is strikingly beautiful. Della Robbia's work was in high demand for churches, religious shrines, and homes of the well-to-do. *Courtesy of The Metropolitan Museum of Art, Gift of the Edith and Herbert Lehman Foundation, 1969.*

13

Renaissance and Discovery

The Renaissance

In what ways was the Renaissance a "rebirth"?

"Renaissance" means "rebirth" in the French language. The Renaissance was a rebirth in many different ways. It began in Northern Italy about 1350, right after the Black Death had ravaged the country, killing from a third to half the population. One of the earliest pieces of Renaissance literature was the *Decameron*, written by GIOVANNI BOCCACCIO (1313-1375). The Decameron is a compilation of 100 short stories told by 10 men and women who journeyed to a country villa to escape the plague, which was ravaging Florence in 1348. Unsure whether they would catch the deadly disease, these young men and women did not pray or volunteer to take care of the sick in the city. Instead, they told each other racy stories about worldly pleasures. Boccaccio wrote the *Decameron* in the vernacular or everyday language of Italian.

The Renaissance was a rebirth in another sense. It was a rebirth of classical learning and a rediscovery of ancient Rome and Greece. Renaissance artists and scholars looked back to this Classical past. They deliberately rejected the scholarship and religious thought of the Middle Ages. For them, the Middle Ages were a Dark Age. Nothing original and creative had happened since the fall of Rome. They sought to imitate

What is the theme of Boccaccio's *Decameron*?

What was the attitude of Renaissance artists and scholars towards the Middle Ages?

What was their attitude toward classical Greece and Rome?

In what sense is the Renaissance an historical turning point?

the art of Classical Greece with its realistic depiction of the human form. They thought that the classical Latin written by Virgil, Cicero, or Julius Caesar was much superior to the Church Latin spoken during their own time. They wanted to purify Latin of its medieval corruptions. In the process of doing so, ironically, they helped to destroy the living Latin of the Middle Ages and turned it into the dead language which it is today.

The Renaissance was a rebirth of the human spirit, a rebirth of creativity. While taking the classical past as its model, the Renaissance was one of the most creative periods in human history, comparable only to the Golden Age of Hellenic Athens in the fifth century before Christ. Florence has often been called the Athens of the Renaissance because so many great artists were born or worked there.

The Renaissance in Italy

The Italian Renaissance marks an important turning point in human history. Just as the Germanic invasions of the fifth century of our era marked the end of the Classical Period of history and ushered in the Middle Ages, so the Renaissance is the beginning of our own Modern Period of history and marks the ending of the Middle Ages. There are some contemporary scholars who have suggested that we are now in a post-modern period. If so, whatever new age may be in the works, its characteristics have not become clear. In most ways, our age continues to be a product of the Renaissance.

What, then, is the Renaissance and why did it begin in Italy? One can often define an age, era, epoch, or period by comparing and contrasting it to another. The Middle Ages were an Age of Faith. In the West, the religion of Christianity gave definition to the Middle Ages. The search for salvation was the primary motivation for most people within Christendom. The Middle Ages was God-centered. In contrast, the Renaissance, and the Modern Period of which it is a part, is man-centered. It is secular rather than spiritual. This does not mean that religion and salvation are not important today, but they are not the focal point of most people's lives.

The Middle Ages were a relatively static period. Society was predominantly agrarian. It was ruled by a warrior nobility. Manorialism provided the economic underpinnings and feudalism gave a limited political stability. The Roman Catholic Church with its priests, monks, and bishops formed the First Estate. The pope was not only a spiritual leader but a powerful political force. During the High Middle Ages, medieval towns and feudal monarchy added further elements to what has been called the Medieval Synthesis. The ideal of the Middle Ages was a universal Church within a universal Empire. While never realized, it remained an ideal.

This medieval synthesis broke down shortly after 1300. The Holy Roman Empire under the Hohenstaufen dynasty had been destroyed by the Papacy and its allies. But the political might of the Papacy had itself been crushed by the ruthlessness of the rising French Monarchy. The Papacy moved from Rome to Avignon, apparently under French tutelage, and remained there during the initial phase of the Renaissance till 1377. The Italian peninsula was free temporarily from outside interference: the Empire, the Papacy, and other major powers. The Avignon Papacy was followed by the Great Schism, when two or sometimes three popes denounced each other, until 1417. France, after humiliating

Compare the Renaissance with the Middle Ages.

Name some events that helped break down the medieval synthesis.

Is there an overlap between the Late Middle Ages and the Renaissance? Explain.

Why did the Renaissance begin in Italy?

the Papacy, became itself embroiled in the Hundred Years' War with the English monarchy from 1334 to 1453. And Spain became a unified country only with the marriage of Isabella of Castile and Ferdinand of Aragon in 1469.

When one age ends and another begins, there are cross currents. The declining or Late Middle Ages are usually dated from 1300 to 1500. It should be noted that this time overlaps with the Renaissance. The glass is either half empty or half full. It depends on one's perspective.

The Renaissance started in Italy because the crises within Christendom during the Late Middle Ages benefited Italy. It gave Italy an independence and freedom which it had not previously enjoyed. It must also be noted that the ruins of Roman civilization were more visible in Italy than elsewhere. The Italians had never quite forgotten that heritage even during the Dark Ages. Urban life had never disappeared entirely in Italy, the way it had in the many places in Europe. When trade and towns revived, the Italian communes had flourished most of all. As we have noted earlier, the Lombard League had fought the centralizing efforts of the Hohenstaufen emperors and its member cities had become virtually independent city states. Feudalism and a landed nobility had never become as entrenched in Italy as elsewhere. Upper middle class merchant families formed an urban ruling class that gradually came to dominate even in the countryside. Italy was ahead of the rest of Europe in economic development. In Italy, the Renaissance was a natural progression from the High Middle Ages.

Renaissance writers were wrong to slander the Middle Ages as a Dark Age. We have seen how varied that 1000-year period of history was. They also overemphasized just how radical a break they were making with the medieval past. In many ways the Renaissance built on the culture of the High Middle Ages. DANTE ALIGHIERI (1265 - 1321) is considered to be a figure of the Middle Ages, yet he wrote his *Divine Comedy* in the Florentine dialect and thereby created the literary language of modern Italian.

The Renaissance began in the Italian city-states because they had the wealth from the commerce and trade of the Middle Ages. For some time, Venice had outfitted the crusaders and was the conduit for the silk and spice trade from India and China. Furthermore, the Byzantines and the Moslems cross-fertilized these urban city-states with their cultural ideas. Merchant banking families, such as the Medici in Florence, were able to profit from these commercial endeavors and became the ruling elite. These wealthy bankers were able to finance and patronize the arts, providing employment for the famous painters, sculptors, and architects of the time.

In addition, Italy had many reminders of the Roman past: the road network, the aqueducts, the public buildings, the monuments. Wealth, a standing heritage from the past, the freedom of the urban elite—all of these factors contributed to a shift in attitude that made the Renaissance.

The Political Situation

Italy can be conveniently divided into three regions: North, Central, and South. In the South, the destruction of the Hohenstaufen dynasty led to the establishment of a Kingdom of Sicily ruled by Spain and a Kingdom of Naples ruled on and off by France. This once prosperous and culturally advanced region became impoverished by foreign misrule. It also brought Spain and France into Italian politics. Foreign intervention and

Were the Renaissance intellectuals actually indebted to the Middle Ages? Explain.

What made the Italian city-states favorable environments for Renaissance endeavours?

Describe the political geography of Italy at the time of the Renaissance.

occupation increased again after 1494 with the invasion of Italy by Charles VIII of France. In the center, the Papal States were ruled by the popes. Even during the Avignon Papacy, nominal control was maintained by the papacy. In the North, a miniature state system had formed by the time of the Renaissance. The Republic of Venice, the Duchy of Milan, The Republic of Florence, the Republic of Genoa, the Duchy of Savoy, with its capital at Turin, were the main "powers" in the North. Lesser city-states that made significant contributions to Renaissance culture included Mantua, Ferrara, Siena, Pisa, Lucca, and Urbino. These were all small city-states compared to the new national states that were developing during the fifteenth and sixteenth centuries in Spain, France, England, Austria, Prussia, and Russia. Indeed, the North Italian state system can be compared to that of ancient Greece. Perhaps this relative smallness is what stimulated the individualism and creativity in both ancient Greece and Renaissance Italy.

Humanism

Why were the humanists interested in the classical past?

"Humanism" is the name given to the basic philosophical orientation of the Renaissance. It entailed, as we have already said, a strong desire to recover and understand the classical heritage of Rome and Greece. This interest in the past was more than an antiquarian's curiosity. There was the belief that much of importance to the present could be learned from the past. For example, many of the Italian city states that had been republics were being torn apart by class struggles and were becoming tyrannies. Rome had been a republic until internal strife transformed it into the principate. What lessons could be learned from Roman history? The humanists wanted to re-examine classical history without the distorting lenses of Christianity. The Romans had been pagans. What had these pagan practices been? What did Stoics like Cicero really say?

FRANCISCO PETRARCH (1304-1374), is known as the Father of Humanism. He labeled the Middle Ages as "a time of darkness." Petrarch's goal was to unearth classical writings. He discovered fragments of Livy's *History of Rome*, as well as the letters and orations of Cicero in old monasteries and churches. His scholarship set a standard of excellence for other humanists to emulate. In Latin, he wrote *Letters to the Ancient Dead* and *Lives of Illustrious Men*, which glorified his Roman heroes of the past. His greatest honor was to be crowned poet laureate by the King of Naples. No poet had been awarded this honor since Roman times. Petrarch is, however, best remembered for his poetry, *Sonnets to Laura* (1360), which was written in Italian rather than Latin. He was almost ashamed of these writings.

Another Latin scholar LORENZO VALLA (1406-1457) developed the technique of critical textual analysis through the study of language (philology). Valla proved that a document allegedly written in the fourth century A.D., The Donation of Constantine, could not have possibly been written then. It used Latin words unknown in the fourth century. It was, instead, an eighth century forgery. Valla's *On the False Donation of Constantine* (1444) was a thorough textual investigation that influenced many subsequent scholars. Although he had discredited important papal claims to territorial sovereignty over the entire Western Roman Empire and spiritual authority over the whole Christian church, the Renaissance pope, Nicholas V (1447-1455), hired Valla to be Apostolic Secretary. Nicholas V shared the ideals of the

What role did Petrarch play in the rise of Renaissance humanism?

How did Lorenzo Valla illustrate his scholarship?

In what sense was the papacy a supporter of Valla's work?

What is Neoplatonism?

Do the Medicis of Florence play a role in fostering Neoplatonism? Explain.

Discuss the work of Marsilio Ficino.

humanists and founded the Vatican Library as a repository for ancient manuscripts. The Vatican Library, today, houses the world's largest collection of classical writings.

Neoplatonism

Humanism appealed to the upper bourgeoisie who dominated the Italian city-states and had a fierce civic pride in their communities. Classical ideals of beauty appealed to them. Many were attracted to Neoplatonism. Neoplatonism, as developed during the Renaissance, was a strange movement that blended classical thought with Christian doctrine, and sometimes astrology. It must be noted that when COSIMO DE'MEDICI (1389 - 1464) founded the Platonic Academy in 1450, there were no available copies of Plato's works in Latin. Cosimo commissioned MARSILIO FICINO (1433-1499) to make translations from the Greek into Humanist Latin. Plato's work called *The Parmenides* contains an element of mysticism, which, while downplayed by Plato himself, had inspired Plotinus (204-270) to develop an elaborate philosophy whereby levels of reality emanate from the unknowable Form of the One. Ficino was deeply influenced by the Neoplatonism of Plotinus. Ficino's *Theologia Platonica* (*Platonic Theology*, 1482) expounded this revived Neoplatonism. The contemplation of beauty formed an important aspect of this hybrid theology. Renaissance Neoplatonism was an important antidote to the increasingly arid Aristotelianism embodied in Medieval Scholasticism.

PICO DELLA MIRANDOLA (1463-1494) was a true Renaissance man. He sought to reconcile Aristotelianism with Platonism and to synthesize Judaism, Christianity, and philosophy. Following Neoplatonic beliefs, he thought that there were three realms: the super-celestial realm of God, the celestial realm of the sun and planets, and the terrestrial. In his *Oration on the Dignity of Man*, Pico accorded humans a special rank in the universe, somewhere between the beasts and angels. But because of the spark of divinity implanted in man by God, there are no limits to what man can accomplish. "...O supreme generosity of God the Father, O highest most marvelous felicity of man! To him it is granted to have whatever he chooses, to be whatever he wills."[1] Here again you have the emphasis on man and his potential in this world.

On a lighter side, the Academy held birthday parties for Plato. Many famous artists, such as Michelangelo and Botticelli, became advocates of Neoplatonism.

Machiavelli

One memorable humanist historian and forerunner of modern political thought was NICCOLO MACHIAVELLI (1469-1527). He looked at the realities of politics, not the ideal Christian moral behavior that was promulgated in the Middle Ages. His most famous book is called *The Prince*. It is a "how to" book that has been read and followed by many rulers, such as Napoleon. In it he describes unscrupulous, amoral behavior by rulers in the pursuit of defending their state. He holds that rulers use any means to gain power and princes may have to be deceitful to maintain power. The ruler must be powerful like the lion and cunning like the fox in order to rule a state effectively. Machiavelli also suggests that a ruler who is feared may be more successful in keeping a turbulent state together than one who is loved. He writes:

How is the work of Pico della Mirandola illustrative of Renaissance ideals?

Was Niccolo Machiavelli's description of rulers realistic?

Does Machiavelli make a convincing argument that it is better for a ruler to be feared than loved?

Why doesn't such a rule seem to apply to contemporary politicians such as the President of the United States?

Was Machiavelli advocating immoral conduct? Explain.

Here the question arises; whether it is better to be loved than feared or feared than loved. The answer is that it would be desirable to be both but, since that is difficult, it is much safer to be feared than to be loved, if one must choose. For of men in general this observation may be made: they are ungrateful, fickle, and deceitful, eager to avoid dangers and avid for gain, and while you are useful to them they are all with you, offering you their blood, their property, their lives, and their sons so long as danger is remote, as we noted above, but as it approaches they turn on you... Men have less hesitation in offending a man who is loved than one who is feared, for love is held by a bond of obligation which, as men are wicked, is broken whenever personal advantage suggest it, but fear is accompanied by the dread of punishment which never relaxes.[2]

What do you think of Machiavelli's description? Machiavelli wrote *The Prince* in 1513 while in exile from his beloved city-state of Florence. He dedicated it to one of the Medicis, the family who had been responsible for his exile, in a possible bid to return to that town. His work gave new meaning to the realities of power politics. If the safety of the state is at stake, he advises the Prince to use any means, including force, to gain and retain power. Many of the monarchs of the fifteenth and sixteenth centuries seemed to have acted in the way Machiavelli predicted they would.

Machiavelli has often been denounced for being immoral. But Machiavelli's writings were not so much immoral, as amoral. In studying the behavior of successful rulers, he discerned certain patterns. Moral rulers have sometimes failed because the ruler was too lenient with his enemies. Machiavelli identified power as the key element of politics. In doing so, he broke with a two thousand year tradition, since Plato that held that the purpose of the state was to provide justice and that a ruler had to be a moral person. Machiavelli identified the national interest, as we call it today, in whose cause almost any crime can be justified. The term "Machiavellian" has come to mean power politics. It may include bad faith, treachery, and dishonesty in diplomatic dealings as long as the greater interests of the country are thereby, allegedly, served. Machiavelli sheds light on the dark side of the Renaissance and of our own Modern Age.

Renaissance Art

For most people the greatest achievements of the Renaissance are in the field of art. While gaining inspiration from classical sources, Renaissance artists created new masterpieces that surpassed the ancients. Three technical developments provided the underpinnings for this outpouring of creativity. Renaissance artists sought to represent the human form and other natural objects realistically. They came to realize that a better understanding of anatomy would help in painting more realistic human figures. An understanding of muscle and bone structures would help artists to paint more naturalistically. For the first time since the fall of Rome, and in opposition to the Catholic Church, which wanted the dead to be given a decent Christian burial, dissections of human cadavers were undertaken to learn more about anatomy. Not only artists profited from these illegal dissections, but new scientific knowledge was gained which aided in the development of medicine.

How was Machiavelli different from political theorists who had preceded him?

What do you understand by the term "Machiavellian"?

How did Renaissance artists acquire a better understanding of anatomy?

What was new about Renaissance art?

Secondly, the laws of perspective were developed to give depth to pictures. Perspective is an applied form of mathematics. A new stimulus was being given to geometry. Third, the use of oil paints required an applied knowledge of chemistry, and mixing colors entails the application of physics. Artists were thus in the forefront of scientific knowledge. They also had close links to the humanists and Neoplatonic philosophy. New artistic themes drawn from Greek and Roman legends inspired many and popularized old, pre-Christian, ideals.

Over the 200-year period of the Italian Renaissance, from 1350 to 1550, new techniques evolved in the fields of painting, sculpture, and architecture. Figures show emotion in their movement and facial expressions. The beauty of the human body reveals itself, as it did to the classical Greeks, in the nude as an art form. In what was called naturalism, artists focused primarily on showing the beauty of nature. The laws of linear perspective, making flat two-dimensional drawings appear as three-dimensional, were discovered. Along with the invention of oil paint (rather than quick-drying tempera or wet plaster painting), the shading of areas and the use of shadows are introduced. Because of the use of oils on a canvas medium, the artist could now blend color, create a haze, and work much longer and more effectively.

How was Giotto di Bondone an innovator?

Although painting still focused on the religious themes of the Middle Ages, a change gradually occurred in the figures and subjects of the times. It was a Florentine, GIOTTO DI BONDONE (c.1267-1337) who broke away from the stiff, expressionless, elongated figures of Byzantine and medieval art. He developed the perspective technique of "foreshortening" of figures, which draws objects in the background proportionally smaller than in the foreground. His frescoes (wall paintings made with fresh plaster) included scenes from the lives of Christ and of St. Francis of Assisi. Other Renaissance artists, such as Michelangelo, studied Giotto's work.

LORENZO GHIBERTI (1378-1455) won a design competition for bronze doors to a baptistery in Florence in 1401. For 50 years, Ghiberti worked on his panels depicting Old and New Testament scenes. The panels, called "The Doors of Paradise" by Michelangelo, required 16 castings per panel until they achieved Ghiberti's standard of perfection. FILIPPO BRUNELLESCHI (1377-1446), who discovered new techniques for showing perspective, designed the dome of the Florentine Cathedral of Santa Maria Del Fiore. Although he borrowed from Roman architects, he still used innovative techniques, including a self-supporting double shell to bear the weight of the 27,000 ton Cathedral dome, which had a diameter of over 130 feet.

Among Brunelleschi's circle of friends was DONATELLO (1386-1466), another Florentine. Donatello gave birth to a full-size equestrian bronze statue, the *Gattamelata*, the first since Roman times. His free-standing bronze statue of *David* is notable for its nudity and realistic detail—quite unlike medieval models.

The Florentine sculptor, LUCA DELLA ROBBIA (c.1400-1482), used both marble and clay in his works. He established a family workshop that originally used enameled terra cotta (ceramic clay) to produce decorative accessories to larger marble sculptures. Later, terra cotta became a popular medium for Madonnas, altarpieces, and other religious subjects. A Madonna by ANDREA DELLA ROBBIA (1435-1525), the highly-skilled nephew of Luca, is pictured in this book.

What did Lorenzo Ghiberti do?

Why was Filippo Brunelleschi important?

For what was Donatello notable?

For what was the della Robbia family known?

Figure 5.2. Raphel Santi (1483-1520). *Alba Madonna*, c. 1510. Known for pointing sweet, tender Madonnas in the tradition of his native Umbria, Raphael studied under Michelangelo and Da Vinci. This Renaissance painting has symbolic meanings. Notice that Jesus is in the forefront accepting the cross from John the Baptist while both the Madonna's and Jesus' eyes are focused on John. *Andrew W. Mellon Collection. 1937. National Gallery of Art, Washington, D.C.*

A contemporary painter from Florence, SANDRO BOTTICELLI (1445-1510), was much indebted to the patronage of the Medici, and he was influenced by the Neoplatonism of the Medici court. Botticelli's work exploits both Christian themes such as the *Madonna of the Magnificat* and scenes from classical mythology like the *Birth of Venus*. During the last years of his life, perhaps under the sway of the fanatical friar, Girolamo Savonarola (1452-1498), Botticelli displayed more religious intensity in such paintings as the *Mystic Nativity* and the *Pieta*.

High Renaissance Art

The creative genius of Renaissance art reached its peak with the well-known Italian names of Raphael, da Vinci, and Michelangelo, who dominated Renaissance art in the late 1400's and early 1500's, a period called the High Renaissance. Much of their work has never been equaled. These artists were no longer the craftsmen from medieval times, but "all-around" geniuses who took on a "superhero" status to the people of their times. For emphasis, Michelangelo was called "The Divine One." These artists were celebrated like rock or movie stars are today.

Achieving balanced composition (one side must equal the other), mathematical proportions, awe-inspiring colors, RAPHAEL SANTI (1483-1520) excelled in painting tender, sweet Madonnas with the infant Jesus, using live Italian women as models. Some of the Madonnas, like the *Alba Madonna* and *The Sistine Madonna*, have appeared on modern Christmas cards. His portrait of *Pope Leo X* illustrates psychological insight into character, whereas his fresco *The School of Athens* painted on the walls of the Vatican Library shows balance, harmony, and the use

What are some of Boticelli's better-known works?

Who are the big three artists of the High Renaissance?

Can you identify the figures in the Raphael painting on the opposite page?

What is unusual about the work of Leonardo da Vinci?

of the laws of perspective. The classical philosophers Plato and Aristotle, framed in a series of Roman arches, are surrounded by famous philosophers and scientists: Socrates, Euclid, Ptolemy, and their students. This fresco proclaims the spirit of humanism interwoven with classical inspiration.

LEONARDO DA VINCI (1452-1519) worked on one of the most famous paintings of all time, *La Giaconda* (the *Mona Lisa*) for about four years, and still left it in an unfinished state. Besides being a consummate artist, da Vinci dissected cadavers to learn anatomy. His notebooks, written backwards so one has to use a mirror in order to read them, illustrate skeletal and muscular structures of humans, birds, plants, and technological innovations far ahead of his time, including sketches of the submarine, tank, and machine gun battery. Because da Vinci was so well-respected, his ideas helped to promote the growth of science.

Figure 5.3. Da Vinci, Leonardo (1452-1519). *Genevra de Benci*, c. 1474. Not as familiar as the *Mona Lisa*, this portrait displays the techniques of chiaroscuro (modeling of light and shade) and sfumato (haze) for which Leonardo Da Vinci became famous. Closely examine the details of the background of the painting for its three-dimensional effect and the photographic effect of the delicate curls on Genevra de Benci's forehead. *Ailsa Mellon Bruce Fund. 1967. National Gallery of Art, Washington, D.C.*

Many art historians and critics acclaim MICHELANGELO BUONAROTTI (1475-1564) to be the greatest sculptor of all time. Believing his figures were imprisoned in blocks of marble, he just *had* to release them. *The Pieta*, sculpted when Michelangelo was only 26 years old, portrays the emotion of Mary cradling a dead Christ in her arms. The citizens of Florence paraded the 18-foot marble statute of *David* around the city for three days in triumph and ecstasy before according it a place of honor in front of the city hall. Both the Medici rulers of Florence and the popes recognized Michelangelo's talents and fought for his services. He received commissions from four popes. Employed by Pope Julius II (1503-1513), Michelangelo spent four years crouching, standing, lying on a scaffold, paint dripping into his eyes and face, in order to paint and create the ceiling of the Sistine Chapel. Over 340 powerful figures adorn the huge ceiling (128 by 44 feet); the scenes include *God Dividing the Light from Darkness*, *The Creation of Adam*, and *The Flood*. His architectural genius must also be recognized, and the designs of the Laurentian Library and the dome of St. Peter's stand as monuments to his universal accomplishments.

Name some of the well known works of Michelangelo Buonarotti.

How popular was Michelangelo in his own time?

What do you think was Michelangelo's greatest achievement?

Mannerism

In his later years, Michelangelo was tormented by his desire for eternal salvation. His sculptures and paintings changed from the classical Greek style of balance, correct proportion, and harmony to one of emotional exaggeration. The bodies become elongated, contorted, and full of powerful feelings. For

What are the features of Mannerism?

Name some Mannerist artists and mention some of their works.

Why is the picture on the opposite page a good example of Mannerism?

example, in *The Deposition,* Christ's twisted torso is held up by Joseph of Arimathea, who resembled Michelangelo. This style of art is referred to as MANNERISM, "in the manner of Michelangelo."

Some of the most interesting artists of the Mannerist school are El Greco (Domenikos Theotokopulos, c.1541-1614), who was born in Crete and did his most notable work in Spain, and the Venetian painter Tintoretto (1518-1594). Working on enormous canvasses, TINTORETTO theatrically painted religious themes including *The Crucifixion* and other aspects of Christ's passion. One project he undertook was reminiscent of Michelangelo. Tintoretto painted Old Testament scenes, such as *Moses Striking Water from the Rock*, on the ceiling of a room. EL GRECO used elongated figures, bizarre colors, such as green skin, and movement to heighten the viewer's emotion. An art historian would say that El Greco (the Greek) was a forerunner of modern surrealist painting; his work was not appreciated in his time period. Look at the *Laocoon* at the National Gallery in Washington, D.C. or *The View from Toledo* at the Metropolitan Museum in New York City and see what feelings they evoke within you.

A one-time pupil of Michelangelo was BENVENUTO CELLINI (1500-71) whose statue, *Narcissus*, shows clearly the influence of mannerism. Cellini, however, had diverse styles and occupations. He was an exquisite goldsmith, and a vivid, candid writer, as well as a sculptor. Cellini described the making of his most famous sculpture, the bronze *Perseus*, in his *Autobiography*, parts of which are presented at the end of this chapter.

Figure 5.4. El Greco (Domenikos Theotokopoulos, 1541-1614). *Laocoon,* c. 1610-1614. Using elongated, tormented figures, El Greco (the Greek) depicts on canvas the violent emotion of a mythological story of a Trojan priest and his two sons being strangled by a sea serpent. El Greco's technique is almost surreal with distorted figures and unusual colors. *Samuel H. Kress Collection. 1946. National Gallery of Art, Washington, D.C.*

The Northern Renaissance

How did the political and social environment of Northern Europe differ from that of Italy?

Europe on the North side of the Alps was much more rural, feudal, and aristocratic. It was much less commercial, urbanized, and bourgeois. Spain, France, and England were dominated by great cities, Madrid, Paris, and London, where the courts of the newly developed absolute monarchs ruled their countries. These were also centers of commerce and intellectual life. The old Holy Roman Empire, which at times included parts of Northern Italy and what is today the Netherlands, was more decentralized and lacked any single great city. Significant commercial centers existed along the Rhine river and in the old Burgundian lands of Flanders. Rich burghers served as patrons for the arts and their sons at the universities were open to the ideas of the Italian humanists.

Northern Renaissance Art

What was notable about Jan van Eyck's work?

The great period of Flemish art was contemporaneous and independent of developments in Italy. The Master of Flémalle, whose real name we do not know, was among the first to use the new medium of oil paint. His *Merode Altarpiece* (c.1425-27) is a profound combination of late Gothic symbolism and realism. JAN VAN EYCK (c.1390-1441) further developed the medium of oil paint, putting layers on top of each other to create rich, translucent colors. His style was extremely realistic. For example, *The Arnolfini Wedding* (1434) has a little terrier in the foreground whose every hair is meticulously painted, showing dark and light contrasts. His

realistic, almost photographic, pictures satisfied his wealthy patrons' desires for portraits.
Van Eyck effectively used the principles of
perspective, which had been pioneered by the
Italian masters, to give depth to his pictures.
Flemish art, in turn, was greatly admired by
the Italians.

Figure 5.5. Jan van Eyck (Flemish, c. 1390-1441). *The Annunciation*, c.
1434-36. This northern Renaissance artist's attention to detail is evident
in the intricate design of the robe of the archangel, the stained glass
window, and the floor tiles. Van Eyck's forms are said to have weight and
volume intertwined with religious symbolism in every part of the panel.
For example, the triple windows of the lower floor symbolize the Trinity.
Van Eyck is responsible for substituting oil paints, a new medium of the
Renaissance, for tempera, a previously used egg yolk-based paint. *Andrew
W. Mellon Collection, 1937, National Gallery of Art, Washington, D.C.*

In what mediums did Albrecht Durer work?

Two German artists must also be mentioned. ALBRECHT DURER (1471-1528) has been called the German Leonardo. He used the art form of engraving in metal and wood with exceptional artistry. He produced sixteen woodcuts dealing with the Revelation of St. John. While obviously a medieval theme, the technical proficiency of the woodcuts makes them Renaissance masterpieces. Dürer also did some copper engravings with classical themes, such as Apollo, Diana, and Hercules. He was honored wherever he traveled throughout Europe. HANS HOLBEIN THE YOUNGER (1497-1543) illustrated Erasmus's book *In Praise of Folly*. His portraits of Erasmus, Sir Thomas More, Henry VIII, Christina of Denmark, and Ulrich Zwingli are psychological masterpieces. In 1532, Holbein settled in London to escape the increasing dogmatism brought on by the Reformation in Germany.

For what is Hans Holbein famed?

Northern Humanism

Northern humanists were as scholarly in their Greek and Latin translations as those in Italy, but they always remained more respectful of religion. DESIDERIUS ERASMUS (1469-1536), was a Dutch monk, who sought to create a more perfect world based on Christian ideals. His advice was sought on a variety of questions, for he was the leader of a group that criticized the weaknesses and abuses of the Church. Erasmus of Rotterdam, as he was called, introduced humanism into England during his term as a scholar at Oxford. His most famous work, *In Praise of Folly*, is a satire on the frailties and foibles of all classes of mankind; he delighted in poking fun at monks and other members of religious orders. He is known as a Christian humanist because his emphasis is on reforming and

What is the best known book of Desiderius Erasmus?

What does he do in this work?

IMAGO · ERASMI · ROTERODA-
MI · AB · ALBERTO · DVRERO · AD
VIVAM · EFFIGIEM · DELINIATA ·

ΤΗΝ · ΚΡΕΙΤΤΩ · ΤΑ · ΣΥΓΓΡΑΜ
ΜΑΤΑ · ΔΙΞΕΙ

· MDXXVI ·

Figure 5.6. Albrecht Dürer (German, 1471-1528). *Erasmus of Rotterdam.* Intaglio Print. This brilliant humanist, Desiderius Erasmus of Rotterdam (c. 1466-1536), was a scholar, who prepared a new edition of the New Testament in Latin based on his translation from the original Greek sources. He advocated church reform using stinging wit and satire in his *Praise of Folly* and *Colloquies. Courtesy of The Metropolitan Museum of Art, Fletcher Fund, 1919. (19.73.120)*

Describe the exchange between Erasmus and Martin Luther.

Why was Erasmus's edition of the New Testament important?

What is the theme of Thomas More's *Utopia*?

educating within the Church. A contemporary of Martin Luther, Erasmus challenged Luther over the issue of free will. Erasmus argued that man has control over his salvation, whereas Luther's position is that only God has the ultimate authority in the afterlife. Not capitulating to Luther, Erasmus remained an independent thinker and a Catholic to the end. His objective was to reform the Church from within. He wanted to return to the original message of simple piety preached by Jesus and the Apostles. Erasmus prepared a new edition of the New Testament in Latin based on his translation from the original Greek sources. This edition was used by Protestant reformers as a basis for their translations of the Bible into German and other vernacular languages.

A friend of Erasmus was the English statesman and author, SIR THOMAS MORE (1478-1535). More went on several diplomatic missions for King Henry VIII of England and served as his Lord Chancellor. However, More was executed by Henry in 1535 when his former Lord Chancellor, a loyal Catholic, refused to recognize the king as the supreme head of the Church of England. More's most famous work was *Utopia*, which literally means "no place." On this imaginary island, land is held in common, religious toleration is granted, and everybody receives an education. No wonder utopia has come to mean an ideal but unrealizable state! The book was intended as a satire to criticize the oppression of the poor and other social evils of More's day.

National Literatures

In many countries besides Italy, writers experimented with the vernacular and developed new national literatures. In Spain, MIGUEL DE CERVANTES (1547-1616) wrote *Don Quixote*. It is a satire on chivalry. Don Quixote, a romantic knight, focuses on a quest for adventure while his faithful, practical squire, Sancho Panza, keeps telling his master to see things as they really are and not as he imagines them to be. Ironically, at the novel's conclusion, the roles are reversed, so that the reader obtains the insight that perhaps the two points of view are necessary for man's/woman's being.

Representative of English literature is the gentleman most English-speaking critics consider the world's greatest playwright, WILLIAM SHAKESPEARE (1564-1616). Writing and producing 37 plays in his lifetime, Shakespeare epitomized the ideal of the "universal man" of the Renaissance. As a poet, psychologist, and dramatist, he is unmatched. Shakespeare's *Hamlet, Prince of Denmark* emphasizes the Renaissance view of man and his potential in this world when he says in Act 2, Scene 2:

> What a piece of work is man! How noble in reason! how infinite in faculties! in form and moving, how express and admirable! in action, how like an angel! in apprehension, how like a god! the beauty of the world! the paragon of animals!

In France, FRANÇOIS RABELAIS (c.1494-1553) wrote a satirical series about the giants *Gargantua* and *Pantagruel* that poked fun at the institutions of his time, especially the Catholic Church and Scholastic learning.

In Germany, Martin Luther was not only one of the founders of Protestantism, but his translation of the Bible helped to make German into a literary language. ULRICH VON HUTTEN (1488-1523), a German humanist and reformer, wrote the satire *Letters of*

What is the theme of *Don Quixote*?

How is Shakespeare illustrative of Renaissance humanism?

What did Rabelais write?

What did he appear to enjoy ridiculing?

Who contributed to the development of German literature in the Renaissance period?

Obscure Men, which mocked monasticism and medieval Scholasticism.

Invention of the Printing Press

The spread of the Renaissance thought throughout Europe was helped along by the invention of the printing press attributed to Johann Gutenberg (c.1398-1468) and others. Gutenberg used moveable metal type in a device derived from a wine press to print whole pages. Books, and the ideas contained in them, became available to a much wider audience because they no longer had to be laboriously copied by hand. Literacy for the masses became feasible.

Why was the printing press such an important technological breakthrough?

The first book printed was the Bible, about 1455 in Mainz, Germany. The Bible, Biblical commentaries, and the works of Desiderius Erasmus and Lorenzo Valla were used by the Protestant reformers in their attacks upon the established Catholic Church. We will soon meet Martin Luther, who wanted every man and woman to be able to read and to interpret the Bible for himself or herself. This was possible only after the invention of the printing press.

The Voyages of Discovery

Europeans had traveled overland to Asia intermittently. The most famous account of such a journey in the Middle Ages was the *Travels of Marco Polo* (1254-1324), which described an overland journey to the court of Kublai Khan, the Mongol Emperor of China, and seventeen years of service to the Emperor. With the breakup of the Mongolian

Empire and the rise of the Ottoman Turks, established trading connections were severed.

The fall of Byzantium to the Ottoman Turks in 1453 disrupted the flow of commerce to Western Europe. Spices, silks, and other luxury items no longer reached Western markets because the Muslims refused to trade with the Venetians and other Westerners. The economic decline of Northern Italy began once the Mediterranean was again dominated by the followers of Islam. The center of trade and commerce shifted to the countries on the Atlantic. First the Portuguese, then the Spaniards, Dutch, French, and English explored the oceans in search of wealth, souls, and glory.

The European exploration of the world and subsequent colonization used to be described as a glorious achievement. Contemporary histories treat this subject more soberly by pointing out the high price paid by those who were discovered. Most of the existing Amerindian cultures were destroyed. The African slave trade took on a new dimension with at least ten million persons forcibly removed from their homelands to work as slaves on plantations on the newly discovered American continent. The European impact on Asia, while apparently less severe, has yet to be fully assessed.

However one wants to assess the legacy of the Voyages of Discovery, for about five hundred years, from 1450 to 1950, Europeans dominated the world. They created the first global economy in all of history. They laid the foundations for the first world civilization which is in the process of evolving.

What prompted European exploration?

Why might some non-Europeans be less than enthusiastic about the Western adventurers?

Portuguese Explorations

The Portuguese led the way in discovering an alternate sea route to Asia, though their initial interest was in Africa rather than

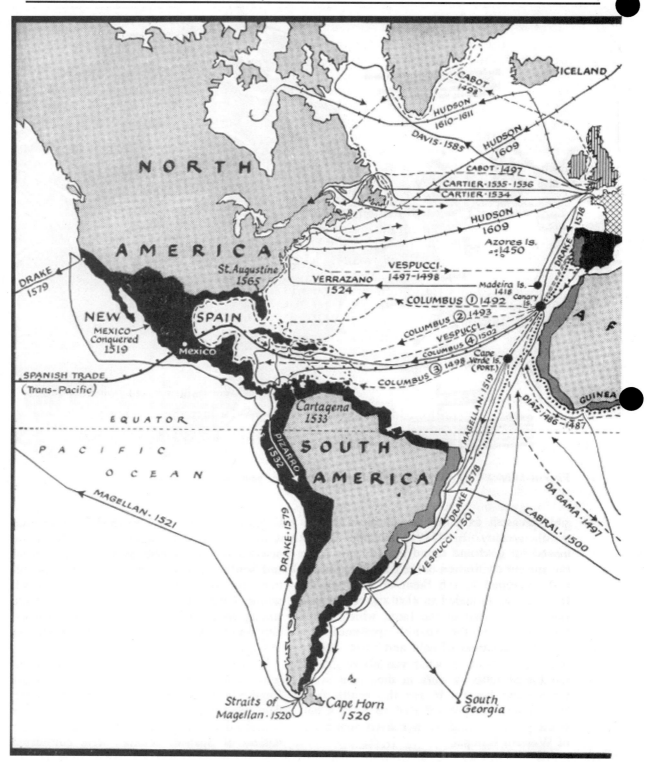

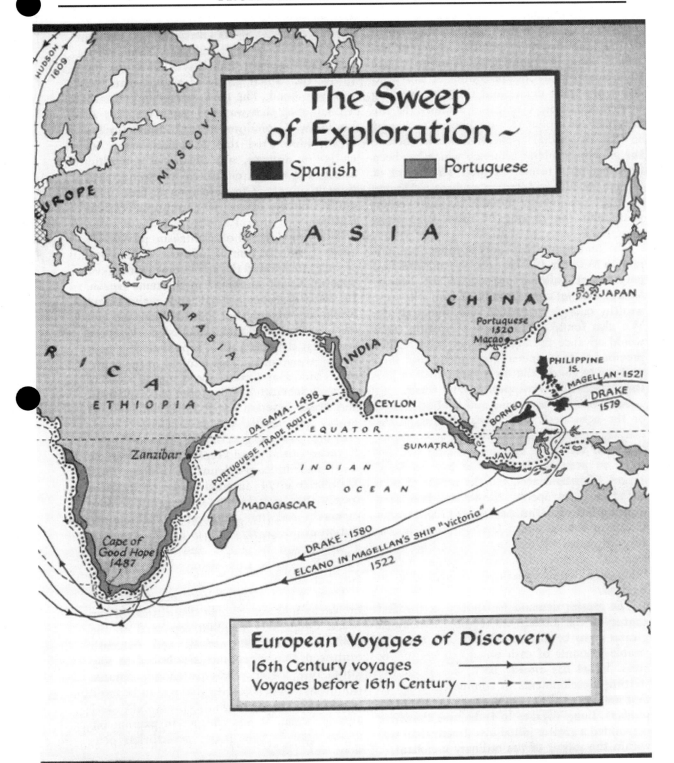

The Sweep of Exploration ~
Spanish   Portuguese

European Voyages of Discovery
16th Century voyages
Voyages before 16th Century

Who was Prince Henry the Navigator? For what was he looking?

in Asia. Even before the fall of Constantinople, Prince HENRY THE NAVIGATOR (1394-1460) established a school for sea captains and sponsored naval expeditions down the coast of Africa. Henry was the third son of King John I of Portugal (c.1385-1433). Prince Henry was apparently searching for the legendary Christian kingdom of Prester John. He hoped to find an ally against the Muslims and to gain access to African gold through direct trade with sub-Saharan Africa—bypassing Arab middlemen. The fall of Constantinople merely increased these motivations and added the imperative to find an alternate route to the pepper, nutmeg, and other spices of the Indies.

By the time of Prince Henry's death in 1460, the Portuguese had settled the Azores, Madeira, and Cape Verde island chains in the south Atlantic and had reached Sierra Leone on the coast of Western Africa.

Name some islands colonized by the Portuguese.

As they explored down the coast of Africa, the Portuguese established trading stations and began trading in slaves and gold. Slaves were used first mainly as domestic servants, but, with the colonization of the Cape Verde islands in the 1460s, slave labor was used on the sugar plantations.

What were the technological advantages of the caravels?

The technological knowledge needed for longer ocean voyages was gradually acquired. In the 1440's, the Portuguese developed broad-beamed sailing vessels called CARAVELS. These ships could be sailed great distances from the shore until they caught the favorable winds and currents to carry them in the direction they desired. Caravels could also withstand the recoil of cannon on their decks, which gave them a comparative advantage over the smaller, more lightly armed vessels encountered in the Indian Ocean. The astrolabe had long been available to help measure latitude, or degrees of distance from the equator. Techniques for measuring longitude, or distances east or west of a location, were not to be perfected until the eighteenth century.

Both skill and luck played roles in the discovery of an all water-route around Africa to India. Bartholomew Dias (c.1450-1500), while sailing along the Atlantic coast of Africa in 1487, was blown off course by a storm and unintentionally rounded the tip of Africa. On his way home he spotted what he called the Cape of Storms, but what came to be known as the Cape of Good Hope, at the southern end of Africa. When the Portuguese heard of Columbus's claim to having reached the Indies by sailing west across the Atlantic, they sent Vasco da Gama (c.1460-1524) on an expedition to reach India by sailing around Africa. Da Gama, with the assistance of Arab and Indian pilots, reached Calicut on the southwestern Indian coast in 1498. He found it difficult to trade in Calicut. The woolens and trinkets he brought were not desired by the Indians, and the Arab traders of Calicut were not receptive to new rivals. Nonetheless da Gama did manage to collect a cargo of spices that was worth, when he returned to Portugal in 1499, many times the cost of outfitting his expedition.

The Portuguese king gave Pedro Cabral (c.1468-1520) command of a fleet the following year, 1500, that was supposed to duplicate the voyage of da Gama. Cabral, however, sailed too far west and discovered Brazil before he eventually reached India. The Spanish and the Portuguese had agreed in the 1494 TREATY OF TORDESILLAS to divide up the rights to the non-Christian world. The Spanish could claim everything west of a line 370 leagues west of the Cape Verde Islands, and the Portuguese could claim all non-Christian lands east of that point. Since Brazil jutted out into the western Atlantic, the Portuguese found themselves with a claim to territory in the western hemisphere!

What did Dias, da Gama, and Cabral discover?

What did the Treaty of Tordesillas presume?

How did America acquire its name?

The Portuguese Empire

Amerigo Vespucci (1454-1512), an Italian navigator working at different times in both the services of Portugal and of Spain, explored the coast of Brazil. He gave saints' names to many areas along the shore. His own first name was adapted as AMERICA for the new continent by a German mapmaker who published an account of Vespucci's voyages. In Brazil, Portugal established large colonial plantations to satisfy the European demand for sugar. Captaincies, resembling feudal estates, were granted to some twelve individuals favored by the crown. At first, the Indians were used for slave labor on these plantations. When the Jesuit missionaries succeeded in restricting the supply of Indian slaves available to the colonists, the importation of slaves from Africa was greatly increased and did not cease until the middle of the nineteenth century. In 1549, a governor-general was appointed at Bahia, which was to be the capital until 1763. The Portuguese successfully fought off French and Dutch intrusions, and Brazil was to remain a Portuguese colony until it declared its independence in 1822.

How did Portuguese activities in Brazil differ from their activities in Asia and Africa?

The story in Africa and Asia was quite different. What the Portuguese did on these continents was to build a trading empire. Commercial and naval bases were established at strategic locations along the coasts of Africa and Asia. The Arabs had long dominated trade in the Indian Ocean and brought spices and other goods to the Venetians and other Italian city states, who in turn sold them to the rest of Europe. The Portuguese, who set out to destroy this trading pattern, experienced no compunction in killing the hated followers of Islam. In 1509, off Diu Island near the western coast of India, the superior fire power of the Portuguese overcame a Muslim fleet of 100 ships—five times the size of the Portuguese fleet!

Alfonso de Albuquerque (1453-1515), who was appointed governor-general of India in 1508, was a chief architect in building the trading empire. He captured Hormuz, which controlled the Persian Gulf. Along the Indian coast, he seized Goa, which became the center of Portuguese activity in the Far East. Portugal lacked the population and the financial resources to create large colonies in heavily-populated Asia. But it did succeed in diverting much of the spice trade to its ships and created an all-water route around the tip of Africa for transport of this valuable cargo to Europe. The Arabs did not merely lose trade. Albuquerque is reported to have cut off the noses of women and the hands of men he met along the Arabian coast!

Portugal and Spain were united from 1580 to 1640. The Dutch, who were at war with Spain, used the union to justify seizing much of the Portugal's eastern empire and Holland supplanted Portugal as the dominant European trader in the East.

Spanish Explorations

Spain owed its great empire in the Americas to the explorations of Christopher Columbus (1451-1506), who was seeking to reach the Indies by sailing west—across the Atlantic Ocean. Columbus, born in Genoa, Italy, was the son of a weaver and was largely self-educated. Most learned people of the time understood that the earth was round. More uncertain was its size. Columbus underestimated the extent of the globe, believing Japan

What did Alfonso de Albuquerque do?

Why do you think the Dutch and the Portuguese were rivals?

What was the background of Columbus?

Where and when did Columbus first land in the Americas?

Did he make any mistakes? Explain.

was only 2,760 nautical miles[3] off the Canary Islands, when in fact it was more than four times that distance. Columbus first sought backing for his expedition from King John II of Portugal (1481-1495). The Portuguese, realizing that Asia was farther west than Columbus thought, refused his request for financial support. It was only then that Columbus turned to Isabella I[*] of Castile (1474-1504). After seven years of fruitless persuasion, Columbus was ready to move on to France when an agreement for Spanish funding of the expedition was reached. Though the funds were modest, he outfitted three small ships with a crew of about 90.

The Explorations of Columbus

Columbus and his three ships set out from Palos, Spain on August 3, 1492. After stopping off in the Canaries, Columbus and his men reached an island in the Bahamas on October 12, 1492. He named the island San Salvador (Holy Savior) and called the natives Indians, since he believed that he had reached the Indies. (At that time the *Indies* was a rather inclusive term. Even Japan was then considered to be part of the Indies.)

Columbus made a total of four voyages to America. The first encampment he established on the island of Hispaniola (now divided into Haiti and the Dominican Republic) was destroyed, in his absence, by the Indians who resented the Europeans' lust for gold and women.

Columbus founded other settlements, but he was not a good administrator and in the end lost the confidence of the Spanish crown. The king and queen wanted more

---

[*] Isabella was married to Ferdinand II of Aragon (1479-1516). Under their offspring, the two kingdoms were united into modern Spain.

wealth and were disturbed by his treatment of the natives. Columbus, who never found the great amount of gold he expected in the Indies, sought to compensate economically by using the Amerindians as slaves. As early as 1494, he shipped 550 Indians to Spain for sale. Other Indians were raped, mutilated, and murdered. The Indians had no immunity to the diseases brought by the Europeans. Consequently, the Indian population in the Caribbean area quickly declined. There may have been a million natives when Columbus first arrived. By 1520, the number of natives was closer to 30,000; by 1648, the Indian population in the Caribbean was almost nil.

When he died in 1506, Columbus still believed he had reached Asia. While he failed to reach his own goals, his discovery helped to make the Americas a part of the European orbit.

Magellan Finds the Western Route to Asia

Other explorers soon realized that, not Asia, but a new land mass had been discovered. Vasco Nunez de Balboa (1475-1519), a Spaniard, in 1513 had made a journey across Panama and saw the Pacific Ocean which he called the South Sea. The problem was to find an all-water route around the Americas to the Pacific Ocean.

Ferdinand Magellan (c. 1480-1521) was the Portuguese native, who found the sea passage through the Americas to Asia. In the service of the king of Portugal, Magellan had previously sailed to Asia by way of Africa. He had been wounded in battle in Morocco fighting for his country. When the king refused to increase his pension, Magellan offered his services to the new Spanish king, Charles I (1516-1556), who also became Charles V of the Holy Roman Empire.

How did Columbus treat the Indians?

Was he a success or a failure? Explain.

What did Balboa and Magellan discover?

Describe Magellan's adventures.

The plan Magellan proposed was to sail across the Atlantic, find a passage through the American continents to the Pacific Ocean, and then go across the Pacific to the Moluccas or Spice Islands (now part of Indonesia). Portugal had already established trade with the Spice Islands, but Magellan thought it was possible that the islands were within that half of the non-Christian world granted to Spain by the 1494 Treaty of Tordesillas. (He mistakenly believed the Moluccas to be much closer to the Americas than they actually were.)

The Spanish king approved the plan and Magellan left Seville on September 20, 1519, with five ships and a crew of about 270. They reached Brazil in December of 1519, but it was not until October of 1520 that they found the passageway, later called the Strait of Magellan, which led to the Pacific Ocean. Magellan reached the Philippines, where he converted some of the natives to Christianity. Engaging in a fight against natives who opposed his convert group, he was killed on April 27, 1521. Magellan and his crew had not had an easy time before that. Mutiny had reared its head, as well as shipwreck and starvation, on the long trip across the Pacific.

Was he a success or a failure? Explain.

Only two ships remained to sail from the Philippines to the Spice Islands, where they were indeed able to purchase a cargo of spices. One of these ships was later captured by the hostile Portuguese. The other ship, the *Victoria*, under the command of Juan Sebastian del Cano (d. 1525), continued around the world by way of Africa. When it arrived in Spain on September 8, 1522, only 17 Europeans and 4 East Indians had survived the journey! The loss of so much life was hardly worth a modest cargo of spices. But Europeans now understood the vastness of the oceans they were determined to subdue. Other

Spanish adventurers sought to dominate the peoples of the newly discovered lands.

Cortes Conquers the Aztecs

In 1519, the same year Magellan set out from Spain to find the Spice Islands, Hernan Cortes (1485-1547) departed Cuba to explore the mainland. He landed on the coast of Mexico and established the city of Vera Cruz. Cortes's force, at most, numbered 600 men and 16 horses. Nevertheless he was able to capture the Aztec city of Tenochtitlan, near present-day Mexico City, with a population of probably 200,000. A combination of daring, Indian allies, advanced technology, and luck led to his success.

Cortes burned his ships after he landed at Vera Cruz so that his troops could not turn back. The Aztecs controlled an empire of 489 cities ranging from the Atlantic to the Pacific. The empire had been established and held together by force. Not only did the conquered peoples pay tribute in food and precious metals, but also in human prisoners who were sacrificed to the Aztec god, Huitzilopochtli. Subjugated tribes hated the Aztecs and some, such as the Tlaxcala, became the willing allies of Cortes. The horses and guns of the Spaniards terrorized and intimidated Indian opponents.

When Montezuma II (c.1502-1520), the leader of the Aztecs, heard of Cortes's approach, he first lavished gifts on the Spaniards, which only served to whet the appetite of Cortes for conquest. When the gifts did not serve as a deterrent, Montezuma permitted Cortes to enter the capital in November 1519 and received him at court. The Indian leader was taken prisoner and later died under mysterious circumstances. Allegedly Montezuma's will to resist was weakened by an

Did Spain gain much from Magellan's trip?

Why was Cortes able to conquer the Aztecs?

Did Montezuma make mistakes in his dealings with Cortes? Explain.

Indian legend that Quetzalcoatl, the feathered serpent god, would one day return to reclaim his lands from the Aztecs. Cortes was taken to be Quetzalcoatl.

An Aztec revolt forced Cortes to withdraw in June 1520, but he returned with reinforcements and retook the city in August 1521, after many of its defenders had died in an epidemic. Cortes became the governor of Mexico and received recognition from the emperor, Charles V.

Pizarro Conquers the Incas

What were the consequences of Cortes's success?

Cortes was the most famous of a group of Spanish adventurers in the new world of the sixteenth century, who came to be known as CONQUISTADORS or conquerors. Another famous conquistador was Francisco Pizarro (c.1475-1541), an uneducated Spanish adventurer who had been with Balboa when he discovered the Pacific Ocean in 1513. Pizarro also had explored parts of Peru on an expedition in 1526-28. In June 1530, after reaching agreement with Charles V on terms for the conquest of Peru, Pizarro set out in three ships from Panama with 180 men and 27 horses.

Peru was under the control of an Amerindian tribe known as the Incas, who had begun to expand from Cuzco in the southern Andes mountains in the late 1400's. By 1530 their empire, which included an estimated 12 million people, extended 2,500 miles from Ecuador to central Chile and included parts of what are now Bolivia and Argentina.

The ruler of the Incas was Atahualpa (c. 1500-1533), who in 1532 beat his brother in a civil war for control of the Inca empire. Atahualpa was at the regional capital of Cajamarca when he heard of Pizarro's approach. The Indian chief, probably out of curiosity, allowed the Spaniards into his presence. Pizarro quickly took Atahualpa captive and held the chief for ransom. Pizarro was paid a ransom in gold and silver estimated to be worth $30 million—allegedly filling a room 22 feet by 17 feet to a height of seven feet! After the ransom was paid, Pizarro treacherously strangled Atahualpa. Then Cuzco, the Inca capital, was conquered. Though resistance continued among relatives of the chief until the 1570's, Pizarro was able to found a new capital, Lima, in 1535 and to become a member of the Spanish nobility. His life of privilege was cut short in 1541 when he was assassinated by the disgruntled followers of a rival conquistador whom he had executed.

Comment on the morality of the actions of Cortes and Pizarro.

Spanish Colonial Government

Charles V and his son, Philip II, established the structure of Spanish colonial government. A Council of the Indies was established at the royal court in Spain to oversee colonial affairs. This Council was wholly the creature of the crown. In the New World, authority was divided between two viceroyalties. The viceroyalty of New Spain was established in 1535. The viceroy, who was headquartered in Mexico City, had jurisdiction over what is presently the southwestern United States, Mexico, Florida, Central America, Venezuela, and the Philippines. The viceroyalty of Peru was established in 1544. From Lima, its viceroy presided over the rest of South America. The viceroys, who were personal representatives of the Spanish king, were assisted by the *audiencias* or regional courts, which had both judicial and administrative functions. There were ten of these audiencias in sixteenth-century Spanish America. The *audiencias* were staffed by royal judges. At a still more local level were

What were the viceroyalties?

Describe the structure of Spanish colonial government.

the *corregidores,* who corresponded roughly to town mayors.

The intention of the Spanish crown in creating this detailed structure was to ensure its absolute control over the colonies. In practice this was hard to achieve—given the great distances involved and the determination of the conquistadors and their successors to exploit the opportunities for power and wealth.

Other European Explorations

Identify Verrazano, Cartier, and Champlain.

Other explorers helped to establish overseas claims for different European nations. Giovanni da Verrazano (c. 1485-1528) was a Florentine navigator who sailed for France during the reign of King Francis I. Verrazano, while searching for a passage to China, explored the Carolina coast line and New York harbor. Jacques Cartier (1491-1557), a Frenchman, discovered the St. Lawrence River, helping to establish France's claim to what is now eastern Canada. However, the real founder of New France, France's North American empire, was Samuel de Champlain (c. 1570-1635), who founded Quebec and discovered Lakes Champlain and Ontario.

England's claim to Newfoundland was laid in 1497 when John Cabot (c. 1451-1498) from Genoa discovered it. Cabot and his son, Sebastian, sailed for Henry VII. Under Henry's granddaughter, Elizabeth I, there were a number of English adventurers who explored the world and robbed their Spanish enemies. The most famous of these was Sir Francis Drake (c.1541-1596), who emulated Magellan by sailing around the world in the period 1577-1580. He sacked towns both in Spain and in New Spain.

A favorite of Elizabeth was Sir Walter Raleigh (c.1552-1618), who founded the unsuccessful colony of Roanoke Island in North Carolina in the 1580's. It mysteriously vanished. The first permanent English settlement in North America was established at Jamestown, Virginia in 1607. The Puritans, who came over on the *Mayflower,* settled the Plymouth Colony in Massachusetts in 1620.

It was an English navigator, Henry Hudson (d.1611), who first explored, in 1609, the Hudson River in the service of the Dutch East India Company. His exploration gave the Dutch claim to the river valley that they made the center of their colony of New Netherland. In 1664, New Netherland was taken over by the English, who gave the name New York to its capital. The Dutch had called it New Amsterdam.

Which explorers helped to establish English and Dutch claims to portions of the New World?

The Impact of Exploration and Colonization

What plants did the Europeans find in the Americas? What plants and animals did the Europeans introduce to the Americas?

Today, we take such foods as corn (maize), potatoes, peanuts, and chocolate for granted. These foods, as well as such harmful products as tobacco and cocaine, were unknown to Europeans before the discovery of the Americas. The Europeans, in turn, introduced many plants and animals to the New World. Horses, cattle, pigs, and goats were brought in. The use of these animals for food and transportation, as well as the introduction of wheat, rye, and oats changed the New World environment radically—in many cases overwhelming native plants and animals.

What impact did colonization have on native Americans?

What impact did the slave trade have on Africans?

The impact of European exploration and colonization upon the Amerindians was profound. In what was to become the eastern half of the United States, the settlers followed a policy of virtual extermination of Native Americans. Even more devastating was the effect of diseases, previously unknown, brought from Europe. The natives' immune systems did not protect them from smallpox, measles, diphtheria, and typhoid fever. In some areas, such as the Caribbean, the native population was wiped out. In other areas, it was substantially reduced. By 1510, the Indian population of Mexico had declined by 75 percent from its preconquest level.

There is also the matter of cultural domination. Native religions were replaced by Christianity, though later investigations have revealed that many native beliefs were mixed syncretically with the new Christian religion. For example, in Mexico Our Lady of Guadeloupe (the Virgin Mary) was endowed with some of the attributes of the Aztec fertility goddess Tonantzin. Nevertheless, the overall impact was the destruction of Native American culture as European religious, political, and social models were introduced in a conscious effort to recreate the Old World order in the New World.

Africans were also impacted by European expansion. Many were forcibly removed from Africa to become slaves in the New World. The figure of ten million is frequently used as the estimate of those enslaved in modern times—it might be even higher. The number touched by slavery certainly exceeded ten million when those who died in the process of capture or en route are taken into account. The horrors of the crowded slave galleys are not easily exaggerated. Perhaps twenty percent died in passage—the sick and the dead were simply cast overboard. Those who survived lost not only their culture, but what today we would describe as basic human rights. Since the slave trade occurred over several centuries, its impact on Africa itself is hard to measure. While some Africans who participated in the trade may have prospered, the social and political patterns of much of sub-Saharan Africa were disrupted, both by the rise of the slave trade in the late 15th century and its curtailment in the 19th century.

Europeans themselves were affected in several ways. They were the prime beneficiaries of an expanding global economy. They became the middlemen in the increased world trade. Most colonies were regulated, through a system that came to be known as mercantilism, so as to ensure a favorable balance of trade for the European mother country. The capital subsequently accumulated in Europe helped to finance the Industrial Revolution that made Europe even wealthier compared to the rest of the world.

There was also a price revolution in Europe. Prices in Spain increased fourfold in the sixteenth century, and other European countries experienced huge increases in inflation. For the poor, who had to pay higher food prices, and those living on fixed incomes, this was a very bad thing. For debtors and the new entrepreneurs, inflation presented opportunity. The influx of gold and silver from the New World appears to have played some role in this inflation. But the population of Europe was also on the increase. Increased demand, correlated to the increased population, was also a contributor to inflation. There were other consequences for Europeans as well. For instance, their knowledge of the world increased, as well as their sense of superiority over those non-Europeans they met and dominated.

On the positive side, it must be noted that the European colonial powers built

What was the impact of expansion on the Europeans themselves?

Overall, do you think European exploration and colonization were positive or negative happenings? Why?

flourishing cities, founded universities, and laid the basis for the modern states of South and North America, including the United States.

14

The Reformation

Have you ever wondered why there are so many religious denominations that call themselves Christians? The Reformation, a "protest" movement that occurred in the 1500's, led to multiple and varied forms of religion and continues to have tremendous impact on our social, political, and economic life.

The medieval church had been the unifying factor in an uncertain world where the life expectancy was approximately 30 years. Worshippers aspired to get to heaven in the universal Catholic church by partaking in the sacraments, going on pilgrimages, venerating relics (wood of the cross, bones, or clothing of the saints), and receiving indulgences. (An indulgence released the sinner, whether living or dead in purgatory, from the punishment due to sin.)

The Decline in Church Morals

With every believer's eye on heaven, scandals and corruption in the Church helped to provoke a spiritual crisis. During the Babylonian Captivity (1309-77), when the popes were under the aegis of the French king, Philip IV, the papacy was moved from Rome to Avignon, France. This relocation severely strained the Catholic Church. It

Why was the Reformation significant?

What was the Babylonian Captivity of the late Middle Ages?

Why was the Great Schism such a scandal?

lasted 73 years, during which time the French popes lived in luxury and appeared to care little for the ordinary person. Shortly after the popes returned to Rome in 1377, the Great Schism (split) rocked the Church. There were soon two people claiming to be pope—one in Avignon and the other in Rome. (Will the REAL Pope please stand?) In 1409, the Council of Pisa (an Italian city) was convened to settle this horrendous dispute. The Council attempted to depose the rival popes and to elect a new pope in their place. Instead, when the old popes refused to step down, there appeared for a time to be three popes. Finally, after several popes were deposed, the Council of Constance in 1417 elected Martin V as pope, thus ending this schism. However, this Schism fostered the development of the Conciliar Movement, which gave church councils higher standing than popes. While the popes eventually succeeded in squashing the Conciliar Movement, both the Movement and the Great Schism greatly weakened papal authority and prestige.

What were some of the abuses affecting the Catholic Church?

Also devastating to the prestige of the papacy was the debauchery and worldliness of the popes at the start of the Reformation. The Renaissance popes were more interested in political control, promoting the arts and literature (for example, the ceiling of the Sistine Chapel painted by Michelangelo, who was patronized by Pope Julius II) than in providing moral leadership. Another example was Pope Alexander VI (1492-1503), who not only fathered illegitimate children, but used his office to help one of them, Cesare Borgia, gain a principality for himself.

In addition to the lack of effective church leadership at the pinnacle, ordinary parishioners were paying their tithes (1/10 of their income) to absentee priests. Some parish priests held multiple offices (pluralism) because of the need for income, while the bishops who bought their bishoprics ineffectively supervised them. The sale of church goods or offices to the highest bidder, known as SIMONY, occurred frequently. So did trade in numerous religious articles, such as the bones, teeth, or hair of a saint. These practices led the Christian humanists, new orders such as The Brethren of Common Life, and ordinary lay persons to cry out for reform.

Because of the invention of the printing press with its movable type in the mid-1400's, new translations of the Bible in Greek and in Latin were disseminated throughout Europe. The printing press helped spread the new scholarly learning of the Renaissance advanced by the Christian humanists. Erasmus of Rotterdam's *In Praise of Folly* (1509) poked fun at monks and established religion as it was then practiced. His writings focused on restoring the spirit of Christ and Christianity back into the Church. This model Christian humanist advocated reform but not religious revolution.

Lutheranism

Now we look at a very religious German Augustinian monk, MARTIN LUTHER (1483-1546), who caused the Reformation. Did he plan to start a new religion? No! Let's see how it happened. Martin Luther, not satisfied studying law, entered the monastic order of the Augustinian Hermits in 1505. He then became a professor of the Bible at the University of Wittenberg, which was within the Electorate of Saxony, a part of the Holy Roman Empire. No matter how hard Luther tried during his tenure as a monk or university professor, he could not find in his religious life the inner peace he sought.

Did the Renaissance encourage the Reformation? Explain.

Who was Martin Luther?

Figure 5.7. Workshop of Lucas Cranach, the Elder (1472-1553). *Martin Luther*. German. 16th Century. By questioning the sale of indulgences, this former Augustinian monk and university professor started the Protestant Reformation. His followers, called Lutherans, became very inluential in the Holy Roman Empire (now Germany) and the Scandinavian countries. *Courtesy of The Metropolitan Museum of Art, Gift of Robert Lehman, 1955. (55.220.2)*

Whatever his good deeds, he did not think any of them adequate in the eyes of God to assure him of salvation. This quandary had perplexed him for a long time. Then he came upon a passage in the New Testament Epistle of Paul to the Romans (1:17) that pointed a way for him: "The just shall live by faith." As he wrote of his revelation:

> Night and day I pondered until I saw the connection between the justice of God and the statement that "the just shall live by his faith." Then I grasped that the justice of God is that righteousness by which through grace and sheer mercy God justifies us through faith. Thereupon I felt myself to be reborn and to have gone through open doors into paradise.[4]

This "justification by faith" merited by God's divine grace rather than good works is one of the primary beliefs of Lutheran Protestants.

He stressed first of all that the grace of God bestows salvation freely on humans; believers no longer had to worry about salvation. To be saved one needed to believe, rather than to do good deeds. Secondly, the Bible is the only source of authority in religious affairs, not the pope, not a church council. Thirdly, every baptized Christian can be his or her own priest. There is no sacrament of Holy Orders; there is no hierarchy of priests, bishops, archbishops, cardinals or a pope. (Is it any wonder why Luther was declared a heretic?) According to Luther's understanding of the New Testament, which he wanted every Christian to be able to read for himself, there are only two sacraments: baptism and communion. Luther also felt Jesus was physically present in the bread and wine at the commemoration of the Lord's Supper. This physical inherence of Christ in the bread and wine was called *consubstantiation*. The Catholic Church, in contrast, held the doctrine of *transubstantiation*—that the

Why didn't Luther find inner peace?

What were the principal teachings of Luther?

What were the *Ninety-Five Theses?*

How was Luther helped by the struggle between the emperor and the princes of the Holy Roman Empire?

bread and wine were changed into the Body and Blood of Christ.

Because of Luther's challenge to the blatant selling of indulgences by a Dominican friar, Johann Tetzel (c.1465-1519), in his hometown of Wittenberg, he set the ball in motion for a nationwide "protest" movement. On October 31, 1517, Luther's *Ninety-Five Theses* (propositions) were supposedly tacked on the door of the castle church as an invitation to debate in the usual scholarly fashion. Disseminated throughout Germany via the printing press, the *Theses* declared that every Christian has a share in the blessings of Christ and the Church—without the sinner buying a pardon to release him from purgatory. Though he denied it, the *Ninety-Five Theses* were the opening salvo in what came to be Luther's war challenging PAPAL AUTHORITY.

This controversy turned out to be more than a religious one; in fact, it had political and social consequences. Luther was excommunicated by the pope in 1520 and his doctrines were condemned. He appeared before the Emperor Charles V at the Diet of Worms in 1521. When he refused to recant his views, an edict was issued making Luther an outlaw in the Holy Roman Empire. While Charles wished to enforce the ban against Luther, many of the German princes opposed such action. Luther was hidden by his patron, Frederick the Wise, the Elector of Saxony, in his castle's basement, where he translated the New Testament into German. Luther had appealed to the German nobility to take the lead in church reformation.

Indeed, after he alienated many peasants by his wholehearted condemnation of the Peasants' Revolt (1524-1526), Luther's dependence on princely support increased. Many nobles remained loyal to Catholicism, but other princes, especially in the north, converted to Lutheranism. The impetus for conversion varied. Nobles were attracted to Luther's teachings from religious conviction, from the wealth to be had by acquiring church property, and as a way of gaining more political independence by weakening the power of the Catholic emperor.

The question is why didn't the emperor act vigorously at once to crush Lutheranism. The answer appears to be that Charles V was too consumed by affairs outside the Holy Roman Empire and too much in need of the help of all the German princes in his struggles with the French and the Turks. Charles alternated between demands for religious conformity and attempts at reconciling conflicting theological viewpoints within Germany. He hoped that a general council of the church would meet and settle the religious dispute for him.

The threat of civil war became more obvious after the 1530 Diet of Augsburg at the end of which Charles had given the Protestants six months to reconsider their position or be suppressed by force. In 1531, the Lutheran princes and free cities joined together to resist the emperor in an alliance called the League of Schmalkalden. Facing a renewed threat from the Turks, the emperor backed down. It was not until 1546 that Charles actually took to battle against the forces of the League. Luther had died earlier in the year, but the Lutheran Church by that time included more than half of the Holy Roman Empire and four of the seven imperial electors. The imperial forces defeated the forces of the League at the Battle of Mühlberg in 1547. The subsequent peace left the Protestant side discontented, and the presence of Spanish and Italian troops in Germany offended many. Fighting was renewed in 1552 after the Schmalkaldic League had formed an alliance with Henry II of France. This time,

Why didn't Emperor Charles V immediately squash Lutheranism?

Discuss the Lutheran challenge to the imperial forces.

Explain the provisions of the Peace of Augsburg.

the fighting went poorly for the imperial forces. At the subsequent Diet of Augsburg, Ferdinand, Charles V's brother, was authorized to negotiate the PEACE OF AUGSBURG (1555), which settled relations between Catholics and Lutherans within the Holy Roman Empire. The Peace provided that each prince of the Empire could choose between Catholicism and Lutheranism and impose that choice on his subjects. People not willing to accept the ruler's choice of religions were free to move to other territories. The Lutherans could retain all Catholic Church property that had been confiscated prior to 1552. If a Catholic churchman turned Lutheran later, he could not bring his titles or territories into the Lutheran embrace. The provisions of this peace did not apply to other Protestants, such as Calvinists. This failure to establish a more comprehensive peace contributed later to the Thirty Years' War (1618-1648).

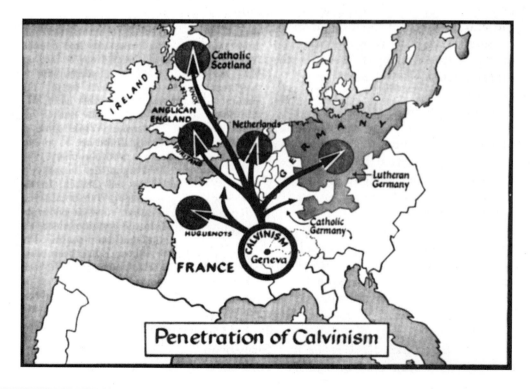

Penetration of Calvinism

The introduction of Lutheranism into Scandinavia was largely the work of the Swedish and Danish kings. In the 1520's, the King of Sweden took over much church property and introduced Lutheranism in Sweden and Finland. In the 1530's, the King of Denmark made Lutheranism the state religion, and established it in Norway. (These countries are still 95% Lutheran today.)

Besides much of Germany, what other countries became Lutheran?

Calvinism

The revolt of Luther encouraged other reformers, among them Ulrich Zwingli (1484-1531) in Zurich, Switzerland, and Menno Simons (1496-1561) in Germany (Have you heard of the Mennonites?). But no other reformer was as successful as John Calvin (1509-1564), who was born in France, trained as a lawyer and humanist, experienced a religious conversion to Protestant Christianity in 1533, and accepted a call to help the reformed church in Geneva in 1536. Calvin was to stay at Geneva, except for a brief exile, until his death. He made the city a model of theocracy (a state ruled by church officials) for the Reformation in the rest of Europe. He was a much more systematic thinker than Luther and spread his influence especially through *The Institutes of the Christian Religion* (1536).

Described very clearly in *The Institutes* is Calvin's doctrine of predestination:

> By predestination we mean the eternal decree of God, by which He has decided in His own mind what He wishes to happen in the case of each individual. For all men are not created on an equal footing, but for some eternal life is pre-ordained, for others eternal damnation...[5]

Where did the Frenchman, Jean Calvin, establish his headquarters?

What was Calvin's most important written work?

Explain Calvin's doctrine of predestination.

God in His infinite wisdom has already decided your future—Heaven or Hell—without regard to your good deeds. Only a few would be among the elect. How do you know if you have been chosen? You must act as though you are heaven-bound in this life, for you will not know until death. Thus free will was denied by Calvin. Humans could not choose their ultimate destiny, only God could.

Scripture was the final authority in religious matters. The sermon was the central focus of the service. The Church was to be purified (hence in England we have the Puritans) of anything not sanctioned by the Bible. Vestments, holy water fonts, statues of saints, and stained glass windows were out. An ideal Calvinist church had four bare walls, a pulpit, and a communion table. Only two sacraments remained for Calvin: baptism and the Lord's Supper (communion), in which Jesus was present spiritually in the bread and wine, not physically.

What were Calvin's chief teachings?

Calvin's *Ecclesiastical Ordinances* established the structure of a presbyterian form of church government. The local congregation was governed through councils of elected lay elders, thus setting a stage for a form of democracy. Above the congregations were assemblies called synods, where clergy and elders shared governance. This type of organization was ever so different from the Catholic Church's hierarchy. Calvinists were required to attend church six hours on Sunday, as well as during the week. There were prohibitions, with forms and degrees of punishments, against adultery, blasphemy, speaking out against ministers, dancing, card playing, heavy drinking, theater attendance, etc. (Did the Calvinists have any fun?) However, they had an exemplary community where capitalism flourished and idleness was discouraged. The Calvinists became bankers and moneylenders engaging in all types of com-

Describe the structure of the Calvinist Church.

mercial activity. From this group, we get the Protestant work ethic. ("Idle hands are the Devil's playground. By the sweat of your brow, you will earn your daily bread.")

Calvinism spread under many guises to the rest of Europe and the colonies. Calvinism came to dominate Holland as the Reformed Church and Scotland as the Presbyterians. Calvinistic Huguenots were strong opponents of the established church and government in France, causing a series of religious wars. Supported by Spain, French Catholic kings attempted to suppress the Huguenots, but Protestantism survived as a minority religion even in predominantly Catholic France.

Economically, Calvinism has been credited with helping to foster capitalism and, politically, with encouraging democracy. Certainly Calvinism was been more successful at limiting the influence of the state on the church than Lutheranism had been. By the middle of the sixteenth century, Calvinism was the most militant form of Protantism. Calvinists led in overthrowing the authority of the king in the Netherlands in the sixteenth century and in deposing two kings in seventeenth-century England.

Was Calvinism influential? Explain.

Anglicanism

Who were Henry VIII and Catherine of Aragon?

Henry VIII (1509-1547) was the second Tudor king of England. His first wife, Catherine of Aragon (daughter of the Spanish rulers Ferdinand and Isabella, and aunt of the Holy Roman Emperor, Charles V), had borne him six children after ten attempts. All died at birth or infancy except Mary. Henry desperately needed a male heir to the throne to insure the continuity of the House of Tudor (remember the War of the Roses), and was

Why would the story of Henry VIII make a good soap opera?

What supporting roles did Anne Boleyn, Clement VII, and Thomas Cranmer play?

simultaneously attracted to racy Anne Boleyn (1507-1536), a lady-in-waiting to Catherine.

By 1527, Henry had decided to petition Pope Clement VII for an annulment of his marriage to Catherine on the grounds it was cursed since Catherine had previously been married to Henry's brother. The Pope, who was fearful of offending Charles V, Catherine's nephew, played a waiting game, hoping Henry's passion for Anne Boleyn would cool. Instead, Henry, who eventually had six wives, proceeded to marry the seven-months pregnant Anne (1533) and appointed Thomas Cranmer (1489-1556) as Archbishop of Canterbury. Cranmer annulled Henry's marriage to Catherine. Parliament obliged the king by passing the Act of Supremacy (1534), which made Henry the head of the church in England. Another act gave the right of royal succession to Henry and Anne's heirs; yet another dissolved the monasteries and their wealth was given to the crown.

A few who resisted the King's policies paid with their lives; Sir Thomas More and Bishop John Fisher were executed in 1535. Most English people went along with the changes, for Henry's religion was basically Catholic in services and doctrines; but now Henry was the head of the Church of England, not the Pope. Henry's advisors, Thomas Cranmer and Thomas Cromwell, sponsored and enacted Lutheran reforms in the now state-controlled Anglican church service. However, it was not until the reign of Henry's son Edward VI (1547-1553) that Protestantism made great advances. Archbishop Thomas Cranmer introduced the *Book of Common Prayer* (1549) and encouraged Protestant ministers to come to England. Forty-two Articles, adopting such Protestant doctrines as justification by faith and the sole authority of the Bible (now translated into English), received official sanction.

Figure 5.8. Probably by Pietro Torrigiano (1472-1522). *Henry VIII, King of England.* Painted Terra Cotta Bust. Florentine, First Quarter of 16th Century. With the Act of Supremacy of 1534, this English king declared himself head of the Church in England. He severed the Anglican Church's ties to the Papacy, closed the monasteries confiscating their property, and began the Reformation in England. His actions caused religious dissension for years to come. *Courtesy of The Metropolitan Museum of Art, Fletcher Fund, 1944. (44.92)*

What changes occurred in the reign of Edward VI?

The reign of Henry's much desired male heir, Edward, by his third wife, Jane Seymour (c.1509-1537), did not last long. Edward VI died from tuberculosis at age fifteen in 1553. Now the pendulum swung in the opposite direction. Catholicism was restored with a vengeance. For next in line to the throne was Mary Tudor (1553-1558), the daughter of Henry VIII by Catherine of Aragon, his first wife. Mary earned the nickname of "Bloody Mary" (hence the tomato juice and vodka cocktail) because she had over three hundred Protestants put to death, including Archbishop Cranmer and other dissenters. Her reign became increasingly unpopular not only because of the fiery executions, but also because of her marriage to Philip II of Spain. The average person could cope with a return to Catholicism, but not an alliance of England with Spain. When Mary died, who do you think became the next reigning monarch? Another woman: Elizabeth I (1558-1603), Mary's half-sister and the daughter of Henry VIII and Anne Boleyn.

Was Mary Tudor a popular English monarch? Explain.

What was the Elizabethan Settlement?

The Elizabethan Settlement

Elizabeth's religious policies were moderate, although she too had dissenters executed. She desired religious conformity for the sake of political unity. Repealing her predecessor's acts, Elizabeth restored a revised version of the Edwardian reforms. She became the "supreme governor" rather than the "supreme head" of the church. Attendance at Church of England services on Sundays was mandatory. The services were said in English by priests who were free to marry. Although the liturgy itself closely resembled that of traditional Catholicism, *The Book of Common Prayer* was brought back along with Thirty-Nine Articles that embodied ambiguously phrased Protestant dogma (doctrine). Adopted by the vast majority of English persons, this middle-of-the-road path, called The Elizabethan Settlement, was a long-lasting success. The Church of England survived the attacks of the Puritans during the seventeenth-century English Revolution. The Church of England is still the official church today with several churches in other countries as derivatives. Thus members of the Church of Ireland in Ireland and of the Episcopalian Church in the United States are Anglicans.

Anabaptism

Anabaptism represents the most radical movement within the Protestant Reformation. Justification by faith and belief in the primary authority of the Bible are shared with other Protestants, but Anabaptists pushed these ideas to logical extremes. The literalness of their reading of the Bible led them to reject all practices not found in the Bible.

Jesus had been baptized as an adult, not as a child. Baptism should signify a conscious decision to follow Christ; it should not be a rite imposed on a baby without understanding of what is happening to him or her. Since adult baptism usually implied a second baptism and most of the original Anabaptists had been christened as children, this violated an ancient prohibition dating to the Justinian Code, which imposed the death penalty on rebaptism. Catholics, Lutherans, Zwinglians, Calvinists, and Anglicans agreed that the Anabaptists were dangerous heretics who should be exterminated. Everywhere Anabaptists were persecuted.

Anabaptists believed in a simple Christian life. Many thought that property should be held in common, as it was in the early Church. They were the first to advocate that

Was the Elizabethan Settlement a success?

Is the Anglican Church, or the Church of England, still around today? Explain.

What were the major religious doctrines of the Anabaptists?

What were the political ideas of the Anabaptists?

Name some Anabaptist leaders.

Church and State should be strictly separated. Most were pacifists who refused to serve in the military. Some refused to pay taxes to the government. Many were inspired by the Holy Spirit, or what they called the Inner Light. Those who had received Grace from God did not require either formal training or the guidance of priests, ministers, or other authorities. The priesthood of all believers was a principle of the Anabaptist movement.

While some of the early Anabaptist leaders where highly educated humanists, the movement appealed especially to the poor and more oppressed social classes. The Peasant's Revolt in Germany, which Luther so stridently denounced, may have been inspired by the Anabaptist doctrines of Thomas Münzer. It is easy to understand why the propertied classes were frightened by the Anabaptist movement. Anabaptists seemed to threaten the existing social order and all authorities.

The Anabaptists did not produce a single great leader, like Luther or Calvin. It was a diverse movement that arose in several places. Conrad Grebel founded the Swiss Brethren in opposition to Ulrich Zwingli in Geneva. In Luther's Wittenberg, the Zwickau Prophets expressed Anabaptist views. Melchior Hoffmann founded the Melchiorites in the Netherlands. Menno Simons (1496-1561) became a leader of the sect in the 1540s after more than twenty years of dreadful persecutions. The Brethren came to be called the Mennonites after his death. Many emigrated to America to escape persecution.

In the 1530s, the German bishop's see of Münster became a center of Anabaptist sectarians. Contrary to their usual beliefs of pacifism and withdrawal from public life, a radical faction, believing God's Second Coming was at hand, seized power on February 25, 1534 and established an Anabaptist Kingdom of Münster. Those who refused rebaptism were expelled from the town. The leaders of the movement, following the practice of the patriarchs of Israel, became polygamous. The New Jerusalem only lasted till June 25, 1535 when the armed forces of the Bishop took the town. The Saints of Münster were brutally put to death. Most Anabaptists denounced this radical experiment of an ecstatic Heavenly Vision and returned to their quietist ways. For the mainstream Christians, the Münster excesses confirmed their hatreds of Anabaptism.

Discuss the events in Münster during 1534 and 1535.

The Catholic Reformation

Renaissance popes Leo X (1513) and Clement VII (1523-1534) were preoccupied with worldly concerns, including the latter's captivity by the Holy Roman Emperor Charles V's army, and were both unable or unwilling to devote their energies to meeting the challenge of the Protestant Reformation. Pope Paul III (1534-1549), while capable of making his grandsons cardinals, saw the wisdom of appointing men of ability to high church office. (Remember the former practice of simony—the selling of church offices with incomes attached.) Paul III helped to initiate a movement of Catholic reformation, which is often called the COUNTER-REFORMATION. Several learned men became cardinals during his reign. The Inquisition to weed out heresy was instituted within the Papal States and the Council of Trent was called. The Papacy in the second half of the sixteenth century was filled by upright men who stressed virtue in making clerical appointments, thereby eliminating some of the former abuses that had gotten the Church into trouble.

Who initiated the Catholic Reformation?

The Council of Trent

What were some of the reforms of the Council of Trent?

The Council of Trent, which encountered major disruptions because of religious and political disagreements, met intermittently at an Italian town under the control of the Holy Roman Emperor from 1545 to 1563. While it did not succeed in restoring the unity of Western Christianity, it formulated important rules for reform. The sale of church offices and indulgences were forbidden. The Council called for establishing seminaries in every diocese for the education of priests, reiterated the celibacy of the clergy, and emphasized preaching and instruction to lay persons. Doctrinally, there was no compromising with the heresy of Protestantism; if anything, Catholic dogma was more rigidly prescribed. For example, justification by faith was denied. Transubstantiation (the miraculous transformation by the priest of the bread and wine into the body and blood of Christ) was reaffirmed; the sacraments, which remained at seven, were defined as indispensable to salvation. The authority of the Pope was held to be indisputable, while Biblical interpretation was held to be the sole prerogative of the Church authorities. As you can see for yourself, Catholicism did not reconcile with Protestantism as many reformers hoped, but it clarified its position, clearly delineating the lines of doctrinal belief that had been fuzzy for decades and perhaps centuries.

Were the changes brought by the Council of Trent chiefly in procedure or mainly in dogma? Explain.

The Society of Jesus

A number of religious orders contributed to the Catholic revival. These included the Theatines for men established by Gaetano Thiene and Gian Pietro Caraffa (later Pope

Paul IV) and the Ursulines for women founded by Angela Merici. But the most famous new order of the sixteenth century was the Society of Jesus, or Jesuits, founded in 1540 by IGNATIUS OF LOYOLA (1491-1556).

A Spanish nobleman and soldier, St. Ignatius experienced a spiritual conversion while recuperating with a shattered leg from a cannonball wound. His *Spiritual Exercises,* a training manual for spiritual development, helped motivate members of the Society for their tasks. The Jesuits were called upon in the *Exercises*:

> To be right in everything, we ought always to hold that the white which I see, is black, if the Hierarchical Church so decides it, believing that between Christ our Lord, the Bridegroom, and the Church, His Bride, there is the same Spirit which governs and directs us for the salvation of our souls.[6]

Chief among the goals of the Jesuits, who were organized along military lines, was missionary work in the areas of Europe that had turned Protestant and overseas, especially in India and Japan. Much of southern Germany, Poland, and Hungary were reclaimed for Catholicism. Success overseas was more limited. Besides serving as missionaries, the Jesuits ("the shock troops of the Papacy" as they were called) helped reinvigorate Catholicism through their work in education, by establishing colleges and seminaries, and as confessors to kings and queens. They indeed brought many converts back to the Church and prevented many more from leaving.

The Inquisition

The Inquisition was a committee of Catholic churchmen with the power to arrest,

What is the popular name for the Society of Jesus? Who founded it?

What did new religious orders, such as the Jesuits and the Ursulines, accomplish?

What was the Inquisition? Where did it find its greatest support?

imprison, and in obstinate cases, call for the state execution of those charged with heresy. There were really two Inquisitions in the sixteenth century. The Roman Inquisition had its chief locus in the Papal States, whereas the Spanish Inquisition affected Spain and Spanish possessions, such as Sicily and Sardinia. Hearsay evidence, unidentified witnesses, and torture were tools of the Inquisitions. Fortunately, the influence of the Catholic Inquisitions on Europe as a whole was limited. Unfortunately, Protestant churches and states also felt threatened by heresy and were willing to use similar methods to rid themselves of the "treasonous" dissenters.

The Index of Prohibited Books

What was the *Index of Prohibited Books*?

The Council of Trent had decided that certain books could not be used in religious services. The *Index of Prohibited Books,* first issued in 1559 by the Congregation of the Inquisition, was a list of books considered dangerous to the faith of Catholics and which should only be read with special permission. The Index was circulated in Catholic countries and underwent several revisions. Over the years some famed intellectuals made this list, including Thomas Hobbes, David Hume, and Jean-Paul Sartre. Interestingly, this *Index* was not abolished until the Second Vatican Council so decreed in 1965; thus, for over four hundred years it was an effective method of suppressing dissenting ideas.

Results of the Reformation

The immediate effect of the clash of religious ideals was an increase in religious fervor and intolerance and a decrease in civility. Luther called reason the "devil's whore." Religion was a prime factor in inter-societal strife well into the seventeenth century. In that century we have the Thirty Years' War in Germany and the English Revolution.

To religious dissent can be attributed more positive, longer range effects. Max Weber has linked Protestantism to the spread of capitalism. Others have seen the Calvinist form of governance as a precursor to modern democracy. Certainly many decided that religious toleration was the only way to deal with irreconcilable religious differences. It can also be argued that the breakup of monolithic religious thinking in the West helped prepare the intellectual soil for the Scientific Revolution and the Enlightenment.

The 1555 Peace of Augsburg gave the ruler the right to determine the religion of his subjects. The most general result of the Reformation was to make the state the ultimate arbiter of church affairs. In the modern era, political concerns in the West were to have priority over religious concerns.

What was the immediate effect of the Reformation?

What were the longer term consequences of the Reformation?

15

The Wars of Religion

Opposition to the Hapsburgs

What territories did Charles V rule?

The greatest political figure of the first half of the sixteenth century was the Holy Roman Emperor Charles V (1519-1556), who was born in Ghent, then a part of Flanders, now a part of Belgium, in 1500. He died in retirement at Yuste, Spain in 1558. Charles's political power resulted from the vast territories he inherited. From his father, Philip the Handsome, a Hapsburg, he received in 1506 the Netherlands (present-day Belgium, Holland, and Luxembourg) and Franche Comté (now a part of France, but at one time forming a separate county of Burgundy). These were known as his Burgundian possessions.

When his maternal grandfather, Ferdinand II of Aragon, who had married Isabella of Castile, died in 1516, he became Charles I, ruler of Spain and the Spanish territories in America, as well as Naples, Sardinia, and Sicily. When his paternal grandfather, the Holy Roman Emperor Maximilian I died in 1519, Charles was elected Holy Roman Emperor as Charles V (He was the fifth Charles to serve as Holy Roman Emperor, but the first Charles to serve as King of Spain). From Maximilian he also gained Austria and some smaller German possessions.

Charles, who was brought up in the Netherlands, had to struggle to gain accep-

How did he acquire these lands?

Who were the major opponents of Charles V?

Why did Francis I fear Hapsburg Encirclement?

What happened at Mohács and Lepanto?

tance from the Spanish nobility. But he succeeded and, in fact, Castilian support became an increasingly important prop for his empire. Sustained opposition to Charles came from three sources: the Lutherans within Germany, the French, and the Ottoman Turks outside his domains.

The French and the Turks

The Valois king of France, Francis I (1517-1547), feared HAPSBURG ENCIRCLEMENT. Charles, a Hapsburg, ruled the Netherlands to the north of France, the Holy Roman Empire to the east and Spain to the south.

Francis I and his son Henry II (1547-1559) fought sporadic wars against the Holy Roman Emperor. In 1559, after Charles V was dead, the fighting ended with the Treaty of Cateau-Cambrésis, agreed to by Henry II of France and Philip II of Spain. The French gave up to the Spanish their claims in Italy. However, they retained control of the bishoprics of Metz, Toul, and Verdun along the border with the Holy Roman Empire. These last territories were fruits of French cooperation with the German Protestants.

The Ottoman Turks, followers of Islam, were the other major external enemy of Charles. They advanced northward into eastern Europe, winning a major victory against the Hungarians at MOHÁCS in 1526. Ladislas II, (1516-1526) King of Bohemia and Hungary, was killed. About two-thirds of Hungary was lost to the Turks. Much of the remaining part, as well as Bohemia, recognized Ferdinand, Charles's brother, as king. Fighting between the Hapsburgs and the Turks continued on and off during the rest of Charles's reign. It was after Charles's death that a naval victory at LEPANTO in 1571, by a Christian alliance of Spain, Venice, and the papacy effectively crushed Ottoman chances of dominating the Mediterranean. The Turkish threat to eastern Europe remained well into the later part of the next century.

The Lutherans

Neither Charles nor his successors succeeded in their attempts to crush Protestantism in Germany. After Luther was declared a heretic, excommunicated by the Pope and declared an outlaw by the Holy Roman Emperor, he was protected by many princes within Germany who wanted to limit the power of the pro-Catholic emperor. In 1555, after Luther's death, we saw that his followers arranged the Peace of Augsburg with Charles V. Both Catholicism and Lutheranism were given legal recognition in the Holy Roman Empire. Each prince decided the religion of his particular principality ("Whoever rules, his religion.") More details on this Peace and other matters were provided earlier in this chapter in the section on "Lutheranism."

Charles did not like the provisions of the Peace of Augsburg because they were an admission of his failure to crush Lutheranism. His failure to maintain Catholic exclusivity within Germany contributed to his decision to abdicate his various offices in 1555-1556. Charles left his brother Ferdinand in charge of the Holy Roman Empire and his son Philip to rule Spain and the Netherlands. The German princes within the Holy Roman Empire were not willing to accept his son Philip, as their ruler. They regarded Philip as a Spanish foreigner. Charles V had ruled an expanse of European territory so extensive that he rivaled the achievements of Charles the Great (or Charlemagne) back in the ninth century,

How did Charles V react to the Peace of Augsburg?

How did Charles divide up his empire? Why do you think he did so?

Can you think of administrative structures available to such empire builders as Charlemagne and Caesar Augustus that Charles V lacked?

Contrast the upbringing of Charles V with that of his son, Philip II.

but the empire of this later Charles was a personal empire without the administrative and legal structures needed for permanence. He could not pass on his empire intact to his son, nor could his son later hold together the disparate territories of Spain and the Netherlands.

The Revolt in the Netherlands

The Netherlands, to the north of France, experienced religious and political conflict in the last half of the sixteenth century. The ruler of the Netherlands or Low Countries was not a native of the region, but the Hapsburg King of Spain, Philip II (1556-1598), the son of Charles V. Charles, as we saw, had been brought up in a region of the Low Countries known as Flanders. Though he later became King of Spain (1516) and Holy Roman Emperor (1519), he retained a fondness for the region of his birth. The Flemish and the other Netherlanders were also comfortable with Charles.

How did the Netherlanders differ from the Spanish?

Problems

In contrast with his father, Philip, born in 1527, had been brought up in Spain. He resided in the Netherlands for only a brief period from 1555 to 1559. He was not culturally comfortable with the Netherlanders, nor they with him. Philip was an ardent Catholic and shared with the Spanish the crusading spirit that had reconquered the Iberian peninsula from the Islamic Moors. The seventeen provinces of the Netherlands had no such military history. Wool production and commerce were for centuries well established in the Low Countries. Each province was jealous of its local traditions and reluctant to agree to increased taxes for Spanish wars unrelated to their own interests.

When Philip left for Spain, he appointed his half-sister, Margaret of Parma (1522-1586), as regent. There was a Council of State including members of the nobility, many of whom belonged to the Order of the Golden Fleece, a prestigious body of knights. But Margaret was secretly instructed to rely on an inner council of three led by the churchman Antoine Granvelle (1517-1586). Real power was still in the hands of Philip, who was a notorious procrastinator when it came to making decisions. Governmental organization was an obvious problem in the Netherlands. The nobility were excluded from meaningful participation in the making of government policy. The regent depended on a small cabal for policy input. The king, the ultimate authority, was in Spain—physically and culturally remote.

There was also a religious problem. Calvinism began, from about 1560, to make rapid progress. While not a majority, the Calvinists made inroads among the skilled laborers, merchants, and nobility. In many cases, they wanted not only religious toleration, but to strip the churches of statues and other papist (Catholic) symbols. Many Catholics of the Netherlands were unsympathetic to the methods of the Spanish Inquisition and were more inclined to religious toleration. The government had a financial problem too. Great debt had been incurred as a result of the wars with France in the first part of the century. When the king or the regent sought tax increases, the States General made demands that threatened royal authority. In 1559, Philip actually agreed to remove Spanish troops from the Netherlands

Describe the various problems facing the Netherlands in the last half of the sixteenth century. Which of these do you think was the most important?

Why do you suppose the Netherlanders were particularly resentful of tax increases?

in return for a tax increase! (The last of these Spanish troops were withdrawn in 1561.) Since Spain continued to wage wars on several fronts during the second half of the sixteenth century, there were continuing requests for more taxes and continuing confrontations.

William of Orange

Who was William of Orange?

Gradually, the nobility developed a leader in their confrontations with the regent. He was William of Orange (1533-1584), sometimes called William the Silent because he was careful not to reveal his private thoughts. Born in the Holy Roman Empire and a member of the German nobility, he inherited extensive territories in the Netherlands, which he made his permanent residence. In religious matters he was extremely flexible. He was raised as a Lutheran, became a Catholic, was a Lutheran again, and finally converted to Calvinism. His political needs apparently determined his religious beliefs.

Why was there opposition to Philip's reorganization of the Catholic Church in the Netherlands?

The Revolt Begins

It was the religious issue that led to the revolt. Philip wanted to reorganize the Catholic Church in the Netherlands. In 1561, the pope obliged by creating fourteen new dioceses to replace the old ones. Philip was given the power to appoint the new bishops, removing these offices as sources of patronage for the local nobility. Granvelle was made a cardinal and primate of the Church in the Netherlands. There was a storm of opposition from the nobility, from the Calvinists who feared increased Spanish-style orthodoxy, and even from abbots whose monastic revenues were to support some of the bishops. William of Orange and his noble cohorts focused their opposition on Granvelle and succeeded in getting him removed in 1564 (ostensibly he went to visit his aging mother).

With Granvelle gone, the Calvinists held more open meetings and many more gentry joined their movement. Philip insisted that the edicts against heresy be enforced. In April 1566, a group of nobles went to Margaret, the regent, with a petition demanding that the Inquisition be halted. The group that sponsored the petition were known as the "Compromise." An antagonist referred to the petitioners as BEGGARS, a nickname they eagerly adopted.

Pro-Calvinist riots broke out in August 1566 when gangs roamed the town streets, broke into churches, smashed statuary and stained glass windows, and roughed up the clergy. Some four hundred towns, including such major cities as Antwerp and Utrecht, experienced this violence. Margaret hired mercenaries and got the cooperation of the great nobles to break up the Calvinist gangs, but she also agreed to suspend the Netherlands version of the Inquisition.

Attempts at Suppression

King Philip, not satisfied, decided on a harder line. He sent the Duke of Alba (1507-1582) with a Spanish army to the Netherlands. Alba (or Alva) arrived in August of 1567. Margaret resigned shortly afterwards. Local government was replaced by a Council of the Troubles, through which the duke implemented a policy of political repression and ruthless extermination of heresy. Some 12,000 were condemned by the Council for their part in the disturbances. The Counts of Egmont and Horn, members of the high nobil-

Who were the Beggars?

How did the revolt in the Netherlands start?

What was Philip II's response?

Who were the Sea Beggars?

Explain the Spanish Fury and the Pacification of Ghent.

Identify Alessandro Farnese?

ity, were beheaded in June 1568. William of Orange had prudently left the country for Germany in April of 1567. He returned with a mercenary army in October of 1568, but his ill-disciplined troops made no headway against Alba's forces.

It looked as if Alba would enforce Spanish domination. But the Spanish managed to ignite more determined opposition by raising new taxes, which were especially objectionable to the merchants. In April 1572, a rebellious naval force, known as the Sea Beggars, seized the small port of Brill in the north. From there the Beggars spread out among the towns of Holland and Zeeland. Alba launched a counter-offensive, but he could not reach the core of Holland and Zeeland. By opening the dikes, those areas were rendered impenetrable to Spanish land armies. Alba lacked the required sea power to overcome this tactic. In 1573, Philip II recalled Alba.

The opposition to Spanish rule intensified in November of 1576 with an event known as the SPANISH FURY. Unpaid Spanish troops in Antwerp rebelled and looted the city for several days. Over seven thousand were killed. The outrage led sixteen of the seventeen provinces (Luxembourg was the exception) to sign the Pacification of Ghent, proclaimed on November 8, 1576. The Pacification called for the withdrawal of Spanish troops from the Netherlands and the use of the States General to settle religious differences.

Two other governors-general followed Alba and tried to subdue the Netherlands without success. Finally, Alessandro Farnese (1545-1592), the son of Margaret of Parma, was appointed governor-general in 1578. He enjoyed considerable success especially in the predominantly Catholic southern provinces, which formed the Union of Arras in 1579.

The largely Calvinist northern provinces formed the rival Union of Utrecht. Farnese used both persuasion and military power, capturing Antwerp in 1585. Though William of Orange, the revolutionary leader, had been assassinated in 1584, Farnese could not retake the northern provinces, which had declared themselves to be an independent republic. The dikes and canals of the north constituted a natural line of defense that was not easy to penetrate. Moreover, the English, unwilling to tolerate Spanish success across the Channel, formed an alliance with the Dutch in the north.

Distinguish between the Union of Arras and the Union of Utrecht.

The Armada

In 1588, Philip launched the Spanish fleet, known as the Armada, in part to halt English aid to the rebels in the Netherlands. 130 ships and 30 thousand soldiers and sailors left Lisbon for the English Channel. The plan was for the Armada to rendezvous with Farnese's army and launch an invasion of England. Philip actually believed that English Catholics would rebel and, with the help of the Spanish army, overthrow Queen Elizabeth. The plan was ludicrous; the execution was disastrous. Farnese's troops were bottled up in the Netherlands in shallow ports that the large Spanish galleons could not reach, but shallower Dutch rebel ships easily blockaded. The Spanish naval forces ran out of ammunition in their engagement with the English, who were clearly superior seamen. Storms wrecked havoc on the fleet. The Spanish commander, the Duke of Medina Sidonia (1550-1619), was forced to take the long way home around Scotland and Ireland. He lost about half of his ships and two-thirds of his men.

What was the Armada? Why did it fail?

Estimate the losses of the Armada.

Who was Maurice of Nassau?

Gaining Independence

Spain's war against the rebels in the northern Netherlands continued after the defeat of the Armada. But there was a change in Spanish leadership. Farnese died in 1592 and Philip in 1598. The Dutch were fortunate in finding in William of Orange's son, Maurice of Nassau (1567-1625), a very capable commander. The Spanish were driven out of the north. In 1609, a truce was reached granting the Dutch virtual independence. Fighting began again during the Thirty Years' War. With the Peace of Westphalia of 1648, the independence of the northern provinces, or the United Provinces, was recognized by the international community. The most important of these provinces was Holland, whose name came to represent all of the Dutch Republic. The independent United Provinces prospered in the seventeenth century, whereas the Spanish state suffered military and economic decline.

When did Holland become independent?

What was the religion of the Huguenots? Where were the Huguenots strongest? Where were they weakest?

The Religious Wars In France

France was the country of John Calvin's birth. Anxious to convert his homeland, Calvin sent many missionaries from Geneva into France. The Calvinists, known as Huguenots in France, enjoyed some success. Inroads were made among university professors, professionals such as doctors and lawyers, the lower clergy, especially the friars, and among the nobility. The movement was strongest in the commercial centers and in the south of

France. It was weakest in Paris, which was staunchly Catholic.

The kings of France resisted Protestantism. Like other rulers of the time, they believed that if all their subjects were members of one religious faith, the kingdom would be stronger. Besides, Catholicism was a financial blessing for the royal coffers. King Francis I had reached an agreement with Pope Leo X, in 1516, known as the Concordat of Bologna. The agreement gave the French kings the right to nominate bishops, abbots, and priors in France. Consequently, the financially pressed monarchs often sold these religious offices to the highest bidders. The monarchs would lose this source of income if Protestantism made substantial inroads in France. Ironically, the unworthy character of the higher Catholic clergy, chosen by the kings for political and financial considerations, helped the Protestant cause.

In 1559, the Peace of Cateau-Cambrésis ended a long series of wars between Spain and France. Henry II, the French king, celebrated this peace with a tournament. When a lance split open his eye, Henry died. His heir was Francis II, who was only fifteen years old. The stage was set for what became a series of religious and political struggles in France.

The Rival Families

The royal family was the most important of the noble families of France. Henry II was a member of the VALOIS dynasty. His wife, the queen-mother, was Catherine de' Medici (1519-1589), who was half French and half Florentine. She had four sons and two daughters. The three eldest sons were to rule France: Francis II (1559-1560), Charles IX (1560-1574), and Henry III (1574-1589).

What was the Concordat of Bologna?

Why did the French kings resist Protestantism?

Who were the most prominent members of the Valois family?

How deep were the religious convictions of Catherine de' Medici?

Who were the most prominent members of the Bourbon family?

Who were the Guises?

None of them had surviving male heirs. The youngest son was Francis, the Duke of Alençon, who died in 1584. One daughter, Elizabeth, married Philip II of Spain. The other daughter, Margaret, married the Huguenot leader, Henry of Navarre, who eventually became Henry IV of France. Catherine, who dominated her weak sons, had no strong religious convictions. She followed a generally pro-Catholic policy more from a desire to guarantee Valois succession than from religious conviction. Her attitude towards the Huguenots vacillated from toleration to seeking the extermination of their leadership, depending on the political need of the moment.

The BOURBON family was related to the reigning Valois family. Both dynasties could be traced back to Saint Louis IX, who died in 1270. The Bourbons, as "princes of the blood," would be next in line for the French throne if the male line of the Valois should die out. The leader of the Bourbons in 1559 was Anthony (1518-1562), who by marriage to Jeanne was also King of Navarre. Anthony's brothers were Louis (1530-1569), Prince of Condé, and Charles, Cardinal of Bourbon (died 1590). Anthony, for a time served as leader of the Huguenots, though he later reconverted to Catholicism for political reasons. Much more steadfast in their loyalty to the Huguenot cause were Jeanne, his wife, and Condé, his brother. The association of the Bourbons with the Huguenot cause was important in advancing the prestige of the Reform movement in France. The Bourbons were particularly strong in the south and in Picardy.

The Catholic cause found its most ardent champions among the GUISE family. The Guise leaders were Francis (1519-1563), Duke of Guise, and his brother Charles (1524-1574), Cardinal of Lorraine. Their sister, Mary, (1515-1560) had married James V of Scotland. The daughter of that union was Mary, Queen of Scots, who had married Francis II of the Valois family. While the Guises had vast properties in eastern France, they were distrusted by some of the French because of their descent from a foreign dynasty, the house of Lorraine.

Another influential family must be mentioned—the MONTMORENCY. Anne of Montmorency (1493-1567), the leader of the family, had been raised to the dignity of constable of France. He remained a Catholic, but his nephew, Admiral Gaspard de Coligny (1519-1572), became a Huguenot leader. The Montmorency had large estates in the north and in central France.

Who were the Montmorencys?

Describe the reign of Francis II.

The Start of Hostilities

Most historians suggest that the wisest policy for Francis II, who was only fifteen when he ascended the throne in 1559, would have been to play off the rival families against one another so that the royal family would hold the balance of power. Francis was legally of age, but he was dominated by his seventeen-year old wife, Mary, Queen of Scots. This made her relatives, the Guises, ascendant in the affairs of the kingdom, much to the distress of the Huguenots. In order to bring a halt to religious persecution, in March 1560 some of the Huguenots hatched a plot to kidnap the young king. The attempted kidnapping failed and inevitably heightened tensions.

On December 5, 1560, Francis II died. His successor was his nine-year old brother, who became Charles IX. His mother, Catherine de Medici, quickly asserted herself to become the regent. She attempted to reconcile

What did Catherine de Medici do when Francis II died?

Explain the Colloquy of Poissy and the Edict of January.

How did the civil war start?

What was the Pacification of Amboise?

Why did Catherine change from a policy of Huguenot toleration?

both Catholics and Huguenots by calling together a conference in which both sides could discuss their theological differences. This was the Colloquy of Poissy in the summer of 1561. The attempt at reconciliation failed. Nevertheless, Catherine issued the Edict of January (1562), which made concessions to the Protestant side. The Huguenots were permitted to hold assemblies outside of towns and to hold services within private homes. Catholic resentment grew. The actual spark that started the civil wars occurred on March 1, 1562, when Francis of Guise happened upon a Huguenot service being held in a barn within the town of Vassy—contrary to the edict of January. In the disturbance that followed over thirty Huguenots were killed and about 120 wounded. The fighting ended, temporarily, the following March with the Pacification of Amboise, which granted the Huguenots freedom of conscience but severely limited the celebration of Protestant services for those who were not members of the nobility. Anthony of Navarre was killed in battle. Francis, the Duke of Guise, was assassinated by a Huguenot who, under torture, falsely implicated Coligny, a major Huguenot leader.

The Civil War Resumes

As Catherine became more convinced that the majority of the French people were unprepared to accept Protestantism, her policy became increasingly pro-Catholic. The Huguenots decided on a desperate gamble and in September 1567 attempted to kidnap Charles, as they had once tried to kidnap his brother. This attempt also failed, but resulted in the restarting of the civil wars, which were to continue on and off for another twenty two years—until 1589. They were marked by many victories, peace treaties, assassinations, and atrocities on both sides.

In attempting to reach a more permanent peace, Catherine arranged to have her daughter, Margaret, marry the Huguenot prince, Henry of Navarre, who was the son of the deceased Anthony of Navarre. This attempt at reconciliation had the support of a new party, known as the *Politiques*. These were moderate Catholics, more interested in peace within the French kingdom than the extermination of the Huguenots, which was the policy favored by the radical Catholics, who supported the Guises. The marriage was scheduled for August 18, 1572. The Huguenot influence at the royal court was growing. Condé had died in battle, but Coligny had come to the court and had become a trusted counselor to King Charles IX.

The Saint Bartholomew's Day Massacre

The relationship between Coligny and the young king worried the king's mother, Catherine de Medici, who had been the dominant influence in Charles' life. She also distrusted the anti-Spanish foreign policy Coligny had persuaded the king to follow. Deciding to have Coligny assassinated, she convinced Henry of Guise, who blamed the death of his father on Coligny, to arrange for the killing. On August 22, 1572, four days after the wedding, Coligny was shot, but he was wounded rather than killed.

The cover-up of the bungled attempt on Coligny's life gave rise to the most infamous incident of the religious wars in France—the Saint Bartholomew's Day Massacre. In an effort to hide her complicity in the assassination attempt, Catherine persuaded her son

Who were the *Politiques*?

Why did Catherine want Coligny assassinated?

Describe the circumstances that led to the St. Bartholomew's day Massacre.

What happened during the St. Bartholomew's Day Massacre?

What was the reaction to the Massacre?

Who were the three Henrys?

Charles that the angry Huguenots, who had come to Paris for the wedding, were plotting against him. The king agreed to a surprise massacre of the Huguenot leaders. The killing began in the early morning of August 24, 1572 (the feast day of St. Bartholomew). Coligny was finished off, and many of the other Huguenot leaders were caught in their beds. The murders spread beyond Paris into the provinces. There is no certain count of the number killed, but possibly 13,000 died by the end of October. Young Henry of Navarre, the groom, kept his life by temporarily converting to Catholicism.

In the aftermath of the St. Bartholomew's Day Massacre, there was rejoicing by the Pope and in Catholic states and horror in Protestant countries. Within France, the civil wars were restarted. The intricacies of these battles are beyond the scope of this book. It will suffice to mention some of the leadership changes. Henry of Navarre escaped Paris and became the leader of the Huguenots. King Charles IX died in March 1574 and was replaced by his brother, who became Henry III. When the childless Henry III's youngest brother died in 1585, France was faced with the ironic prospect that the next in line to the throne was none other than the leader of the Huguenot opposition, Henry of Navarre.

Three Henrys Die Violently

Assassination continued to be a prominent feature of French political life. Henry III arranged for the assassination of the popular Catholic, Henry of Guise, who had been allied with Spain and who the king feared might overthrow him. Henry III, in turn, was assassinated on August 1, 1589 by a fanatical

Dominican friar. The next in line of succession, Henry of Navarre, the Bourbon leader of the Huguenots, decided that Paris was "worth a Mass." Henry reconverted to Catholicism so that he could gain the acceptance of the majority of the French and he ascended the French throne as Henry IV.

Henry IV (1589-1610) issued the Edict of Nantes in 1598 to meet the Protestant grievances. The Edict granted the Huguenots freedom of conscience and the right to worship in certain places. They also obtained many political rights, including the right to garrison with their own troops 200 fortified towns. Unfortunately, Henry IV was himself stabbed to death by a mad monk in 1610.

The French consider Henry IV to have been one of their great kings. Although the Edict of Nantes was undone later, the religious wars were not to be renewed. Perhaps his own religious flexibility—at times a Huguenot, at times a Catholic—demonstrated the triumph of the ideas of the Politiques. Religious considerations were subordinated to the needs of the state.

The Thirty Years' War

Background

We conclude our discussion of religious wars with the Thirty Years' War[7] in Germany, which lasted from 1618-1648. In the seventeenth century there was no national state called Germany. Instead, there was a political conglomeration known as the Holy Roman Empire, which had existed since at least 962. Since 1438, it had been customary to elect

Explain how each of the three Henrys died?

What were the provisions of the Edict of Nantes?

What was the Holy Roman Empire?

How did the seventeenth century Empire differ from countries like England or France?

members of the Hapsburg family or dynasty as Holy Roman Emperors. The electors were seven princes or churchmen from different parts of Germany. While the emperors traditionally claimed jurisdiction over Italy and Burgundy as well as Germany, the area they actually controlled was only Germany. In fact, their control of Germany was much less certain than the control of their kingly counterparts over England or France. The emperor, representing the Empire as a whole, and the princes who were the various dukes, counts, and bishops who ruled its components, struggled continuously over who should exercise more political power. The emperor wished to create a strong, more centralized, nation-state after the model of France or England, but the princes preferred decentralization and local autonomy.

What were the sources of conflict within the Holy Roman Empire?

To complicate matters further, the seventeenth-century Holy Roman Empire was also deeply divided along religious lines. The 1555 Peace of Augsburg had attempted to settle the religious disputes in Germany by allowing each prince to determine whether his particular territory was to be Catholic or Lutheran. It also sought to prohibit Catholic churchmen, who became Lutheran after 1552, from transforming Catholic property into Lutheran territory. By 1618, when the Thirty Years' War began, the Holy Roman Empire had a significant number of Calvinists, who were not included under the Peace of Augsburg. More territories of the Catholic Church had become Protestant possessions.

The Phases of the War

Historians usually divide the Thirty Years' War into four phases. The first phase is the BOHEMIAN PHASE (1618-1625). The Kingdom of Bohemia (part of the present-day Czech Republic) was ruled by the Hapsburg Ferdinand of Styria, who would soon become Ferdinand II (1619-37), the Holy Roman Emperor. Ferdinand attempted to force Catholicism upon his Protestant Czech subjects. They revolted and in 1618 tossed two Hapsburg ambassadors out the window of a Prague castle. Though they fell some 50 feet, they landed in a dung heap and lived. The event is known as the DEFENESTRATION (the act of throwing out of a window) OF PRAGUE. In place of Ferdinand, the Czechs chose Frederick V, the Elector of the Palatinate, as their king. Frederick was also the leader of a Protestant Union, designed to defend the gains Protestantism had made throughout the Empire. From the start, the war had an international dimension. The Bohemians received money from the Dutch and the forces of Transylvania harassed the Emperor from the rear. Ferdinand received troops from Bavaria within the Empire, and from Spain outside the Empire, and money from the Pope. In 1620, Ferdinand's forces defeated the Bohemians at the Battle of the White Mountain near Prague. Frederick became known as the Winter King (since he was king only for a short period in 1619 and 1620). He was pushed out of not only Bohemia, but his own Electorate of the Palatinate as well.

The next phase of the war is the DANISH PHASE (1625-29). The king of Denmark, Christian IV (1588-1648), intervened on behalf of the Protestants. He most likely hoped to gain some northern bishoprics for himself or his son. The Emperor commissioned Albert of Wallenstein (1583-1634) to raise an army on his behalf. The campaign ended in disaster for the Danes. Christian was beaten by Wallenstein and other imperial

How did the Thirty Years' War start?

Who were involved in the Bohemian Phase of the War?

What was the outcome of the Danish Phase?

What interest did the Swedish king, Gustavus Adolphus, have in the conflict?

generals. The overconfident Emperor issued, in 1629, the Edict of Restitution, which restored to the Catholic Church all property secularized since 1552 and forbade Calvinist worship. The Protestant princes of the Holy Roman Empire were alarmed and quickly found new allies outside Germany.

The next phase, the SWEDISH PHASE of the war, lasted from 1630 to 1635. The Swedish king, Gustavus Adolphus (1611-1632), wanted to rescue the German Lutherans and to protect his Baltic interests from possible imperial intrusion. He received financial aid from the French, who did not want to see the Empire ruled by a strong monarch. Gustavus Adolphus was a superb general, with an army seasoned by previous battles with Russia and Poland. He defeated an imperial army at Breitenfeld in 1631, and the following year won a major victory at Lutzen. However, Gustavus Adolphus lost his life at Lutzen, while Wallenstein, who had begun to negotiate peace independently of the Emperor, was assassinated on February 25, 1634. In September of that year the Swedes, without Gustavus Adolphus, were badly defeated at Nordlingen. It looked as if there might be a reconciliation between Ferdinand II and the princes of the Empire. The Emperor even agreed to annul the Edict of Restitution and made peace with the Saxons, who had been allies of the Swedes.

The German principalities in 1635 were ready to make peace, but peace did not come. By this time, the war had become an international struggle involving the French, the Swedes, the Spanish, and the Dutch, as well as the Germans. Each of these powers had its own agenda. The chief French minister was Cardinal Richelieu (1585-1642). Although a Cardinal of the Catholic Church, he decided not only to supply funds, but also troops for the Protestant cause. His major objective was to weaken the Hapsburgs, whose territories bordered France on the east (Ferdinand II of the Holy Roman Empire) and on the south (Philip IV of Spain). In 1635, the fourth phase of the war began, the FRENCH-SWEDISH PHASE, which lasted until the making of peace in 1648. Much of this phase was spent in looting the cities and the countryside. The French and Swedish armies managed to maintain the upper hand. There was much loss of civilian life. Some have estimated that, for the whole war, the cities lost one third of their population, while the population in the countryside was reduced by two-fifths. If correct, this would represent an overall decrease in population from perhaps 21 to 13 million.

Why did the French, under Cardinal Richelieu, become directly involved in the war?

The Peace of Westphalia

The 1648 Peace of Westphalia, which ended the Thirty Years' War, is considered by many historians to be a turning point in modern Western civilization. After 1648, political rather than religious considerations predominate in international relations. In most areas of Europe, the division between Catholic and Protestant stabilized. The Hapsburg Holy Roman Empire and Hapsburg Spain were on the losing side in the conflict. Germany would not become a united, modern nation-state until the latter half of the nineteenth century. France was free to establish itself as the dominant power on the European continent.

The Peace of Westphalia permitted the 300-odd principalities of the Holy Roman Empire to conduct their own foreign diplomacy and to make treaties. The Empire, which could not raise taxes or declare war without the consent of the principalities, was de-

What did the Peace of Westphalia mean for the Holy Roman Empire?

How was the rest of Europe affected by the end of the Thirty Years' War?

stroyed as an effective political entity for modern times. The Hapsburg rulers (Ferdinand III was Holy Roman Emperor from 1637 to 1657) henceforth concentrated their attention on Austria and other hereditary holdings. Each prince within the Holy Roman Empire could determine the religion of his territory, whether it might be Catholic, Lutheran, or Calvinist. Dissatisfied individuals were free to migrate to other territories. Church territories confiscated by Protestants after 1552 remained Protestant.

In early 1648, the independence of the Dutch from Spain was recognized. The French and Spanish did not make peace until the 1659 Treaty of the Pyrenees. Both Holland and the Swiss Cantons were recognized as independent of the Holy Roman Empire. The French and the Swedes received some border territories of the Holy Roman Empire. Sweden was left in a dominant position in the Baltic, France in most of continental Europe.

Which of the events covered in this chapter do you believe were most significant in ushering in modern times? Why?

Conclusion

This chapter began with the new ideas ushered in by the Renaissance, discussed the spread of Europeans overseas, and ends with the split of Western Christianity into competing, warring sects. These are events that have an inherent interest in themselves. We can imagine what it would have been like to be present when Columbus encountered Amerindians for the first time or when Luther tacked the *Ninety-Five Theses* on the door of the Wittenberg church.

Yet those who were contemporaries of these and related events suffered what was often emotional shock and great physical danger. The Indians and the African slaves paid a dreadful price for the European discovery of the New World. Within Europe, religious differences were not suffered lightly. Heretics were burned by both sides. Paris gleefully massacred the Huguenots on Saint Bartholomew's Day.

For those who witnessed the events, the changes described were not merely disconcerting in the way new things are often disturbing for older persons. The changes were truly revolutionary! Their vision of the world and of the place of religion in the world changed. These happenings were steps along the passage to the modern world. If you want to know more about the modern world, perhaps you will join the authors in *Exploring Western Civilization: 1600 to the Present*[8], which is the companion volume to this book.

NOTES

[1] Quoted in Jackson J. Spielvogel, <u>Western Civilization</u>, <u>Volume I: To 1715</u>, 2nd ed., (Minneapolis/St. Paul: West Publishing, 1994), p.425.

[2] Nicollo Machiavelli, <u>The Prince</u>, 1513, trans. by Thomas G. Bergin (New York: Appleton-Century-Croft, 1947), p. 48.

[3] John Noble Wilford, <u>The Mysterious History of Columbus</u> (New York: Alfred A. Knopf, 1991), p. 80. Samuel Eliot Morison gives Columbus's estimate as 2,400 miles in <u>The Great Explorers</u> (New York: Oxford University Press, 1978). p. 370.

[4] Quoted in Roland Bainton, <u>Here I Stand: A Life of Martin Luther</u> (New York: Abington Press, 1950), 65.

[5] Quoted in Eugen Weber, <u>The Western Tradition</u>, Volume 1, Fourth Edition (Lexington, Mass.: D. C. Heath, 1990), p. 344.

[6] Ignatius of Loyola, Saint: <u>Spiritual Exercises.</u> Translated from the autograph by Father Elder Mullan, S.J., The Christian Classics Ethereal Library (Internet, <http://hkein.ie.cuhk.hk/Education/Religion/Christ/library/ignatius/exercises/exercises.html>, 25 March 1997).

[7] The material on the Thirty Years' War is taken from the companion volume to this book by Thomas J. Kehoe, Jose M. Duvall, and Lawrence J. Hogan, <u>Exploring Western Civilization: 1600 to the Present</u> (Dubuque, Iowa: Kendall/Hunt Publishing, 1994), pp. 3-8.

[8] Ibid.

BENVENUTO CELLINI

The Autobiography of Benvenuto Cellini

At the end of Chapter III, selections from St. Augustine's *Confessions* were presented. Augustine stressed his dependence on God to find the strength to lead the Christian life. Bevenuto Cellini's *Autobiography* has a very different tone. Cellini boasts of his artistic achievements and brags about killing a man who had insulted him. His braggadocio offers a startling contrast to the humility of a St. Augustine. Cellini's *Autobiography* gives us an insight into the mind of a Renaissance artist who glories in human accomplishments, just as the *Confessions* gave us an insight into the mind of an early Christian saint.

Cellini's masterpiece, the *Perseus*, illustrates the Renaissance interest in the pre-Christian Greek and Roman world. The theme of the statue is from Greek mythology. The hero Perseus, having slain the monster Medusa, holds her bloody head aloft in triumph. We learn about his struggle to produce the statue in the passages which follow. Cellini was also greatly influenced by contemporary artists, especially the mannerism of Michelangelo.

Cellini, born in Florence in 1500, was trained as a goldsmith. His work includes many fine coins, jewelry, and a most elaborate salt-cellar made for King Francis I of France. His other patrons included Pope Clement VII, Pope Paul II, and Cosimo I de' Medici of Florence. Cellini died in Florence in 1571.

Cellini Gets Revenge[1]

While I [Cellini] was sitting in the street with several of my friends, Pompeo [who had mistakenly reported to Pope Clement VII that Cellini had killed a man] went by, attended by ten men very well armed; and when he came just opposite, he stopped, as though about to pick a quarrel with myself. My companions, brave and adventurous young men, made signs to me to draw my sword; but it flashed through my mind that if I drew, some terrible mischief might result for persons who were wholly innocent. Therefore I considered that it would be better if I put my life to risk alone. When Pompeo had stood there time enough to say two Ave Marias, he laughed derisively in my direction; and going off, his fellows also

---

[1]The shaded titles are by the authors of this book. The selections are from Benvenuto Cellini, *The Autobiography of Benvenuto Cellini*, trans. by J. Addington Symonds, Vol. XXXI of *The Harvard Classics*, ed. by Charles W. Eliot (New York: Colier & Son, 1910), pp. 148-152, 389-399.

laughed and wagged their heads, with many other insolent gestures. My companions wanted to begin the fray at once; but I told them hotly that I was quite able to conduct my quarrels to an end by myself, and that I had no need of stouter fighters than I was; so that each of them might mind his business. My friends were angry and went off muttering. Now there was among them my dearest comrade, named Albertaccio del Bene, own brother to Alessandro and Albizzo, who is now a very rich man in Lyons. He was the most redoubtable young man I ever knew, and the most high-spirited, and loved me like himself; and insomuch as he was well aware that my forbearance had not been inspired by want of courage, but by the most daring bravery, for he knew me down to the bottom of my nature, he took my words up and begged me to favour him so far as to associate him with myself in all I meant to do. I replied: "Dear Albertaccio, dearest to me above all men that live, the time will very likely come when you shall give me aid; but in this case, if you love me, do not attend to me, but look to your own business, and go at once like our other friends, for now there is no time to lose." These words were spoken in one breath.

In the meanwhile my enemies had proceeded slowly toward Chiavica, as the place was called, and had arrived at the crossing of several roads, going in different directions; but the street in which Pompeo's house stood was the one which leads straight to the Campo di Fiore. Some business or other

made him enter the apothecary's shop which stood at the corner of Chiavica, and there he stayed a while transacting it. I had just been told that he had boasted of the insult which he fancied he had put upon me; but be that as it may, it was to his misfortune; for precisely when I came up to the corner, he was leaving the shop and his bravi [thugs] had opened their ranks and received him in their midst. I drew a little dagger with a sharpened edge, and breaking the line of his defenders, laid my hands upon his breast so quickly and coolly, that none of them were able to prevent me. Then I aimed to strike him in the face; but fright made him turn his head round; and I stabbed him just beneath the ear. I only gave two blows, for he fell stone dead at the second. I had not meant to kill him; but as the saying goes, knocks are not dealt by measure. With my left hand I plucked back the dagger, and with my right hand drew my sword to defend my life. However, all those bravi ran up to the corpse and took no action against me; so I went back alone through Strada Giulia, considering how best to put myself in safety.

I had walked about three hundred paces, when Piloto the goldsmith, my very good friend, came up and said: "Brother, now that the mischief's done, we must see to saving you." I replied: "Let us go to Albertaccio del Bene's house; it is only a few minutes since I told him I should soon have need of him." When we arrived there, Albertaccio and I embraced with measureless affection; and soon the whole flower of the young men of the Banchi [Banks], of all nations except the Milanese [Pompeo was from Milan], came crowding in; and each and all made proffer of their own life to save mine. Messer Luigi Rucellai also sent with marvellous promptitude and courtesy to put his services at my disposal, as did many other great folk of his station; for they all agreed in blessing my hands,[1] judging that Pompeo had done me too great and unforgivable an injury, and marvelling that I had put up with him so long.

Cardinal Cornaro,[2] on hearing of the affair, despatched thirty soldiers, with as many partisans, pikes, and arquebuses, to bring me with all due respect to his quarters. This he did unasked; whereupon I accepted the invitation, and went off with them, while more than as many of the young men bore me company. Meanwhile, Messer Traiano, Pompeo's relative and first chamberlain to the Pope, sent a Milanese of high rank to Cardinal de' Medici, giving him news of the great crime I had committed, and calling on his most reverend lordship to chastise me. The Cardinal retorted on the spot: "His crime would indeed have been great if he had not committed this lesser one; thank Messer Traiano from me for giving me this information of a fact of which I

had not heard before." Then he turned and in presence of the nobleman said to the Bishop of Frulli,[3] his gentleman and intimate acquaintance: "Search diligently after my friend Benvenuto; I want to help and defend him; and whoso acts against him acts against myself." The Milanese nobleman went back, much disconcerted, while the Bishop of Frulli come to visit me at Cardinal Cornaro's palace. Presenting himself to the Cardinal, he related how Cardinal de' Medici had sent for Benvenuto, and wanted to be his protector. Now Cardinal Cornaro, who had the touchy temper of a bear, flew into a rage, and told the Bishop he was quite as well able to defend me as Cardinal de' Medici. The Bishop, in reply, entreated to be allowed to speak with me on some matters of his patron which had nothing to do with the affair. Cornaro bade him for that day make as though he had already talked with me.

Cardinal de' Medici was very angry. However, 1 went the following night, without Cornaro's knowledge, and under good escort, to pay him my respects. Then I begged him to grant me the favour of leaving me where I was, and told him of the great courtesy which Cornaro had shown me; adding that if his most reverend lordship suffered me to stay, I should gain one friend the more in my hour of need; otherwise his lordship might dispose of me exactly as he thought best. He told me to do as I liked; so I returned to Cornaro's palace, and a few days afterwards

---

[1]*Tutti d' accordo mi benedissono le mani.* This is tantamount to approving Cellini's handiwork in murdering Pompeo. [This and subsequent footnotes for this reading are by the translator, J. Addington Symonds.]

[2]This was Francesco, brother to Cardinal Marco Cornaro. He received the hat in 1528, while yet a layman, and the Bishopric of Brescia in 1531.

[3]Forli. The Bishop was Bernardo de' Medici.

the Cardinal Farnese was elected Pope.[1]

After he had put affairs of greater consequence in order, the new Pope sent for me, saying that he did not wish any one else to strike his coins. To these words of his Holiness a gentleman very privately acquainted with him, named Messer Latino Juvinale, made answer that I was in hiding for a murder committed on the person of one Pompeo of Milan, and set forth what could be argued for my justification in the most favourable terms.[2] The Pope replied: "I knew nothing of Pompeo's death, but plenty of Benvenuto's provocation; so let a safe-conduct be at once made out for him, in order that he may be placed in perfect security." A great friend of Pompeo's, who was also intimate with the Pope, happened to be there; he was a Milanese, called Messer Ambrogio.[3] This man said: "In the first days of your papacy it were not well to grant pardons of this kind." The Pope turned to him and answered: "You know less about such matters than I do. Know then that men like Benvenuto, unique in their profession, stand above the law; and how far more he, then, who received the provocation I have heard of?" When my safe conduct had been drawn out, I began at once to serve him, and was treated with the utmost favour.

---

[1]Paul III., elected October 13, 1534

[2]Latino Giovenale de' Manetti was a Latin poet and a man of humane learning, much esteemed by his contemporaries.

[3]Ambrogio Recalcati. He was for many years the trusted secretary and diplomatic agent of Paul III.

Making the *Perseus*

The waxen model [of Perseus] produced so fine an effect, that when the Duke [Cosimo de' Medici] saw it and was struck with its beauty—whether somebody had persuaded him it could not be carried out with the same finish in metal, or whether he thought so for himself—he came to visit me more frequently than usual, and on one occasion said: "Benvenuto, this figure cannot succeed in bronze; the laws of art do not admit of it." These words of his Excellency stung me so sharply that I answered: "My lord, I know how very little confidence you have in me; and I believe the reason of this is that your most illustrious Excellency lends too ready an ear to my calumniators, or else indeed that you do not understand my art." He hardly let me close the sentence when he broke in: "I profess myself a connoisseur, and understand it very well indeed." I replied: "Yes, like a prince, not like an artist; for if your Excellency understood my trade as well as you imagine, you would trust me on the proofs I have already given. These are, first, the colossal bronze bust of your Excellency, which is now in Elba;[4] secondly, the restoration of the Ganymede in marble, which offered so many difficulties and cost me so much trouble, that I would rather have made the whole statue new from the beginning; thirdly, the Medusa, cast by me in bronze, here now before your Excellency's eyes, the execution of which was a

---

[4]At Portoferraio. It came afterwards to Florence.

greater triumph of strength and skill than any of my predecessors in this fiendish art have yet achieved. Look you, my lord! I constructed that furnace anew on principles quite different from those of other founders; in addition to many technical improvements and ingenious devices, I supplied it with two issues for the metal, because this difficult and twisted figure could not otherwise have come out perfect. It is only owing to my intelligent insight into means and appliances that the statue turned out as it did; a triumph judged impossible by all the practitioners of this art. I should like you furthermore to be aware, my lord, for certain, that the sole reason why I succeeded with all those great arduous works in France under his most admirable Majesty King Francis, was the high courage which that good monarch put into my heart by the liberal allowances he made me, and the multitude of workpeople he left at my disposal. I could have as many as I asked for, and employed at times above forty, all chosen by myself. These were the causes of my having there produced so many masterpieces in so short a space of time. Now then, my lord, put trust in me; supply me with the aid I need. I am confident of being able to complete a work which will delight your soul. But if your Excellency goes on disheartening me, and does not advance me the assistance which is absolutely required, neither I nor any man alive upon this earth can hope to achieve the slightest thing of value"

It was as much as the Duke could do to stand by and listen to my pleadings. He kept turning first this way and then that; while I, in despair, poor wretched I, was calling up remembrance of the noble state I held in France, to the great sorrow of my soul. All at once he cried: "Come, tell me, Benvenuto, how is it possible that yonder splendid head of Medusa, so high up there in the grasp of Perseus, should ever come out perfect?" I replied upon the instant: "Look you now, my lord! If your Excellency possessed that knowledge of the craft which you affirm you have, you would not fear one moment for the splendid head you speak of. There is good reason, on the other hand, to feel uneasy about this right foot, so far below and at a distance from the rest." When he heard these words, the Duke turned, half in anger, to some gentlemen in waiting, and exclaimed: "I verily believe that this Benvenuto prides himself on contradicting everything one says." Then he faced round to me with a touch of mockery, upon which his attendants did the like, and began to speak as follows: "I will listen patiently to any argument you can possibly produce in explanation of your statement, which may convince me of its probability." I said in answer: "I will adduce so sound an argument that your Excellency shall perceive the full force of it." So I began: "You must know, my lord, that the nature of fire is to ascend, and therefore I promise you that Medusa's head will come out famously; but since it is not in the nature of fire to descend, and I must force it downwards six cubits by artificial means, I assure your Excellency upon this most convincing ground of proof that the foot cannot possibly come out. It will, however, be quite easy for me to restore it." "Why, then," said the Duke, "did you not devise it so that the foot should come out as well as you affirm the head will?" I answered: "I must have made a much larger furnace, with a conduit as thick as my leg; and so I might have forced the molten metal by its own weight to descend so far. Now, my pipe, which runs six cubits to the statue's foot, as I have said, is not thicker than two fingers. However, it was not worth the trouble and expense to make a larger; for I shall easily be able to mend what is lacking. But when my mould is more than half full, as I expect, from this middle point upwards, the fire ascending by its natural property, then the heads of Perseus and Medusa will come out admirably; you may be quite sure of it." After I had thus expounded these convincing arguments, together with many more of the same kind, which it would be tedious to set down here, the Duke shook his head and departed without further ceremony.

Abandoned thus to my own resources, I took new courage, and banished the sad thoughts which kept recurring to my mind, making me often weep bitter tears of repentance for having left France; for though I did so only to revisit Florence, my sweet birthplace, in order that I might charitably succour [help] my six nieces, this good action, as I well perceived, had been the beginning of my great misfortune. Nevertheless, I felt convinced that when my Perseus was accomplished, all these

trials would be turned to high felicity and glorious well-being.

Accordingly I strengthened my heart, and with all the forces of my body and my purse, employing what little money still remained to me, I set to work. First I provided myself with several loads of pinewood from the forests of Serristori, in the neighbourhood of Montelupo. While these were on their way, I clothed my Perseus with the clay which I had prepared many months beforehand, in order that it might be duly seasoned. After making its clay tunic (for that is the term used in this art) and properly arming it and fencing it with iron girders, I began to draw the wax out by means of a slow fire. This melted and issued through numerous air-vents I had made; for the more there are of these, the better will the mould fill. When I had finished drawing off the wax, I constructed a funnel-shaped furnace all round the model of my Perseus.[1] It was built of bricks, so interlaced, the one above the other, that numerous apertures were left for the fire to exhale at. Then I began to lay on wood by degrees, and kept it burning two whole days and nights. At length, when all the wax was gone, and the mould was well baked, I set to work at digging the pit in which to sink it. This I performed with scrupulous regard to all the rules of art. When I had finished that part of my work, I raised the mould by windlasses and stout ropes to a perpendicular

---

[1]This furnace called *manica*, was like a grain-hopper, so that the mould could stand upright in it as in a cup. The word *manica* is the same as our *manuch*, an antique form of sleeve.

position, and suspending it with the greatest care one cubit above the level of the furnace, so that it hung exactly above the middle of the pit, I next lowered it gently down into the very bottom of the furnace, and had it firmly placed with every possible precaution for its safety. When this delicate operation was accomplished, I began to bank it up with the earth I had excavated; and, ever as the earth grew higher, I introduced its proper air-vents, which were little tubes of earthenware, such as folk use for drains and such-like purposes.[1] At length, I felt sure that it was admirably fixed, and that the filling-in of the pit and the placing of the air-vents had been properly performed. I also could see that my workpeople understood my method, which differed very considerably from that of all the other masters in the trade. Feeling confident, then, that I could rely upon them, I next turned to my furnace, which I had filled with numerous pigs of copper and other bronze stuff. The pieces were piled according to the laws of art, that is to say, so resting one upon the other that the flames could play freely through them, in order that the metal might heat and liquefy the sooner. At last I called out heartily to set the furnace going. The logs of pine were heaped in, and, what with the unctuous resin

of the wood and the good draught I had given, my furnace worked so well that I was obliged to rush from side to side to keep it going. The labour was more than I could stand; yet I forced myself to strain every nerve and muscle. To increase my anxieties, the workshop took fire, and we were afraid lest the roof should fall upon our heads; while, from the garden, such a storm of wind and rain kept blowing in, that it perceptibly cooled the furnace.

Battling thus with all these untoward circumstances for several hours, and exerting myself beyond even the measure of my powerful constitution, I could at last bear up no longer, and a sudden fever,[2] of the utmost possible intensity, attacked me. I felt absolutely obliged to go and fling myself upon my bed. Sorely against my will having to drag myself away from the spot, I turned to my assistants, about ten or more in all, what with master-founders, hand-workers, country-fellows, and my own special journeymen, among whom was Bernardino Mannellini of Mugello, my apprentice through several years. To him in particular I spoke: "Look, my dear Bernardino, that you observe the rules which I have taught you; do your best with all despatch, for the metal will soon be fused. You cannot go wrong; these honest men will get the channels ready; you will easily be able to drive back the two plugs with this pair of iron crooks; and I am sure that my mould will fill miraculously. I feel more ill than I ever did in all

---

[1]These air-vents, or *sfiatatoi*, were introduced into the outer mould, which Cellini calls the *tonaca*, or clay tunic laid upon the original model of baked clay and wax. They served the double purpose of drawing off the wax, whereby a space was left for the molten bronze to enter, and also facilitating the penetration of this molten metal by allowing a free escape of air and gas from the outer mould.

---

[2]*Una febbre efimera.* Lit., *a fever of one day's duration.*

my life, and verily believe that it will kill me before a few hours are over."[1] Thus, with despair at heart, I left them, and betook myself to bed.

No sooner had I got to bed, than I ordered my serving-maids to carry food and wine for all the men into the workshop; at the same time I cried: "I shall not be alive tomorrow." They tried to encourage me, arguing that my illness would pass over, since it came from excessive fatigue. In this way I spent two hours battling with the fever, which steadily increased, and calling out continually: "I feel that I am dying." My housekeeper, who was named Mona Fiore da Castel del Rio, a very notable manager and no less warmhearted, kept chiding me for my discouragement; but, on the other hand, she paid me every kind attention which was possible. However, the sight of my physical pain and moral dejection

---

[1]Some technical terms require explanation in this sentence. The *canali* or channels were sluices for carrying the molten metal from the furnace into the mould. The *mandriani*, which I have translated by *iron crooks*, were poles fitted at the end with curved irons, by which the openings of the furnace, *plugs*, or in Italian *spine*, could be partially or wholly driven back, so as to let the molten metal flow through the channels into the mould. When the metal reached the mould, it entered in a red-hot stream between the *tonaca*, or outside mould, and the *anima*, or inner block, filling up exactly the space which had previously been occupied by the wax extracted by a method of slow burning alluded to above. I believe that the process is known as casting *à cire perdue*. The *forma*, or mould, consisted of two pieces; one hollow (*la tonaca*), which gave shape to the bronze; one solid and rounded (*la anima*), which stood at a short interval within the former, and regulated the influx of the metal.

so affected her, that, in spite of that brave heart of hers, she could not refrain from shedding tears; and yet, so far as she was able, she took good care I should not see them. While I was thus terribly afflicted, I beheld the figure of a man enter my chamber, twisted in his body into the form of a capital S. He raised a lamentable, doleful voice, like one who announces their last hour to men condemned to die upon the scaffold, and spoke these words: "O Benvenuto! your statue is spoiled, and there is no hope whatever of saving it." No sooner had I heard the shriek of that wretch than I gave a howl which might have been heard from the sphere of flame. Jumping from my bed, I seized my clothes and began to dress. The maids, and my lads, and every one who came around to help me, got kicks or blows of the fist, while I kept crying out in lamentation: "Ah! traitors! enviers! This is an act of treason, done by malice prepense [forethought]! But I swear by God that I will sift it to the bottom, and before I die will leave such witness to the world of what I can do as shall make a score of mortals marvel."

When I had got my clothes on, I strode with soul bent on mischief toward the workshop; there I beheld the men, whom I had left erewhile in such high spirits, standing stupefied and downcast. I began at once and spoke: "Up with you! Attend to me! Since you have not been able or willing to obey the directions I gave you, obey me now that I am with you to conduct my work in person. Let no one contradict me, for in cases like this we need the aid of hand and hearing, not of advice." When I had uttered these words, a certain Maestro Alessandro Lastricati broke silence and said: "Look you, Benvenuto, you are going to attempt an enterprise which the laws of art do not sanction, and which cannot succeed." I turned upon him with such fury and so full of mischief, that he and all the rest of them exclaimed with one voice: "On then! Give orders! We will obey your least commands, so long as life is left in us." I believe they spoke thus feelingly because they thought I must fall shortly dead upon the ground. I went immediately to inspect the furnace, and found that the metal was all curdled; an accident which we express by "being caked."[1] I told two of the hands to cross the road, and fetch from the house of the butcher Capretta a load of young oak-wood, which had lain dry for above a year; this wood had been previously offered me by Madame Ginevra, wife of the said Capretta. So soon as the first armfuls arrived, I began to fill the grate beneath the furnace.[2] Now oak-wood of that kind heats more powerfully than any other sort of tree; and for this reason, where a slow fire is wanted, as in the case of gun-foundry, alder or pine is preferred. Accordingly, when the logs took fire, oh! how the cake began to stir beneath that awful heat, to glow and sparkle in a blaze! At the same time I kept stirring up the channels, and sent men upon the roof to stop the

conflagration, which had gathered force from the increased combustion in the furnace; also I caused boards, carpets, and other hangings to be set up against the garden, in order to protect us from the violence of the rain.

When I had thus provided against these several disasters, I roared out first to one man and then to another: "Bring this thing here! Take that thing there!" At this crisis, when the whole gang saw the cake was on the point of melting, they did my bidding, each fellow working with the strength of three. I then ordered half a pig of pewter to be brought, which weighed about sixty pounds, and flung it into the middle of the cake inside the furnace. By this means, and by piling on wood and stirring now with pokers and now with iron rods, the curdled mass rapidly began to liquefy. Then, knowing I had brought the dead to life again, against the firm opinion of those ignoramuses, I felt such vigour fill my veins, that all those pains of fever, all those fears of death, were quite forgotten.

All of a sudden an explosion took place, attended by a tremendous flash of flame, as though a thunderbolt had formed and been discharged amongst us. Unwonted and appalling terror astonied every one, and me more even than the rest. When the din was over and the dazzling light extinguished, we began to look each other in the face. Then I discovered that the cap of the furnace had blown up, and the bronze was bubbling over from its source beneath. So I had the mouths of my mould immediately opened, and at the same time

---

[1]*Essersi fatto un migliaccio.*

[2]The Italian Is *brocciatuola*, a pit below the grating, which receives the ashes from the furnace.

drove in the two plugs which kept back the molten metal. But I noticed that it did not flow as rapidly as usual, the reason being probably that the fierce heat of the fire we kindled had consumed its base alloy. Accordingly I sent for all my pewter platters, porringers, and dishes, to the number of some two hundred pieces, and had a portion of them cast, one by one, into the channels, the rest into the furnace. This expedient succeeded, and every one could now perceive that my bronze was in most perfect liquefaction, and my mould was filling; whereupon they all with heartiness and happy cheer assisted and obeyed my bidding, while I, now here, now there, gave orders, helped with my own hands, and cried aloud: "O God! Thou that by Thy immeasurable power didst rise from the dead, and in Thy glory didst ascend to heaven!" . . . . even thus in a moment my mould was filled; and seeing my work finished, I fell upon my knees, and with all my heart gave thanks to God.

After all was over, I turned to a plate of salad on a bench there, and ate with hearty appetite, and drank together with the whole crew. Afterwards I retired to bed, healthy and happy, for it was now two hours before morning, and slept as sweetly as though I had never felt a touch of illness. My good housekeeper, without my giving any orders, had prepared a fat capon for my repast. So that, when I rose, about the hour for breaking fast, she presented herself with a smiling countenance, and said: "Oh! is that the man who felt that he was dying? Upon my word, I think the blows and kicks you dealt us last night, when you were so enraged, and had that demon in your body as it seemed, must have frightened away your mortal fever! The fever feared that it might catch it too, as we did!" All my poor household, relieved in like measure from anxiety and overwhelming labour, went at once to buy earthen vessels in order to replace the pewter I had cast away. Then we dined together joyfully; nay, I cannot remember a day in my whole life when I dined with greater gladness or a better appetite.

After our meal I received visits from the several men who had assisted me. They exchanged congratulations, and thanked God for our success, saying they had learned and seen things done which other masters judged impossible. I too grew somewhat glorious; and deeming I had shown myself a man of talent, indulged a boastful humour. So I thrust my hand into my purse, and paid them all to their full satisfaction.

That evil fellow, my mortal foe, Messer Pier Francesco Ricci, majordomo of the Duke, took great pains to find out how the affair had gone. In answer to his questions, the two men whom I suspected of having caked my metal for me, said I was no man, but of a certainty some powerful devil, since I had accomplished what no craft of the art could do; indeed they did not believe a mere ordinary fiend could work such miracles as I in other ways had shown. They exaggerated the whole affair so much, possibly in order to excuse their own part in it, that the majordomo wrote an account to the Duke, who was then in Pisa, far more marvellous and full of thrilling incidents than what they had narrated.

After I had let my statue cool for two whole days, I began to uncover it by slow degrees. The first thing I found was that the head of Medusa had come out most admirably, thanks to the air-vents; for, as I had told the Duke, it is the nature of fire to ascend. Upon advancing farther, I discovered that the other head, that, namely, of Perseus, had succeeded no less admirably; and this astonished me far more, because it is at a considerably lower level than that of the Medusa. Now the mouths of the mould were placed above the head of Perseus and behind his shoulders; and I found that all the bronze my furnace contained had been exhausted in the head of this figure. It was a miracle to observe that not one fragment remained in the orifice of the channel, and that nothing was wanting to the statue. In my great astonishment I seemed to see in this the hand of God arranging and controlling all.

I went on uncovering the statue with success, and ascertained that everything had come out in perfect order, until I reached the foot of the right leg on which the statue rests. There the heel itself was formed, and going farther, I found the foot apparently complete. This gave me great joy on the one side, but was half unwelcome to me on the other, merely because I had told the Duke that it could not come out. However, when I reached the end, it appeared that the toes and a little piece above them were unfin-ished, so that about half the foot was wanting. Although I knew that this would add a trifle to my labour, I was very well pleased, because I could now prove to the Duke how well I understood my business. It is true that far more of the foot than I expected had been perfectly formed; the reason of this was that, from causes I have recently described, the bronze was hotter than our rules of art prescribe; also that I had been obliged to supplement the alloy with my pewter cups and platters, which no one else, I think, had ever done before.

Having now ascertained how successfully my work had been accomplished, I lost no time in hurrying to Pisa, where I found the Duke. He gave me a most gracious reception, as did also the Duchess; and although the majordomo had informed them of the whole proceedings, their Excellencies deemed my performance far more stupendous and astonishing when they heard the tale from my own mouth. When I arrived at the foot of Perseus, and said it had not come out perfect, just as I previously warned his Excellency, I saw an expression of wonder pass over his face, while he related to the Duchess how I had predicted this beforehand. Observing the princes to be so well disposed towards me, I begged leave from the Duke to go to Rome. He granted it in most obliging terms, and bade me return as soon as possible to complete his Perseus; giving me letters of recommendation meanwhile to his ambassador, Averardo Serristori. We were then in the first years of Pope Giulio de Monti [Julius III].

Questions for Critical Thinking and Discussion

1. Why do you think Cellini's *Autobiography* has a lasting interest to students of the Renaissance? Support your opinion.

2. Is the murder of Pompeo premeditated or accidental? Do you feel Cellini wanted to get back at him in some manner?

3. When the Pope gives Cellini a pass of safe conduct after the murder of Pompeo, the Pope says Cellini is "above the law." What prompts him to say this? Do you agree or disagree that Cellini is above the law?

4. Cellini's description of his casting of the *Perseus* is filled with action and vitality. What do you learn about the casting of bronze sculptures from the reading? Give specifics.

5. Why did Pope Paul III wish Cellini's services? Who else wanted to use his talent?

6. Why did Cellini feel the hand of God was controlling his art?

7. Do you think Cellini is too egotistical in his explanations of his worth to Cosimo de Medici? Explain your position.

Figure 5.9. Perseus with Head of the slain Medusa. By Benvenuto Cellini. *From the bronze statue in the Musee Nationale, France.*

Self-Test

Part I: Identification

Can you identify each of the following? Tell who, what, when, where, why, and/or how for each term.

1. Prince Henry the Navigator
2. Caravels
3. Vasco da Gama
4. Treaty of Tordesillas
5. Amerigo Vespucci
6. Hispaniola
7. Ferdinand Magellan
8. Hernan Cortes
9. Conquistadors
10. Francisco Pizarro
11. Viceroys
12. Samuel de Champlain
13. Price Revolution
14. Reformation
15. Babylonian Captivity
16. Council of Constance
17. Simony
18. Erasmus
19. Indulgences
20. Transubstantiation
21. *Ninety-Five Theses*
22. League of Schmalkalden
23. Peace of Augsburg
24. John Calvin
25. Predestination
26. Huguenots
27. Anglicanism
28. Henry VIII
29. Act of Supremacy
30. Mary Tudor
31. The Elizabethan Settlement
32. Puritans
33. Counter-Reformation
34. Council of Trent
35. Society of Jesus
36. *Spiritual Exercises*
37. Inquisition
38. Index of Prohibited Books
39. Charles V
40. Hapsburg-Valois rivalry
41. Peace of Cateau-Cambrésis
42. Lepanto
43. Philip II
44. William of Orange
45. Sea Beggars
46. Spanish Fury
47. Pacification of Ghent
48. Armada
49. Peace of Westphalia
50. Valois dynasty
51. Henry IV of Navarre
52. Bourbon dynasty
53. Mary, Queen of Scots
54. St. Bartholomew's Day Massacre
55. Edict of Nantes
56. Thirty Years' War

Part II: Multiple Choice Questions

Circle the best response from the choices given.

1. All of the following are correctly matched except:
    a. Prester John — ruler of legendary Christian kingdom.
    b. John Cabot — sought northwest passage to the Indies.
    c. Francisco Pizarro — discovered Brazil.
    d. Magellan — circumnavigated the globe.

2. The viceroy of New Spain was:
    a. headquartered at Havana, Cuba.
    b. able to promote Montezuma's revenge.
    c. included parts of Bolivia, Argentina, and Chile.
    d. assisted by regional courts called *audiencias*.

3. Which of the following was not a motive for exploring unknown seas?
    a. to spread Christianity.
    b. to discover gold and silver.
    c. to settle excess population.
    d. to find new routes to the source of the spice supply.

4. The greatest mariners in the late fifteenth century Age of Discovery were the
    a. English.   b. Russians.
    c. Spanish.   d. Portuguese.

5. Francisco Pizarro:
    a. was paid an extravagant ransom for Atahualpa.
    b. was able to use llamas to conquer the Carib.
    c. became governor of Mexico and received accolades from the Holy Roman Emperor, Charles V.
    d. terrorized and intimated the Aztecs.

6. Which of the following gentlemen did not expand Spain's interest in the New World?
    a. Alfonso de Albuquerque.
    b. Christopher Columbus.
    c. Vasco Nunez de Balboa
    d. Hernan Cortes.

7. The Treaty of Tordesillas:
   a. gave the Spice Islands to Spain.
   b. established commercial and naval bases at Goa and Diu.
   c. divided the rights to the non-Christian world between Spain and Portugal.
   d. divided South and Central America between the conquistadors, Hernan Cortes and Francisco Pizarro.

8. The Renaissance period of history lasted approximately from

   a. 950 -1300 A.D.   b. 1200-1350 A.D.
   c. 1350-1600 A.D.   d. 1500-1700 A.D.

9. Italian humanism consisted primarily of
   a. the creation of works of art depicting the human form realistically.
   b. the liberalization and democratization of Italian social and political life.
   c. a quest for Greek and Latin literary manuscripts and the development of a secular philosophy of life.
   d. both a and c.

10. The chief reason for Leonardo da Vinci's extensive studies of anatomy, physics, and other sciences was his desire to
   a. understand the innermost workings of nature for the sake of his art.
   b. present a faithful representation of the surface appearance of things.
   c. gain wealthy patrons who were interested in the new science.
   d. become a professor of natural science.

11. The teachings of Martin Luther include all but one of the following:
   a. Every Christian should be able to read the Bible.
   b. There are only two sacraments: baptism and communion.
   c. belief in justification by faith; that is, "The just shall be saved by faith."
   d. belief in the power of indulgences to release sinners' souls from purgatory upon payment of a fee.

12. Under John Calvin, Geneva:
   a. became a theocracy.
   b. was governed by elected lay elders.
   c. became a model city characterized by austere living.
   d. all of the above.

13. The English Supremacy Act of 1534 declared _____ to be the head of the Church of England.
    a. Mary Tudor.   b. Anne Boleyn.
    c. Edward VI.   d. Henry VIII.

14. The doctrine of predestination, where eternal life is foreordained for the elect, is described in:
    a. *The Institutes of the Christian Religion*.
    b. *The Ninety-Five Theses*.
    c. *The Book of Common Prayer*.
    d. *The Divine Comedy*.

15. The Council of Trent approved all but <u>one</u> of the following:
    a. *The Index of Prohibited Books*.
    b. the special powers of the priesthood.
    c. the doctrine of transubstantiation.
    d. a reconciliation with the Lutherans.

16. All of the following religious denominations came from the Reformation <u>except</u>:
    a. Anglicans.   b. Puritans.
    c. Chartists.   d. Calvinists.

17. As a result of the Protestant Reformation,
    a. religious conflict continued for at least a century.
    b. religious toleration was immediately practiced in all churches.
    c. the spirit of secularism grew faster than ever.
    d. Catholicism was driven out of Europe.

18. Which group was NOT one of Charles V's opponents?
    a. the Lutherans.
    b. the Castilians.
    c. the Ottoman Turks.
    d. the French.

19. The Netherlanders in the mid-1500's were disgruntled with Spanish rule because:
    a. Philip II of Spain taxed the Netherlanders in order to pay for his previous wars with France.
    b. A regent, Margaret of Parma, had been appointed to rule them.
    c. The Calvinists were seeking religious toleration.
    d. all of the above.

20. The Duke of Alva was extremely unpopular in the Netherlands for which <u>one</u> of the following reasons:
    a. He encouraged members of the high nobility to join the Calvinist church.
    b. He implemented a policy of political repression.
    c. He demanded that the Inquisition be halted.
    d. He appointed himself governor-general of the Netherlands.

21. In 1588 the Spanish Armada failed in its invasion plans of England in part because:
    a. The English by forming an alliance with the Dutch successfully blockaded the Spanish galleons in Japanese ports.
    b. The Spanish navy ran out of ammunition.
    c. The French joined in an alliance with the English to help sink the Spanish fleet.
    d. all of the above.

22. Religious conviction was set aside for political reality by king:
    a. Henry III. b. Henry IV.
    c. Francis II. d. Charles IX.

23. Which one of the following statements is <u>false</u>?
    a. In the sixteenth century the Catholics and the Huguenots were divided along religious lines.
    b. The Catholic cause was championed by the Guise family of France.
    c. Catherine de Medici issued the Edict of Nantes, which granted limited religious toleration to the Huguenots.
    d. The effect of the St. Bartholomew's Day Massacre was horror in Protestant countries.

24. Which one of the following statements is <u>true</u>?
    a. The Peace of Westphalia (1648) recognized the independence of Belgium.
    b. The Concordat of Bologna (1516) permitted French kings to nominate men of their own choice to the highest offices in the French church.
    c. Elizabeth I had her rival Mary Tudor beheaded.
    d. The *Politiques*, a Huguenot group, had Catherine de Medici plan the St. Bartholomew's Day Massacre.

25. In 1555-56 the Emperor Charles V
    a. divided the Hapsburg states into Austrian and Spanish monarchies.
    b. announced the policy of separation of Church and state in Spain.
    c. announced the loss of Spain to Hapsburg rule
    d. conquered Austria and converted it to Protestantism

Part III: Review and Thought Questions

1. Explain the competition between the Portuguese and the Spanish explorers. Why did the overseas explorations occur when and where they did?

2. Compare and contrast the tactics of Cortes and Pizarro in the New World.

3. What role did each of the following explorers — Amerigo Vespucci, Samuel de Champlain, Giovanni da Verrazano, and Henry Hudson — have on the Age of Exploration?

4. What abuses in the Catholic Church prompted Martin Luther to post his *Ninety-Five Theses?*

5. Explain why Lutheranism appealed to the German princes and to the Scandinavian kings. What about the German peasants?

6. What were the primary ideas of John Calvin's theology? What caused it to spread?

7. What did the Council of Trent accomplish? If this Council was convened 50 years earlier, would it have changed the course of history? Why or why not?

8. What were the effects of the Reformation on the Catholic Church? Give examples.

9. What were the principal concerns of Charles V, and how did he try to deal with them?

10. Describe the conflict between England and Spain in the late sixteenth century.

11. What was Elizabeth I's contribution to the Reformation?

12. Why did the Netherlands rebel against Philip II and what were the consequences of this revolt?

13. If you were living in sixteenth century France, would you have sided with the Protestant Huguenots? Why or why not?

Part IV: Full-Length Essays

1. Discuss how the European lust for gold and spices impacted both Europeans and non-Europeans.

2. Compare and contrast the theology of Lutheranism with that of Calvinism.

3. Describe the reign of Charles VI as king of Spain and Holy Roman Emperor.

4. Evaluate the measures of the Counter-Reformation to halt the spread of Protestantism.

5. Describe the abuses within the Catholic Church prior to the Reformation.

6. From 1562 to 1598, religious wars diminished the power of the French throne. Refute or support this statement.

7. Trace how Anglicanism evolved in England under the reigns of Henry VIII, Edward VI, and Elizabeth I.

8. What were the doctrinal beliefs of the Anabaptists? Contrast how they were treated by political authorities with the treatment accorded to the Lutherans? What do you think accounts for the difference?

Figure 5.10. Andrea del Verrocchio (Florentine, 1435-88). *Lorenzo de'Medici*, c. 1485. Decending from a prominent banking and political family in Florence, Italy, Lorenzo the Magnificent (1469-1492) patronized such artists and Michelangelo, Sandro Botticelli, and the artist who sculpted his terra cotta bust, Andrea del Verrocchio. *Samuel H. Kress Collection. 1943. National Gallery of Art, Washington, D.C.*

Answers to Multiple Choice Questions

Chapter 1, pp. 96-99.

1. a	8. d	14. d	20. d
2. c	9. b	15. d	21. a
3. b	10. d	16. d	22. c
4. d	11. d	17. c	23. b
5. d	12. b	18. b	24. b
6. b	13. b	19. c	25. a
7. a			

Chapter 2, pp. 208-211.

1. d	8. d	14. a	20. d
2. c	9. a	15. b	21. d
3. b	10. b	16. c	22. c
4. d	11. a	17. b	23. a
5. b	12. d	18. a	24. c
6. c	13. d	19. b	25. c
7. b			

Chapter 3, pp. 306-309.

1. d	8. d	14. d	20. d
2. c	9. b	15. b	21. b
3. b	10. b	16. b	22. c
4. c	11. a	17. d	23. c
5. c	12. c	18. b	24. d
6. d	13. b	19. c	25. b
7. d			

Chapter 4, pp. 402-405.

1. b	7. d	13. a	19. a
2. a	8. c	14. a	20. b
3. c	9. d	15. d	21. a
4. c	10. c	16. b	22. a
5. d	11. d	17. b	23. d
6. d	12. b	18. d	24. a

Chapter 5, pp. 514-517.

1. c	8. c	14. a	20. b
2. d	9. d	15. d	21. b
3. c	10. a	16. c	22. b
4. d	11. d	17. a	23. c
5. a	12. d	18. b	24. b
6. a	13. d	19. d	25. a
7. c			

Index

Check also the **EXPANDED CONTENTS FOR EACH SUBCHAPTER** *which begins on page v for a detailed outline of the subjects discussed in this worktext.*

Nero, 152, 186, 224, 225, 236, 248, 289
Nerva, 226, 227, 289
Netherlanders, 480, 482
Netherlands, 287, 430, 465, 470, 477, 478, 479, 480, 481, 482, 483, 484, 485, 486
New Amsterdam, 451
New Comedy, 134
New Kingdom, 27, 28, 41, 43, 46
New Netherland, 451
New Testament, 241, 247, 265, 423, 434, 459, 460
New York, 138, 428, 450, 451
Newfoundland, 450
Nibelungenlied, 333
Nicaea, see Council of Nicaea
Nicene Creed, 254
Nicholas II, 338
Nicholas of Cologne, 360
Nicholas V, 417
Nicias, Peace of, 80
Nicomachean Ethics, 126, 128
Nile, 17, 33, 38, 44, 153
Ninety-Five Theses, 460, 498
Nineveh, 30
Noah, 25
Nogaret, William de, 352
Nomes, 39
Norman, 344, 369, 370
Normandy, 288, 365, 366, 369, 372
Normans, 368, 369, 370
Norsemen, 288
Northern Renaissance, 430
Northumbria, 263
Northumbrian, 333
Norway, 463

Notre Dame, Cathedral of, 331, 332
Noumena, 233
Novels, 273
Nubia, 41
Numidia, 172
Nut, 37
Oath of homage, 317
Octavia, 186
Octavian, 185, 186, 217, 218
Odes, 235
Odoacer, 259, 261
Odyssey, 129, 235
Oil Paint, 422, 430
Old Age, 235
Old Assyrian Period, 28
Old Babylonian Kingdom, 24
Old Comedy, 130, 133, 134
Old Kingdom, 36, 39, 40, 44
Old Market Woman, 157
Oldowan, 7, 13
Olduvai Gorge, 10
Oligarchy, 127, 181, 182
Olympia, 108, 141, 142
Olympiad, 108
Olympian Games, 108
Olympian, 107, 108, 114, 147, 234
Olympians, 107
Olympic, 108
Olympus, Mount, 107, 108
On Generation and Corruption, 128
On Interpretation, 128
On the False Donation of Constantine, 417
On the Heavens, 128
On the Soul, 128
Ontario, 450
Optimates, 175, 185
Oracle at Delphi, 108, 116

Oral tradition, 53, 243-245
Oration on the Dignity of Man, 419
Order of the Golden Fleece, 481
Oresteia, 131
Orestes, 131
Orpheus, 251
Orphic, 148
Orthodox, 264, 265, 273
Osiris, 37, 38
Ostracism, 77, 78 323
Ostrogothic Kingdom, 260, 261
Ostrogoths, 259, 260
Otho, 289
Otto I the Great, 341
Otto IV, 366
Otto of Brunswick, 350
Ottoman Turks, 31, 255, 271, 437, 478
Our Lady of Guadeloupe, 452
Overseers, 250
Ovid, 222, 235
Oxford, 326, 377
Pacific, 445, 446, 447, 448
Pacification of Amboise, 490
Pacification of Ghent, 484
Painted Porch, see *Stoa Poikile*
Pakistan, 139, 153
Palatinate, 495
Paleolithic Period, 13
Paleolithic, 11, 12, 13, 18, 19, 26, 33, 54, 159
Palestine, 15, 27, 30, 40, 41, 42, 43, 45, 47, 144, 145, 270, 277, 361
Palos, 444
Panama, 445, 448
Panhellenism, 145

Verrazano, Giovanni da, 450
Vespasian, 225, 230, 248, 289
Vespucci, Amerigo, 442
Vesta, 233
Vestal virgins, 161, 234
Vesuvius, Mount, 225
Vezelay, 330
Vicar of Christ, 265
Viceroyalty of New Spain, 449
Viceroyalty of Peru, 449
Vienna, 326
View from Toledo, 428
Viking, 329, 369
Vikings, 288
Virgil, 160, 222, 235, 325, 412
Visigoths, 256, 259, 260
Vitellius, 289
Vitruvius, 232
Voelkerwanderung, 26, 259
Vulcan, 234
Vulgate, 264
Waiblingen, 351
Waldenses, 339
Wales, 263
Wallenstein, Albert of, 495, 496

Wanax, 62
War of the Roses, 385, 386
Warfare, organized, 18
Wasps, 134
Waterwheel, 320
Welf(s), 350, 351
Wessex, 263
Western Roman Empire, see Roman Empire, Western
Westphalia, 486, 497
Whitsunday, 334
William of Orange, 482, 483, 484, 485, 486
William the Bastard, see William the Conqueror
William the Conqueror, 369, 377
William the Silent, 482
Windmill, 320
Winged Victory of Samothrace, 156
Winter King, 495
Wittenberg, 457, 460, 470
Works and Days, 129
World-Soul, 123
Worms, 347, 460
Writing system, 18

Wuerm glaciation, 10, 13
Xerxes, 55, 75
Yahweh, 46
Yathreb, 276
York, House of, 385
Yorkist, 385
Yorkists, 385
Zacharias, 284
Zagros, 28
Zakros, 60
Zama, Battle of, 171
Zara, 360
Zarathustra, see Zoroaster
Zealots, 243, 245
Zeeland, 484
Zeno, 152, 261
Zeus Amon, 138
Zeus, 50, 106, 107, 108, 139, 234
Ziggurat(s), 19, 22, 31, 36
Zoroaster, 55, 56
Zoroastrianism, 55, 56, 148
Zoser, 36
Zurich, 463
Zwickau, 470
Zwingli, Ulrich, 432, 463, 470
Zwinglians, 469